PRINCIPLES OF MICRO-ECONOMICS

Ryan C. Amacher
Chairman, Department of Economics
Professor of Economics
Arizona State University

Richard James Sweeney
Professor of Economics
Claremont Men's College

Consulting Editor:
Lloyd M. Valentine
Professor of Economics
University of Cincinnati

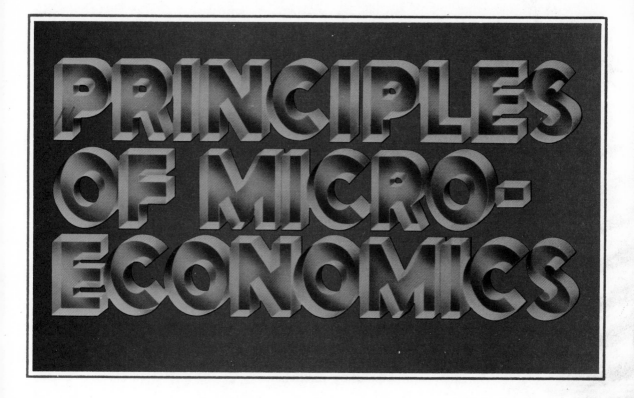

PRINCIPLES OF MICRO-ECONOMICS

Published by

H13   **SOUTH-WESTERN PUBLISHING CO.**

CINCINNATI   WEST CHICAGO, ILL.   DALLAS   PELHAM MANOR, N.Y.   PALO ALTO, CALIF.

PREFACE

THE ECONOMIC APPROACH

In the early 1970s, the economics profession and the teachers of introductory economics courses went through an exhaustive search for "relevance," in large part because students demanded it. Unfortunately, this search for relevance produced a large number of "cute" applications aimed superficially at catching students' (or instructors') eyes. We learned, for example, that supply and demand can be applied to markets for illegal drugs and marketable sex. The results of this rush toward relevance, however, were predictable. Some students were offended, others were amazed, and many were bored. Instructors for the most part then fell back on the tested (and familiar) ways of approaching the subject of economics.

Our goal in writing this book has been to show students the relevance of the economic approach as it applies both to important real-world situations and to economic policymaking. This is not easily accomplished. Today's students are not deceived by slick marketing techniques. If the economic approach is a relevant way to approach social and political problems, students must be convinced through application and example. This book is intended to accomplish that difficult task.

We proceed by presenting the basic tools of economic analysis at a rapid, rigorous pace, geared toward those students seriously interested in learning the principles of economics well enough to follow policy debates in an informed, enlightened way. This, of course, is not enough. To demonstrate the usefulness of these tools, we show through example the powerful insights they yield for solving social problems. These insights can provide valuable input to both the policymaker and the voter who, in the final analysis, makes the policy choices.

In developing these basic tools of economic analysis and the economic approach, we continually stress two important aspects of basic theory. First, we show how the theory evolved in the history of ideas and how economic conditions prompted the development of the theory. This gives students a hook on which to hang what might otherwise appear to be irrelevant economic insights. Second, we make an effort to point out the areas in which economists agree and disagree. The public often views economists as being in constant disagreement. Yet students are often left with the impression that economists agree on almost everything. This book presents a balanced approach, showing students that there is sometimes more than one way to view an economic problem.

UNIQUE FEATURES

In the preface of each introductory economics book, the author(s) spends a great deal of time extolling the differentiated (but not too differentiated) features of the book. We believe we have included some worthwhile features that contribute to a unique product.

Organization

This book is organized to allow students to see the power of economic analysis very quickly. After elementary tools are developed in Chapters 1 through 3, Chapter 4 shows how the basic tools covered in the first three chapters can be applied to a wide range of social policy questions.

Chapters 5 and 6 allow the instructor to present the theory of consumer behavior using utility analysis or indifference curve analysis (or both) without any loss of continuity.

After the theory of the firm has been presented in Chapters 7 through 11, Chapter 12 takes a look at the American economy to apply the theory that has been developed. In this chapter students can grapple with some of the difficulties of applying theory to practical economic problems.

Chapter 13 takes up the topic of factor markets, with particular emphasis on the redistribution of income within the United States, while Chapter 14 examines the labor movement, its history, and its economic significance within the American economy.

Chapter 15 examines the role of government in the market system. Reasons for calling upon government to solve problems are discussed, and the consequences of governmental activity are outlined. The purpose of this chapter is to show students that neither markets nor governments conform to textbook ideals and that solutions to problems often must be found by selecting the best of two imperfect mechanisms.

Chapter 16 provides an introduction to international transactions, while Chapter 17 examines the economics of alternative systems.

In Chapter 18 we present a wide-ranging discussion of economics and economists. We look at what economists do, what they are paid, how they are educated, and why students might decide to major in economics. This chapter offers answers to a host of questions that potential economics majors may have about economics as a career option. No other book on the market includes such a feature.

Important Economists and Important Economic Institutions

Each chapter contains at least one pictured insert of a contemporary or historical economist. In some cases a significant economic institution is substituted for the biographical insert. These inserts are closely related to the material in the chapter and are intended to highlight the way a particular theory was developed or how it is being applied to important problems.

References, Questions, and Reading Suggestions

Since one of our major goals is to demonstrate the relevance of the economic way of thinking, we have included numerous references that are intended to direct interested students to more information on the same or related subjects. The carefully selected *Suggestions for Further Reading* at the end of each chapter serve this same purpose. We also have included *Questions for Discussion* at the end of each chapter. These questions are intended to generate interest in the material that has been presented in the chapter. The questions can serve as a foundation for more in-depth understanding of economic policymaking. Suggested answers to all of the questions appear in the instructor's manual.

Glossary

All terms that appear in boldface type in the book are defined in the *Glossary*.

TEACHING AND STUDY AIDS

This book has teaching and study aids contained in it. In addition, a study guide, instructor's manual, and test bank are available.

The Text

The appendix to Chapter 1 contains a review of the graphing techniques used in the text. Each text chapter begins with a set of *Learning Objectives* for that chapter. Students can use these as a handy guide to areas which may require more work or as a review technique. At the end of each chapter there is a *Summary* which presents a useful review of the chapter. *New Terms* are listed at the end of each chapter in the order in which they appeared in the chapter. All these new terms are found in the *Glossary*. The *Questions for Discussion* at the end of each chapter provide a test of students' understanding of each chapter.

The Study Guide

The study guide has a chapter that corresponds to each chapter in the text (with the exception of the final chapter). Each study guide chapter includes

1 learning objectives for that chapter,
2 a list of important terms and concepts,

3 completion questions based on the list of important terms and concepts,

4 problems requiring numerical and graphical solutions,

5 multiple choice questions,

6 short-discussion questions,

7 complete answers to all questions in the study guide.

Extensive class testing of the study guide has shown it to be an effective way for students to improve their understanding and performance.

The Instructor's Manual

The instructor's manual has a chapter that corresponds to each chapter in the text (with the exception of the final chapter). Each of these chapters includes

1 a short discussion of the purpose of the chapter,

2 a chapter outline based on the headings within the text chapters,

3 the learning objectives that are found in the text and study guide,

4 a summary of the chapter,

5 the new terms (with definitions used in the text) that appear in that chapter,

6 selected reference notes that expand on chapter themes,

7 answers to all end-of-chapter questions.

The Test Bank

A test bank is available to adopters. This set of nearly 1,000 multiple choice questions has been classroom tested. None of these questions have been used in the study guide, so questions selected from the study guide will not duplicate those taken from the test bank. The questions are on $2\frac{1}{2}'' \times 4\frac{1}{4}''$ cards in a file system to facilitate test preparation.

ACKNOWLEDGMENTS

Any project as complex as this takes a number of dedicated and talented people to insure that it doesn't remain just another "book in progress." We are extremely grateful to these people.

Lloyd Valentine, the consulting editor, spent a great deal of time suggesting revisions in the manuscript through its many drafts. So much time, in fact, that any errors or omissions could be blamed on him! We bow to tradition, however, and accept all responsibility for errors or omissions.

Closer to home, we would like to thank Jon Ozmun and James Pinto who, in addition to preparing the test bank and study guides, gave detailed comments on each draft. Special thanks go to our typists, Gladys Smith, who prepared first drafts from scrawl we sometimes couldn't read ourselves, and Lynnette Winkelman, who produced magnificent revisions under tight deadlines.

Closest to home, we thank our wives, Susan Amacher and Joan Sweeney, and the Sweeney daughters, Robin and Erin. They didn't complain too often about all the time we spent working on the manuscript. Indeed, they more often complained because we weren't working on it!

RYAN C. AMACHER

RICHARD JAMES SWEENEY

CONTENTS

CHAPTER 1

THE SCOPE AND METHODOLOGY OF MICROECONOMICS

LEARNING OBJECTIVES

After studying the materials found in this chapter, you should be able to do the following:

1 Define microeconomics.

2 Describe the *economic approach* to problem solving using the concepts
   (a) model,
   (b) simplifying assumption,
   (c) hypothesis,
   (d) marginal approach.

3 List the characteristics of the economic models used by Friedman, Samuelson, Tullock, and Boulding.

4 Use a diagram to illustrate a production possibilities model.

5 Calculate the opportunity cost reflected in the principle of increasing cost.

6 List the characteristics of the three types of economic systems.

7 Compare and contrast how each type of economic system answers the four basic economic questions.

This first chapter presents a wide-ranging discussion of microeconomics, the scientific method in economics, and some elements of the economic approach. The fundamental economic problem of scarcity is discussed, and different ways of economizing are introduced. Most importantly, the economic way of thinking is stressed. An appendix which reviews some elementary relationships in graphic form concludes the chapter.

WHAT IS MICROECONOMICS?

Many of you have already completed a course in *macroeconomics*, where you studied the aggregate economy and were concerned with such policy issues as the level of unemployment in all markets and the overall price level and changes in it (inflation). In this course and in this book you will be studying *microeconomics*, which is the study of individual market interactions. We will concentrate on the interaction of consumers and producers in markets for particular goods and services.

It makes little difference if you study "macro" or "micro" first. Many economists would argue that it makes more sense to begin with microeconomics and then build from the micro to the macro. However, many universities teach macro before micro. So don't worry if this is your first course in economics. Except perhaps for knowing a few buzzwords, your fellow students who have taken macro are not at a significant advantage.

THEORY

Theory often suffers from bad press. Theory is sometimes viewed as abstract and useless, maybe even "too hard." In part, the complaints are justified. Theory for theory's sake is a waste of time for most people. *Theory* is valuable, however, in that it allows the development of a set of principles that can be used to untangle the web of different forces involved in social problems. Principles will then develop into a framework for thinking. We might call this way of thinking the *economic approach*. This approach will allow you to analyze and understand a wide range of social interactions.

All economists have the same tool kit of ideas to use on the particular problem they wish to analyze. In this book and its companion, we present the basic tools in that kit. There are many specializations in economics — international finance, industrial organization, and labor economics, to name only a few. Economists in each of these specialties may not be aware of the institutional factors in the others, but they will all use very similar theoretical tools. This causes economists to approach problems in very similar ways. Despite this common approach, economists argue about many issues. If you look at your daily newspaper or at weekly newsmagazines such as *Newsweek* or *Time*, it seems that most news about economists concerns disagreement over issues. This is in large part because disagreement makes good news. We will see in this book that economists agree on many issues. However, there is legitimate disagreement among economists on many issues, and we plan to explain these differences so that you can start to decide for yourself who is right. In this respect our approach may be different from others in that we don't plan to "sell" you on a particular view but rather to present the facts as we know them and then let you draw your own conclusions.

Theorizing and the Scientific Method

The chapters to follow will develop the theoretical models of microeconomic *science* so that you can then use this science to develop operational hypotheses about the world and analyze a wide range of social policy problems. Science consists of appealing to facts in a systematic manner. The early scientists did little more than systematize and classify the facts that they uncovered. If you have taken an introductory course in botany or zoology, you are familiar with this methodology. Such an approach can very quickly lead to diminishing returns unless your mind works like a giant filing cabinet. It is very easy to get lost and bogged down in the facts, and unless you are preparing for an appearance on College Bowl, this approach is not very appealing. As an alternative, economic theorists make assumptions that simplify a problem and then develop a theoretical model that will yield a ***testable hypothesis***. This hypothesis can then be checked by appealing to the facts.

The role of theory is an important one in everything we do. Any interpretation we make about the environment around us has a theory implicit in it. Our senses receive information and we interpret that information. How we interpret this information will affect how we behave, and our interpretation is based on a theory about the world that we have developed over time. These theories are, for most people, constantly being revised and improved. The only difference with the theory in this book and the theory you use in daily life is that we will make this theory explicit and examine its implications in detail.

As an example, we might develop a theory that leads to a hypothesis that if we hold supply constant and increase demand, price will rise. We could then empirically examine situations in which this has happened and determine if price did rise. Such experiments are often referred to by economists as *ceteris paribus* experiments. The economist changes one variable in the theoretical model (demand, in this example) and then hypothesizes what will happen *ceteris paribus*, or "holding everything else constant." In this example, if demand rises *ceteris paribus* (with all else held constant), it is hypothesized that price will rise. In many of the theoretical chapters that follow, we will venture into a never-never land that has been created by the assumptions we make. This never-never land could be compared to the frictionless world often assumed in physics courses.

We plan to "tell it like [we think] it is," and here is the first point where there is disagreement among economists. This disagreement on the role of assumptions is the crux of an often bitter (and often not too valuable) debate between Paul Samuelson, of The Massachusetts Institute of Technology, and Milton Friedman, who was at the University of Chicago for many years, both Nobel prizewinners in economics. The traditional view, taken by Samuelson, is that once a theory is proven to be logically correct, its usefulness can be tested by examining whether the assumptions it makes are realistic. Friedman disputes this view, arguing that the purpose of theory is to abstract from the unimportant aspects of reality, and the test of the theory is, Does it work? Does it describe what happens to the important aspects of reality? Although the debate has never been resolved, in part because it hinges on semantics, it offers some important points. **Assumptions** can fulfill very different roles. Some are fundamental to the analysis; others are not. Some simplify the problem and reduce it to manageable proportions. These fundamental and simplifying assumptions are the key to economic theorizing and policy analysis. They are valuable because they permit the economist to come to grips with the key element of a problem and then to explain the problem to noneconomists.

In this book, we will concentrate on simple (basic) models because they require less knowledge (facts) to analyze a given set of phenomena. In this sense, it might appear that we are closer to Friedman's position in the debate. However, very little of what we have to say in this book leads us to the methodological views of either Samuelson or Friedman. This is because there is a wide area of agreement in economics. Most economists would agree that the importance of assumptions in theory is that they allow the model specified to be logically consistent and to express the fundamental aspects of any social process. For most economists, an important way of judging theory is to consider how well it predicts behavior *vis-à-vis* alternative theories.

The Self-Interest Hypothesis

Perhaps our most basic assumption in economics is that people behave in a selfish, *self-interested* manner. A question almost always raised about this assumption concerns the question of whether Homo sapiens are basically self-interested and whether selfish behavior accurately describes the real world. Gordon Tullock, professor of economics at Virginia Polytechnic Institute, states that economists, in order to test their theories, have assumed, usually implicitly but sometimes explicitly, that people under study have desires for their own well-being which are roughly similar to the economist conducting the study and that they act on these desires, say, 90 percent of the time. Tullock refers to this assumption as the *90 percent selfish hypothesis*. Accordingly, if a human is basically self-interested, then economists' models will be descriptive and

Milton Friedman and Paul A. Samuelson

Public Info/U. of Chicago

Milton Friedman (1912–   )

MIT Photo, News Offices, Massachusetts Institute of Technology, Room 5-111, 77 Massachusetts Avenue, Cambridge, Mass.

Paul A. Samuelson (1915–   )

Milton Friedman and *Paul A. Samuelson* are two of the best known contemporary economists. They both have been recipients of the Nobel Prize in Economics — Samuelson in 1970 and Friedman in 1976. The two men represent polar extremes in the economic policy advice they offer. Samuelson is a liberal activist who sees an important role for government in the modern industrial society. Friedman advocates a position of laissez-faire economic policy, arguing that the market economy operates very well and that the interventions Samuelson supports cause more harm than good. Samuelson represents the "Eastern Establishment" brand of economics, while Friedman represents the "Chicago School." Friedman was recently quoted in *People* magazine as saying, "There is no such thing as a free lunch. That is the sum of my economic theory. The rest is elaboration." You can see the juxtaposition of these differing views on social problems in the columns that Friedman and Samuelson write on alternate weeks for *Newsweek*.

Samuelson, a professor at M.I.T., was awarded an A.B. degree from the University of Chicago and an A.M. and Ph.D. in economics from Harvard University. Samuelson's Ph.D. dissertation, *Foundations of Economic Analysis*, written when he was only 23 years old, still ranks as a monumental work in the application of mathematics to neoclassical economics. Present-day graduate students still study Samuelson's *Foundations*. Samuelson is largely responsible for making M.I.T.'s economics program one of the best in the country. He took a job there after receiving his degree at Harvard and helped to attract to M.I.T. what some people consider to be the leading graduate faculty in economics.

Friedman presently is retired from the University of Chicago, where he taught for 30 years, and is a Senior Research Fellow at the Hoover Institute at Stanford University. Friedman received a B.A. degree from Rutgers (where he took courses from Arthur Burns), an A.M. degree from the University of Chicago, and a Ph.D. from Columbia University. Friedman has published many articles and books, but his ideas are readily available in your library in two books, *Essays in Positive Economics* (1953) and *Capitalism and Freedom* (1962).

5

will be very useful in predicting actual behavior of the "if A, then B" variety.

Of course, economists recognize that people are motivated by complex forces. However, these complex forces are not important in the examination of all questions. Hence it is often possible to obtain predictive results based on this very simple assumption about human motivation. It is not that economists view the world in a simpleminded fashion but rather that simplifying assumptions about human behavior allows the economist to make powerful predictive statements without becoming a victim of a quagmire of behavioral questions concerning human motivation which can never be effectively concluded. This does not mean that the economist does not know that individual behavior is or can be vastly different from what the assumptions presume or that the economist is denigrating the importance and origins of different types of individual behavior. It only means that for some problems the economist finds the effects of these differences not significant enough to warrant special attention.

In addition, the economist does not view the concept of self-interest narrowly. Individual choice is simply characterized as utility-maximizing behavior. (We will develop this in detail in Chapter 5.) Many human motivations, including those of love and altruism, can be seen to derive from self-interest or selfish behavior. For example, one of the authors has two daughters. He cares about these daughters and many of his actions can be fitted into this hypothesis. Say he has enough discretionary income to purchase a tricycle or 10 bottles of scotch. It is consistent with our self-interest hypothesis for him to purchase the tricycle if the satisfaction he receives from his daughter's happiness exceeds the satisfaction he would receive from the scotch. He may be behaving in his own self-interest by purchasing the tricycle. What is important for an economic model is not what an individual maximizes but how predictable the behavior is, and in order to be able to predict how any one individual will choose, it is necessary to have some knowledge of what motivates people. This is the role of the self-interest hypothesis.

This assumption of self-interest or selfish behavior does not imply that economists think that people cannot change or that their preferences cannot be influenced by outside forces. If we turn the economist's self-interest assumption on its head, it is possible to envisage a world of selfless people. But the critic who argues this view is logically required to develop consistent and predictive models of this form of behavior. Indeed, such models, based on an economy of love, if you will, may be quite relevant to describing some forms of human behavior. However, there is competition even in a world of saints between different views of the general welfare. Consider the competition between different religions, for example.

In general, political economists, from their behavioral perspective that people behave in a narrowly self-interested way 90 percent of the time, are interested in institutions, such as markets, that minimize the need for "good" action to solve social problems. In other words, economists seek to design institutions that channel self-interest into socially desirable patterns. They do not believe that social policy should be based on appeals to love of humanity or should attempt to build character.

Economists using the self-interest assumption often think in a calculating way about things that often have a highly emotional element. This leads to the caricature of the economic human by those who are critical of the economic approach and the conclusions economists reach. Kenneth Boulding, professor of economics at the University of Colorado, in his presidential address to the American Economic Association, argued that this attack arises from the economist's neglect of the heroic. While "economic man" may be a clod to some, Boulding argues that "heroic man" is a fool, and he wonders how economic institutions have survived so long given the fact that "economic man" is so unpopular. Somewhere between the extremes of the clod and the fool are real people. The important point is that economic theory does not depend on purely economic humans to be valid. The accepted theory of how markets operate makes reasonably meaningful predictions as long as people base a substantial part of their behavior on their own self-interest.

It is important to keep in mind that the economist does not use the concept of self-interest to predict any one individual's behavior, but rather the economist uses the concept to predict group, average, or normal behavior. It is similar to how insurance companies use attributes of certain groups to predict behavior. Insurance companies tend to grant lower auto rates to young female drivers than to young male drivers. This is because they predict that, as a class, young women have fewer accidents than do young men. This says nothing about how any one individual young man or young woman will do relative to the group.

A SHORT GUIDE TO THE ECONOMIC APPROACH

We now turn to a short discussion of the basic elements of the economic approach. The list is not meant to be exhaustive, although we hope that we have captured the essential aspects of the economic approach. Our list is not arranged in any particular order and, as usual in any listing process, there is some redundancy. This redundancy is unavoidable and we hope the repetition will aid the cause of better understanding. If this guide seems difficult to understand at this point, that's because it represents much of the material you will be exposed to in upcoming chapters.

1 Economic theory is *positive*, or *nonnormative*; that is, it consists of a set of refutable propositions about "what is" rather than individual, *normative* value judgments about "what ought to be." This does not mean that economists do not, or should not, make

their personal preferences known in the process of giving economic advice, but the reader needs to be aware of the particular personal bias of the economist giving policy advice. To summarize, economic theory, as such, is not biased although its applier may be. This is a very simple methodological view. It basically implies that the science of economics does not offer policymakers a guide as to how things "ought" to be organized. Rather, it presents a way to infer how certain conditions or policies will affect consumption and production or other economic variables in which we may be interested.

2 Economic theory cannot predict the future but can only explain the consequences of certain occurrences. Economic theory allows "if A, then B" types of statements and does not predict the occurrence of A. Yet economists sometimes do offer predictions of future events. This should not be taken as the substance of economic theory. When economists do venture predictions, these predictions are, as often as not, a subject of much disagreement among economists because the predictions are not based just on theory but rather on estimates of the future. These predictive statements are the ones you see economists disagreeing about so often in the news media.

3 Economists tend to look to private market processes for solutions to social problems. In a narrow sense the economist is opting for the general efficiency characteristics of the market process, especially in solving the problem of providing reliable information on issues of resource allocation. The preference for a market process in this sense does not stem from an inherent conservative bias but rather from a desire to generate an efficient resource allocation. However, in a broader sense, this preference stems from a desire to see solutions obtain from the system rather than being forced upon it. And in its broadest sense, this preference shows the premium that the economist places on individual freedom and decentralized decision-making processes.

4 Economists tend to spend a great deal of effort clarifying options and making the cost of a given choice as clear as possible. This is quite distinct from, say, a purely political approach which instead might seek to find a consensus without ever asking serious questions about the efficiency of a project. This tendency to draw attention to the cost of various choices often makes the economist appear as an agitator, frustrating the attainment of political consensus. However, we note that agitation of traditional political thinking can be quite healthy, and in a sense this is the role of the economist as a social accountant, protecting economic efficiency from those who would violate its dictates in search of agreement.

5 Economists are likely to recognize the opportunity for substitution among options that exist. Because of this, the political economist

is more likely to be critical of an all-or-nothing approach to public policy; that is, the economist will probably not be impressed by claims that a project or program has to be undertaken at a certain all-or-nothing size to be successful, unless clear evidence of the economies of such lumpiness in the project is convincingly presented. As a corollary to this general point, an economist would be likely to suggest a great deal of experimenting on a small scale for public policies.

6 A closely related point is that economists employ an incremental or *marginal* approach. Economists are more inclined to examine the merits of a small contraction or expansion in a public program. They will look carefully at the *change* in costs and benefits from changes in policy; that is, they look at *marginal* costs and benefits. In government, economists try to use this approach even where the "margin" must be broadly interpreted to include not only a change in the effectiveness of a single project but also differences in the compared costs and benefits among a number of projects and programs.

7 Economists tend to take an individualistic approach to social analysis; that is, they regard the decisions and behavior of individuals as an important influence on the formulation of public policy and the organization of the economy. There are several reasons for this individualistic approach (which stands in stark contrast to some political science or sociological approaches to public policy). Perhaps most important, it economizes on the need for information. For example, suppose people begin to demand more soybeans. As we will see in later chapters, this will drive up the price of soybeans and farmers will produce more of them. Note, the farmer does not need to know *why* the price of soybeans increased sharply, only that it did. Economists consider this decentralized decision-making process to be highly efficient.

8 Economic theory is applicable to all economic systems. The legal institutions among systems may differ, but the theory that is applied to these systems is not different. It is possible, then, for the economist to apply the tools, which historically have been extensively developed to analyze Western market economies, to examine socialist economic relations and a wide variety of essentially non-market behavior. We shall apply this theory to other systems in Chapter 17.

THE ECONOMIC PROBLEM

The *resources* of any society, which represent all the inputs that can be used to produce goods and services, are *scarce*. We do not live in the garden of Eden, we do not have Aladdin's lamp, we haven't found Big

Rock Candy Mountain, and Li'l Abner's shmoos exist only in the newspapers' comic sections. There are never enough resources to produce what everyone would like to have because individuals' *wants*, what individuals desire to have, are insatiable. These wants can thus never be satisfied with a certain level or composition of consumption. Wants are insatiable and resources are scarce. This scarcity, then, forces individuals to make choices. Individuals must *economize*. This simple fact of life is very important because without scarcity, it would not be necessary to economize or to make decisions on the priority of wants, and there would be no need to study economics.

Because of scarcity, every decision to consume or produce means that we forego consuming and producing something else. In fact, the cost of engaging in some activity, say going to a football game, is whatever is given up in order to attend. Economists use the term *opportunity cost* to designate such costs. The cost of attending the game is the most valuable other thing you could have done during that three-hour time period. Suppose you would have studied for an economics exam coming up the following week but instead went to the game. The opportunity cost is the price of the ticket plus the difference in the test score that three more hours of study could have produced.

An interesting way of using opportunity cost was put forward in discussions several years ago when politicians were debating the volunteer army. Some politicians said we "couldn't afford" the volunteer army. Economists viewed this as a foolish statement. Take yourself as an example. If your two alternatives were to earn $10,000 selling insurance or to be drafted or volunteer and earn $4,000, which would you do? Using our self-interest assumption, we would conclude you would decide to sell insurance. The government would need to raise salaries to $10,001 to get you to volunteer. This would cause the price of the volunteer army to go up. But wait! What if you're drafted? You earn $4,000 but you could have earned $10,000, your opportunity cost. Truly, the government, if it drafts you, is taking $6,000 from you and "giving" it to all taxpayers in the sense that they now have to pay smaller taxes to raise an army. So really you have been taxed $6,000 to raise an army. In essence, then, the cost of the volunteer army is the same as the cost of a drafted army. The difference is that in one instance taxpayers have to pay the cost and in the other instance those drafted have to pay the cost. The military draft, then, is a very discriminatory (unfair) tax because it is a tax levied only on a small subset of the population, i.e., young, healthy males. Beyond this, if society thinks each soldier only costs $4,000 per year, it will use more soldiers than it would if it knew each was really costing $10,000. Also, by thinking it's cheaper to use soldiers than it really is, society will rely more on soldiers and less on machines and equipment for defense than it would if it knew the true costs of using soldiers.

Let us develop a simple model to view choice under scarcity. Given the resources and technology in our hypothetical economy, we can produce only so much butter and so many guns. Table 1-1 gives a numerical example of the combination of guns and butter that can be produced assuming that only these two outputs can be produced. We see that the only way to receive more of one good is to give up some of the other. The opportunity cost of getting five billion pounds of butter at combination B, for example, is the three million guns that had to be given up in moving from combination A to combination B.

TABLE 1-1   Production Possibilities

Combinations	Butter (Billions of Pounds)	Guns (Millions of Guns)
A	0	40
B	5	37
C	10	32
D	15	25
E	20	15
F	25	0

This concept is even more illuminating if we translate Table 1-1 into a graph, which we call a **production possibilities curve**, as in Figure 1-1. In Figure 1-1 we see that moving from combination C to combination D means that seven million guns are given up in order to get 5 billion additional pounds of butter. The particular point of consumption on the curve will depend on the tastes of the consumers and on the type of economic system that the curve represents. In a free market economy the choice would be made by consumers while in a command economy the choice would be made by central planners (more on this later).

The particular shape of the production possibilities curve depends upon the technology and resources an economy has available. An increase in resources or an improvement in technology would shift the boundaries of the curve outward. Such a shift is depicted as the move from PP to P_1P_1 in Figure 1-2. Such a shift would enable the economy to produce more guns *and* more butter; at point A, b_1 units of butter and g_1 units of guns are produced and at point B, b_2 units of butter and g_2 units of guns are produced. A change in technology that only applied to one of the products would shift the curve, but not in a parallel fashion as with P_1P_1. We say in a parallel *fashion* because it is not mathematically correct to call this a parallel shift. The shift, if the technology only applied to guns, might look like the production possibilities curve represented by the dashed line in Figure 1-2.

FIGURE 1-1   **Production Possibilities Curve**

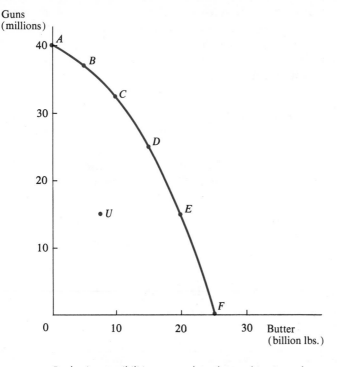

Production possibilities curves show the combinations of two goods that
can be produced given the resources and technology available. Points on
the curve represent full employment of the available resources. At point
U there are unemployed resources.

We have also drawn the production possibilities curve concave from
below to depict an important principle — the ***principle of increasing
costs***. Start at combination *A* in Table 1-1 and Figure 1-1. In order to
increase the amount of butter, we have to give up a certain amount of
guns. As we produce more and more butter, moving from *B* to *C* and
from *C* to *D*, we are forced to give up larger and larger numbers of guns.
The reason is that in most economies, resources are not all equally sub-
stitutable for each other. As we produce more and more butter, we have
to take resources, such as land and labor, that are better at producing
guns and switch them to butter production. As a result, the cost, in terms
of foregone guns, increases. If all resources in an economy were perfectly
interchangeable in producing all commodities, the production possibilities curve would be a straight line rather than a curved line.

The production possibilities curve can even tell us about efficiency
in the employment of resources in our hypothetical economy. If all resources are fully and efficiently employed, we are on the *frontier* at any of

FIGURE 1-2   Shifts in Production Possibilities Curves

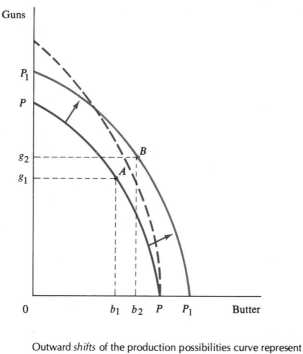

Outward *shifts* of the production possibilities curve represent
improvements in technology or increases in available resources. A
parallel shift means the technological growth is neutral. The dashed line
represents *biased* technological growth in that it affects only one of the
goods.

the points A through F in Figure 1-1. Suppose for a moment we aren't
on the frontier, but instead are at point U on Figure 1-1. It is possible at
point U, by using resources more efficiently, to put underemployed resources to better use *or* to put unemployed resources to work to produce
more guns and more butter, and the production of one output can be
increased without decreasing the production of the other. In other words,
if resources are unemployed or inefficiently employed, there may not be
an opportunity cost to increased production. This is one of the problems
we discuss in our companion macroeconomics text.

Fundamental Questions

Because of the fundamental problem of scarcity that all economies
face, there are *fundamental questions* that must be answered. These
questions can take many forms but they reduce to four basic questions.

1 What is to be produced?

2 How much is to be produced?

3 In what way, or how, are things to be produced?

4 Who will have the right to consume the goods and services produced, and how much will each person get?

Each of these questions is addressed in every society, and microeconomic theory concentrates on the way different types of economic systems affect the answers to these questions.

Economists divide economic systems into three major groups — the traditional economy, the planned economy, and the market economy. Of course, no economy fits neatly into any of these classification schemes because all economies are mixed. A *mixed economy* contains elements of tradition, planning, and the market.

The *traditional economy*, sometimes called the subsistence economy, answers the fundamental questions by appeals to tradition. What is produced is what the young have been taught by their parents to hunt, to gather, or to plant. The techniques of production, or how to produce, are also passed on, often without change, from generation to generation. The amount of production is, of course, highly dependent on good fortune, but often there are traditional limits. The answer to the last question concerning distribution is also traditionally determined. If you have studied cultural anthropology, you know that such traditional societies often have hard and fast rules on how the spoils of the hunt or the harvest are to be divided. In a traditional society, particular goods and services are produced and distributed in a given manner because they always have been and always will be (at least, the people believe so). Most of you recognize that some elements of tradition exist even in societies as modern as our own. Throughout the United States, for example, there are many small rural Pennsylvania Dutch and Amish communities almost untouched by modern farming techniques. There are other farming areas where the most modern farming techniques are avoided. In recent years, such life-styles and techniques have even been pursued by some groups in our society as a "better" way of life.

The *planned economy* answers the fundamental questions through planning or through central command and control. The decision of what, how, and how much to produce is carefully spelled out and documented. Detailed plans and orders are sent to producers and they carry the weight of law. A large part of the question of who receives what is determined in the same way because planners determine wage rates and the amount of production of consumer goods. In this way, the distribution is a function of the plans. Such planning is the primary method of organization in the USSR and other countries in Eastern Europe. In Chapter 17, we will go into a detailed explanation of the benefits and costs of such economic organization. Centralized planning, however, exists in some form in all economies, including our modern economy. Both Washington-based and local bureaucrats determine to some extent what is produced and the manner in which it is produced. Governmental policies also affect the distribution of income and thus affect the determination of who gets what.

The third economic organization that operates, again, to some degree, in all economies, is the *market*. Much of what follows in this book develops theories that explain how the market influences the resolution of the fundamental questions.

The Market Resolution

The organizing principles in a market economy are the forces of *supply and demand*. The determination of what to produce is made by consumers. The impersonal force of demand causes prices to go up for those products that consumers want the most. In a sense, consumers "vote" with their dollar expenditures. The result of this voting process determines what will be produced and how much of various goods and services will be produced. Suppliers, combining resources, determine how goods and services are to be produced. Assuming suppliers seek to maximize their profits, they will tend to combine inputs to produce any good or service at the lowest cost possible. This determination, then, depends on the prices of resources. Suppliers will use more of relatively abundant resources because they are relatively cheap. This, in turn, helps conserve the scarcer (expensive) resources. The goods are then distributed to consumers who have the purchasing power to buy them. Those who have more purchasing power receive more goods. This purchasing power is in part determined by the quantity and quality of the skills the individual sells; in the United States, for example, approximately 75 percent of income is labor income. Those with scarce, high quality skills receive higher incomes and can thus purchase more production. In a sense, these people have more votes.

Such a system is not without problems (as we shall see), but its advantage is that it generates valuable information at low cost and passes only the needed information on to consumers and producers. As an example, suppose that for some reason, say an earthquake closing some copper mines, the supply of copper is suddenly cut by one half. In a command economy, the central planners would have to investigate, determine the possible effects of this shortage, and estimate how long it will last. They then would have to notify all consumers of copper that they should start to use less of it. Instructions would be sent to firms producing generators, for instance, commanding them to substitute other metals for copper. Contrast this to a market system. When the mine closes, copper prices rise. Consumers of copper know immediately that the price has gone up. They then search for cheaper substitutes. All this happens very quickly with no need to process and send information. What the market has done is to economize on the amount of costly information that is needed to make production and consumption decisions.

The basic institution needed for the market resolution to work is the institution of ***property rights***. Markets and exchange will happen only if individual buyers and sellers possess the property rights to the goods and services they exchange. Slavery is not a market process, but rather a command system process. If workers possess the property right to their own labor, they are then free to sell that labor to the highest bidder. A market system, therefore, requires legal enforcement of property rights and freedom to exchange these property rights. However, if the cost of protecting the property right becomes too high, the market process will break down. Consider buying a bicycle. Would you buy a bicycle if the probability of it being stolen is 95 percent? Probably not. But what if you could reduce the possibility of theft to .1 percent with the purchase of a $5 lock. In this case, the cost of enforcing your property right probably isn't too high, so the market process works. What we need, then, is a legal system or other mechanism that works reasonably well in insuring the protection and exchange of property rights.

Summary

This has been a wide-ranging chapter that has introduced a way of thinking that will be expanded in the remainder of the book. The basic elements of the market system and the economic way of thinking have been discussed. Although we will spend much time examining the market resolution in detail, the principles derived will be applicable to command and traditional economies. The forces of supply and demand are operating in all systems. The difference in the market resolution is that these forces are permitted to direct consumption and production without direction from outside authorities or rules.

Microeconomics is the study of individual market interactions. Economic theory is an abstract way of thinking that allows the development of principles, or tools, that can be used to examine complex social issues.

The self-interest hypothesis is a very basic assumption of economic theory. Although economists recognize that human behavior is a complex process, we assume in economics that human beings pursue their own self-interest.

The economic approach is positive, or nonnormative. It can't predict the future but predicts events of an "if A, then B" type. Economists tend to look to the market to solve social problems because of their individualistic approach. In analyzing problems, economists spend a great deal of time clarifying options and looking at costs. In looking at possibilities for substitution, economists examine costs and benefits at the margin.

Resources are scarce and wants are insatiable. This creates the economic problem of scarcity. As a result, individuals must make choices.

Opportunity cost is a measure of the things given up in order to consume or undertake some alternative. Opportunity cost is the benefit foregone by the act being undertaken. Production possibilities curves depict opportunity cost by showing that the cost of one good is the foregone production of some other good.

Every society must answer four fundamental questions: What is to be produced? How much is to be produced? How is it to be produced? for whom is it to be produced? Each of these questions is answered in every mixed economy regardless of whether it is primarily a traditional, market, or planned economy.

New Terms

microeconomics
macroeconomics
theory
economic approach
testable hypothesis
ceteris paribus
assumptions
self-interest
positive (nonnormative) economics
normative economics
marginal
resources
scarcity

wants
economize
opportunity cost
production possibilities curve
principle of increasing costs
fundamental questions
mixed economy
traditional economy
planned economy
market economy
supply and demand
property rights

Questions for Discussion

1 The famous British economist, J. M. Keynes, once remarked: "The object of our analysis is not to provide a machine, or method of blind manipulation, which will furnish an infallible answer, but to provide ourselves with an organized and orderly method of thinking out particular problems.... This is the nature of economic thinking." (*The General Theory of Employment, Interest, and Money* [New York: Harcourt, 1936], p. 297.) Does this statement more closely fit the position of Samuelson or Friedman in their debate on methodology?

2 What is the difference between facing scarcity and being poor?

3 If a government ruled that a technology presently in use should no longer be used because of environmental considerations, what effect would this ruling have on the shape of the production possibilities curve?

4 Write four statements about the energy crisis (it doesn't matter if they are based on correct economic reasoning). Then classify each statement as being positive or normative.

5 Do you think people exhibit behavior patterns that confirm the self-interest hypothesis? Does your own behavior confirm the self-interest hypothesis? Can you develop any theory based solely on this assumption?

6 Why do economists theorize rather than attempt to describe reality?

Suggestions for Further Reading

Amacher, Ryan, Robert Tollison, and Thomas Willett. *The Economic Approach to Social Policy Questions*. Ithaca: Cornell University Press, 1976, Chapter 1.

Boulding, Kenneth. "Economics as a Moral Science?" *American Economic Review* (March, 1961).

Buchanan, James M. "Toward an Analysis of Closed Behavioral Systems." In James Buchanan and Robert Tollison (eds.), *Theory of Public Choice*. Ann Arbor: University of Michigan Press, 1972.

Friedman, Milton. *Essays in Positive Economics*. Chicago: University of Chicago Press, 1953, Chapter 1.

Samuelson, Paul. "Discussion — Problems of Methodology." *American Economic Review* (May, 1963).

Tullock, Gordon. "Economic Imperialism." In James Buchanan and Robert Tollison (eds.), *Theory of Public Choice*. Ann Arbor: University of Michigan Press, 1972.

APPENDIX: WORKING WITH GRAPHS

Economic ideas, theories, and models are often expressed as relationships among variables. These relationships can be put into mathematical form, and if you decide to major in economics, you may want to take some calculus. Instead of putting these relationships into mathematical form, we will often express these relationships in graphical form. It is important to be comfortable with graphs because, while economics is not *about graphs*, graphs allow us to illustrate our theories and models in ways that make them easier to remember and apply to the real world. Remember that everything that can be said in graphs can also be said in words. Don't get hung up on graphs; if you can master their use it will make this book and the course you are now taking much easier. It is also important that you don't memorize graphical relationships; understand them, don't memorize them. They are an aid to understanding the theory, not ends in themselves.

Relationship Between Variables

One of the most common ways to represent the relationship between two variables is through the use of a graph. A graph shows how the quantity of one variable changes when the other changes. Table 1A-1 shows how much corn is produced on an acre of land as the rainfall is varied. We could graph this relationship. Before we do, however, we need to discuss graphs in general.

Figure 1A-1 depicts a typical graphing quadrant system. The vertical line is referred to as the *y-axis* and the horizontal line is referred to as the *x-axis*. The x-axis and y-axis divide the graph into four quadrants. The point of intersection of the axes is the *origin*. The intersection represents zero value for both the x variable and the y variable. As you move upward from the origin, above the x-axis, the y variable takes on positive values. Below the x-axis, movement along the y-axis represents negative values for the y variable. Likewise, as you move away from the origin along the x-axis to the right of the y-axis, positive values for the x variable are represented. Leftward movement from the origin represents negative values for the x variable.

TABLE 1A-1 Relationships Between Variables

Rainfall in Inches/Month	Bushels of Corn/Acre
1	1
2	10
3	40
4	80
5	100
6	110
7	115
8	110
9	100
10	70

FIGURE 1A-1 Quadrant System

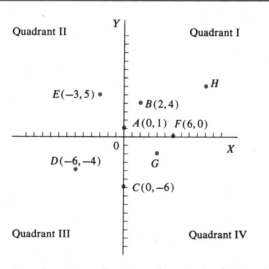

A quadrant system allows us to plot points in a horizontal and vertical dimension. The four quadrants represent combinations of positive and negative values in the two dimensions. Point C, for example, thus represents a zero x value and −6 y value.

You can now locate points on the graph. Each point has a *coordinate*, which is a pair of numbers, one representing the x value and one representing the y value. For example, point B on Figure 1A-1 represents the value 2 for the x variable and 4 for the y variable. The x value is always given first. For example, point E represents $x = -3, y = 5$. Can you give the coordinates of points G and H?

In this book we will almost always be plotting lines in Quadrant I. This is because the data from which we will plot our lines is almost always positive. In the few cases where we deal with negative numbers, we are usually most concerned with where they become negative, which is where they cross the x- or y-axis.

Now we can plot the relationship between rainfall and corn which we listed in Table 1A-1. Figure 1A-2 plots the relationship with rainfall as the x variable and corn output as the y variable. You will note that we could represent the amount of rainfall and the production of corn by selecting almost any scale on the axis that we would want. The scale should be chosen to suit the problem. We can then connect the plotted points with a smooth curve to produce a graph. The value of the graph is that it gives you a visual picture of the mathematical relationship between the variables. In Figure 1A-2 we can easily see that as rainfall increases up to 7 inches per month, corn output increases, and then more rain causes a decrease in output.

FIGURE 1A-2   **Rain and Corn Output**

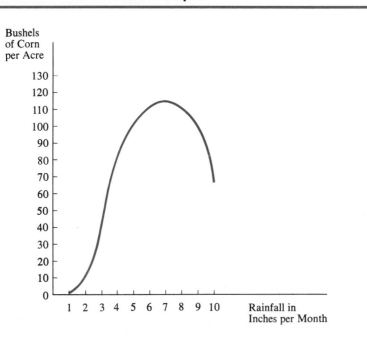

A graph is usually plotted with the dependent variable on the y-axis and the independent variable on the x-axis. This graph shows that as the independent variable, rainfall, increases, the dependent variable, corn output, increases and then decreases.

When plotting lines in economics we usually plot the dependent variable as the y variable and the independent variable as the x variable. In this case bushels of corn per acre is the dependent variable because it is a function of the independent variable, rainfall. Therefore, we plot the corn output on the y-axis. In economics there is one important exception to this principle. When we plot demand and supply curves, which you will be doing in the next chapter, we plot price as the y variable and quantity as the x variable even though quantity is the dependent variable and price is the independent variable.

Slopes and Relationships Between Variables

When we are studying and describing graphs, it is often very convenient to consider the graph in terms of slopes. The *slope of a line* is the ratio of the change in the y value to the change in the x value. This is seen in Figure 1A-3, where the slope of line A is equal to $+1/2$ because

FIGURE 1A-3   Positively Sloped Lines

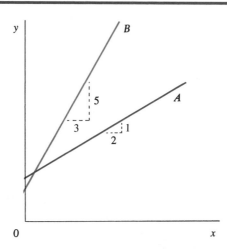

The slope of a line is the ratio of the change in the y value to the change in the x value. A line sloping upward to the right indicates a positive slope. We say a positive slope represents a positive relationship between the variables; as one increases, the other increases.

the y value changes by one unit for each two-unit change in the x value. The slope of line B is $+1.67$. It is very important to keep track of the sign of the slope because the sign tells you the relationship between the two variables. If the variables move in the same direction, that is, if when y is increasing x is also increasing, we say we have a *positive relationship*.

A slope with a positive sign designates a positive relationship. If, on the other hand, the variables move in opposite directions, we have an *inverse relationship*. An inverse relationship is one in which increases in the *y* variable result in decreases in the *x* variable, and vice versa. Such a relationship is graphed in Figure 1A-4. A line depicting an inverse relationship will have a negative slope.

FIGURE 1A-4   **Negatively Sloped Line**

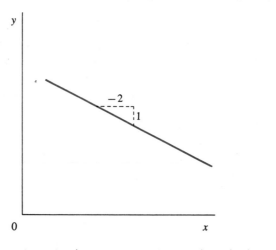

A negative slope represents an inverse relationship between the variables; as one of the variables increases, the other decreases.

Slopes of Curves

A straight line graph, like those in Figures 1A-3 and 1A-4, has the same slope along the entire line, but the slope of the curve varies along the curve. The *slope of a curve* is defined as the slope of the straight line tangent to the curve at that point. A *tangent line* is a line that touches a curve without crossing it. Calculating the slope of the curved line in Figure 1A-5 gives us a slope of +1 at point *A* and a slope of −1.5 at point *C*. The slope of the curve at point *B* is equal to 0. This is because changes in *x* occur but there are no changes in *y* on the straight line tangent to the curve at point *B*.

Graphs Without Numbers

We have plotted graphs and calculated slopes of graphs using explicit relationships between variables. These relationships were explicit because there was a set of numbers from which we actually plotted the

FIGURE 1A-5   **Slopes of Curves**

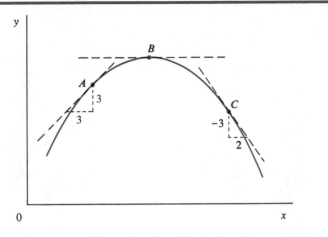

A curved graph has a slope that changes along the curve. The slope of
the curve at any point is the slope of a straight line tangent to the curved
line at that point.

graph. In economics, however, we sometimes plot graphs of theoretical
concepts without having a set of numbers from which to plot the graph.
In these cases the graph represents a conceptualization of an abstract
principle we wish to depict. For example, we might theorize that there is
a negative relationship between price and the quantity demanded of any
good that people consume. If price is the y variable and quantity demanded the x variable, the relationship we have theorized would be expressed by a negatively sloped line similar to the one in Figure 1A-4. It
doesn't matter that we don't have specific coordinates to plot; instead we
have graphed an abstract idea. Much of the graphing in economics is of
an abstract nature.

CHAPTER 2

THE ECONOMICS OF SUPPLY AND DEMAND

LEARNING OBJECTIVES

After studying the materials found in this chapter, you should be able to do the following:

1 Define supply and demand and list the factors influencing each.

2 Translate the concepts of supply and demand among the following media:
    (a) words,
    (b) numbers or functions,
    (c) graphs.

3 Identify on a graph the differences between

    (a) changes in demand and changes in the quantity demanded,
    (b) changes in the supply and changes in the quantity supplied.

4 Identify on a graph the excess quantity supplied or excess quantity demanded when the price is at other than the equilibrium price.

The subject matter of this chapter is basic to the study of economics. Many economists contend that economics is 90 percent supply and demand analysis and that the remaining 10 percent is the study of what causes supply and demand to be what they are. To begin, it is essential to reemphasize that economists view *demands* as desires to consume at certain prices, not needs or wants that can be measured in some social or biological way. The concept of need is reserved for *welfare economics*, which evaluates the economic order from an ethical perspective, or for the realms of the biologist, the sociologist, and the cleric. In addition, for these needs and wants to be demands, they must be viewed as what people actually will do when confronted with different sets of prices. We are not talking about wishes but rather demonstrated action to consume specified amounts at certain prices.

DEMAND

When we talk about demand, we need first to isolate the factors that can affect the demand for a good or service. We generally focus on a few, namely:

1 the price of the good or service itself,
2 the tastes of the group,
3 the income and wealth of the group,
4 the prices of other goods and services, and
5 expectations concerning *1* through *4* above.

All things that affect demand work through one of these factors. The weather, for example, may affect the demand for beer by changing people's taste for beer. These factors become the *ceteris paribus* conditions we discussed in the last chapter. We hold all but one factor constant and determine what happens when we change the factor under consideration.

The Law of Demand

Initially we want to focus on what happens when the price of a good or service changes relative to the prices of other goods and services. We focus on price and hold all the other factors that affect demand constant. We can thus state the *law of demand*:

> The *quantity demanded* of a good or service is an inverse function of its price, *ceteris paribus*.

In other words, we are saying that, holding all else constant, consumers will purchase more of a good or service at a lower price; and as price rises, *ceteris paribus*, consumers will demand a smaller quantity of a good or service. It is important to note that we are saying *quantity demanded* is

Alfred Marshall

Alfred Marshall (1842–1924)

Alfred Marshall is perhaps the most important "modern" economist and may be the most influential economist of all time, in large part because of the great number of students he influenced through his teaching and writing.

Marshall was the great synthesizer and expositor of the *neoclassical school of economics*. The neoclassical school consisted of a regeneration of much of classical economics after Karl Marx (and others) had criticized the errors in classical analysis. Most present-day microeconomic theory can be directly traced to this neoclassical school of economic thought.

Born in London, Marshall came to the study of economics by a circuitous route. Marshall's father, William Marshall, was a strict disciplinarian who pushed brilliant Alfred to the point of mental and physical exhauston after endlessly drilling him in Latin and Greek until midnight. Marshall was offered a scholarship at Oxford which would have led to the ministry. Instead, he enrolled at Cambridge to study mathematics. This was in part a rebellion against his father, who had forbidden him to study mathematics. Later, Marshall began to study political economy, but he made extensive use of mathematics in developing his economic theory.

After marrying a former student, Marshall returned to Cambridge. There he belonged to what he called "a small cultural society of great simplicity and distinction." At Cambridge, Marshall generated a tremendous impact on the economists profession. At first, this impact was felt primarily through his influence as a teacher of almost all the major British economists of the twentieth century. Later, his book *Principles of Economics* (1890) influenced still larger numbers of students. Generations of economists learned economics from Marshall's *Principles*. In fact, if you had taken a course in economics before 1950, it is very probable that you would have studied from Marshall's book.

a function of price. This is not just semantics; it allows us to make some important distinctions, as you will soon see.

We can now generate a hypothetical *demand schedule* for an individual. A demand schedule shows the quantity demanded at various prices. Such a schedule is created in Table 2-1. You will notice that there is a time dimension attached to the demand schedule. It wouldn't make any sense if we didn't know the time period under investigation; we need to talk about the demand for beer per day, per week, per year, etc. Table 2-1 conforms to our law of demand and demonstrates that Freddy Foghorn demands larger quantities of Pabst Blue Ribbon beer at lower prices. We can now convert the demand schedule of Table 2-1 to a graphical representation that we call a *demand curve*. Such a curve is drawn in Figure 2-1. The demand curve is the line graph representing the demand schedule. When we draw a demand curve, we designate the y-axis as the price per unit variable and the x-axis as the quantity per time period variable.[1] It is important to always designate the quantity as quantity per unit of time. Often this can be done by labeling the x-axis as x/t, meaning quantity of x per time period.

TABLE 2-1   Freddy Foghorn's Demand for Pabst Blue Ribbon

Price Per Can	Quantity Demanded Per Day
50¢	1
40¢	7
30¢	13
20¢	19
10¢	25
5¢	28

Market Demand

We have now generated a demand schedule and a demand curve representing Freddy Foghorn's demand for Pabst Blue Ribbon beer. This, however, is of little interest unless we wish to examine only Freddy's behavior in isolation. We are more concerned with the *market demand* curve for Pabst Blue Ribbon or even the market demand curve for all beer. This market demand could be found by adding all the individual

---

[1]If graphing the schedule is confusing, review the appendix to Chapter 1. We usually draw linear curves for convenience.

FIGURE 2-1   **Freddy Foghorn's Demand for Pabst Blue Ribbon**

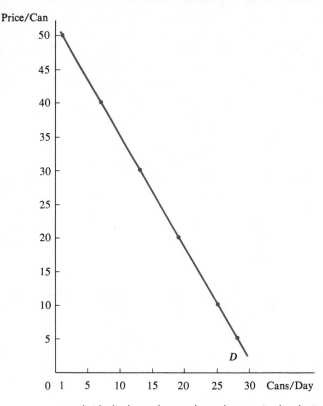

An individual's demand curve shows the quantity that the individual will purchase at different prices.

demand schedules or by a horizontal geometric summation of all the individual demand curves. Figure 2-2 is a market demand curve for beer. It tells us the total quantity demanded at various prices.

As price changes in the market, the quantity demanded changes inversely. In Figure 2-2, 13,000 cans of beer are purchased at a price of 35¢ per can. If price falls to 20¢, the quantity demanded increases to 25,000 cans, or if price rises to 45¢, the quantity demanded decreases to 5,000 cans.

Changes in Demand

We will now see how the other factors affect the market demand for the commodity. To keep things simple, we will continue to use the beer example.

FIGURE 2-2   **Market Demand for Beer**

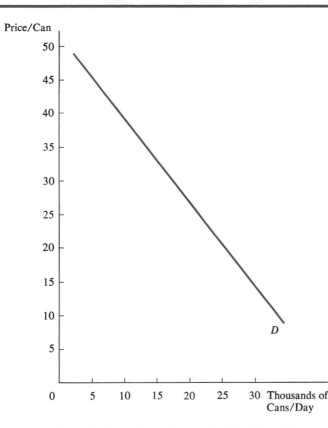

A market demand curve is a graphical depiction of how much will be purchased by the market at various prices. It is the aggregation of all the individual demand curves.

Suppose the tastes of the group change. The reason for a change in tastes is best left to a field like psychology. Let's just assume that people's tastes change in favor of beer; perhaps beer drinking has become more glamorous because famous people are beer guzzlers. Such a change in taste is reflected in Figure 2-3 as an ***increase in demand***. At every price, consumers demand a larger amount than before. The demand curve shifts from D to D_1 in Figure 2-3. The opposite would have occurred if tastes changed away from beer. Such a change in tastes would cause a ***decrease in demand***, represented by a shift from D to D_2 in Figure 2-3.

If income changes, we have similar shifts in demand, again represented geometrically by shifts in the demand curve. The first consideration in assessing the effect of income changes on demand is to determine if the good under consideration is a ***normal good*** or an ***inferior***

FIGURE 2-3   **Effects of Changes in Tastes on the Demand for Beer**

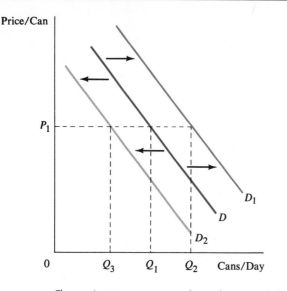

Changes in tastes can cause a demand curve to shift. If the tastes of the group change in favor of the item, more will be demanded at every price and the curve will shift to the right, as from D to D_1. A change in tastes away from the good causes a shift to the left, as from D to D_2.

good. A normal good is a good for which demand increases as income increases. If you reflect on it, you will quickly realize that most goods are normal goods. It is very hard to think of goods that people as a group consume less of when their income increases. If this happens, we call such a good an inferior good. If we define goods quite narrowly, it is possible to define some inferior goods. Consider, for example, poorer cuts of meat, such as hamburger. If, as an individual's income increases, the individual consumes less hamburger and more steak, hamburger is an inferior good and steak is a normal good, but meat or beef is still considered a normal good.[2] In terms of our geometric analysis, an increase in income causes demand in Figure 2-4 to increase to D_1 if good x is a normal good. If good x is an inferior good, the shift to D_1 is caused by a decrease in income. The opposite changes in income cause a decrease in demand. Again consider Figure 2-4. The decrease in demand represented by the shift in demand from D to D_2 represents a decrease in income if x is a normal good or an increase in income if x is an inferior good.

---

[2]Perhaps the best example of an inferior good was suggested to one of the authors by a student. The student suggested that outhouses were inferior goods. As a community's income rises, its demand for outhouses decreases.

FIGURE 2-4   Effects of Changes in Income on the Demand for Good X

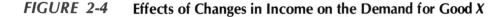

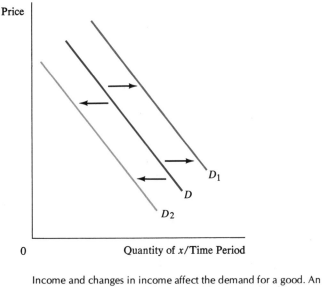

Income and changes in income affect the demand for a good. An increase in income causes the demand for a normal (inferior) good to increase (decrease), as depicted in the shift from D to D_1. A decrease in income causes the demand for a normal (inferior) good to decrease (increase), as depicted in the shift from D to D_2.

The fourth factor that we held out for consideration was the price of other goods and services. Here it is important to determine what type of other good is under consideration. There are two classes of these other goods, **complements** and **substitutes**. Complementary goods are those goods that are jointly consumed. If consuming goods together enhances the consumption of both, such as bacon and eggs, lox and bagels, or hamburgers and ketchup, we refer to them as complements. Substitute goods have just the opposite relationship. Rather than enhancing the consumption of the other good, substitute goods replace the consumption of it. Orange juice and grapefruit juice, Miller High Life and Pabst, and bacon and sausage would be examples of this type of relationship.

After we determine if goods are complements or substitutes, we can examine how changes in the price of one affect the other. Examine, for example, the demand for complementary good x (bagels), as represented in Figure 2-5. If the price of complementary good y (lox) goes up, the demand for bagels will decrease, shifting from D to D_2 in Figure 2-5. This is because consumers will now consume fewer lox, and thus fewer bagels, at every price than before. The opposite would obtain if the price of good y (lox) fell. Consumers would now want to consume more lox, and thus more of good x (bagels), at each price. This would be geometrically depicted as a shift from D to D_1 in Figure 2-5.

FIGURE 2-5   **The Price of Other Goods and the Demand for X**

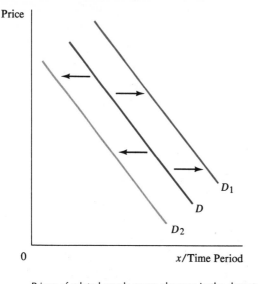

Prices of related goods cause changes in the demand for the good under
analysis. An increase (decrease) in the price of a substitute (complement)
causes an increase in demand for the good, represented by the shift from
D to D_1. A decrease (increase) in the price of a substitute (complement)
will, for similar reasons, cause a decrease in demand for the good, as
demonstrated by the shift from D to D_2.

Now consider what happens when we have a substitute relationship
between the two goods. Good x (Miller High Life) and good y (Pabst) are
substitutes and we can again use Figure 2-5. Curve D represents the
demand for good x (Miller High Life). The price of good y (Pabst) now
increases relative to the price of good x. This makes good x more attractive to consumers and at every previous price consumers will now demand more of good x. This is geometrically represented by the shift from
D to D_1 in Figure 2-5. If instead the price of the substitute good y decreased relative to good x, the opposite would happen. Consumers would
now find good x less attractive and would desire less good x at each price
as they shift consumption to good y. This is a decrease in demand for
good x, represented by the shift from D and D_2 in Figure 2-5.

The last of the *ceteris paribus* factors that affects demand is *expectations*. If individuals expect demand to change in the future, they will
take action now that brings that change into effect. For example, if you
expect that the demand for automobiles will be so high next year that
price will rise, you may take action to demand a car now to avoid the
higher price. If enough people act on that same expectation, the price
will be higher now because of the expectation. The same situation will,
of course, hold for other factors. If you expect your income to be higher

in the future, you may demand more goods now and expect to pay for them later.

What we have seen is that economists spend a lot of time distinguishing clearly between changes along a demand curve and changes (or shifts) of the curve itself. Changes along the curve are *changes in quantity demanded* caused solely by a change in the *price* of the good. Changes (or shifts) of the curve are *changes in demand* caused by changes in any of the *ceteris paribus* conditions.

SUPPLY

Supply is the quantity of goods offered for sale at a particular time or at a particular price. When we talk about supply, we need, as when we examined demand, to isolate the factors that affect the supply of a good or service. When examining supply, we usually concentrate on three factors as being most important. These are:

1 the price of the good,
2 the price of the factors of production, and
3 the level of technology.

All things that affect supply work through one of these factors. For example, if there is a natural disaster that affects society by destroying large amounts of capital, the price of that factor of production will rise.

We should be careful to avoid confusing the words **cost** and **price**. The cost of a factor of production includes both price and productivity. Thus, the cost of a factor could rise even if its price remained the same if the productivity of the factor fell.

The (Not Quite) Law of Supply

Initially we want to focus on what happens when the price of the good or service under consideration changes. We want to make this a *ceteris paribus* experiment by holding constant everything but the price of the good or service. We can thus state the *(not quite) law of supply*:

> The *quantity supplied* of a good or service is *usually* a positive function of price, *ceteris paribus*.

In other words, we are saying that, holding all else constant, suppliers will usually supply less of a good or service at lower prices; and as prices rise, the quantity supplied will increase. It is important to note that we are saying that *quantity supplied* is a function of price. This distinction is important just as it was when we considered demand. But note we said *usually*. This is why we call it a "not quite" law. There are some exceptions to this relationship (which we shall be concerned with later).

We can now generate a hypothetical *supply schedule* for an individual supplier, which we will call a firm. A supply schedule shows the quantity supplied at various prices. Such a schedule is created in Table 2-2. You will notice that, just as when we considered demand, there is a time element attached to the supply schedule. It wouldn't make any sense to talk about supply without knowing the period of time. Table 2-2 conforms to our (not quite) law of supply and demonstrates that Suzy Sizzle supplies larger quantities of lemonade at higher prices. We can now convert the supply schedule of Table 2-2 to a graphical representation we call a *supply curve*. Such a curve is drawn in Figure 2-6. As when graphing demand, we put price per unit on the *y*-axis and quantity per time period on the *x*-axis. We generally draw supply curves as linear curves for convenience, and they usually are drawn with a positive price intercept, indicating that at some low price none of the commodity may be supplied.

TABLE 2-2   Suzy Sizzle's Supply of Lemonade

Price Per Glass (Cents)	Quantity Supplied Per Day
5	0
10	5
15	10
20	15
25	20
30	25

Market Supply

We have now generated a supply schedule and a supply curve depicting Suzy Sizzle's supply of lemonade. What we really want to obtain is the *market supply* curve. This could be found by summing all the individual supply schedules or by a horizontal geometric summation of all the individual supply curves. Figure 2-7 is a market supply curve for lemonade. It tells us the total quantity supplied at various prices.

As price changes in the market, the quantity supplied changes as a positive function of this price change. In Figure 2-7, 5,000 glasses of lemonade are supplied at a price of 10¢. If price fell to 5¢, the quantity supplied would decrease to zero glasses, and if price rose to 20¢, the quantity supplied would increase to 15,000 glasses. These changes occur because most producers are willing to offer more units for sale if the price rises enough to cover the additional, higher costs of production.

FIGURE 2-6   **Suzy Sizzle's Supply of Lemonade**

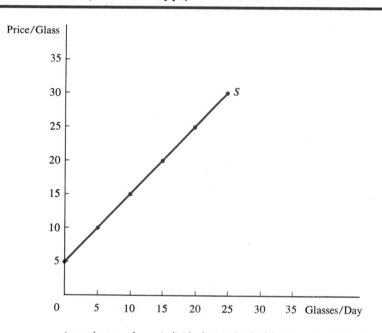

A supply curve for an individual (or individual firm) graphically depicts
how much will be offered for sale at various prices.

Changes in Supply

We can now see how the other factors affect the market supply of a
good or service. Suppose technology changes and this change is a positive technological change. For instance, assume we are looking at the
supply of beef and that the "ag" researchers at the State Agricultural
Research Center develop a very inexpensive pill to feed cattle which
causes a young steer to double in weight very rapidly. This technological
advance would mean that more beef would be supplied at each previous
price. There would be an *increase in supply*. Such an increase in supply
is represented in Figure 2-8 as the outward shift from S to S_1. A negative
technological change would have the opposite effect. Suppose the government discovers that a drug now in use for steer fattening has harmful
side effects on humans, and farmers are therefore prohibited from giving
it to steers. This would mean that less beef would be supplied at each
previous price. There would be a *decrease in supply*, and this decrease
would be represented as a shift from S to S_2 in Figure 2-8.

Now consider changes in the prices of the *factors of production*.
These factors of production are *land, labor, capital*, and *entrepreneurship*. The price paid for the use of land is *rent*. The price paid for labor

FIGURE 2-7   **Market Supply of Lemonade**

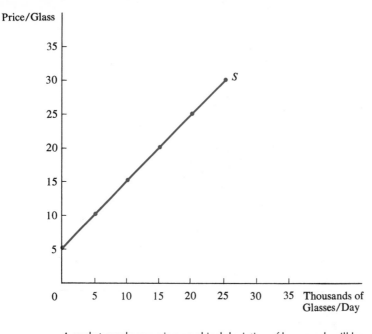

A market supply curve is a graphical depiction of how much will be offered for sale at various prices. It is the aggregate of all the individual supply curves.

services is **wages**. The price paid for using capital is **interest**, and the price paid for entrepreneurship is **profit**. If the price of a factor, say, labor services, goes up, it will affect supply. It will mean that less of the good will be supplied at each of the previous prices. That is to say, supply will decrease because the costs of production have gone up. Suppose that S in Figure 2-9 represents the market supply of beef. Assume the wage rate of meat cutters increases. This will mean less will be supplied at each price; supply will decrease. This is represented as a shift from S to S_2. Another way of looking at this is to see that before the increase in wages, amount OQ_1 was supplied at price OP_1. When S decreases to S_2 after wages go up, suppliers will only supply the old amount (OQ_1) at a higher price (OP_2).

The same principle holds for any factor of production: A rise in the price of a factor of production, *ceteris paribus*, causes a decrease in supply. This happens because the producer will now find the cost of supplying the same quantity has increased. We will thus find that after the price rise in a factor of production, less will be supplied at the old price or the same amount will only be supplied at a higher price. This is graphically

FIGURE 2-8   Changes in Technology and Supply

Changes in technology can cause the supply curve to shift. A positive change in technology would cause more to be supplied at each previous price. This increase in supply is represented by the shift from S to S_1. A negative change in technology causes the supply to decrease, as from S to S_2.

represented by a shift in the curve. The opposite also holds true. Any decrease in the price of a factor of production will cause an increase in supply. Such an increase in supply is geometrically depicted as a shift from S to S_1 in Figure 2-9.

MARKET EQUILIBRIUM

We can now combine market supply and market demand schedules or curves for a good or service and determine the *market equilibrium*. The equilibrium is the price and quantity that will exist in the market if no impediments are placed on the free working of the market. To see how equilibrium comes about, examine Figure 2-10 and Table 2-3. In Figure 2-10 we have market demand and market supply curves for coffee corresponding to the supply and demand schedules in Table 2-3. Examine Table 2-3 first. At a price of $2.00 suppliers *want* to supply 4 million pounds of coffee and demanders *want* to purchase 8 million pounds. This is a difference of 4 million pounds. The quantity demanded exceeds the quantity supplied by 4 million pounds at a price of $2.00. This means that at $2.00 some consumers will be frustrated by not being able to purchase the desired amount. Since markets are free, these consumers will

FIGURE 2-9   Changes in the Price of Factors of Production and Supply

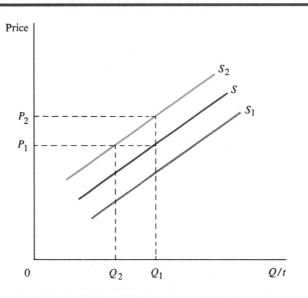

Increases and decreases in the prices of the factors of production cause
increases and decreases in supply. An increase in the price of a factor of
production can cause a decrease in supply. Such a decrease is depicted
by the shift from S to S_2. A decrease in the price of a factor of production
can cause an increase in supply, as the shift from S to S_1 represents.

offer more and bid the price up. As the price rises, the quantity supplied
will rise and the quantity demanded will fall. This will continue until
the price reaches $3.00. At $3.00, the amount consumers wish to purchase is exactly equal to the amount suppliers wish to sell. This is equilibrium. We also say that $3.00 is the ***market clearing price***. It is the
market clearing price because there are no frustrated purchasers or
suppliers.

To see the same process from the other side, assume a price higher
than the market clearing price. At $4.00 per pound, suppliers offer 8 mil-
lion pounds per month for sale. Consumers only wish to purchase 4 million pounds per month at a price of $4.00 per pound. We thus have an
excess quantity supplied of 4 million pounds per month. Suppliers having unsold coffee will lower the price. As the price falls, the quantity
supplied decreases and the quantity demanded increases. This continues
until the equilibrium price of $3.00 is reached. This $3.00 price again
clears the market.

You should understand that the point representing equilibrium price
and equilibrium quantity is not the same thing as the point where the
amount sold equals the amount bought. Quantities bought and sold are

FIGURE 2-10 Supply and Demand of Coffee

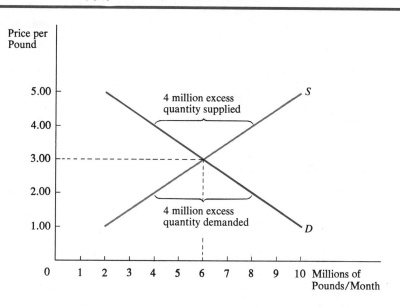

The supply and demand curves produce an equilibrium. At equilibrium, the amount demanders wish to purchase is equal to the amount suppliers wish to sell. The price established at equilibrium is called the market clearing price because there are no frustrated purchasers or suppliers.

TABLE 2-3 Supply and Demand of Coffee

Price Per Pound	Pounds Supplied Per Month	Pounds Demanded Per Month	Difference
$1.00	2 million	10 million	8 million excess quantity demanded
$2.00	4 million	8 million	4 million excess quantity demanded
$3.00	6 million	6 million	equilibrium
$4.00	8 million	4 million	4 million excess quantity supplied
$5.00	10 million	2 million	8 million excess quantity supplied

always equal. At \$2.00 and \$4.00, 4 million pounds per month were bought and sold. The key to equilibrium is that at the equilibrium price, the amount demanders *wish* to purchase is equal to the amount suppliers *wish* to sell.

Figure 2-10 demonstrates the same process. The equilibrium price is \$3.00 and 6 million pounds per month are sold at equilibrium. At \$4.00 there is an excess quantity supplied and price will fall, causing the quantity demanded to increase and the quantity supplied to decrease. The opposite happens at a price of \$2.00 per pound.

A THEORY OF PRICE FORMATION

We have been using the law of demand and the (not quite) law of supply and have developed a very powerful theory of price formation in free markets. We have used the assertions that:

1 demand curves always have a negative slope and
2 supply curves almost always have a positive slope,

and we have generated a theory that says that when the quantity demanded exceeds the quantity supplied ($QD > QS$), price will rise; when the quantity demanded is less than the quantity supplied ($QD < QS$), price will fall; and when the quantity demanded equals the quantity supplied ($QD = QS$), price will remain the same. We can now combine this theory with the possible *ceteris paribus* shifts to examine further the effects of various factors on free markets.

Changes in Demand and Supply

When changes occur in any of the other factors (our *ceteris paribus* conditions) that affect demand, we can trace out the effect on market equilibrium. Assume first that there is an increase in demand, that is, an upward or rightward shift of the entire curve. This increase in demand could be a result of: (1) an increase in income if this is a normal good (or a decrease in income if this is an inferior good); (2) a change in tastes in favor of the good; (3) an increase in the price of a substitute; or (4) a decrease in the price of a complement. The increase in demand is geometrically represented by an outward shift in the demand curve from D to D_1, as drawn in Figure 2-11. The effect of this increase in demand is to cause the equilibrium price to rise from OP_e to OP_{e1}. This price increase causes the quantity supplied to increase to OQ_{e1}, the new equilibrium quantity. Consumers are now demanding a larger quantity of the good at every price than before the shift in demand.

Now consider a decrease in demand. A decrease in demand means that consumers will demand less of the good at every price. A decrease in demand would result from: (1) an increase in income if this is an inferior

FIGURE 2-11   **Changes in Demand**

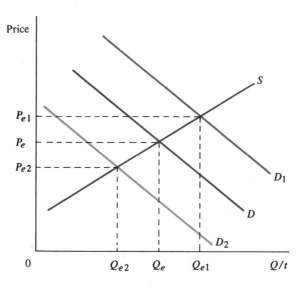

An increase in demand from *D* to *D*₁ causes equilibrium price to rise from *OP*ₑ to *OP*ₑ₁ and the quantity supplied to increase from *OQ*ₑ to *OQ*ₑ₁. A decrease in demand from *D* to *D*₂ causes the equilibrium price to fall from *OP*ₑ to *OP*ₑ₂ and the quantity supplied to fall from *OQ*ₑ to *OQ*ₑ₂.

good (or a decrease in income if this is a normal good); (2) a change in tastes away from this good; (3) a decrease in the price of a substitute; or (4) an increase in the price of a complement. The decrease in demand can be geometrically represented by the leftward shift in the demand curve from D to D_2 in Figure 2-11. The decrease in demand causes equilibrium price to fall from OP_e to OP_{e2}. As a result of the decrease in price, the quantity supplied falls from OQ_e to OQ_{e2} and consumers are consuming OQ_{e2}.

Changes in the factors that affect supply cause changes in supply that we represent by shifts in the supply curve. Consider first an increase in supply. This would be caused by a positive change in technology or a decrease in the price of a factor of production. The increase in supply would be represented by the downward and outward shift in the supply curve, from S to S_1 in Figure 2-12. This increase in supply would cause the equilibrium price to fall from OP_e to OP_{e1}. The decrease in price would cause an increase in the quantity demanded from OQ_e to OQ_{e1}.

A decrease in supply would be geometrically represented by a shift in the supply curve in an upward and inward direction. Such a decrease in supply could result from a negative change in technology or an increase in the price of a factor of production. This decrease in supply is represented by the shift of S to S_2 in Figure 2-12. This decrease in supply

FIGURE 2-12   Changes in Supply

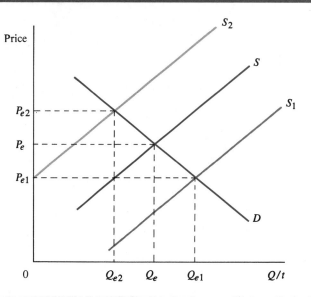

An increase in supply from S to S_1 causes equilibrium price to fall from
OP_e to OP_{e1} and the quantity demanded to increase from OQ_e to OQ_{e1}. A
decrease in supply from S to S_2 causes price to rise from OP_e to OP_{e2} and
the quantity demanded to fall from OQ_e to OQ_{e2}.

causes equilibrium price to rise from OP_e to OP_{e2}. This increase in price
causes the quantity demanded to decrease from OQ_e to OQ_{e2}.

Shifts and Movements

We can now analyze many problems of today's economy in terms of
simple supply and demand theory. Many economists in government and
business spend much of their time analyzing problems with these basic
tools. In Chapter 4, we will examine a range of social problems in terms
of basic supply and demand theory. As we proceed you should keep in
mind the difference between changes in demand and supply (that is,
changes in the position of the curve, or shifts) and changes in quantity
demanded and quantity supplied (that is, changes along the curve, or
movements). The importance of this difference will become very clear
later as you attempt to untangle situations where you proceed through
several changes in *ceteris paribus* conditions.[3] It is also important to real-

---

[3]To test yourself, work through these shifts. You need to be able to geometrically
determine the effect on price and quantity of changes in demand and supply. For example,
ask yourself, What is the effect on equilibrium of an increase in demand coupled with a
decrease in supply?

ize that we are looking for the most salient effect and are not trying to trace through all the implications of a price change or change in *ceteris paribus* conditions. For example, if we know that the price of a substitute has gone up, we know that the demand for the good under consideration will increase. But the rise in price of the substitute good also means (as you will learn later) that real income (actual purchasing ability) has fallen. The effect of the decrease in real income would be to decrease the demand for the good under consideration. This decrease in demand, however, is insignificant relative to the change brought about by the substitute relationship between the two goods. We are primarily interested in the most significant response to a change in one of the *ceteris paribus* conditions.

One final word is in order. You will note that we have said nothing about what constitutes a "fair" or a "just" price. We are developing ***positive theory*** and simply predicting, for example, that if demand increases, *ceteris paribus*, price will rise and the quantity supplied will increase. If this price rise means that some group can no longer afford the item, you may want to argue that we shouldn't allow the price to rise because this is not fair or equitable. Try to hold this response in check for now, as we will return to your concern in Chapter 4.

Summary

Demand depends on the tastes of the consuming group, the incomes of that group, the prices of related goods, the price of the good or service in question, and expectations concerning all these factors. The law of demand states that the quantity demanded of a good or service is an inverse function of its price.

Changes in a good's price affect the quantity demanded of that good. Changes in other factors that affect demand cause demand to either increase or decrease. It is important to separate changes in demand from changes in quantity demanded.

When income increases, the demand for a normal good will increase while the demand for an inferior good will decrease. Goods are complements when a price increase in one will cause a decrease in demand for the other. Similarly, goods are substitutes if an increase in price of one good causes an increase in demand for the second good.

Supply depends on the prices of the factors of production, the level of technology, and the price of the good or service being supplied. The (not quite) law of supply states that the quantity supplied of a good or service is usually a positive function of its price.

Changes in a good's price affect the quantity supplied of that good. Changes in other factors that affect supply cause supply to either increase or decrease. When the prices of factors of production increase, there will be a decrease in supply. A technological advance will usually cause supply to increase.

The market clearing price is the price at which the amount consumers wish to purchase is equal to the amount suppliers wish to sell.

New Terms

demand
welfare economics
law of demand
quantity demanded
demand schedule
demand curve
market demand
increase in demand
decrease in demand
normal good
inferior good
complements
substitutes
expectations
supply
cost
price
(not quite) law of supply

quantity supplied
supply schedule
supply curve
market supply
increase in supply
decrease in supply
factors of production
land
labor
capital
entrepreneurship
rent
wages
interest
profit
market equilibrium
market clearing price
positive theory

Questions for Discussion

1 If you buy at an auction, you save the middleman's markup and get a better deal. Is this true?
2 Does the fact that some people appear to buy more of some goods, such as mink coats or diamonds, as their price goes up negate the law of demand?
3 How can the belief in a change in the future availability of gasoline affect the demand for automobiles?
4 Pat, a professional student, failed principles of economics and decided to sell flowers on a street corner to make ends meet. A second flower seller established a business directly across the street from Pat. Pat, unconcerned, came up with the following hypothesis: When supply increases, demand will increase, and therefore I will be just as well-off now as I was before the second flower seller arrived. Did Pat deserve to fail economics? Why or why not?
5 A market clearing price is the price at which the amount sold equals the amount purchased. Is this correct?
6 List all the factors that can decrease demand or supply.
7 List all the factors that can increase demand or supply.
8 Why is it so important to distinguish changes in demand and changes in supply from changes in quantity demanded and changes in quantity supplied?

Suggestions for Further Reading

Ferguson, C. E., and S. Charles Maurice. *Economic Analysis*. Homewood, Ill.: Richard D. Irwin, 1978, Chapter 2.
Kamerschen, David R., and Lloyd M. Valentine, *Intermediate Microeconomic Theory*. Cincinnati: South-Western Publishing Co., 1977, Chapter 2.

CHAPTER 3

THE ECONOMICS OF RESPONSIVENESS: ELASTICITY

LEARNING OBJECTIVES

After studying the materials found in this chapter, you should be able to do the following:

1 Define elasticity.

2 Calculate the coefficients of elasticity for the following measures:
   (a) price elasticity of demand,
   (b) income elasticity of demand,
   (c) cross elasticity of demand,
   (d) price elasticity of supply.

3 List and define the values for the coefficient of price elasticity of demand when the demand is
   (a) elastic,
   (b) inelastic,
   (c) unit elastic.

4 List and define values for the coefficient of the income elasticity of demand when the good is
   (a) inferior,
   (b) normal.

5 List and define the values of the coefficients of cross elasticity of demand when two goods are
   (a) substitutes,
   (b) complements,
   (c) independent.

In this chapter we develop yet another tool of the micro economist, the elasticity measurement. *Elasticity* is the economist's measure of the *sensitivity* or *responsiveness* of quantity demanded or quantity supplied to changes in price (and other factors). We will develop several elasticity measures and then demonstrate the usefulness of such measures for discussions of public policy.

ELASTICITY AS A GENERAL CONCEPT

In general, elasticity measures the way one variable changes in response to changes in other variables. The *dependent variable* is the variable that changes in response to some other variable, called the *independent variable*. In formula form we express the dependent variable (x) as a function of an independent variable (y), as in equation (3-1).

$$x = f(y_1, y_2, y_3, \ldots, y_n). \tag{3-1}$$

Elasticity measures show how the x variable responds to changes in any one of the different y variables. The formula to determine this responsiveness can be expressed as in equation (3-2).

$$E_1 = \frac{\%\Delta x}{\%\Delta y_1}, E_2 = \frac{\%\Delta x}{\%\Delta y_2}, \ldots, E_n = \frac{\%\Delta x}{\%\Delta y_n}. \tag{3-2}$$

E denotes elasticity, and the formula says the elasticity is the percentage change in the dependent variable divided by the percentage change in the particular independent variable we are looking at.

In examining demand, we are interested in how the quantity demanded responds to changes in price as well as to how the quantity demanded responds to changes in the other *ceteris paribus* factors that affect demand. The quantity demanded of good x (QD_x) is thus the dependent variable, and the independent variables are the price of x (P_x), income (I), tastes (T), the price of complements (P_c), and the price of substitutes (P_s). We can thus rewrite equation (3-1) as

$$QD_x = f(P_x, I, T, P_c, P_s). \tag{3-3}$$

We can then determine how QD_x responds to any of the factors by holding all but one constant and then calculating the elasticity coefficient using equation (3-2). For example, to see how the quantity demanded responds to price, we would calculate

$$E_d = \frac{\%\Delta QD_x}{\%\Delta P_x}, \tag{3-4}$$

where E_d is defined as the coefficient of price elasticity of demand. This formula gives us the *price elasticity of demand*.

PRICE ELASTICITY OF DEMAND

The famous English economist, Alfred Marshall, writing in the late 1800s, developed the concept of elasticity to compare demands for various products. When comparisons are to be made, it is necessary to concentrate on the *relative* responsiveness of the quantity demanded to price rather than concentrating on the absolute responsiveness. We are interested in relative comparisons because we want to be able to measure and then label the sensitivity of the demand relationship. To understand this concept, examine Figure 3-1. Two demand curves are drawn — one is the demand curve for coffee, the other is the demand curve for orange juice. As the price increases by the same amount for each curve, we see different changes in the quantity demanded. The two goods have different sensitivities to the price change; they have different elasticities.

FIGURE 3-1   Demand Curves with Different Elasticities

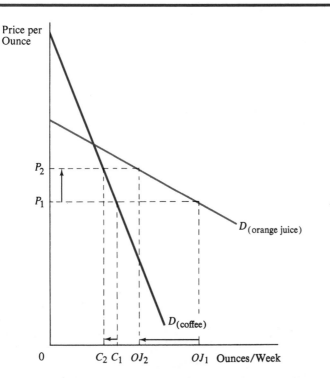

Demand curves may have different elasticities or exhibit different responses to changes in price. The same price change can be seen to have quite a different impact on the quantity demanded of coffee and orange juice. The price change has a much greater impact on the quantity of orange juice demanded, so we say the demand for orange juice is more elastic than the demand for coffee.

The *coefficient of price elasticity of demand* (E_d) is defined as the percentage change in quantity demanded divided by the percentage change in price. The equation for the price elasticity of demand is, as we saw above,

$$E_d = \frac{\%\Delta QD_x}{\%\Delta P_x}. \tag{3-5}$$

Since what we mean by the relative change (or percentage change) is the change in the variable divided by the base amount of the variable, this reduces to

$$E_d = \frac{\dfrac{\Delta QD_x}{QD_x}}{\dfrac{\Delta P_x}{P_x}}. \tag{3-6}$$

With market demand curves the elasticity coefficient will vary along the curve; however, to begin our discussion of price elasticity of demand, we should note that some demand curves have a *constant* price elasticity of demand. This is not the normal state of affairs, but we shall first examine these cases.

Figure 3-2 depicts a vertical demand curve, showing that quantity demanded is totally unresponsive to changes in price. As price changes from OP_1 to OP_2, there is no change in the quantity demanded. If we calculated the elasticity coefficient, we would find:

$$E_d = \frac{\dfrac{OQ_1 - OQ_1}{OQ_1}}{\dfrac{OP_1 - OP_2}{OP_1}} = \frac{0}{\dfrac{OP_1 - OP_2}{OP_1}} = 0.$$

This is a limiting case which violates the law of demand and is not known to exist in the real world. This curve is called a *perfectly inelastic* demand curve. Although it doesn't exist in the real world, there may be demand curves that are very close to it, such as curve D_1, represented by the dashed line in Figure 3-2. We would refer to this curve as a *relatively* inelastic demand curve. A highly inelastic demand would probably exist for goods such as heroin for an addict or heart medicine for someone with a heart condition. These individuals will probably not respond very much to changes in price, particularly if they are quite wealthy.

In Figure 3-3, which depicts a horizontal demand curve, we have another limiting case. At OP_1 or at any price below OP_1 an infinite quantity of the good would be demanded; if price rises above OP_1, the quantity of the good that would be demanded is zero. If we calculate the coeffi-

FIGURE 3-2   Perfectly Inelastic Demand Curve

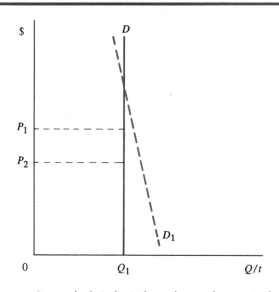

On a perfectly inelastic demand curve, the quantity demanded has no responsiveness to changes in price. A relatively inelastic demand curve is a demand curve which is not very responsive to changes in price.

cient for a price change from OP_1 to OP_2, we get:

$$E_d = \frac{\dfrac{\infty}{OQ_1}}{\dfrac{OP_1 - OP_2}{OP_1}} = \infty.$$

We refer to such a curve as a *perfectly elastic* demand curve because the response to changes in price is infinite or perfect. We would refer to a curve such as D_1, the dashed demand curve in Figure 3-3, as a *relatively* elastic demand curve. A highly elastic demand exists for wheat in the United States. The price of a bushel of wheat is determined by the market. At that price (or any lower price), all of the wheat that is available will be demanded. But if a farmer raises the price even slightly, demand for that farmer's wheat will go to zero.

A third constant elasticity curve is drawn in Figure 3-4. It is represented by a rectangular hyperbola. Any percentage decrease or increase in price is met by an exactly equal increase or decrease in the percentage change in the quantity demanded. This means that the elasticity coefficient at any point along the demand curve is equal to one. For example, if we calculated the elasticity coefficient for a price change from OP_1 to

OP_2, we would find that:

$$E_d = \frac{\dfrac{OQ_1 - OQ_2}{OQ_1}}{\dfrac{OP_1 - OP_2}{OP_1}} = 1.$$

We refer to such a curve as **_unit elastic_**.

FIGURE 3-3   **Perfectly Elastic Demand Curve**

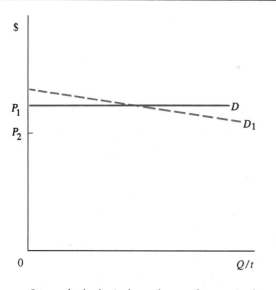

On a perfectly elastic demand curve, the quantity demanded has an infinite response to changes in price. A relatively elastic demand curve is a demand curve which is very responsive to changes in price.

Most demand curves are not shaped like the curves in Figure 3-2, 3-3, or 3-4. Most straight line demand curves have a shape similar to the one drawn in Figure 3-5. Demand curve *D* in Figure 3-5 has a *range* of elasticity coefficients from infinitely elastic (at the *y*-axis intercept) to infinitely inelastic (at the *x*-axis intercept). Table 3-1 presents a handy guide to the nomenclature of demand elasticities. When the coefficient is *less* than one, we refer to the elasticity as being inelastic. This is because the change in quantity demanded is less than the change in price. When the coefficient is *greater* than one, we refer to the elasticity as elastic because the quantity demanded changes more than the change in price. Of course, there are degrees of responsiveness. As the coefficient becomes larger, the responsiveness or elasticity is increasing.

FIGURE 3-4   **Unitary Elastic Demand Curve**

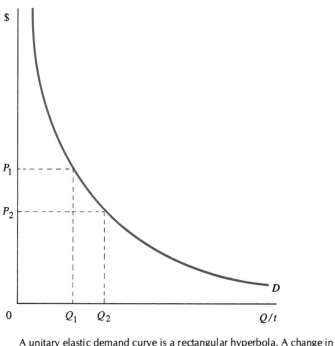

A unitary elastic demand curve is a rectangular hyperbola. A change in price brings about an equal relative change in quantity demanded.

The best way to understand elasticity is to calculate some elasticity coefficients. Using Figure 3-5, which is produced from the demand schedule in Table 3-2, we can calculate elasticity coefficients for the demand curve in Figure 3-5. First, however, we need to get some technicalities straight. The first problem is whether we are calculating the elasticity at a point or between two points. In mathematics we are technically measuring the elasticity at a point by assuming infinitesimally small changes in price and quantity demanded, but when we use arithmetic to calculate particular coefficients, we are working with a sizable discreet change.[1] This is no problem for our purposes as long as we are careful to limit our price changes so that they are not "too large." A second technicality is that the formula will always produce a negative number because demand curves are negatively sloped. This means that there is an inverse

---

[1]Elasticity at a particular price can be measured by the formula $E = \dfrac{\dfrac{dQ}{Q}}{\dfrac{dP}{P}}$.

FIGURE 3-5   **Straight Line Demand Curve with Changing Elasticity**

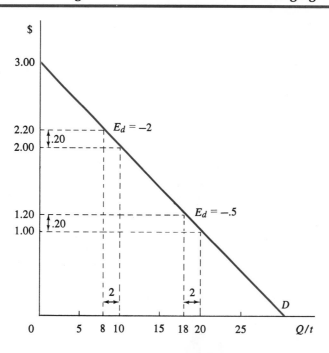

A straight line demand curve has changing elasticity coefficients from the
y-axis intercept to the x-axis intercept.

TABLE 3-1   **A Guide to Elasticity Coefficients**

Numerical Coefficients	Responsiveness of Quantity Demanded to a Change in Price	Terminology
$E_d = 0$	NONE	perfectly inelastic
$E_d > 0 < 1$	Quantity changes by a smaller percentage than the percentage change in price	inelastic
$E_d = 1$	Quantity changes by an equal percentage as the percentage change in price	unit elastic
$E_d > 1 < \infty$	Quantity changes by a larger percentage than the percentage change in price	elastic
$E_d = \infty$	Quantity goes to zero or to all that is available	perfectly elastic

TABLE 3-2   Demand Schedule for Figure 3-5

Price	Quantity Demanded
$ .50	25
1.00	20
1.20	18
1.40	16
1.60	14
1.80	12
2.00	10
2.20	8
2.40	6
2.60	4
2.80	2
3.00	0

relationship between the variables.[2] In practice, we ignore the sign and consider an E_d of -5 larger than an E_d of -4. It will be important later, when considering other elasticity measures, to keep track of the sign, but when considering price elasticity of demand, we ignore it.

We can now calculate some price elasticity of demand coefficients using the demand schedule of Table 3-2. The formula again is

$$E_d = \frac{\text{percentage change in quantity demanded}}{\text{percentage change in price}}.$$

For analytical purposes, this reduces to

$$E_d = \frac{\dfrac{\Delta Q}{Q}}{\dfrac{\Delta P}{P}}.$$

We will now compute the elasticity coefficients for two different changes on the demand curve in Figure 3-5. First, the elasticity coefficient for the increase in price from $1.00 to $1.20.

$$E_d = \frac{\dfrac{20\text{-}18}{20}}{\dfrac{1.00 - 1.20}{1.00}}$$

---

[2]See the appendix to Chapter 1.

$$E_d = \frac{.10}{-.20}$$

$$E_d = -.5.$$

Now for the elasticity coefficient for the increase in price from $2.00 to $2.20.

$$E_d = \frac{\dfrac{10-8}{10}}{\dfrac{2.00 - 2.20}{2.00}}$$

$$E_d = \frac{.20}{-.10}$$

$$E_d = -2.$$

You can see that the elasticity is different at different points along this constant slope demand curve.[3] In fact, all constant slope or linear demand curves except those that are perfectly vertical or horizontal have points that range from elastic to unit elastic to inelastic. On a demand curve such as D in Figure 3-6: all points above price OP_1 have an elasticity coefficient greater than one and are elastic; at price OP_1 the elasticity is equal to one (unit elasticity); and all points below OP_1 have an elasticity coefficient less than one and are inelastic.

Elasticity and Substitutability

Price elasticity of demand is in large part a function of the number of substitutes a product has. If a product, such as table salt, has relatively few substitutes, it will have a relatively inelastic demand. This is just another way of saying that the quantity demanded of a good like table salt isn't very responsive to changes in price over a wide range of prices. Because of this, the elasticity coefficients for general groups of commodities will be lower than for specific commodities. For example, the elasticity of salt in general will be lower than the elasticity of Morton salt.

A related point is that the longer the period of time consumers have to adjust, the more elastic the coefficient of price elasticity. This is because there are more opportunities to modify behavior and substitute products over a longer time period. A good example would be the price

---

[3]You should note that the exact coefficient will depend on what numbers are used as the base quantity and price in making the calculation. In these examples we used the beginning prices, $1.00 and $2.00, and the beginning quantities, 20 and 10. If you were to calculate the coefficient for a decrease in price from $1.20 to $1.00 (or from $2.20 to $2.00), you would get a different coefficient than the one previously calculated. This does not matter much if we only calculate elasticity coefficients for small changes. For the sake of consistency, always use the beginning price and beginning quantity as the base number.

FIGURE 3-6   **Varying Elasticity Demand Curve**

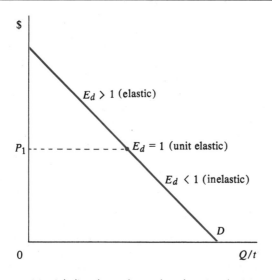

A straight line demand curve has changing elasticity coefficients from the
y-axis intercept to the x-axis intercept. At all prices above the unit elastic
price (OP_1), demand is elastic. At all prices below the unit elastic price,
demand is inelastic.

elasticity of demand for natural gas. In the short run it is likely very
inelastic; but over time, as industry and homes can convert to other
sources of energy, the price elasticity will increase. To give you a feel for
the price elasticity of demand for a range of commodities, see Table 3-3,
which lists some estimated elasticity coefficients.

TABLE 3-3   **Selected Estimated Elasticities**

	E_d
Air Transportation	1.10
Bacon	0.88
Butter	0.70
Furniture	3.04
Jewelry	2.60
Milk	0.31
Pork	0.45
Sugar	0.44

Source: David R. Kamerschen and Lloyd M. Valentine, *Intermediate Microeconomic Theory* (Cincinnati: South-Western
Publishing Co., 1977), Chapter 3, p. 54.

Price Elasticity of Demand and Total Revenue

When we are dealing with demand curves, we are dealing with price and quantity relationships. Quantity, or the number of items sold, multiplied by price is, of course, the *total revenue* generated. We can now use the principle of elasticity to establish a pricing technique and can examine the relationship of total revenue to price elasticity of demand. In order to grasp the relationship, consider a famous illustration in economics. The famous French mathematician and economist, Augustin Cournot, wondered what the owner of a mineral spring should charge for the spring's water, which was wanted for its healing powers. Cournot assumed that the spring cost nothing to operate, it produced an unlimited quantity of output, and the owner wanted to be as wealthy as possible under the principle of self-interest.

To determine the correct price, we must first recognize that a price change has two (opposite) effects on total revenue. The first effect is that a price decrease will decrease total revenue. The other is that with a price decrease, quantity demanded increases, thus increasing total revenue. The net effect on total revenue will depend on whether the relative price decrease exceeds the relative quantity demanded increase or vice versa. This is exactly what the price elasticity of demand coefficient tells us. Consider, for example, a situation where total revenue is given by

$$TR = OP_1 \times OQ_1.$$

On Figure 3-7, a decrease in price from OP_1 to OP_2 will decrease total revenue if the coefficient of price elasticity of demand is inelastic. This results because the percentage increase in quantity demanded would be less than the percentage decrease in price.

To see the same principle in numerical form, consider Figure 3-5 and Table 3-2 once more. At a price of $2.00, the total revenue (TR) is $20.00. An increase in price from $2.00 to $2.20 causes TR to fall from $20.00 to $17.60. This is because the 10 percent increase in price caused an even larger percentage decrease in quantity demanded. The elasticity was greater than one. Conversely, if price rises from $1.00 to $1.20, TR increases from $20.00 to $21.60 because the percentage increase in price was greater than the percentage decrease in quantity demanded. The elasticity was less than one.

To see the principle in a more general way, consider Figure 3-8. On both demand curves the price falls from OP_1 to OP_2 and output increases from OQ_1 to OQ_2. This change causes the total revenue to change. Some revenue is lost and some revenue is gained due to the price change. In Figure 3-8 the crosshatched area represents revenue that has been lost and the shaded area represents revenue that has been added. In the case of the relatively elastic curve, panel (b) of Figure 3-8, the decrease in price has brought about an increase in total revenue; in panel (a), the decrease in price has brought about a decrease in total revenue.

Antoine Augustin Cournot

Historical Pictures Service, Chicago

**Antoine Augustin Cournot
(1801–1877)**

Antoine Augustin Cournot was one of the first economists to view economic theory as a set of tools that could be used to analyze economic and social problems. Cournot was one of the first to show that both supply and demand determine price, and that, in time, price influences both supply and demand. Cournot used simple two-dimensional diagrams to demonstrate these relationships.

Cournot is now recognized as a great economist, but this was not always the case. He had one of the great original minds in economic theory, but his life was a tragic one. Cournot studied mathematics at the École Normale in Paris. He had an insatiable appetite for reading, which he pursued despite very poor eyesight and eventual blindness. While a student, Cournot worked as a secretary to one of Napoleon's generals. In 1834, with the help of the famous statistician Poisson, Cournot became a professor of mathematics at Lyons. In 1838, Cournot published his great work in mathematical microeconomics, *Researches into the Mathematical Principles of Theory and Wealth*. This book did not have much impact and was hardly noticed. Some sources indicate that not a single copy was sold! In later years, as his sight was failing, Cournot published less mathematical versions of his previous work, which were more widely read. When Cournot died in 1877, his highly original and innovative work in economic theory was largely unnoticed.

The irony of Cournot's life is that, although he was not well known during his own lifetime, his vision of economics as a set of highly mathematical tools that could be used to examine a large number of social problems is very close to the thinking of most present-day economists. If Cournot were to return today, he would surely be surprised to see how his vision has come to be the practiced role of the economist.

FIGURE 3-7   **Total Revenue and Elasticity**

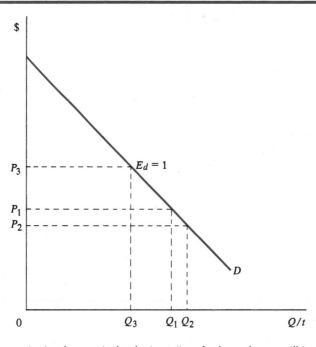

A price decrease in the elastic portion of a demand curve will increase
total revenue. A price decrease in the inelastic portion of a demand
curve will decrease total revenue.

In other words, we can determine what will happen to total revenue when we change price if we know the elasticity coefficient. A reduction in price will always cause an increase in quantity demanded, but total revenue will decrease with inelastic demand and increase with elastic demand. Likewise, a rise in price will cause total revenue to fall with elastic demand and to rise with inelastic demand. These relationships are summarized in Table 3-4.

A good real-world example of this principle occurred in the U.S. airline industry in the late 1970s. The airline industry, believing that the elasticity of demand for air travel was inelastic, had historically been against lower fares and the deregulation of the industry that would produce lower fares. When deregulation was forced in the late 1970s, the revenues of the airline companies increased dramatically in the face of lower fares. The experience indicates that the demand for air travel is relatively elastic or at least much more elastic than the airlines had thought.

We can now answer Cournot's question. The owner of the mineral spring should not try to charge the highest possible price or sell the larg-

FIGURE 3-8   Changes in Total Revenue

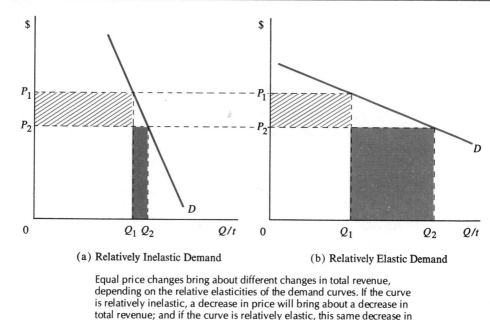

(a) Relatively Inelastic Demand   (b) Relatively Elastic Demand

Equal price changes bring about different changes in total revenue,
depending on the relative elasticities of the demand curves. If the curve
is relatively inelastic, a decrease in price will bring about a decrease in
total revenue; and if the curve is relatively elastic, this same decrease in
price will bring about an increase in total revenue.

TABLE 3-4   Elasticity and Total Revenue

Price Change	Quantity Demanded Change	Elasticity	Total Revenue
Rise	Decrease	$E_d > 1$	Decrease
Rise	Decrease	$E_d = 1$	Unchanged
Rise	Decrease	$E_d < 1$	Increase
Fall	Increase	$E_d > 1$	Increase
Fall	Increase	$E_d = 1$	Unchanged
Fall	Increase	$E_d < 1$	Decrease

est possible amount. The owner should set price where the elasticity coefficient is *unitary*. To see why, set price where the elasticity is, say, $-.5$,
or inelastic. If the owner raises price, quantity demanded will decrease,
but by only one-half the rate of the price increase, so *TR* will rise. On the
other hand, if the $E_d = -2$, or is elastic, the owner should decrease price.

If the price is lowered, the quantity demanded increases at twice the rate of the price decline. The owner will maximize total revenue when $E_d = -1$, or is unitary elastic. So the mineral spring owner would set a price of OP_3 in Figure 3-7. At price OP_3, the area $OP_3 \times OQ_3$ represents maximum total revenue.

Price Elasticity of Demand and Public Policy

Using a hypothetical example based on some "reasonable" estimates of consumption, price, and price elasticities, we can see how useful a tool price elasticity of demand is to the economist who is a policy adviser. Suppose you are picked by the president to be an adviser to his "energy czar." On your first day on the job, the czar, after meeting with the president, calls you in and tells you that as part of a new "Project Independence" the consumption of gasoline must be decreased by 3 billion gallons per year. You discuss the matter and decide against lowering the speed limit, patriotic appeals, or legislated rationing. You decide that the market should ration the quantity available and that the best solution is to raise price by putting an additional excise tax on gasoline. Your job then becomes one of determining what the appropriate tax should be.

You return to your office and check the latest figures on gasoline consumption, which you find to be 30.5 billion gallons per year. Next it is necessary to determine what the price elasticity of demand for gasoline happens to be. A trip to your library and some research into statistical work by economists leads you to the conclusion that the best estimates appear to be that the long-run price elasticity of demand for gasoline in the U.S. is .45, with estimates for individual states ranging between .4 and .5. The short-run elasticity, in sharp contrast, is approximately .09, with estimates ranging between .07 and .11.[4] Remember that as the time under consideration is lengthened, the elasticity increases. This is borne out in this case where the long-run elasticity is five times that of the short-run elasticity. Over a period of time people will buy more fuel-efficient cars, but they won't do it overnight. It will happen in the normal course of car replacement. Of course, a huge increase in price might speed up the replacement process.

It is now a simple matter to compute the tax necessary to have the desired effect on consumption. For simplicity, assume the current price is $1.00 per gallon. If the $E_d = .45$ and you wish to decrease consumption by 3 billion gallons in the long run, *ceteris paribus*, you need only to substitute into the formula to determine the tax.

$$E_d = \frac{\% \Delta QD}{\% \Delta P} = \frac{\dfrac{3 \text{ billion}}{30.5 \text{ billion}}}{\% \Delta P}$$

---

[4]Data Resources, Inc. *A Study of the Quarterly Demand for Gasoline and Imports of Alternative Gasoline Taxes* (Lexington, Massachusetts: December, 1973).

$$E_d = \frac{.098}{\%\Delta P}$$

$$.45 = \frac{.098}{\%\Delta P}$$

$$\%\Delta P = 21.8$$

Thus, in order to have the 9.8 percent decrease in quantity demanded, it is necessary to have a 21.8 percent increase in price. The required additional excise tax would, therefore, be 21.8 cents per gallon of gasoline ($1.00 × 21.8%), making the price of gasoline $1.22 per gallon.

In this hypothetical case, you have used a simple economic tool in a way that economists giving policy advice would use it. Although it was hypothetical, the estimates were real and the exercise is similar to exercises performed many times by government economists in contingency planning exercises during recent energy crises.

PRICE ELASTICITY OF SUPPLY

The equation for the *price elasticity of supply* is

$$E_s = \frac{\text{percentage change in quantity supplied}}{\text{percentage change in price}},$$

which again reduces into the more workable formula of

$$E_s = \frac{\frac{\Delta Q}{Q}}{\frac{\Delta P}{P}}. \tag{3-7}$$

As with E_d, if $E_s = 1$, it is unit elastic. If $E_s > 1$, it is elastic; and if $E_s < 1$, it is inelastic. The analogy to price elasticity of demand stops there. A major difference is that the *coefficient of the price elasticity of supply* (E_s) is normally positive because we normally have positively sloped supply curves. Since the curves are positively sloped, the relationship between elasticity and total revenue that we established for price elasticity of demand doesn't hold; higher prices result in higher total revenue, regardless of whether supply is elastic or inelastic.

We can designate some supply curves as perfectly inelastic, unit elastic, or perfectly elastic. The designations again, of course, measure the responsiveness of changes in quantity to changes in price.

Consider Figure 3-9. The quantity supplied is totally unresponsive to changes in price. It is perfectly inelastic. Examples of perfectly inelastic supply curves are infrequent, but in the very short run it is often impossible to produce more of a good regardless of what happens to price. This

FIGURE 3-9   Perfectly Inelastic Supply Curve

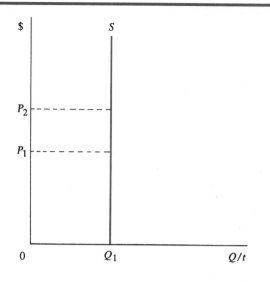

A perfectly inelastic supply curve is a vertical line. It would exist if suppliers dumped a certain stock of a commodity on a market in such a short time that changes in price would not affect the quantity supplied.

inability to produce more will, of course, affect the supply curve, which depicts the amount people are willing to supply at various prices. Consider the supply of Rembrandts, as an example, or the supply of Rose Bowl tickets. A rise in the price of Rembrandts (even in the long run) or Rose Bowl tickets (in the short run) does not cause the stock of these items to increase. We usually represent these stock supply curves as being perfectly inelastic.

Figures 3-10 and 3-11 depict a perfectly elastic and unit elastic supply curve, respectively. Any straight line supply curve that is drawn through the origin, as in Figure 3-11, is unit elastic over its entire range. This is because the percentage changes of the two variables will always be equal to each other. Throughout their range, other linear, or straight line, supply curves are elastic if they intersect the price axis and inelastic if they intersect the quantity axis, though elasticity changes along both curves. Two such curves are drawn in Figure 3-12.

Price Elasticity of Supply and Cost

The elasticity of supply depends to a large degree on how the cost structure in the market for the good under consideration responds to changes in output. If costs rise rapidly as output is expanded, the quantity supplied will not be very responsive to changes in price; the curve

FIGURE 3-10   **Perfectly Elastic Supply Curve**

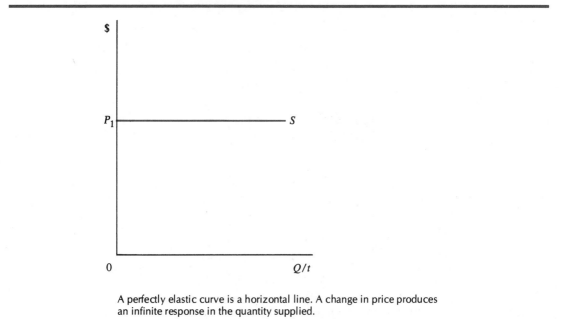

A perfectly elastic curve is a horizontal line. A change in price produces
an infinite response in the quantity supplied.

FIGURE 3-11   **Unit Elastic Supply Curve**

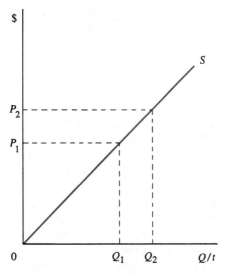

A straight line supply curve drawn through the origin has a unitary
coefficient of elasticity along the entire curve.

FIGURE 3-12   Inelastic and Elastic Supply Curves

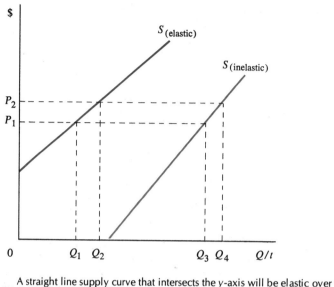

A straight line supply curve that intersects the y-axis will be elastic over
its entire length, and a straight line supply curve that intersects the x-axis
will be inelastic over its entire length.

will be inelastic. Alternatively, if costs don't increase very much as output is increased, the rise in price will increase the profits of supplying
firms and the output response could be significant. This would be the
case for an elastic curve. We will go into this subject in much greater
detail in Chapters 7 through 11.

Price Elasticity of Supply and Time

Elasticity of supply is our measure of the responsiveness of quantity
supplied to changes in price. The major factor affecting this responsiveness is the availability of inputs that can be attracted away from other
uses. This, of course, in large part depends on the time period under
consideration. As the period of time increases, the possibility of obtaining new and different inputs to increase the supply increases. In our two
examples of stock supply, Rembrandts and Rose Bowl tickets, you will
recognize that in the long run the stadium could be expanded and the
quantity of tickets increased; Rembrandts, however, would always have a
perfectly inelastic supply because new or additional inputs (Rembrandt is
dead) don't exist.

These two factors affecting elasticity of supply, availability of inputs
and time, would lead you to predict that the elasticity of supply coeffi-

cient would be larger as the time frame is increased and for those products that use relatively unspecialized or abundant inputs.

Price Elasticity of Supply and Public Policy

If we examine another hypothetical policy question, but one based on real world data and considerations, we can see how important and useful the elasticity of supply coefficient can be. Suppose that you are hired as an adviser to the Secretary of Defense and you are instructed to determine how to make the volunteer army work better. You determine that the army is presently enlisting 57,500 volunteers per month, but this is 30 percent fewer than needed to keep the ranks at full strength. If you could calculate the elasticity of supply, it would be a simple matter to determine the pay increase necessary to reach full strength. Note that you don't even need to know what the present level of pay happens to be if you can calculate the elasticity.

It happens that during the early 1970s the military commissioned many such studies. You retire to the library and peruse these early studies. Agreement in these studies centers on an $E_s = 1.25$.[5] Thus, working from $1.25 = \dfrac{.30}{\%\Delta P}$, you can now report to your new boss that the army can meet its personnel requirements by raising pay levels by 24 percent $\left(24\% = \dfrac{.30}{1.25} \times 100\right)$. But before you turn this figure in to your boss you have some second thoughts. You know that elasticity of supply depends on availability of inputs, in this case, volunteers. Now not all potential volunteers are equally available; the more intelligent have more options in civilian life in jobs and colleges and would probably be less responsive to the pay increase. This would lead you to forecast that a simple pay increase for all potential enlistees might change the mental mix of enlistees and attract fewer intelligent ones. You gather more data and you find that at present the army breaks its personnel into three groups — Mental Categories I and II, Mental Category III, and Mental Category IV, based on how high they score on the AFQT (Armed Forces Qualifying Test). The test is supposed to be similar to an IQ test, with Categories I and II being the smartest. Assuming the present army has one third of its strength from each group, and speculating that the elasticity coefficients for the three groups are 0.5, 1.25, and 2.0, you now have some important policy information to report. If the pay raise of 24 percent that you just calculated was to go into effect, the number of Mental Category IV enlistments, which have the highest elasticity because the volunteers have fewer options, would increase by 48 percent while the number of Categories I and II enlistments would increase by only 12 percent. This would

[5]For one such study, see *Innovations for Achieving an All Volunteer Army*. General Electric TEMPO (January 3, 1972).

mean the ability (as measured by mental category) of the army would decrease substantially. To counteract this problem, you could suggest a differential pay increase. Assuming you want to keep enlistments by mental category at the present share, you could now calculate the needed increases. Mental Categories I and II pay would have to go up by 60 percent $\left(.5 = \frac{.30}{\%\Delta P}\right)$, Mental Category III pay would have to go up by 24 percent $\left(1.25 = \frac{.30}{\%\Delta P}\right)$, and Mental Category IV pay would only need to go up by 15 percent $\left(2 = \frac{.30}{\%\Delta P}\right)$.

As you can see, an imaginative application of this simple tool can have very important implications for policy. This example, though hypothetical, is very similar to exercises that were actually performed in the early years of the volunteer army.

OTHER ELASTICITIES

As we saw at the beginning of this chapter, we could calculate the elasticity of almost anything because what an elasticity coefficient does is measure the responsiveness of one measurable quantity to another. There are, however, two other elasticity coefficients which are quite common in economics.

The first is the *income elasticity of demand*. This measures the responsiveness of changes in quantity demanded to changes in income, assuming all other things including price are held constant. The formula is expressed as

$$E_I = \frac{\text{percentage change in quantity demanded}}{\text{percentage change in income}}.$$

The sign of the coefficient is important when we calculate income elasticity. If the sign is negative, indicating an inverse relationship between income and demand, the good is an inferior good. If the sign is positive, the good is a normal good.

For normal goods we use the same designations for the elasticity coefficient that we used before. If the coefficient is greater than one, $E_I > 1$, we say the good is income elastic. If $E_I < 1$, we say the good is income inelastic. Goods that have high and positive income elasticities are usually thought to be luxury goods. Indeed, you might use the concept of income elasticity of demand as a definition of what a luxury good is. Necessities, such as salt, would have an inelastic income elasticity coefficient. Luxuries, such as diamonds, would have an elastic income elasticity coefficient.

The other elasticity concept we can make use of is *cross elasticity of demand*. It measures the responsiveness of changes in quantity demanded for one product to changes in the price of another product. It assumes the goods are related; they are either complements or substitutes. Two goods that are completely unrelated (independent of one another) would have a zero cross elasticity of demand. The formula can be stated as

$$E_{x,y} = \frac{\text{percentage change in quantity demanded of good } x}{\text{percentage change in price of good } y}.$$

If the sign of $E_{x,y}$ is negative, we know the relationship is an inverse one and that an increase in the price of good y will bring about a decrease in the quantity demanded of good x. A negative cross elasticity coefficient would thus indicate that good x and good y are complements. A positive coefficient would indicate a substitute relationship between good x and good y because an increase in the price of good y will lead to an increase in the quantity demanded of good x. The size of the coefficient tells us how strong the complementary or substitute relationship is between the two goods.

Summary

Elasticity is the measure of the sensitivity or responsiveness of quantity demanded or quantity supplied to changes in price (and to the other *ceteris paribus* factors). Linear demand curves, except for those that are perfectly vertical or horizontal, have points on them that range from elastic to inelastic and one point that is unit elastic.

Price elasticity is a measure of substitutability. The more substitutes an item has, the more elastic it will be. This simply means that consumers have more options and as a result respond more quickly to changes in price. As time increases, elasticity increases because individuals will have more opportunity to substitute other goods.

Total revenue is dependent on elasticity because a demand curve is a price-quantity line. When price changes, the quantity demanded changes and this changes total revenue. The amount of the change in total revenue will depend on the responsiveness of consumers to changes in price, and this is precisely what elasticity measures.

Price elasticity of supply is a measure of the responsiveness of changes in quantity supplied to changes in price. As time increases, the elasticity of supply increases because the longer the time period, the more chance there is for adjustments to take place.

Income elasticity measures the responsiveness of changes in quantity demanded to changes in income. Cross elasticity of demand measures the responsiveness of changes in the quantity demanded of one good to changes in the price of other goods.

New Terms

elasticity   independent variable
dependent variable   price elasticity of demand

coefficient of price elasticity of demand (E_d)
perfectly inelastic
perfectly elastic
unit elastic
total revenue

price elasticity of supply
coefficient of price elasticity of supply (E_s)
income elasticity of demand
cross elasticity of demand

Questions for Discussion

1 If the government wants to place a tax on a certain commodity for the purpose of generating revenue, should it look for goods that have relatively inelastic or relatively elastic demand curves?

2 Suppose that in your city the manager of the transit authority increases the bus fares and subsequently finds that revenues decline. The bus line is losing money and the manager calls for still higher fares to break even. Can you suggest any other solution?

3 What are the primary factors that cause the demand for one item to be more elastic or inelastic than the demand for some other item?

4 Would the elasticity of demand for Miller High Life beer be higher or lower than the elasticity of demand for beer? Why?

5 How does the fact that demand for gasoline is income elastic and price inelastic frustrate public policy that is aimed at decreasing the importation of oil?

Suggestions for Further Reading

Ferguson, C. E., and S. Charles Maurice. *Economic Analysis*. Homewood, Ill.: Richard D. Irwin, 1978, Chapter 2.

Kamerschen, David R., and Lloyd M. Valentine. *Intermediate Microeconomic Theory*. Cincinnati: South-Western Publishing Co., 1977, Chapter 3.

CHAPTER 4

THE ECONOMICS OF SOCIAL PROBLEMS

LEARNING OBJECTIVES

After studying the materials found in this chapter, you should be able to do the following:

1 Calculate the expected cost of a crime given
    (a) probability of arrest and conviction,
    (b) penalty.

2 Diagram the economic effects of an excise tax to determine the incidence of the tax.

3 Define
    (a) price ceiling,
    (b) price floor,
    (c) shortage,
    (d) surplus,
    (e) black market.

4 Diagram the economic effects of
    (a) rent control,
    (b) minimum wages,
    (c) target prices in agriculture,
    (d) natural gas price regulation.

5 List the economic aspects of the health care crisis.

In this chapter we make use of the basic models and theories that we have developed in the previous three chapters. These simple tools of economics can yield profound insights into social issues of a widely diverse nature. You will see in this chapter how you are now equipped with tools of analysis that can help you understand diverse issues such as crime, taxation, rent control, minimum wages, the energy crises, and the farm problem.

THE ECONOMICS OF CRIME: USE OF THE SELF-INTEREST HYPOTHESIS

We can use one of our assumptions, the self-interest hypothesis, to analyze and give policymakers advice on crime problems and prevention. Let's assume that the criminal is a rational calculator who commits a crime when it is in the criminal's self-interest to do so. A criminal calculates the costs and benefits of each crime and commits those crimes where the benefits exceed the costs. In other words, crime is an economic activity.

We have generated the simple hypothesis that a criminal calculates costs (C) and benefits (B) of criminal activities and commits those crimes where $B > C$. Crime is an economic activity and the criminal behaves like any other entrepreneur.

If we go deeper into the cost and benefit calculation, we can analyze the situation in more detail. The benefits are, of course, what the criminal hopes to realize by the activity. We want to place a value on this. In crimes involving the theft of property, this is relatively easy. The anticipated benefit is the anticipated market value of the take. For other crimes such as murder, illegal parking, or littering, we have to impute some value to the activity.

Now let's look at the cost side. The cost is the penalty (P) adjusted for the probability (π) that the criminal will be caught and the penalty will be imposed. So we need to compare B to $P\pi$. In other words, if the fine for littering is $500, but on average one will be caught and fined for littering only once every 500 times, the expected cost of littering is $1 (=$500 \times 1/500$). The economic model we have just developed thus tells us that if some people get more than $1 worth of benefit from littering, they will litter.

The Economics of Robbery

Our model can now be applied to crimes more serious than littering. If we want to do something about the amount of armed robbery that is taking place in our society, we analyze this crime and its prevention in terms of our model. There are three elements to our model. It says that crime depends on the benefits from the activity so, *ceteris paribus*, as the take goes up we would predict more robbery. Second, it says that, as the penalty goes down (with no change in the probability of being caught), criminal activity will go up. Third, it says that if the probability of being caught goes down, *ceteris paribus*, the amount of robbery will go up.

We can now give advice to policymakers. If we want to decrease the amount of armed robbery, we can do any of three things or some combinations of all three. We could decrease the potential take, or profit. This is sometimes hard to do, but you have probably noticed that most late-night gas stations advertise that they don't keep much cash on hand. We could also increase the penalty. We could say that if a person is caught robbing a gas station and using a gun during the robbery, the criminal will have the hand holding the gun cut off. Now increasing the penalty is sometimes difficult because society deems some penalties too severe. In some countries, the hands of robbers are cut off, but in the United States penalties for robbery are usually limited to prison sentences. Recently, in one suburb outside Washington, D.C., the local police chief announced that squad cars would be equipped with rifles with exploding shells (outlawed by the United Nations as being too inhumane for warfare), and that officers had been instructed to shoot first and ask questions later when investigating robberies. What do you suppose happened? Almost immediately the robbery rate fell in this jurisdiction and increased in adjacent jurisdictions. The reason is predicted by our model which says as the potential penalty rises, criminal activity will fall. Of course, we might object to this behavior by the police even if it does reduce crime. But be careful; economic models are positive, telling us only what the consequences of such a policy will be. They don't say if it's good or bad in a moral sense.

The third activity which could reduce the robbery rate would be to increase the probability of arrest and conviction of would-be robbers. This might be accomplished by more police, speedier justice, television cameras in banks, or other such measures.

The Economics of the Death Penalty

The preceding analysis has probably led you to the conclusion that economists would argue that the death penalty deters crime. Indeed, a University of Chicago economist, Isaac Ehrlic, has statistically argued that the death penalty does act to reduce the amount of murder.[1] If you are a doubter, answer this question: Would you ever litter if the probability of getting caught was one in five hundred and the penalty was death? You would have to place a high value on being able to litter, or a low

---

[1] Again, this does not mean that you should necessarily support the death penalty. You can still be opposed to the death penalty on humanitarian grounds even though you accept the implications of the model. For the study, see I. Ehrlich, "The Deterrent Effect of Capital Punishment: A Question of Life and Death," *American Economic Review* (June, 1975).

value on your own life, if you answered in the affirmative. However, some people argue that murderers have such a distorted view of reality that they underestimate the probability of being caught, convicted, and sentenced to death. Thus, these people would argue, the death penalty provides little deterrence. More importantly, just because positive economic theory says the death penalty provides deterrence does not mean that you, or anyone else, has to accept it on moral, or normative, grounds.

The Economics of Illegal Parking

There are probably some of you who still are skeptical about our simple model of crime, so let's analyze a criminal activity that you have probably committed or at least contemplated committing — illegal parking on campus. On almost all college campuses, parking is in short supply and as a result there are benefits to parking in an illegal parking space. Let's suppose that the fine for illegal parking is $2.00, and you find from experience that you get a ticket one out of every four times you park illegally. The expected value of the cost of the crime is thus $.50 (=$2.00 × .25). Now it would be almost impossible to estimate the benefits that accrue to those who illegally park, but since there are large numbers of violators, we know that benefits are substantial. Now assume you are appointed to a committee formed by the university's president to solve the parking problem. You have three options: you could lower the benefits by buying shuttlebuses to transport students from their parking areas to the classroom buildings; you could hire more police and increase the number of times they check the parking areas; or you could raise the fine. A common way to do this is to tow away illegally parked cars. This raises the fine significantly because violators now have to pay towing fees in addition to the basic fine. This usually includes a great deal of time and trouble.

If you still don't believe the model, here is an empirical test you can carry out. Observe the amount of illegal parking on a nice sunny day. Then the next time it rains, observe the criminal activity again. What does the model predict? On rainy days the benefits of the crime go up, *ceteris paribus*, because the benefit now is the proximity to class plus arriving in class dry. The probability of being caught also goes down, *ceteris paribus*, because campus police don't like to get wet either. Our model thus predicts that there will be more illegal parking on rainy days. Check it out — test the model!

WHO PAYS WHAT TAX: AN EXERCISE IN SUPPLY AND DEMAND

An *excise tax* is a tax that is placed on the consumption of a particular item, such as liquor, cigarettes, or electricity. Excise taxes can be specific, being placed on one particular item, such as cigarettes, or they can be general, being placed on a broad class of goods, such as food. It is even possible to view the income tax as an excise tax on labor. We can look at excise taxes, then, as we try to understand who actually pays an imposed tax.

If you listen to the rhetoric of the debates over taxation, you know it is quite confusing. Consumers are often convinced that they ultimately pay all taxes, yet business often fights hard to prevent tax increases on their products. If consumers pay all taxes, why should business care if it is taxed or not? The answer is not simple. The correct answer to the question of who ultimately pays what tax is: it depends; it depends on the supply and demand conditions in the relevant markets.

Let's examine a case in which we have normally sloped supply and demand curves, as in Figure 4-1, which illustrates the market for beer. Assume we have a market and the market settles at a price of $1.50 per six-pack, with X_e six-packs per week representing the equilibrium quantity. Now suppose the governmental taxing unit places a tax of $.50 per six-pack on beer and collects this tax from producers. This means that the supply curve will shift up by the amount of the tax. The costs of production for the beer producer have been increased $.50 per six-pack. One way to view the tax is that the producer must pay $.50 per six-pack for the permission of the government to produce beer. In terms of Figure 4-1, the supply curve shifts up at all points by $.50. The post-tax supply curve is S_t. Price will rise to $1.75 per six-pack and the new equilibrium quantity is X_t. But note that this new price is less than the old price plus the tax. If the entire tax had been shifted forward to consumers, the consumer would now pay the old price of $1.50 plus the tax of $.50, or $2.00 per six-pack. It is also clear that the amount of money the producer actually receives has fallen. Before the tax the producer received $1.50 per six-pack, but now the producer receives $1.25 per six-pack [$1.75 (price) minus the $.50 tax]. What has happened is that the tax caused prices to rise, which meant the quantity demanded fell. The beer producers must sell the lower quantity at a lower received price than before. In this example, then, part of the tax was paid by consumers and part was paid by producers. Each paid half of the excise tax.

The amount of the tax that each pays will depend critically on the supply and demand elasticities for the goods that are being taxed. To see this more clearly, examine the four panels in Figure 4-2. Using Figure 4-2, we can easily see how the elasticity of supply and the elasticity of demand affect the *tax incidence*. Tax incidence is the economist's phrase for who really pays the tax.

In panel (a) of Figure 4-2, we have a normally sloped supply curve and a perfectly inelastic demand curve. When the excise tax is placed on the good, the supply curve shifts to S_t. The result is that price rises from OP_e to OP_t. Price has risen by the full amount of the tax and the equilibrium quantity is unchanged. In this case, the incidence of the excise tax

FIGURE 4-1   An Excise Tax on Beer

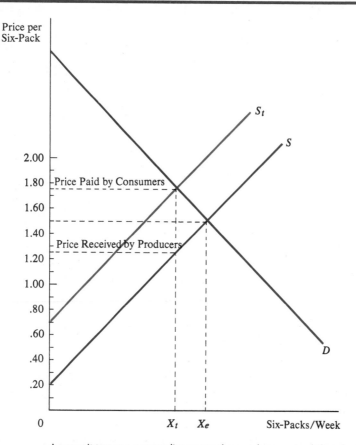

A per unit tax on a commodity causes the supply curve to shift up by the amount of the tax. Less of the commodity is purchased at a higher price. Part of the tax is borne by consumers and part of the tax is borne by producers.

falls fully on the consumers of this good. The tax has been shifted forward to consumers by the full amount of the tax.

In panel (b) of Figure 4-2, we have a normally sloped supply curve and a perfectly elastic demand curve. The post-tax supply curve is S_t. After the tax is imposed, price is unchanged at OP_e and equilibrium quantity falls to OQ_t. Since the price to consumers is unchanged, the producer is paying the entire tax. The incidence of the tax falls fully on the suppliers of this good.

The principle involved in panel (a) and panel (b) is clear. The more inelastic the demand for a good, the more any excise tax placed on the good will fall on consumers of that good. Secondly, the more elastic the

FIGURE 4-2   **Elasticity and Tax Incidence**

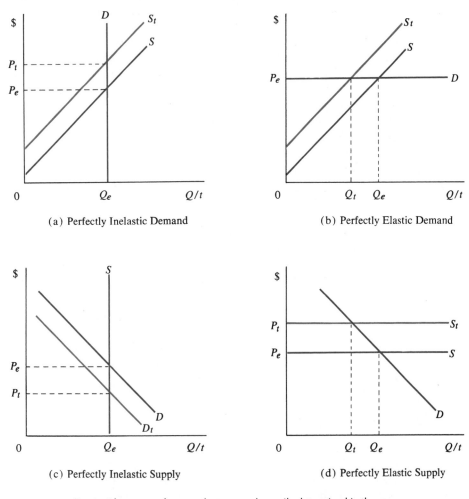

(a) Perfectly Inelastic Demand

(b) Perfectly Elastic Demand

(c) Perfectly Inelastic Supply

(d) Perfectly Elastic Supply

Tax incidence, or who pays the tax, can be easily determined in the case of perfectly elastic or perfectly inelastic demand and supply curves. With perfectly inelastic demand [panel (a)], the consumer pays the entire tax. With perfectly elastic demand [panel (b)], the producer pays the entire tax. With perfectly inelastic supply [panel (c)], the supplier pays the entire tax. With perfectly elastic supply [panel (d)], the consumer pays the entire tax.

demand curve, the more any excise tax placed on the good will fall on the producers of that good.

Now examine the supply curves in panels (c) and (d) of Figure 4-2. In panel (c) we have a perfectly inelastic supply curve. In order to geometrically represent the tax, we now need to shift the demand curve down by the amount of the tax. This is because it is impossible to shift back a perfectly inelastic supply curve because a perfectly inelastic supply curve represents the offering of a fixed amount regardless of price. In this case the tax cannot affect that given quantity. We view the demand curve as the demand curve the industry faces with the amount of the tax netted out. The equilibrium quantity is unchanged after the shift and the price the firm receives falls from OP_e to OP_t. In other words, the entire amount of the tax has been paid by the suppliers of the good. In panel (d) we have a perfectly elastic supply curve. An excise tax shifts the supply curve to account for the higher price at each output. After the shift, the price of the item has increased from OP_e to OP_t, the exact amount of the tax. In this case, consumers are paying the entire tax. Of course, less is being sold so some producers may be worse off, but consumers are paying more for OQ_t, and this increased amount is exactly equal to the amount of the tax.

This exercise in shifting supply and demand curves serves the purpose of developing some general propositions of excise taxation incidence: the more inelastic the demand, the more price rises, meaning that the tax falls on consumers; the more elastic the demand, the less price rises, indicating that the tax falls on producers; the more inelastic the supply, the more the tax is paid by producers; and the more elastic the supply, the more price rises, indicating that the tax is paid by consumers. The answer to the question of who pays an excise tax should now be clear. The answer again is: it depends. It depends on the relative elasticity of supply and demand in the market for the good on which the tax is placed.

INTERVENTION IN MARKETS

In Chapter 2 we saw how free and unfettered markets reach equilibrium. It is possible for this market process to be interfered with, and this inference is sometimes the result of governmental action. *Price ceilings* result when the government establishes a price as a limit and will not allow the market price to rise about the limit. *Price floors* are prices established as minimums and the authority won't permit the market price to fall below the price minimum. Price ceilings and price floors cause disruptions in the market-clearing process, and our economic tools allow us to see the effects of these disruptions.

Price Ceilings

A price ceiling that is set below the equilibrium price prohibits the market from clearing. The amount that consumers wish to purchase at the imposed ceiling is greater than the amount suppliers are willing to supply at this price. Figure 4-3 demonstrates this. In Figure 4-3 the equilibrium price is OP_e and the equilibrium quantity is OQ_e. The govern-

FIGURE 4-3   Price Ceiling

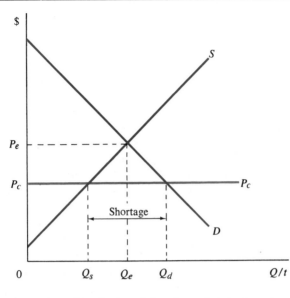

A price ceiling that is set below the market-clearing price creates a
shortage. At the price imposed by the government, potential purchasers
demand a larger quantity of the good than suppliers are willing to sell.

ment imposes a price ceiling of OP_c. The result is that the amount that
consumers wish to consume at price OP_c is OQ_d and the amount the
suppliers are willing to supply at the ceiling is OQ_s. The result is a
shortage. It is important to realize that the shortage is created by the
ceiling. Without the ceiling, price would rise and, as a result of the price
rise, the quantity demanded would decrease and the quantity supplied
would increase until price reached OP_e and the market cleared. If the
ceiling is to be maintained, government must replace the market with
some other way to allocate the goods. Consumers are frustrated as they
try to obtain the good or service at the lower price, and some institution
other than the market must be imposed to determine who will get the
good or service.

In almost all cases where price ceilings are imposed, **black markets**
spring up. Black markets are market processes in which people buy and
sell the goods or services that are controlled by price ceilings at prices
above the imposed price ceiling.[2] We'll have more to say about black
markets a little later.

Rent Control. Price ceilings are frequently used by various levels of

<hr/>

[2]You should be able to show why a price ceiling that is imposed *above* the equilibrium
price has no effect on the market.

government and often produce the crises that we experience in our economy. Later in this chapter we will discuss how price ceilings have created the natural gas crisis which we have today. Consider now the effect of price ceilings on apartment rentals.

Many cities, including New York City and Washington, D.C., have imposed price ceilings on apartment rents. This is usually referred to as *rent control*. At first glance, the goals of rent control are admirable; i.e., to keep rents low so that everyone, including the poor, can find a place to live at a reasonable price. For the effect of rent control, refer again to Figure 4-3. At a price less than the market-clearing price, there will be a shortage of rental units. More people will be looking for rental units than the number available. Something other than the market mechanism will now allocate the rental units. The landlord can now impose criteria on who the tentants will be because for any vacancy, the landlord has a number of people waiting in line to rent the apartment. The landlord can now inexpensively discriminate in a choice of tenant because it is now costless to discriminate. Without rent control, the landlord is more likely to rent to any prospective tenant rather than leave the apartment vacant because the market is clearing. With rent control the landlord can choose from the backlog of prospective tenants. The landlord can exclude those who are young (or old), those who have children (or dogs), or those who are black (or white). The point is that the interference in the market has replaced the nondiscrimination of the market mechanism.

The experience of one of the authors is instructive. Several years ago, Amacher moved to Washington to work with Sweeney. He wanted to live in Georgetown, where there is rent control. To find rental units, one needs to examine the *Washington Post* early in the morning because there are very few listings. With rent control in effect, most vacancies are rented by word of mouth. This discriminates against newcomers who aren't included in the word-of-mouth communication network. Amacher was lucky enough to call a landlord early, before she had rented her vacant townhouse. She invited him over for coffee to talk about the rent. At coffee she looked him over and asked about children, where he was working, the number of pets, and so on. Since Amacher had short hair (relatively), a respectable job (some would say being a bureaucrat isn't respectable), no children, and one small dog, the landlord agreed to rent to him. One wonders if he would have been able to rent the house had he had an afro, worked for a homosexual awareness group, had seven adopted Vietnam orphans, or owned a large German shepherd. The point is simply that markets don't discriminate, but price ceilings make it easy (inexpensive) to discriminate.

Black Markets. The other tendency which we mentioned earlier is for black markets to develop when price ceilings are imposed. Let's examine a black market you have all seen operate. Let's say the market in Figure 4-4 represents the market for tickets to the biggest college football game of the year. Let's say it's for this year's version of the "Game of the

FIGURE 4-4   **The Game of the Decade**

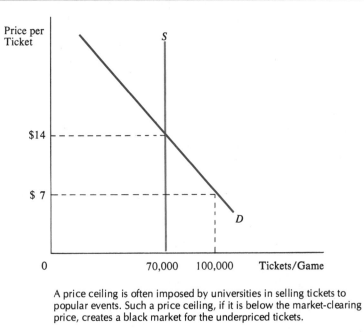

A price ceiling is often imposed by universities in selling tickets to
popular events. Such a price ceiling, if it is below the market-clearing
price, creates a black market for the underpriced tickets.

Decade." The stock of tickets is perfectly inelastic in the short run at the
70,000 seating capacity of the stadium. The university is selling the tickets at a price ceiling of $7.00 per ticket. For this game, the market-clear-
ing price would be $14, so the $7 imposed price has created a shortage of
30,000 tickets. This means that there are going to be a larger quantity of
tickets demanded than there are tickets. The university has to allocate
these tickets by some other means than using the market, so it discriminates; it sells tickets to those fans who are willing to wait in line the
longest or to those who donate to the booster club. The shortage of tickets will produce a black market. Some of those who are able to get the
tickets for $7 will be willing to sell them. These people will engage in
black market activity by selling them to those who are willing to pay
more. In the black market for tickets to such events, these black marke-
teers are sometimes referred to as scalpers. Scalping generally has a bad
connotation. But consider: the scalper is performing the service of transferring tickets from people who value other goods more highly than they
value the tickets to individuals who value the tickets more highly than
other goods, and the scalper is being paid for performing this service.

Why Ceilings? If price ceilings are so disruptive, why do we have
them? One answer is that not all people are hurt by ceilings. Those who
are able to purchase the good or service at the artificially low price are

better off and they, as a result, approve of the ceiling. In the apartment example, if you already have an apartment and you don't want to move, you would be better off with rent control. You would then probably vote for rent control because it would make you better off. In the ticket example, if you don't mind waiting in line, or if you will get a ticket because you are a booster, you would like low ticket prices. It is important to realize, though, that price ceilings do not, as is often claimed, generally help the poor. If there is one ticket left at $7 for the big game, who do you think will get it? A poor fan who likes football more than anything else the $7 would buy, or the governor who thinks it would be good politics to be seen at the game? When the market is replaced, another mechanism must be substituted to allocate goods. This mechanism usually depends heavily on power and influence, and thus the poor are not generally helped by the ceiling because they don't usually have the necessary power or influence.

Price Floors

A price floor that is set above the equilibrium price prohibits the market from clearing. The amount that suppliers offer for sale at the imposed floor is greater than the amount consumers wish to purchase at this price. Figure 4-5 demonstrates this case. In Figure 4-5 the equilibrium price is OP_e and the equilibrium quantity is OQ_e. The government

FIGURE 4-5   Price Floor

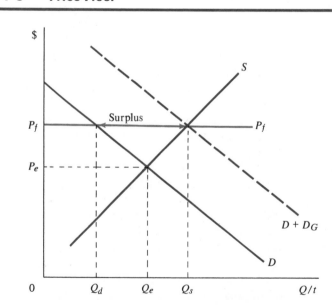

If the government imposes a price above the market-clearing price, a surplus will be created. At the higher than equilibrium price, suppliers will desire to sell more units than consumers will be willing to purchase.

Bruce Hoertel

Alfred E. Kahn (1917–   )

Alfred E. Kahn

Alfred E. Kahn made big news as the economist in charge of airline deregulation. Kahn was appointed chairperson of the Civil Aeronautics Board (CAB) by President Carter. An avid proponent of deregulation, Kahn immediately set out to deregulate the airline industry. When he was sworn in, he remarked, "I will consider it some measure of success in this job, if there is no job when I leave it."[1]

Kahn was spectacularly successful in his term as chairperson of the CAB. The results of his rapid push toward deregulation are obvious to all of us in the lower fares we pay to fly. At the 1978 American Economic Association, Kahn received the plaudits of almost all the economists in attendance, for he had succeeded in a policy application of the most simple economic principle — that government noninterference in an industry promotes competition and thus serves the public interest better than would a government-enforced cartel.

Kahn was born in Paterson, New Jersey. He received a B.A. and an M.A. degree from New York University and later attended Yale, where he received his Ph.D. in 1942. His first academic appointment was as an assistant professor at Ripon College from 1945–1947. He moved to Cornell University, where he presently is R. J. Thorne Professor of Economics. Kahn is a no-nonsense, aggressive administrator, and his style of leadership made headlines when he was chairperson of the CAB. On one occasion he wrote the following memo to his staff: "May I ask you, please, to try very hard to write . . . in straight-forward, quasi-conversational prose — as though you were talking to real people."[2] On another occasion at a CAB meeting, when Kahn supported a new, low-rate international air fare, a veteran CAB staffer warned him, "You have destroyed the North Atlantic fare structure." Kahn replied, "That's a good afternoon's work."[3]

In late 1978, President Carter, in large part because of Kahn's past success, named Kahn his chief inflation-fighter by appointing him chairperson of the Council on Wage and Price Stability. In characteristic fashion, Kahn quickly pointed out, "I became not Mr. Wage and Price Regulator, but Mr. Efficiency in Government, Mr. Deregulator, or Mr. Minimizer of Coercion."[4] It remains to be seen if Mr. Kahn can be as successful at his inflation job as he was at dismantling the power of the CAB.

[1]*Newsweek* (November 6, 1978), p. 32
[2]*Ibid.*
[3]*The Wall Street Journal*, July 3, 1978, p. 5.
[4]*Newsweek* (November 6, 1978), p. 33.

81

imposes a price floor of OP_f, with the result that the quantity supplied at price OP_f is OQ_s and the quantity consumers demand is OQ_d. The result is a **surplus** equal to $OQ_s - OQ_d$. This surplus is created by the price floor. If the floor didn't exist, price would fall and the quantity demanded would increase while the quantity supplied would decrease until the market cleared.

It can be difficult for the governmental unit that imposes a price floor to maintain the floor. Some would-be suppliers will attempt to cut prices in order to sell the desired quantity. The most effective way for the government to prevent this price cutting is to purchase the unwanted quantity supplied. By purchasing the surplus, the government in effect is shifting the demand curve outward to create a new equilibrium at the desired price. In Figure 4-5, the dashed demand curve represents the previous demand curve plus the added governmental demand. Such a shift would allow the price to remain at OP_f. The best example of price floors that worked in this way were the price supports for grain in the period of the 1960s. The government wanted to maintain a price that was above the market-clearing price. To maintain this price floor, it was necessary for the Department of Agriculture to purchase the grain; the effect of this was to shift the demand curve to the right so the higher price could be maintained.

The Minimum Wage

The **minimum wage** is a price floor in the labor market. In terms of Figure 4-5, a minimum wage (OP_f) that is set above the market wage (OP_e) would cause a surplus of labor ($OQ_s - OQ_d$). In terms of our analysis, if the minimum wage is set above the market-clearing wage rate, the amount of labor that laborers will supply at that wage will be greater than the amount of labor that firms will wish to employ. Thus, there will be unemployment.

Economists are generally in agreement that minimum wage legislation causes unemployment to be higher than it would be otherwise. This is particularly true for young people, where the minimum wage might be significantly higher than the market-clearing wage. In 1978 Congress raised the wage floor to $2.65 an hour, up from the $2.30 per hour which was set in 1974. In addition, a formula was adopted which insures automatic increases that will move the wage floor up to $3.35 an hour in 1981. This was done despite the fact that teenage unemployment was almost 18 percent at the time the bill was passed and despite strong statistical evidence from a large number of economists that the increase would raise youth unemployment to even higher levels. Professor Robert Goldfarb of George Washington University and Dr. Edward Gramlich of the Brookings Institution have reviewed, in two independent publications, eight recent empirical studies by economists. The studies overwhelmingly agree that increases in minimum wages cause increases in unemployment. The studies differ, however, as to how significant the impact is. The studies set a range, with the conclusion that the 1978 increase in the minimum wage of 15 percent (from $2.30 to $2.65) would increase teenage unemployment anywhere from 3.4 to 5.3 percentage points.[3]

If there is so much agreement among economists about the deleterious effects of minimum wages, why are they enacted? The reason is very similar to the one we gave when we examined the reason for enacting price ceilings. Not all people are hurt by the floor. Some workers receive pay increases when the legislation is enacted. Those who are laid off or who are unable to find employment at the new minimum wage usually don't understand why they can't find employment. The result is that it is politically popular among some groups, particularly organized labor, to support minimum wage legislation. Remember, economics only tells us that minimum wage legislation causes decreased employment. It does not tell us that minimum wage legislation is a good or bad thing. We may decide that it is better to have fewer people employed at a higher wage rate than to have everyone who wants to work employed at a lower, market-clearing wage rate.

THE MORAL EQUIVALENT OF WAR?

In 1978 President Carter held a fireside chat to talk to the American public about the energy crisis. He declared that the energy crisis was the moral equivalent of war. We can, using the tools developed in the previous three chapters, analyze many aspects of the energy crisis. As an example, we will examine the natural gas shortage.

The Creation of a Crisis: Regulation of Natural Gas

In 1938 Congress passed the Natural Gas Act, and in 1954 the Supreme Court placed all firms selling interstate natural gas under the regulation of the *Federal Power Commission (FPC)*.[4] The law was intended to keep prices "just and reasonable" and to keep prices low for consumers by allowing only a "fair" rate of return. After the 1954 Su-

---

[3]See Edward M. Gramlich, "Impact of Minimum Wages on Other Wages, Employment and Family Incomes," *Brookings Papers on Economic Activity*, No. 2 (1976), pp. 409–451; and Robert Goldfarb, "The Policy Content of Quantitative Minimum Wage Research," Industrial Relations Research Association Proceedings, December, 1974, pp. 261–268.

[4]The brief discussion that follows does not do justice to the complexity of natural gas regulation. The interested reader should see Edward J. Mitchell, *U.S. Energy Policy: A Primer* (Washington: American Enterprise Institute for Public Policy Research, June, 1974). Mitchell's study cites much of the relevant literature on natural gas regulation. See Mitchell for references to the data and the other studies mentioned.

preme Court ruling, the FPC attempted to regulate the price received by each individual producer engaged in the interstate sale of natural gas. The system broke down in 1960 as a giant backlog of hearings developed in response to the attempted regulation of more than 4,000 firms. A former Harvard Law School dean has called this "the outstanding example in the federal government of the breakdown of the administrative process."[5] In response to this administrative breakdown, the FPC ruled in 1965 (affirmed by the Supreme Court in 1968) that it would set prices separately for each geographical area and each individual petroleum commodity. This decision took eight years to be concluded, and during this entire period prices were kept at 1960 levels. This individual commodity approach to pricing is next to impossible to implement because natural gas is jointly produced with crude oil. The FPC method requires that certain costs be allocated to the production of natural gas even though it is produced in a joint process. Recognizing the administrative history and difficulty of these controls, let us determine what the effects of regulation were.

Paul W. MacAvoy, a professor of economics at M.I.T. and a member of President Ford's Council of Economic Advisers, has extensively examined the natural gas industry. In a series of books and articles in professional journals, he has simulated the market for natural gas to determine the effects of regulation. He has concluded that regulation has held prices below free-market levels. Between 1964 and 1967, prices would have been about twice as high without regulation. The result of these artificially depressed prices is that new reserves added to production were 40 percent lower than what would have been added in the free-market context. The result of these lower reserves is painfully obvious to all of us. In the absence of the price-rationing function of the market system, there is a shortage. Existing supplies must then be rationed and consumers (including industry) must substitute more expensive alternative fuels for the cheaper natural gas that is not available. The curious result is that the government, because it did not want the price of natural gas to rise, produced a shortage that requires consumers to buy even more expensive gasified coal, imported liquid natural gas, or some other alternative fuel.

We can see this graphically in Figure 4-6. Initially assume the price set by the FPC was near or at equilibrium. This produced a price represented by P_{1960} and an equilibrium quantity of Q_{1960}. The 1960 decision to set prices on a geographical-area basis represented a price ceiling that was not changed for eight years while the case was in litigation. During this period there were tremendous changes in the *ceteris paribus* demand conditions. For one, income increased substantially during this period. The demand for natural gas is very income elastic. Thus, by 1968 the

---

[5]Quoted in Edward J. Mitchell, *U.S. Energy Policy: A Primer* (Washington: American Enterprise Institute for Public Policy Research, June, 1974), p. 7.

FIGURE 4-6   The Market for Natural Gas

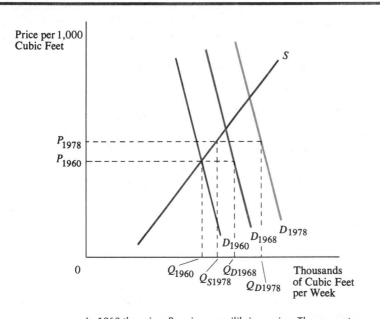

In 1960 the price, P_{1960}, is an equilibrium price. The amount consumers *wish* to purchase is exactly equal to the amount suppliers *wish* to sell. A shortage is created if the price is frozen at P_{1960} and demand increases to D_{1968} and to D_{1978}. Increasing the price ceiling to P_{1978} can reduce the shortage, but as long as the ceiling price is below the equilibrium price, a shortage will exist.

demand curve had shifted to the curve represented by D_{1968}. We now have a shortage. At P_{1960} the quantity supplied is Q_{1960} and the quantity demanded is Q_{D1968}. Ten years later, the problem is still with us. Demand has increased to D_{1978}. To be sure, the FPC has allowed the price to rise, but the price rise lags behind the demand increase. So in 1978 we still have a government-created shortage because at P_{1978} the quantity supplied is Q_{S1978} and the quantity demanded is Q_{D1978}.

It is important to realize that the shortage was caused by the price ceiling. Natural gas is scarce, but scarcity and shortage are quite different concepts. Scarcity simply means that the item is not as plentiful as we would like; with scarcity, rising prices insure equilibrium. Shortage means that at the prevailing price, the quantity demanded exceeds the quantity supplied. This distinction is important because much of the talk about an energy crisis confuses these two concepts.

Predictions of doom for the users of energy are not uncommon. As early as the beginning of the 19th century some commentators were predicting our first energy crisis. In the early 1800s houses were lit by oil-burning lamps. Demand for these lamps was increasing rapidly because of income and population growth. The lamps were fueled by oil from sperm whales. Many people predicted that the whale population would soon be depleted and therefore houses would be dark. In other words, they were predicting greater scarcity of this particular product. What happened? Prices rose rapidly, from about 40 cents per gallon to about $2.50 per gallon in thirty years. These higher prices caused the quantity demanded to decrease as substitutes for the whale oil were sought. The important point is that a shortage did not occur because prices rose in the face of greater scarcity. Shortages can only occur with artificially imposed low prices. It is particularly disturbing that the shortages of natural gas occurred in a market where there was a potentially large and relatively elastic supply. *The Energy Resources and Development Administration (ERDA)* estimated in 1977 that at prices between $2.00 and $3.00 per thousand cubic feet, or about double the current regulated price of $1.34, there was enough natural gas to last a thousand years (at current rates of consumption).[6]

The Dilemma of Earlier Regulation

Perhaps even more disturbing is the lesson that, even after it is generally recognized that government regulation is creating havoc in important markets, it is politically very difficult to remove the controls. This is understandable if we examine the behavior the controls bring about. Those individuals who are lucky enough, or have enough political power, purchase the natural gas at below market prices. When Congress becomes convinced that the crisis may be the result of regulation, it is politically very unpopular to change the law. After all, those people purchasing gas at $1.34 per thousand cubic feet in 1978 would have had to pay up to $3.00 per thousand cubic feet if deregulation had been undertaken. This would have produced a sharp rise in fuel bills, and voters might vote against a member of Congress who voted to deregulate. It is important to realize that if Congress had not interfered with the market mechanism in the first place, voters would probably not hold Congress as responsible for subsequent higher gas prices after deregulation.

It was a major goal of the Carter administration to lift the price ceiling in 1978–1979, and the necessary legislation was approved by Congress in the fall of 1978. The Carter deregulation, which was a hard fought legislative battle, immediately raised prices 25 percent and allowed for a 10 percent increase per year until 1985, when all ceilings on newly found natural gas would be removed. There is, however, disagreement over what impact the bill will have on natural gas consumption. The White House hailed the bill as a major energy victory. Critics disagree, saying that the bill is vague and complex and that it will be too hard to administer.

---

[6]*The Wall Street Journal* (April 27, 1977).

This brief review of natural gas regulation was not meant as a lesson of one industry, but as an illustration of the effect that regulation and political interference can have on market forces. Similar regulation can be found throughout the U.S. economy. One need only to scan the headlines for this month's crisis. Be it the meat shortage, the cement shortage, or the capital shortage, one need not look far for the cause. The distortion is very likely caused by often well-intentioned interference with market forces.

THE HEALTH CARE INDUSTRY

Health care, and particularly the rapidly rising price of health care, is receiving considerable attention from journalists and politicians these days. In large part, this increased interest and concern is a natural outgrowth of the fact that health care has become one of the fastest growing industries in the United States. Between 1950 and 1978, total expenditures on health care increased from $11 billion annually to more than $162 billion annually, and they are expected to more than double again between 1978 and 1983. In 1950 these expenditures represented 4.5 percent of total national income. They are expected to represent more than 10 percent of national income by 1983. Let's look at the potential problems of the health care industry using the basic economic tools we have developed in the previous three chapters.

We can see what is happening in the health care industry by examining Figure 4-7. The market in 1950 is represented by supply curve S_{1950} and demand curve D_{1950}. An equilibrium of OP_1 and OQ_1 obtains. Between 1950 and 1978 there were, of course, substantial changes in the *ceteris paribus* conditions in the health care market. Consider a few. On the supply side, hospitals and doctors greatly increased the sophistication of the care they supply. There has been a virtual explosion in the industries that make diagnostic, surgical, and therapeutic equipment. This equipment is very expensive and increases the cost of supplying health care (even if it does mean improved health care). The effect of all this improved, expensive care has been to shift the supply curve from S_{1950} to S_{1978} in Figure 4-7.

On the demand side, the changes are equally significant. First and foremost, the income of U.S. citizens has risen significantly over this period. Assuming health care is a normal good and that the demand for it is income elastic, the increased income will increase the demand for health care, and the more income elastic this demand, the more significant will be the increase in demand. Second, the very success of medical health care delivery creates more demand for health care in the future. This is because older people demand more health care than younger people. As the health care of the population improves, the population lives longer. More health care is then demanded because the population is now older. For example, one of the reasons we have more people demanding health care related to the heart is because we have an older

FIGURE 4-7   **The Market for Health Care**

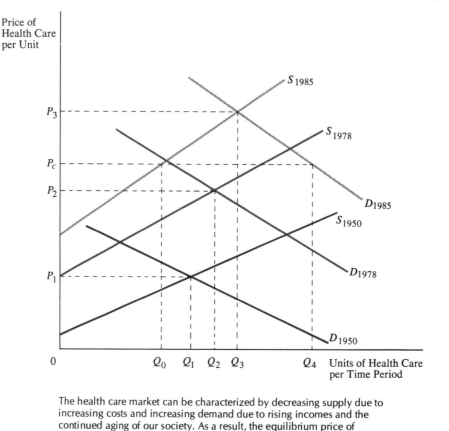

The health care market can be characterized by decreasing supply due to increasing costs and increasing demand due to rising incomes and the continued aging of our society. As a result, the equilibrium price of health care has been rising rapidly.

population. Twenty years ago many of these people would have died of measles, polio, or tuberculosis before they would have been old enough to develop heart problems. In any event, for a myriad of reasons, the demand for health care has increased significantly. This increase is represented by the shift from D_{1950} to D_{1978} in Figure 4-7. The result of these changes in supply and demand has been for price to rise to OP_2 and a new level of consumption to be established at OQ_2.

The Coming Crisis in Health Care

What about the future? Let's speculate as to what might happen, using our basic tools. It is likely that the supply curve will continue to shift upward (leftward), representing an increase in the price of the factors of production used to produce health care. It is also likely that demand will continue to increase as incomes rise and the population ages. We would predict, then, that in response to a shift in demand from D_{1978}

to D_{1985}, and a shift in supply from S_{1978} to S_{1985}, there will be an increase in price to OP_3 and an increase in the equilibrium quantity to OQ_3. But this supposes that the government does not intervene in this market. A quick review of congressional interest in the health care industry would be enough to convince you that this is not a realistic assumption. As it stands now, the most likely governmental solution to the rapidly rising prices is twofold. Currently, the most popular solution is some form of national health insurance. Senator Edward Kennedy has made a national health insurance program a major political issue. The economic effects of such a program are easy enough to predict. Since national health insurance would lower the effective price of health care and make health care affordable to more citizens, it would increase the demand curve even beyond the one represented by D_{1985} in Figure 4-7. This would put even greater upward pressure on prices. While a national health insurance program is seen as an antidote to rising costs, there is also increasing pressure to intervene in the market with price controls. Congress is beginning to talk about the "immorality" of the high price of health care. Wage and price controls have been suggested as a solution. The effect can be predicted by examining Figure 4-7. At a ceiling price of OP_c the quantity supplied would be OQ_0 and the quantity demanded would be OQ_4. There would be a shortage of $OQ_4 - OQ_0$ units. We would have the same type of crisis we discussed earlier when examining the natural gas market. An interesting point is that just at the time Congress is beginning to understand how controls implemented in the 1950s helped create the energy crisis, it is flirting with similar controls for the health care industry.

A Liberal's Dilemma?

Does this discussion and an understanding of these basic economic tools mean that we can't support a national health program that would insure health care to all citizens? Not at all! All that economics tells us is that such a program would increase demand and put upward pressure on prices of health care. We may well decide that this upward pressure on prices is worthwhile and that we want such a program. The point of economics is to tell us that these pressures are there, that we can't ignore them, and that to resort to controls will probably create a crisis.

THE FARM PROBLEM

We hear and read a lot in the news about the demise of the family farm and the crisis in agricultural markets. In some areas of the country, traditionally conservative farmers have even borrowed the tactics of the protest movements in efforts to draw political attention to their economic problems. The farm problem and agricultural economics present some very complicated problems, but our basic tools can provide many insights into what the situation is and how the problem came about.

In the short run the problem is simple enough to understand. First, agricultural production takes place in a very competitive market which closely resembles the basic supply and demand model we developed in Chapter 2. Second, the demand for the products produced in this market tends to be price inelastic. Third, weather plays a significant role in determining the size of any particular crop. These things taken together mean that the revenue a farmer receives in any one year can be highly variable. The irony for farmers is that in good harvest years they may be in worse shape than in poor harvest years. This can be seen by examining Figure 4-8. Let's say that in the previous year farm output sold at a price of OP_1, so OQ_1 units were sold with farmers receiving a total revenue of $OP_1 \cdot OQ_1$. The next year is very good and the crop is bountiful, so the supply curve shifts to S_2. Price falls to OP_2 and consumers purchase OQ_2 units. Since demand is so inelastic, farmers are now making less revenue than they did the year before $(OP_1 \cdot OQ_1 > OP_2 \cdot OQ_2)$; the large fall in price brought only a small increase in sales. An individual farmer can do nothing about the fact that the bountiful harvest caused prices to fall.

FIGURE 4-8   The Market for Farm Output

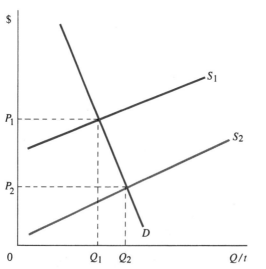

The market for farm output is characterized by erratic supply and inelastic demand. This means that the total revenue a farmer receives in any one year can be highly variable.

The Long-Run Problem

The long-run problem for the farmer is caused by the fact that there have been huge increases in farm productivity in the United States in the last century. These technological advances have been faster in agriculture than in the economy as a whole. This simply means that it takes fewer and fewer farmers to supply the food we need. In the early 1800s, more than half the U.S. labor force was engaged in farming, but now less than 5 percent of the work force is engaged in agriculture. Farmers who enjoy their lifestyle are, of course, against future reductions in the agricultural labor force. Many of the political arguments "to save the family farm" are arguments to stop this trend toward fewer and fewer agricultural workers. If farmers have political power, and some would argue that they have disproportionate political power because reapportionment of political districts lags population shifts, we would expect a governmental response to their calls for action. One such governmental response has been the agricultural support program.

The Political Response

Prior to 1973, the *agricultural support program* consisted of attempts to decrease supply or increase demand. Price floors were enacted to create parity. *Parity* prices are an attempt to define fair prices, that is, prices that are necessary to establish the purchasing power of the farmer at some past level which is selected as the proper level. Farmers like to view 1910–1914 as a "golden age" and often think parity should be established with this period. The idea is to link farm prices to an index of the purchasing power of farmers as it was in the period selected as the appropriate one, such as 1910–1914. Parity then is an argument for higher relative prices in the agricultural sector. In actuality, parity creates price floors, which are prices above equilibrium levels.

We saw the effect of price floors in Figure 4-5. The quantity supplied exceeds the quantity demanded at the imposed price and a surplus develops. If the government is to maintain this price floor, it must act as the buyer of last resort. The government must purchase the surplus. After the government purchases the surplus, it has a dilemma. It can't sell the product on domestic markets or the price will fall back to the equilibrium price. In the 1950s and early 1960s, the government reacted to this dilemma by building storage bins and storing the farm product. At the high point of such storage activity, which occurred in 1961, the government had 1.3 billion bushels of wheat and 1.7 billion bushels of corn in storage.

There are some other things that could be done. The government could destroy the surplus grain, but this can be predicted to upset those who would consider it wasteful.[7] The government could give the produce away, perhaps to poor countries, but this might upset other countries who are trying to sell to these poor countries. The government could sell

---

[7]The Canadian government once destroyed 28 million eggs. See Patrick Howe, "Unscrambling the Egg Market: A Lesson in Economics," *Common Sense Economics*, Vol. 2, No. 2 (Spring, 1977), pp. 42–47.

the grain to other countries if customers could be found. Still another alternative would be to hold on to the surplus for future emergency needs. It is, however, absolutely necessary for the government to buy the surplus it has created.

Managing Production

As early as the mid-1950s, the U.S. government had decided that the purchase and storage of the surplus was too costly and that managing production was a better alternative. The idea was, and is, that the government can maintain the price floor by keeping the quantity supplied at lower levels than would exist without government intervention. In this case, the government is trying to shift the supply curve to maintain the higher price.

The first such attempt to manage production was known as the *soil bank program*. In the soil bank program, which was started by President Eisenhower, farmers were paid to let their land lay idle. This would thus reduce the supply.[8] A second attempt along similar lines was an *acreage allotment*. An acreage allotment sets a limit on the number of acres that can be put into production. The government then must determine who gets what acreage allotment. In producing tobacco, for example, the decision is based on historical levels of production. In other words, if your parents were tobacco producers and you buy or inherit their farm, you would get an allotment equal to their share of past production. Still another way to decrease supply is with a *marketing quota system*. A marketing quota system simply specifies how much a farmer can bring to market.

All of these attempts to manage the production of farms have had profound effects on farmers. In the case of the soil bank, the farmer was paid out of general tax revenues not to produce on the least productive land. In the acreage allotment method, farmers have had an incentive to cultivate the allowed acres very intensively in an effort to produce larger crops on fewer acres. In the marketing quota system, the farmer cannot benefit by increasing productivity and output since the allowed output is specified by the government.

The Political Response Since 1973

Since 1973 and the period when Earl Butz was President Nixon's Secretary of Agriculture, the system of agricultural support has changed. We no longer have price floors or *support prices*, which had been the term for floors in the pre-1973 period. Instead, we now have *target prices*. Target prices are prices the government considers to be fair for

---

[8]Predictably, farmers took their least productive land out of production and the supply didn't change very much.

farmers. The market is allowed to clear and the equilibrium price is compared to the target price. The government then pays each farmer the difference between the target price and the market-clearing price. This can be a sizable amount of money. For example, in the winter wheat market, the 1978 price of winter wheat in the Texas panhandle was as low as $1.92 per bushel. This was compared to a 1977 average price of $3.00 per bushel and an average of between $5.00 and $6.00 per bushel in 1971–1972. The target price in May, 1978, was raised to $3.40 per bushel. It was estimated by the government that the differential between the market-clearing price of $1.92 per bushel and the target price of $3.40 per bushel cost taxpayers $4.4 billion dollars in 1978.

The latest piece of agricultural legislation was the Food and Agriculture Act of 1977. This legislation covered almost all major crops and included dairy products. It covered many of the same programs that previous legislation had covered, such as target prices and acreage reductions, but included at least one new program, a farmer-held *grain reserve program*. The idea of the program is that farmers should store their own surplus grain. For example, a price for wheat is established and if the farmer can't sell at this price, the farmer will receive payments to cover the cost of storage until the price rises to the established floor. The idea is to prevent price instability by withholding grain from the market whenever the price is below support levels. Taxpayers pay the cost of the storage although the actual storage is undertaken by the farmer.

Solutions?

Like the other social problems discussed in this chapter, the tools of economics cannot solve the problem but can point out some fundamental truths. The fundamental truths are that there are too many resources in the agricultural industry and these resources are kept there by transfers from general tax revenues. Taxpayers' income is being redistributed to farmers and this keeps resources in the farm industry that would otherwise be attracted to other industries. The basic tools of economics cannot tell us if this is good or bad, nor can they predict if anything will be done to change the situation. The answer to the first question is a value judgment concerning whether you think it is good or bad to maintain the present level of resources in agriculture. The answer to the second question will in part depend on the political strength of farmers and the farm constituency.

Summary

This chapter used the basic tools developed in the previous chapters to demonstrate how useful economics is in analyzing a wide range of social policy questions. Crime is an economic activity and can be analyzed as a rational decision of the criminal. To decrease criminal activity, one need only decrease the benefits the criminal receives or increase the costs the criminal must pay. This holds for the entire range of crime, from illegal parking to armed robbery or murder.

The concepts of supply, demand, and elasticity can be used to determine tax incidence. The more inelastic the demand for a product and the more elastic the supply, the greater the amount of the tax paid by the consumer. Conversely, the greater the elasticity of demand for a product and the more inelastic the supply, the more the tax is paid by producers. In other words, relative elasticities determine tax incidence.

Price ceilings are attempts to keep prices from rising to their equilibrium level. Price ceilings cause shortages, and black markets often develop in response to the shortage. Rent control is an example of a price ceiling.

Price floors are attempts to keep market prices from declining below a certain level. Price floors cause surpluses that must be absorbed to prevent the price from falling. Agricultural support prices and minimum wages are examples of price floors.

The energy crisis as it pertains to natural gas is a good example of how price ceilings disrupt markets. The lesson is that price ceilings are very difficult to remove even after the damage they cause is well understood. This type of intervention seems likely in the health care industry.

The farm problem has in part been caused by the supply and demand characteristics of the industry and in part by the rapid productivity gains in agricultural production. The government has been active in agricultural markets for a long time and the effects of this activity can be examined by using the concepts of supply and demand.

New Terms

excise tax
tax incidence
price ceilings
price floors
shortage
black markets
rent control
surplus
minimum wage
Federal Power Commission (FPC)

Energy Resources and Development
   Administration (ERDA)
agricultural support program
parity
soil bank program
acreage allotment
marketing quota system
support prices
target prices
grain reserve program

Questions for Discussion

1 Why does a price ceiling that is set above the equilibrium price have no effect on the market?

2 Can you think of other areas where models like the simple economic model

of crime might be formulated? What about the economics of the decision to have children? The economics of marriage and/or divorce?

3 How is the minimum wage maintained at

higher than market-clearing rates? Why don't the unemployed workers agree to work for lower wages and thereby circumvent the imposed price floor?

4 If you were the taxing authority, would you place an excise tax on items with elastic or inelastic demand? Why?

5 Should the government stay out of the farm sector? What would be the consequences for farmers of no government intervention? For consumers?

6 Do you favor price controls on rentals (rent control)? Explain your position.

Suggestions for Further Reading

Fellner, William, (ed.). *Contemporary Economic Problems: 1978*. Washington: American Enterprise Institute for Public Policy Research, 1978.

Hailstones, Thomas J., and Frank V. Mastrianna. *Contemporary Economic Problems and Issues*, 5th ed. Cincinnati: South-Western Publishing Co., 1979.

LaForce, J. Clayburn. *The Energy Crises: The Moral Equivalent of Bamboozle*. Los Angeles: International Institute for Economic Research, 1978.

Leftwich, Richard H., and Ansel M. Sharp. *Economics of Social Issues*, 3d ed. Dallas: Business Publications, Inc., 1978, Chapter 2.

McKenzie, Richard B., and Gordon Tullock. *The New World of Economics*, revised ed. Homewood, Ill.: Richard D. Irwin, 1978.

Miller, Roger LeRoy. *The Economics of Energy: What Went Wrong*. Glenn Ridge, N. J.: Thomas Horton and Co., 1974.

North, Douglass C., and Roger LeRoy Miller. *The Economics of Public Issues*, 4th ed. New York: Harper & Row, Publishers, 1978.

CHAPTER 5

THE ECONOMICS OF CONSUMER BEHAVIOR: I

LEARNING OBJECTIVES

After studying the materials found in this chapter, you should be able to do the following:

1 Define utility.

2 Calculate total utility given marginal utility, and derive a marginal utility curve from a total utility curve.

3 Use the equation for maximizing total utility to determine the consumption pattern for an individual.

4 Derive an individual demand curve for a good based on
   (a) the equation for maximizing total utility,

(b) the principle of diminishing marginal utility.

5 Solve the diamond-water paradox based on
   (a) marginal utility and total utility,
   (b) value in exchange and value in use.

6 Discuss the theory of progressive income taxation based on
   (a) the marginal utility of income,
   (b) interpersonal utility comparisons.

We have spent a considerable amount of time using demand curves to develop predictions concerning the outcome of market processes. Most of our analysis has made use of market demand curves, which we derived by aggregating individual demand curves. Since these individual demand curves form the bedrock of the analysis, we need now to consider the factors that underlie the individual consumer's demand curve.

In this chapter we will discuss the first approach economists took to the examination of consumer demand — the classical approach, which involves the concept of measurable marginal utility. We will then use this approach to examine some problems and suggest some applications. The second approach to consumer demand, indifference curve analysis, will be discussed in the next chapter.

DEMAND AND UTILITY

It is important for economists to be able to derive the demand curve of an individual for a commodity. The demand curves of all individuals for that commodity can then be aggregated to form the market demand curve for the commodity.

Why does a person demand a certain good or service? An obvious answer would be that the good or service is expected to satisfy some need or desire of the consumer. Economists are content with this superficial answer. Psychologists would want to probe much more deeply into the question. They might want to distinguish between "wants" and "needs." Psychologists would also be interested in the qualities or intensities of the needs being satisfied.

There may be moral, or ethical, dimensions to the desires people have. Why do people want to buy guns? pornography? narcotics? sports cars? liquor? cigarettes? These are questions to which psychologists, moralists, and many others devote a great amount of their attention. But economists, as economists, are not generally interested in why desires exist or whether people should buy some things and not others. It is not because they think such questions are unimportant. Indeed, such questions may be much more important than the questions they try to answer as economists, such as, What would happen to sales if the price of Porsches increased by $1,000? or, What would happen to the sales of potatoes if the price of wheat went up $1 per bushel? Economists accept the fact that people have the psychological or ethical makeup they do without approving or disapproving of it, and the analysis starts from there.

UTILITY

In the early years of the development of the discipline of economics, the major issue was the determination of the value of goods and services.

Some saw value as depending on the scarcity of the commodity or the difficulty of producing it. Others looked for some intrinsic or inherent value attached to the consumption of the commodity as the source of its value. It wasn't until the beginning of this century that the great British economist, Alfred Marshall, spelled out the importance of both ideas. One point of view involved supply; the other, demand. In his famous analogy he said that you could no more say whether supply or demand determined value than you could say which blade of a pair of scissors did the cutting. Thus, value, or price, is determined by the interaction of supply and demand.

Let's consider the influence of demand on value first, and ignore supply, or cost, temporarily. Demand theorists used the notion of *utility*. The ordinary meaning and dictionary definitions of utility always include something about "usefulness," but this meaning is much more restricted than the one we use in economics. In economics, if an individual would like to have a commodity, then that commodity has utility. The good or service has whatever qualities that inhere in it, and the individual decides how much utility it has, given those qualities. The same commodity may have a great deal of utility for one person and none or very little for some other person. Like beauty, utility is in the eye (or mind) of the beholder.

Utility is strictly an *ex ante* concept; that is to say, utility measures the way the individual feels about a commodity *before* buying or consuming it. You might see a cake in a bakery window and have a great desire for it — that's utility. If you bought and ate the cake, you might get sick and receive no satisfaction from its consumption — that's irrelevant economically. Utility is the satisfaction you *expect* to get, not what you actually get after the fact. The reason for this distinction is that we use utility in the development of the demand curve, and the demand curve shows the amounts that people will buy based on anticipated satisfaction, not the amounts they would have bought after having made the purchase.

A good unit for the measurement of utility, like pounds or gallons or miles, does not exist, but since utility is unique to the individual, an arbitrary unit called the *util* can be employed. As long as no attempt is made to compare the number of utils of different people, this is a satisfactory measuring device. For example, suppose you tried to construct your *utility function* for some commodity, say a particular brand of beer. First, choose a convenient time period, say, a day for this example. Then for one unit (one can) of beer per day assign a number of utils, say, 20. (You could choose any number at all: 1; 10,000; 1/10; 47 1/2.) Then ask yourself, If I get 20 utils from one can, how many utils would I get if I consumed two cans of beer per day rather than just one? Suppose, after much reflection you say, 38. Ask yourself the same question about three cans of beer per day, four, five, six, and so on.

An economist would expect you to come up with a schedule something like that shown in Table 5-1. The important characteristic of the

TABLE 5-1   Utility Schedule for Beer

Cans of Beer per Day	Total Utility	Marginal Utility
0	0	
1	20	20
2	38	18
3	54	16
4	67	13
5	77	10
6	84	7
7	88	4
8	89	1
9	87	−2
10	82	−5

schedule is that, while the total utility would become larger the more you consumed per day (up to a point), the additions to total utility per unit would become smaller. This feature — the fact that additional, or marginal, utility declines as consumption increases — is called *diminishing marginal utility*.

Marginal utility is defined as the amount of utility that an additional unit of consumption adds to total utility. The formula for determining marginal utility (MU) is

$$MU = \frac{\text{change in total utility}}{\text{change in quantity consumed}}.$$

Marginal utility is thus the change (increase or decrease) in total utility brought about by consuming one more or one less unit of the good. The marginal utility is determined in Table 5-1 by calculating how much each additional can of beer adds to total utility. For example, the first can of beer adds 20 utils to total utility. The fourth can of beer adds 13 utils to total utility. This is found by subtracting the total utility of consuming three beers from the total utility of consuming four beers ($67 - 54 = 13$).

Principle of Diminishing Marginal Utility

The principle of diminishing marginal utility holds that for a given time period, the greater the level of consumption of a particular commodity, the lower the marginal utility. In other words, as you consume more units of a commodity, the additional units yield less of an addition to total utility than the preceding units. For instance, the seventh beer is expected to provide less additional pleasure than the sixth beer. This

William Stanley Jevons

Radio Times Hulton Picture Library

**William Stanley Jevons
(1835–1882)**

William Stanley Jevons had one of the great original minds in the history of economic thought. Jevons combined utility theory with marginal analysis and applied it to consumer choice. He thus constructed the theory that underlies the theory of demand, much as we have done in this chapter.

Jevons led a strange life. He was both an esoteric intellectual and a practical economist. He was born in Liverpool and studied chemistry and mathematics at University College, London. Financial problems caused him to move to Australia to accept a job with the Sydney Mint. He spent five years in Australia, during which time he became very interested in political economy. In 1859 he returned to the University of London and studied political economy until 1865. In 1865 he published a book, *The Coal Question*, which thrust him into prominence in economic circles. His most famous book, *Theory of Political Economy*, was published in 1871.

Jevons accepted a professorship at Owens College, Manchester, in 1866, where he worked on a wide range of intellectual pursuits, from statistical analysis of commodity prices to very abstract economic theory. He even developed a sun spot theory to explain business cycles. His work generated a great deal of interest in political circles, but Jevons himself had little impact on economic policy or on economic thought. This was largely because of his personal habits. He was, perhaps, the original "strange professor." He once wrote to his sister that he had never attended a party "without impressing upon all friends the fact that it is no use inviting me." He didn't regret this solitude; in fact, he argued that reserve and loneliness are necessary to develop ideas. He felt that social intercourse insured that thoughts would "never rise above the ordinary level of the others." A colleague of Jevons wrote: "There never was a worse lecturer, the men would not go to his classes, he worked in flashes and could not finish anything thoroughly, the only point about Jevons was that he was a genius."

Unfortunately for economics, Jevons died at the early age of 47. He drowned while at a health resort in the south of England. At the time of his death, Jevons was working on a massive book entitled *Principles of Economics*. The book, of course, was never completed.

principle is reflected in Table 5-1 and Figure 5-1. In Table 5-1, marginal utility falls from 20 utils for the first beer to 18 utils for the second beer. The seventh beer only adds four utils to total utility.

Figure 5-1, panel (b), shows the marginal utility curve that corresponds to the total utility curve in panel (a). Note that when the total utility curve reaches its maximum, marginal utility is zero. This makes sense because if total utility is to decline, marginal utility must become negative. In Table 5-1, total utility reaches a maximum at eight because the ninth beer has a negative marginal utility. And, the only way a total can decline is for additions to that total to be negative.

Utility and Consumer Behavior

The concept of utility and price can now be combined to show how consumers make choices in the marketplace. You remember that the reason we have an economic problem is that we must choose. When choosing, consumers are confronted with a range of items and also a range of prices. You may not choose the item which has the greatest utility because price and your income are also important. In other words, consumers don't always buy their first choice. Such behavior is commonplace. You may prefer a Porsche to a Vega, but you may purchase the Vega. This is rational behavior, and we can see why by looking at price and utility.

Suppose, for example, you are considering purchasing a six-pack of beer. You are presented the three possibilities listed in Table 5-2. Heineken is your first choice because it yields the most utility. But the relevant question is not which beer has the most utility, but which has the most utility *per dollar*. Therefore, you choose to buy a six-pack of Miller. This choice implies that the extra satisfaction of Heineken over Miller is not worth $1.50, but the extra satisfaction of Miller over Pabst is worth the extra $.75 it costs. Thus, in deciding how to spend your money, you look at marginal utility per dollar rather than marginal utility alone. You do this because money is the common denominator. Dollars can be used to buy any available good. So for the last dollar you spend, you want to choose the item with the highest utility per dollar; and in so doing, you economize by getting the most satisfaction per dollar. There are other things you can do with your money, and you are saying in this example that $1.50 spent on something other than Heineken will yield more utils than the Heineken would but that $.75 spent on other goods will not yield more utils than spending it on Miller.

Maximizing Total Utility

The self-interest hypothesis lets us make the assumption that individuals will act to maximize their total utility. To see how marginal utility and price influence how a consumer maximizes total utility, let's look

FIGURE 5-1   Total and Marginal Utility

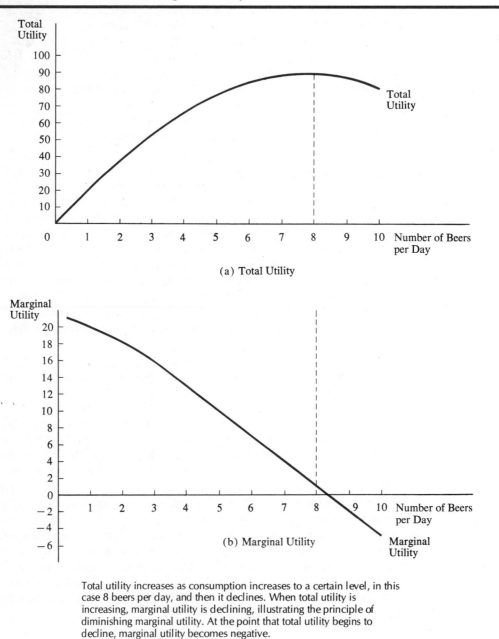

(a) Total Utility

(b) Marginal Utility

Total utility increases as consumption increases to a certain level, in this case 8 beers per day, and then it declines. When total utility is increasing, marginal utility is declining, illustrating the principle of diminishing marginal utility. At the point that total utility begins to decline, marginal utility becomes negative.

at a market with only two goods, beer and pizza, where a unit of beer costs $.50 and a unit of pizza costs $1. The utility schedules for the two goods are presented in Table 5-3.

TABLE 5-2   Utility Per Dollar Comparisons

	Marginal Utility (Utils)	Price	MU per Dollar
Heineken	30.0	$3.00	10
Miller	22.5	1.50	15
Pabst	7.5	.75	10

TABLE 5-3   Utility Schedule

Beer				Pizza			
Quantity per Week (Cans)	MU (Utils)	MU/P (P = $.50)	TU (Utils)	Quantity per Week (Small Pizzas)	MU (Utils)	MU/P (P = $1.00)	TU (Utils)
1	15	30	15	1	32	32	32
2	14	28	29	2	31	31	63
3	13	26	42	3	28	28	91
4	12	24	54	4	24¾	24¾	115¾
5	11	22	65	5	20¼	20¼	136
6	10¾	21½	75¾	6	18	18	154
7	10¼	20½	86	7	17	17	171
8	10	20	96	8	16	16	187
9	9	18	105	9	14	14	201
10	8	16	113	10	12	12	213
11	7	14	120	11	11	11	224
12	6½	13	126½	12	9	9	233
13	5	10	131½	13	7	7	240
14	4½	9	136	14	6	6	246
15	3	6	139	15	5	5	251
16	2½	5	141½	16	4	4	255
17	2	4	143½	17	3	3	258
18	1½	3	145	18	2	2	260
19	1	2	146	19	1	1	261
20	½	1	146½	20	0	0	261

The consumer has a given amount of income, which we call a **budget constraint**. For this example, let's endow our consumer with $13 worth of purchasing power and see how that income will be allocated between the two goods to achieve maximum utility.

The first dollar will obviously be spent on pizza because pizza yields 32 utils of satisfaction compared to 29 utils for $1 worth of beer. The second dollar will also be spent on pizza because it yields 31 utils, which is still greater than the 29 utils for $1 worth of beer. In other words, the consumer buys $2 worth of pizza before buying any beer. The third dollar would be spent on beer because the 29 utils of satisfaction it yields are greater than the 28 utils yielded by a third dollar spent on pizza. This process continues until the income of $13 is spent. In maximizing total utility, the consumer will spend $5 on 10 cans of beer and $8 on 8 pizzas. This allocation produces 300 utils of satisfaction — the maximum total utility that could be purchased with $13 of income. You cannot find an expenditure pattern which would produce more satisfaction (try reducing beer consumption by $1 and increasing pizza consumption by $1, or vice versa).

What we have done is to follow a maximization rule which says that an individual maximizes total utility by consuming where the last dollar spent on A yields the same utility as the last dollar spent on B. In algebraic form, total utility is maximized where $\frac{MU_A}{P_A} = \frac{MU_B}{P_B}$. In our example, the marginal utility of a can of beer when 10 cans per week were consumed was 8 utils, and the price of beer was $.50, so $\frac{MU_{beer}}{P_{beer}} = \frac{8}{\$.50}$, or 16 utils per dollar. For pizza, at the optimum consumption rate the MU was 16 and the price $1, so $\frac{MU_{pizza}}{P_{pizza}} = \frac{16}{\$1}$, or 16 utils per dollar.

This can be generalized to include all goods by saying an individual maximizes utility where $\frac{MU_x}{P_x} = \frac{MU_y}{P_y} = \ldots = \frac{MU_n}{P_n}$. Of course, individuals don't spend all their income on goods $x, y, \ldots, n$. Sometimes individuals hold money (let's use $ as the symbol) as they do any other commodity. We now write our equation for a maximization as $\frac{MU_A}{P_A} = \frac{MU_B}{P_B} = \frac{MU_\$}{P_\$}$. Now, the price of one dollar is one dollar, so $\frac{MU_\$}{P_\$}$ can be simply written as $MU_\$$. We thus have total utility being maximized where $\frac{MU_x}{P_x} = \frac{MU_y}{P_y} = \ldots = \frac{MU_n}{P_n} = MU_\$$. This now is a very complete expression for **utility maximization**. It has been extended to include all commodities, including money, and says that in order to maximize total utility, the marginal utilities per dollar of expenditures have to be equal and also have to equal the marginal utility of money. If this is not the case, a change in consumption patterns, for a given budget constraint, can produce more satisfaction. This is just a formal way of saying that people allocate their income so as to yield the most satisfaction possible. When utility is being maximized, the additional satisfaction from any use of $1 will equal the additional satisfaction from any other use of $1. When this is not the case, the individual will, by reallocating personal income, consume more of the good that yields more additional satisfaction per dollar.

To see how a given consumption pattern can be adjusted to achieve maximum utility, return to Table 5-3. Let's give the individual a $9 income and say that $3 worth of beer and $6 worth of pizza is being consumed. Obviously the expression $\dfrac{MU_{beer}}{P_{beer}} = \dfrac{MU_{pizza}}{P_{pizza}}$ doesn't hold because $\dfrac{21\frac{1}{2}}{1} > \dfrac{18}{1}$. The individual isn't maximizing because the last dollar spent on beer yields more utils than the last dollar spent on pizza. The individual should reallocate consumption outlays. By giving up one dollar's worth of pizza, the consumer would lose 18 utils but would gain 20¼ utils by spending one more dollar on beer. Total utility would thus rise by 2¼ utils. Now substituting back into the equation, we get $\dfrac{20}{1} = \dfrac{20}{1}$ (20¼ rounded off); the consumer is maximizing.

Marginal Utility and the Law of Demand

With the tools we've developed, we can now derive an individual's demand curve for a good. Suppose that there are only two goods, x and y. We could refer to a large number of goods by letting y represent all goods other than x. Remember, we draw demand curves in a *ceteris paribus* experiment so income, tastes, and the prices of all other goods (good y) are held constant. We start with our consumer in equilibrium, maximizing utility when $\dfrac{MU_x}{P_x} = \dfrac{MU_y}{P_y}$. At this equilibrium, MU_{x_1} corresponds to the consumption of x_1 units of x in Figure 5-2. P_{x_1}, the price of x_1, is represented by OP_{x_1} in Figure 5-2. So our equation should now be written, $\dfrac{MU_{x_1}}{P_{x_1}} = \dfrac{MU_y}{P_y}$. Now lower the price of x to OP_{x_2}. This throws the expression out of equality because the denominator on the left side is now smaller, making the left side of the expression larger: $\dfrac{MU_{x_1}}{P_{x_2}} > \dfrac{MU_y}{P_y}$. In order to get the expression back into equality, the individual has to lower the value of the left side of the expression and/or raise the right side. How can this be done? If the individual consumes more of x, MU_x will decline because of the principle of diminishing marginal utility. As consumption moves to Ox_2 on Figure 5-2, $MU_{x_2} < MU_{x_1}$. When this happens, the expression will move toward $MU_x/P_x = MU_y/P_y$. But as more x is purchased, less y is bought, so the MU of y increases as the MU of x is declining.

FIGURE 5-2   **Demand for x**

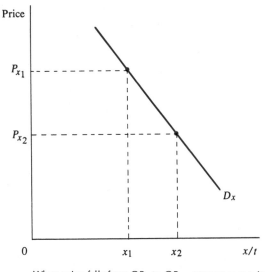

When price falls from OP_{x_1} to OP_{x_2}, consumer maximization is thrown out of equilibrium. Equilibrium will be restored if the consumer increases consumption to Ox_2.

What has happened is that consumer maximization behavior requires that when the price of a commodity falls (as from OP_{x_1} to OP_{x_2} in Figure 5-2), the consumer will increase the consumption of x. Since this is necessary for utility maximization, it proves that the demand curves of individuals must have a negative slope; that is, the lower the price, the greater the quantity demanded.

SOME APPLICATIONS OF UTILITY THEORY

You have practiced and observed the working of utility maximization even though you may not have thought of it in the formal terminology of economics. Suppose for a moment you are organizing the beer concession for a club fund-raising event. There are two ways to finance the concession: you could charge an admission fee to the event and then allow "free" consumption, or you could charge a set price for each beer, say, $.50 per glass. Our theory would predict different levels of consumption and hence different requirements for planning the supply. In the first case, beer drinkers would consume until the marginal utility per glass was zero because the price per additional glass is zero. In the second case, beer drinkers would consume beer until the marginal utility per glass equaled the marginal utility of $.50. You would predict, then, that there would be more drunken, rowdy behavior if the party were financed by an admission charge. If you don't agree with this analysis, reflect back on group parties you have attended. Were the most rowdy ones the pay-as-you-go type or the admission type?

This may seem like an insignificant example because the consumption of beer isn't a very earth-shaking issue. So let's change the good in the example from beer to medical services. If we consider a "free" national health service, what would you predict would happen to the consumption of these services?[1] Of course, people would consume them until the marginal utility was zero! This is exactly what happens in a socialized medicine program. If you have ever participated in such a program in the army, at a university, or under one of the new health maintenance plans, you have probably consumed more of these services than before. Since the services are "free," more are consumed. You may also have noticed that with the "free" system the waiting time is usually longer than with a paid system, the waiting rooms are less comfortable, the workers are less congenial, and so on. The effect of all of this is to reduce the marginal utility and therefore decrease the demand for the service. Lowering the quality of a good or a service is equivalent in many ways to increasing the price.

THE DIAMOND-WATER PARADOX

Classical economists argued that utility (and thus demand) could not be a determinant of price because diamonds, while less useful than water, were more expensive than water. These classical economists spent a great deal of time discussing this problem, which became known as the *diamond-water paradox*. It should be clear that the paradox is caused by the failure to separate total utility and marginal utility. The total utility of water is high, but since there is a great deal in existence and large quantities are consumed, its marginal utility is low. The total utility of diamonds, on the other hand, is relatively low, but since diamonds are rare, their marginal utility is high. Price, then, is determined by marginal utility, not total utility. We say that marginal utility determines *value in exchange* (price) and that total utility determines *value in use*. Scarcity, then, is related to value through utility. If something is scarce and has a low marginal utility, it will have a low price; but if something is scarce and has a high marginal utility, it will be valuable and hence be expensive.

THE UNEASY CASE FOR THE PROGRESSIVE INCOME TAX[2]

One of the main arguments (but not the only one) for a *progressive income tax* is based on the principle of diminishing marginal utility. This

---

[1]By *free*, we mean there is no monetary cost to the patient; i.e., price is zero.

[2]For a comprehensive treatment of this subject, see Walter J. Blum and Harry Klaven, Jr., *The Uneasy Case for Progressive Taxation* (Chicago: University of Chicago Press, 1970).

argument assumes that we can measure utility (which we have seen is impossible), and further, that we can make *interpersonal utility comparisons* or say that individuals all have the same utility schedule for equal increments of income. With these two assumptions, proponents of the progressive income tax argue that we can maximize utility within society by taking income away from the high income individuals who have lower marginal utilities of income and transferring it to the low income individuals who have a higher marginal utility of income.

Proponents of a progressive income tax who apply principles of individual utility maximization to the society as a whole are on very shaky ground, however. First of all, economists are in agreement that interpersonal utility comparisons are meaningless. People are different. There really is no accounting for taste. There is no way you can prove that an additional $100 of income gives less satisfaction to Jacqueline Kennedy Onassis than to Cesar Chavez. In fact, Jackie may get more satisfaction because she is such an expert consumer. It would be impossible to prove that one individual gets more or less satisfaction from an increment to income than does any other individual.

A second and more fundamental problem with this analysis is that it assumes a diminishing marginal utility for income (money). This proposition cannot be verified. The principle of diminishing marginal utility, you will remember, states that the marginal utility of a *particular commodity* declines as consumption is increased. Increased income, however, represents an increase in the consumption of all goods. If wants are insatiable, as we posited in Chapter 1, there is no reason to believe that the principle of diminishing marginal utilty holds for money. Even so, it is probably the case that most people think that money has diminishing marginal utility. What about you? Do you think a $100 bill would give your "rich" economics instructor more or less satisfaction than it would give you?

PROBLEMS WITH UTILITY THEORY

There are two major difficulties with a demand theory based on utility. They center on the indivisibility and immeasurability of utility. In working through the theory, we have traced what happens to the consumer's satisfaction when we vary units of consumption in a given period in which tastes are held constant, and we have seen that adjustments in consumption can be made in order to maximize utility. The theory works well enough when we consider the consumption of certain kinds of goods, such as ice cream cones or beer or shirts. When we consider the purchase of an automobile or a home, however, we see that it is difficult to talk about additional units because the purchase is what economists call *lumpy*. It is difficult to consume a part of a house or a part of a car while it is possible to consume part of a case of beer. The theory is somewhat weakened, then, by the fact that the consumer can't make continuous decisions about successive amounts of consumption.[3]

A greater problem is the inability to measure utility. We have proceeded as if there were a way we could strap a meter to a consumer and with exactness measure the utility expected from consuming one more beer. This is, of course, not possible. Psychology has not yet developed to such a technological level. But before you reject utility theory as useless, remember that we are developing a theoretical tool, much as is done in a physics class. It really isn't that important for our theory that we be able to measure utility. Our purpose is to develop propositions about how quantity demanded will change when prices change, not about how utility changes.

Summary

Economists say that individuals derive satisfaction from consuming goods and services, and that utility is the expectation of that satisfaction. Total utility is the total amount of satisfaction expected from consuming an item or group of items. Marginal utility is the addition to total utility from consuming one more unit of the good. Consumers, in deciding among items, choose those items with the highest marginal utility per dollar.

An individual maximizes total utility by consuming all items so that the marginal utilities per dollar spent are equal. That is, the maximizing rule is $\frac{MU_x}{P_x} = \frac{MU_y}{P_y} = \frac{MU_n}{P_n} = MU_\$$. If marginal utilities per dollar spent are not equal, a reallocation of expenditures can increase total utility.

Utility theory has been criticized on the grounds that utility is not measurable and that items consumed are not perfectly divisible as the theory of utility maximization requires. Despite these criticisms, utility theory is a useful tool for analyzing consumer behavior.

New Terms

utility
ex ante
util
utility function
marginal utility
diminishing marginal utility
budget constraint

utility maximization
diamond-water paradox
value in exchange
value in use
progressive income tax
interpersonal utility comparisons
lumpy

---

[3]This is really not such a debilitating flaw. Consumers can still make adjustments even with most lumpy purchases. Consider a house as an example. Suppose the individual decides after the purchase that the house is too large and that other purchases would yield more marginal utility. Over time, the house can be depreciated by a lessening of routine maintenance so that more can be spent on the other goods which yield a higher marginal utility. Buying a smaller house, or one at a less desirable location, or renting are other alternatives available.

Questions for Discussion

1 Does something have to be useful to have utility? What does it mean for a good or service to be useful?

2 Do you think money (or income) has diminishing marginal utility?

3 Does the fact that water is inexpensive and diamonds are expensive conflict with the theory developed in this chapter? Explain.

4 If the marginal utility of one good is 4 and the price is $2, and the marginal utility of another good is 5 and its price is $1, is the individual consumer maximizing total utility? If not, how could more utility be obtained?

5 Does advertising increase or decrease the utility you get from consuming certain goods? Is this "good" or "bad"?

6 A survey shows that a group of consumers prefers light beer to regular beer. What does this mean in terms of the utility analysis we have presented in this chapter?

7 What would you expect to happen to a normal consumer's total utility curve for bacon if the surgeon general established a link between bacon and cancer? How would this announcement affect the demand curve for bacon?

Suggestions for Further Reading

Easterlim, Richard A. "Does Money Buy Happiness?" *Public Interest* (Winter, 1973).

Hirshleifer, Jack. *Price Theory and Applications*. Englewood Cliffs, N.J.: Prentice-Hall, 1976, Chapter 3.

Kamerschen, David R., and Lloyd M. Valentine. *Intermediate Microeconomic Theory*. Cincinnati: South-Western Publishing Co., 1977, Chapter 4.

CHAPTER 6

THE ECONOMICS OF CONSUMER BEHAVIOR: II

LEARNING OBJECTIVES

After studying the materials found in this chapter, you should be able to do the following:

1 Define indifference curve analysis.

2 List and define the following elements of indifference curve analysis:
   (a) indifference curve,
   (b) budget line,
   (c) the equilibrium point in terms of the slope of the budget line and the marginal rate of substitution.

3 Derive the following, using indifference curve analysis:
   (a) an income-consumption curve,
   (b) a price-consumption curve,
   (c) the income effect and the substitution effect,
   (d) a demand curve.

The primary shortcoming of marginal utility theory was the immeasurability of utility. This shortcoming does not mean that the theory has no value. The value, however, is to be found in the theoretical insights that it offers rather than in any precise applications. Marginal utility theory was first explained in the 1870s. Working in the late 1800s, Italian economist Vilfredo Pareto and British economist F. Y. Edgeworth are credited with the next development in consumer behavior theory, that of *indifference curve analysis*. Although Pareto and Edgeworth are separately credited with the development of indifference curve analysis, it wasn't until 1939, when Nobel prizewinning British economist Sir John Hicks published his classic book *Value and Capital*, that this analysis became popular with economic theorists and teachers. The theory swept the economics profession, and for a while marginal utility analysis fell into disrepute.

Pareto, Edgeworth, Hicks, and others were not trying to dispute utility analysis, but rather they were proposing an alternative way of viewing consumer behavior. Its major improvement is that it does not require the ability to measure utility. All that is necessary is that consumers are able to rank bundles of goods in the order, from low to high, in which they prefer them.

INDIFFERENCES

The concepts of indifference and preference seem to fit much more closely the way consumers actually make decisions than does the concept of utility. Individuals make choices between bundles of goods. For example, you might choose between four tickets to the football game and two tickets to the rock concert. In indifference analysis, we view the consumer as making choices between collections of goods and services. We assume only that the individual is able to state preferences for different bundles of commodities or to profess indifference among some of them. Suppose we offer an individual different combinations of Coke and Miller beer, as indicated in Table 6-1. Carton *A* contains 16 Cokes and 6 beers. When we offer the individual carton *B*, which contains 12 Cokes and 8 beers, the individual states that neither one is preferred over the other; they are equal in the amount of satisfaction the individual expects to derive and therefore the individual is indifferent between the two cartons. Offering the individual the choice among cartons *C*, *D*, and *E* yields the same response, or indifference. The individual has indicated that all five cartons of beer and Coke yield the same amount of satisfaction. We have created an *indifference set* for our consumer. We can geometrically represent this indifference set by drawing an *indifference curve*. An indifference curve corresponding to the indifference set in Table 6-1 is drawn in Figure 6-1. An indifference curve shows all combinations of the two commodities among which a consumer is indifferent. It is the geometric representation of an indifference set.

Sir John R. Hicks

Sir John R. Hicks
(1904–   )

Sir John R. Hicks is one of the most significant contributors to modern microeconomic theory. In his book *Value and Capital* (1939), he reconstructed demand theory using indifference curves. Hicks therefore developed the theories discussed in this chapter. In 1972 Hicks was awarded the Nobel Prize in Economics (along with Kenneth Arrow) for ". . . pioneering contributions to general economic equilibrium theory and welfare theory."

Hicks was born in Leamington Spa, England, and attended Balliol College, Oxford. His first teaching post was at the London School of Economics, where he taught from 1926–1935. He later taught at Cambridge and the University of Manchester. In 1946 he moved to Nuffield College at Oxford and remained at Oxford until his retirement.

Hicks's main contributions to economic literature center on his work on the theory of demand. Hicks showed that if a consumer maximizes something (we call it utility) and if the consumer's choices can be ranked, it is possible to deduce the consumer's reaction to price changes as well as to substitute and complementary goods. Hicks then went on to establish clearly the difference between income and substitution effects by developing the idea of the *compensated demand curve*, which is the demand curve along which an individual consumer's real income is unchanged.

Sir John Hicks made contributions to a host of theoretical economic areas, including international trade, public finance, macroeconomics, and monetary theory. Most of his theoretical work was done in the 1930s and 1940s; he clearly ranks as a major economist in the history of economic theory.

TABLE 6-1   An Indifference Set

Cartons	Good x (Coke)	Good y (Miller)
A	16	6
B	12	8
C	10	10
D	8	14
E	6	18

FIGURE 6-1   Indifference Curve

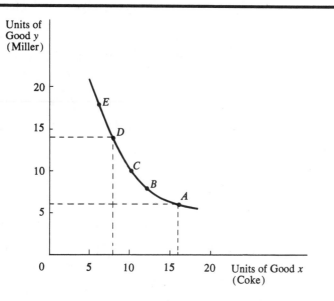

Indifference curves geometrically represent combinations of two goods between which the consumer is indifferent. All combinations represent the same level of satisfaction.

Indifference curves are negatively sloped because there is an inverse relationship between the quantities of the two goods available in each combination. In other words, each combination represents a trade-off. In our example, if carton A is to have more beer, it must have less Coke, since the bundles are to yield the same level of satisfaction. If a carton had more beer and more Coke, or if it had more of one good without having less of the other, it would be preferred and the consumer would no longer be indifferent.

The indifference set represented by a higher indifference curve is preferred to that represented by a lower indifference curve. As we move from I_1 to I_2 to I_3 to I_4 in Figure 6-2, the individual receives more satisfaction. Such a series of indifference curves is called an ***indifference map***. Every individual consumer has such a map, and movement to higher curves on the map represents a gain in utility.

FIGURE 6-2   **Indifference Map**

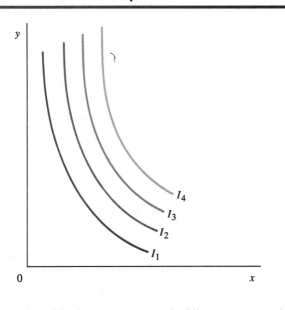

An indifference map is a series of indifference curves. Higher curves on the map represent higher levels of satisfaction.

Extreme Indifference Curves

The shape of the indifference curves shown in Figure 6-2 is considered to be typical for most goods. To understand why this shape is typical, let's look at two extreme shapes first. One extreme is shown in Figure 6-3, where each indifference curve is a straight line (linear curve). On indifference curve I_3, the individual is indifferent among all combinations between 40 units of y and no x, and 20 units of x and no y. For instance, this person is indifferent between a bundle made up of $20y$ and $10x$ and a bundle made up of $10y$ and $15x$. We can generalize and say that the consumer is indifferent between all combinations offering two units

FIGURE 6-3   Linear Indifference Curves

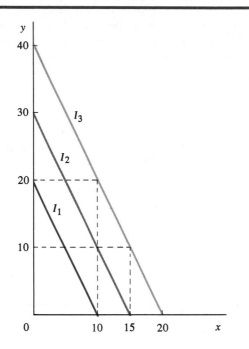

On a linear indifference curve the consumer always has the same
trade-off between the two goods, regardless of the amount of either good
the consumer may have. The two goods are perfect substitutes.

of y in compensation for the loss of one unit of x. The trade-off is always
two (y) to one (x).[1]

Indifference curves like this could happen only if the two commodities, x and y, are the same commodity except for the units in which they
are expressed. Thus, y could be nickels and x, dimes; or y could be a
one-pound bag of candy and x, a two-pound bag of the same candy. In
other words, this is a trivial example, except for the lesson that we learn,
namely, that perfect substitutes have linear indifference curves and that
the closer two commodities are to being perfect substitutes, the closer the
indifference curves are to being straight lines.

The extreme opposite of the linear indifference curve is the indifference curve with a right angle, as shown in Figure 6-4. To see the
significance of this, look at I_1. I_1 indicates that the consumer is indifferent

---

[1]The equation for I_3 is $y = 40 - 2x$, or $x = 20 - 1/2y$. In this case the slope is -2,
meaning that two units of y will compensate the consumer for the loss of one unit of x.
Remember that since this is an indifference curve, any point on the curve has the same
utility as any other point on the curve. The equation for I_2 is $y = 30 - 2x$, and for $I_1, y = 20$
$- 2x$. Obviously I_3 is preferred to I_2, which is preferred to I_1.

between having two units of x and two units of y, and having two units of x and three units of y, or indeed, two x and any number of y greater than two. As long as the individual has two units of each commodity, any additional units of only one of them would contribute nothing to utility.

FIGURE 6-4   Right-Angled Indifference Curves

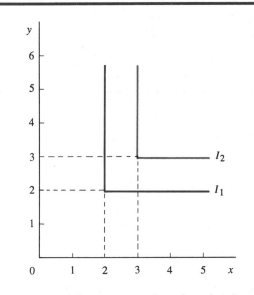

An indifference curve with a right angle indicates that more of one good with a fixed amount of the other adds nothing to satisfaction. The goods are perfect complements.

What kind of goods might these be? The answer is they must be perfect *complements*, and the examples usually given are: y = left shoes and x = right shoes, or x = coats and y = linings. Again, this is a trivial case since perfect complements are usually combined and sold as one good. We can observe from this, however, that goods that are complements to each other will have indifference curves which approach the right-angled ones, being very concave or bowed toward the origin and almost parallel to the axes.

Typical Indifference Curves

The typical indifference curve for two goods will lie between the extremes of perfect substitutes and perfect complements; that is, it will have some curvature and some degree of concavity. It will have a negative slope, which means that for the individual to be indifferent between

two bundles of commodities some positive amount of one good is necessary to compensate for the loss of some amount of the other. Saying the
same thing in another way, every combination of two goods represented
on the same indifference curve will have more of one of the goods but
less of the other than any other combination on that indifference curve.

The concavity feature is of considerable interest. It means that a consumer attains more units of one good and fewer units of the other good,
it takes more and more units of the more abundant good to compensate
for the loss of one unit of the good that is becoming more scarce. See
Figure 6-5 for a depiction of this.

FIGURE 6-5   Concavity Feature of Indifference Curves

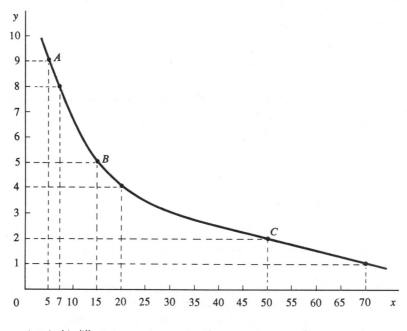

A typical indifference curve is concave. This concavity means that it
takes increasingly larger amounts of the abundant good to compensate
for losses of the good that is becoming more scarce.

At point A the individual would be consuming relatively large
amounts of y and small amounts of x. In order to compensate for a reduction in consumption of 1 unit of y, the person would only require 2 units
of x to be satisfied with such a trade; but at point B, since less of y and
more of x are being consumed compared to point A, it will take a larger
quantity of x (5 units) to compensate for the loss of 1 unit of y. At point
C, the individual now consumes a large amount of x and very little y, so

to give up 1 unit of y, 20 units of x would be needed to retain the same utility as before.

There is no law that says such preference relations must hold, but it is powerfully plausible. First, upon introspection most of us would say that this is about the way we would behave in this trade-off situation. Second, the opposite proposition seems highly unlikely. It would say that the less you had of a good, the less you would want of it relative to other goods, and the more you had of a good, the more valuable additional units of it would become. If this were the case, you would eventually only consume one good! By far the most convincing argument, however, is one that we are not quite ready to present yet. It is that the behavior we observe in the marketplace is consistent with concavity and is not consistent with convexity. We will see this a little later on.

DIMINISHING MARGINAL RATES OF SUBSTITUTION

The trade-off ratio we have been discussing represents the ***marginal rate of substitution***. It is expressed as MRS_{xy} and is defined as the change in y needed to compensate for a given change in x. In symbols $MRS_{xy} = \frac{\Delta y}{\Delta x}$. Geometrically, it is the slope of the indifference curve. In Figure 6-5, the MRS_{xy} at point A is $\frac{1}{2}$; that is, one unit of y is worth two units of x, or when $y = 1, x = 2$. At point B, the MRS_{xy} is $\frac{1}{5}$, and at point C, it is $\frac{1}{20}$. The declining value of MRS_{xy} is a reflection of the ***principle of diminishing marginal rates of substitution***, showing that as more of one good (x) is substituted for the other good (y), the value of good x in terms of good y declines.

BUDGET CONSTRAINTS

An indifference map allows us to compare points representing combinations of goods x and y in such a way that we can say whether the individual prefers or is indifferent to any two of them. We know that all points on any single indifference curve are equivalent to each other in utility. We also know that points on indifference curves located to the right and above other indifference curves are preferred combinations.

The question we must now ask is what combinations of commodities are actually possible for the consumer we are studying. The answer clearly depends on the purchasing power (money, income, or wealth) available to that person and the prices of the commodities in question.

These two factors, income and prices, constrain the individual from buying all that might be desired. Together, the factors form a **budget constraint**, and when shown on a graph the constraint is called the **budget line**.

We shall limit our analysis to two goods (you could think of one of the goods as "all other goods"). Remaining consistent with our earlier example, assume the individual can consume either Miller beer or Coke. Suppose the individual has a disposable income (DI) of $10.00 and Miller and Coke each sell for $.50 per unit. The construction of the budget line is illustrated in Figure 6-6. If the individual spends the entire income (DI) on Miller, 20 units of beer can be purchased. This is determined by dividing the income by the price of the good $\left(\dfrac{DI}{P_y}\right)$. In this case, $\dfrac{\$10.00}{\$.50} = 20$ units of beer. Thus, 20 is the intercept on the y-axis.

The x intercept is calculated in the same manner: $\dfrac{DI}{P_x} = \dfrac{\$10.00}{\$.50} = 20$.

FIGURE 6-6   Budget Line

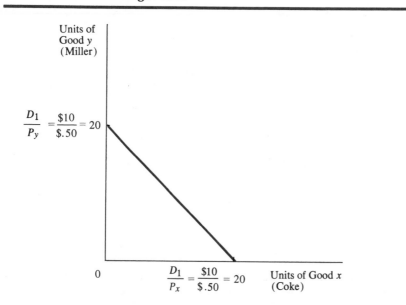

A budget line graphically depicts the consumption combinations that are attainable with a given level of income. Any combination outside (to the northeast of) the line is unattainable.

With a straight line, we connect the two points that represent buying all of good y (Miller) or all of good x (Coke), and we thus express all possible combinations that can be purchased with a given income level. It is a budget line because any combination outside (to the northeast of) the line is unattainable at that income level; it is outside the budget constraint. In other words, the budget line is the dividing line between all attainable combinations of consumption at a given level of prices and a given level of income and those combinations that are unattainable.

CHANGES IN INCOME AND CHANGES IN PRICES

The budget line we just drew was developed holding prices and income constant. We need to see how changes in income and prices will affect the budget line.

An increase in income would mean that more of both goods could be purchased. A doubling of income would mean that twice as much of both goods could be purchased if prices remained constant. Increases in income would thus be represented by parallel outward shifts of the budget line. Correspondingly, a decrease in income would be represented by an inward parallel shift of the budget line. Two such shifts are shown in Figure 6-7.

FIGURE 6-7   The Effect of Income Changes on Budget Lines

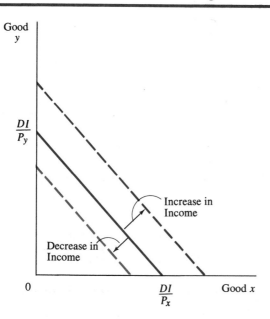

An increase in income is represented by a parallel outward shift of the budget line. A decrease in income is represented by an inward parallel shift of the budget line.

A price change of one good only affects the total amount of that good that can be purchased, not the total amount of the other good that can be purchased. If the price of good x rises and the consumer spends all the income on good y, the price rise has had no effect on the amount of good y purchased. A price rise, then, will only affect the budget line intercept of the good which has experienced the price rise. Such a change is shown in Figure 6-8. A price rise for good x from P_{x_1} to P_{x_2} causes the budget line intercept to move closer to the origin, reflecting the fact that less x can now be purchased with the constant income. A decrease in the price of good x to P_{x_3} would mean more x could be purchased and the intercept would move away from the origin, reflecting increases in the potential consumption of good x.

FIGURE 6-8   The Effect of Price Changes on Budget Lines

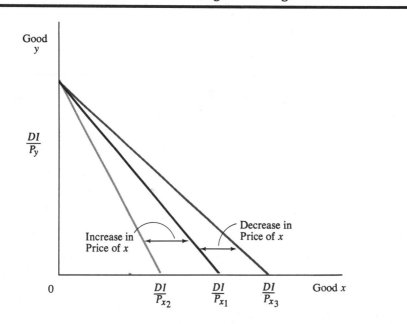

An increase in the price of one good changes the slope of the budget line. An increase in price means that if all disposable income is spent on the item, less of it can be purchased. As a result, the intercept of the budget line will shift closer to the origin. The opposite holds for a decrease in price.

Price changes cause the slope of the budget line to change. The slope of the budget line is, of course, $\frac{\Delta y}{\Delta x}$. Notice that we can compute the slope by dividing the vertical intercept by the horizontal intercept;

the ratio of the intercepts is $\dfrac{DI}{P_y} \div \dfrac{DI}{P_x}$, which is equal to $\dfrac{P_x}{P_y}$, so we can say that the slope of the budget line is equal to the ratio of the prices. The slope has changed because the relative prices of the two commodities have changed. A change in income, on the other hand, represents no change in relative prices, so the slope of the budget line remains the same, as reflected by the *parallel* shifting of the budget line described above.

MAXIMIZATION OF SATISFACTION

We can now demonstrate maximization of consumer satisfaction. Let's combine a set of indifference curves, like those in Figures 6-1 and 6-2, with the budget line in Figure 6-6, to get Figure 6-9. It is now a simple matter to determine the preferred composition of the consumption basket. At point C, on indifference curve I_2, the budget line and indifference curve I_2 are tangent. Any point on I_3, such as point F, is of course preferred to point C, because higher indifference curves represent higher levels of utility. However, point F is not attainable because it is outside the budget line. Point G on I_1 is attainable, but a point on indifference curve I_2 is also attainable, and any point on I_2 represents more satisfaction than any point on I_1. The consumer wants to reach the highest attainable indifference curve. The highest attainable curve would be one which is tangent to the budget line because no higher indifference curve can be reached with the given income and prices. So in this example, our consumer is maximizing utility, or is in equilibrium, at point C on indifference curve I_2.

You may remember from geometry that tangent curves have equal slopes at the point of tangency. We now know that the marginal rate of substitution between the two goods (given by the slope of the indifference curve) is equal to (minus) the ratio of the price of x to the price of y (given by the slope of the budget line) at equilibrium. This may seem like a lot of theoretical mumbo jumbo, but the common sense of it is that the slope of the indifference curve expresses the willingness of the consumer to trade a certain amount of x for a certain amount of y, and the budget line expresses the market's willingness to trade a certain amount of x for a certain amount of y. The impersonal forces of the market impose the relative prices on the consumer, so the consumer adjusts consumption amounts in such a way that his or her trade-off rates are the same as those of the market.

Look at Figure 6-10. Suppose you are consuming 15 units of y and 5 units of x (you are at point A). According to your indifference curve (I_1), you would be willing to give up 5 units of y if you were compensated by 2 units of x; but the market is willing to give you 5 units of x in exchange for 5 units of y (note point B). We should then expect to see you consuming less y and more x. In fact, until your indifference curve says you are

FIGURE 6-9   **Consumer Maximization**

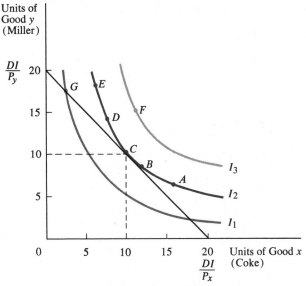

An individual maximizes consumer satisfaction where the budget line is
tangent to an indifference curve. This tangency is with the highest
attainable indifference curve.

willing to give up exactly 1 unit of x in exchange for 1 unit of y when the
prices of the two commodities are the same, as in this example, you will
be able to increase your utility by moving in the direction of the ***tangency*** of some indifference curve and the budget line.

Household Reaction to Income Changes

We can now trace through the adjustment process when a household
experiences a change in income. In Figure 6-11, if the consumer's income is DI_1, and x and y sell for P_x and P_y respectively, the optimum
utility is at point A. A decrease in income is represented by DI_0, and two
increases in income are represented by DI_2 and DI_3. The respective optimum positions representing tangencies of a budget line and an indifference curve are points B, C, and D. If we connect these points, we get
what is called an ***income-consumption curve***. This curve shows how
consumption of the two goods changes as income changes. Now recall
our discussion of the income elasticity of demand in Chapter 3. The
income elasticities of both good x and good y in Figure 6-11 are positive
because consumption of both goods increases as income increases. You

FIGURE 6-10   Tangency Solution Once Again

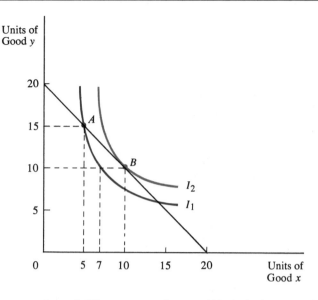

Lower indifference curves that are within the budget constraint represent lower levels of utility than the highest, but still attainable, indifference curve.

should remember that a positive income elasticity indicates that a good is a normal good. An inferior good would have a negative income elasticity since, in that case, as income increases, consumption of the good decreases.

Figure 6-12 shows a case where one commodity, good x, is a normal good for this person until the individual's income reaches DI_3, but when income increases above DI_3, less x is bought as income increases. So x is a normal good up to point A, then becomes inferior as the income-consumption curve bends backward. There is, of course, nothing pejorative about the term "inferior." Your daily newspaper might be considered an inferior good; as income falls, a person buys the paper more often, because it is a less expensive form of entertainment and also because it offers job listings. Beer is generally thought to be an inferior good, as are potatoes. Remember, however, that a normal good to some people may be an inferior good to others.

Household Reaction to Price Changes

We saw in Figure 6-8 how price changes affect the budget line. We can now see how the optimum consumption point will be affected by

FIGURE 6-11   Income Changes and the Income-Consumption Curve

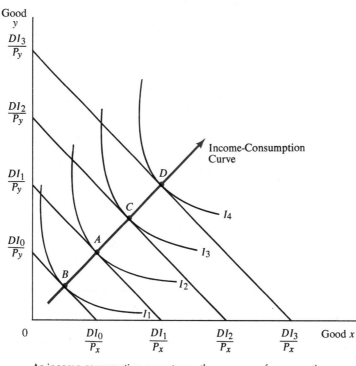

An income-consumption curve traces the response of consumption
patterns to changes in income.

price changes. The consumer is at an initial optimum, or maximizes utility, at point A in Figure 6-13. As the price of x falls from P_{x_1} to P_{x_2}, the
budget line shifts out to intersect the x-axis at $\dfrac{DI}{P_{x_2}}$, and the consumer
can now reach a new optimum at point B on indifference curve I_2. Another decrease in price to P_{x_3} allows the consumer to reach a still higher
indifference curve, I_3, and a new optimum at point C. The points can be
connected and doing so produces a *price-consumption curve*, which
shows how consumption changes when relative prices change.

We will not spell out the theoretical mechanics here, but it is worth
noting that when the price of a commodity falls, there are two forces at
work to cause the consumer to increase purchases of that commodity.
First, when the price of a good falls, the market trade-off, or the *substitution*, rate changes. This is referred to as the *substitution effect*. Second,
the individual has a larger *real income*, meaning that with the same
money income, more of both (or all) commodities can be purchased (and
will be as long as the good is not an inferior good). We refer to this as the
income effect.

FIGURE 6-12   Income-Consumption Curve for an Inferior Good

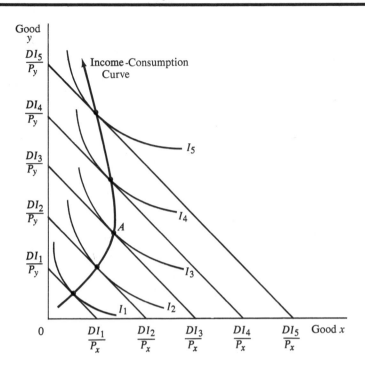

The income-consumption curve for an inferior good bends backward, indicating that less of the good is consumed as income increases beyond a certain level.

INDIFFERENCE ANALYSIS AND THE LAW OF DEMAND

We can now derive an individual's demand curve and demonstrate the law of demand. This is a *ceteris paribus* experiment in which we will change the price of one commodity and observe what happens to the quantity demanded. In Figure 6-14, we have an indifference map and a budget line for goods x and y. Let x be the particular good in which we are interested and let y represent all other goods. The consumer is at an optimum at point A. At point A the individual is consuming O_{x_1} of x at a price of P_{x_1}. This price and quantity is plotted on Figure 6-15 (page 130). Now let the price of x fall to P_{x_2}. As before, this decline in price causes the budget line to rotate outward, as in Figure 6-14. A new optimum is reached at point B, where the new budget line is tangent to indifference curve I_3. The change in price has caused consumption to increase from O_{x_1} to O_{x_2}. This increase in consumption is also plotted on Figure 6-15. If a line is drawn through the two price-quantity points, we have two points on a demand curve which has the negative slope we expect of demand curves.

FIGURE 6-13   **Price-Consumption Curve**

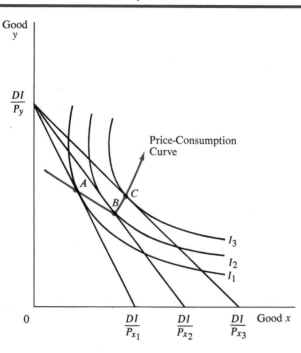

A price-consumption curve graphically depicts how consumption changes when relative prices change.

INDIFFERENCE CURVE ANALYSIS: APPLICATION

Although indifference curve analysis is not one of the basic tools you need for rudimentary economic analysis, virtually every advanced economics course makes extensive use of indifference curves. To demonstrate how useful such analysis can be, we can analyze the effect of a proportional income tax on the work-leisure choice.

With a ***proportional income tax***, all consumers are taxed at the same *tax rate*. An individual's preferences between work and leisure can be depicted on an indifference curve. We assume the two "goods" are income (earned from work) and leisure. The trade-off relationship between these two goods can be graphed as an indifference curve, as in Figure 6-16 (page 131). In this simple scheme, the individual can choose between income and leisure without any constraint. The individual's income is equal to the wage rate (w) times the number of hours per day that the individual chooses to work. The hours of work chosen per day are the difference between 24 hours and the amount of leisure chosen. In Figure 6-16, the budget line is represented by the line SL. The S intercept is 24 hours times the wage rate (w), and the L intercept is 24 hours

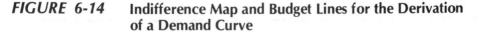

FIGURE 6-14   **Indifference Map and Budget Lines for the Derivation of a Demand Curve**

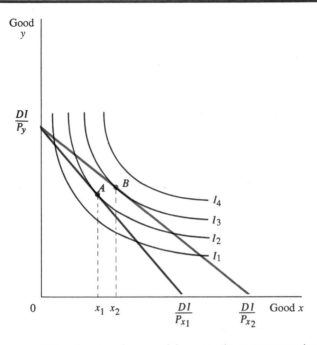

When the price of one good decreases, the consumer reaches a higher
indifference curve. On this higher indifference curve, the consumption of
the good that experienced the decrease in price will have increased.

of leisure. Now, of course, the individual does not choose either to work
24 hours or to consume 24 hours of leisure. As before, the budget line
simply shows the attainable combinations. The individual maximizes
total utility at point A, where an indifference curve (I_2) is tangent to the
budget line. An OS_1 level of income and OL_1 amount of leisure are chosen by this individual.

Now consider the introduction of an income tax that takes the same
percentage of everyone's salary. This means that if the individual worked
all 24 hours, the amount of income would no longer be S but S minus
the amount of the tax. So we get a new intercept for the budget line on
the income axis, $S^\star$. $S^\star$ is equal to 24 hours times the take-home wage
rate (w_1) which is lower by the percent of the tax. The individual now
maximizes total utility at point B, which represents a tangency with the
highest attainable indifference curve, I_1. In effect, the prices of all the
goods the individual buys have increased relative to the price of leisure
(the price of leisure is the income foregone per hour of not working).

FIGURE 6-15   Deriving a Demand Curve

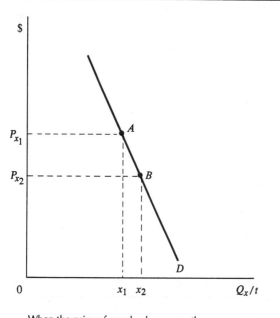

When the price of good x decreases, the consumer can reach a higher
indifference curve, as in Figure 6-14. This increased consumption of
good x at a lower price means that the demand curve must have a
negative slope.

Imposition of the tax has had three effects on the individual. First,
the individual is on a lower indifference curve and is, therefore, at a
lower level of satisfaction or well-being. This ignores what the government did with the tax receipts and implicitly assumes the government
spent them in a way different than our hypothetical individual would
have spent them. This is not too outlandish an assumption because if the
individual would have spent the money in the same way the government
would, there would have been no need for the tax. A second effect is that
the individual's spendable income fell from OS_1 to OS_2. The third effect
is that the individual increased the amount of leisure taken from OL_1 to
OL_2. In other words, the income tax has definitely had an effect on the
work-leisure trade-off.

What you have just worked through is the standard explanation of
how income taxes change the relative price of leisure and thereby create
incentives to take more leisure and work less. Income taxes can thus be
shown to have a disincentive effect on work and the supply of labor.

Summary

Indifference sets and indifference curves show combinations of goods that
yield equal amounts of satisfaction. The slope of an indifference curve shows

FIGURE 6-16   Effects of a Proportional Income Tax

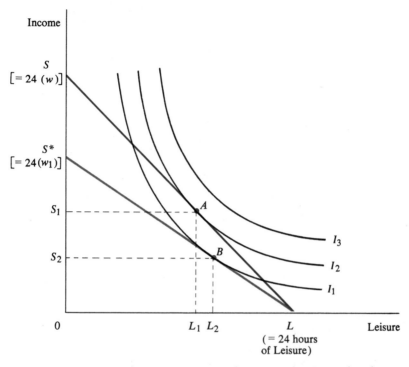

A proportional income tax increases the "price" of income and results in the individual opting for less income and more leisure.

the rates of substitution between the goods. Diminishing marginal rates of substitution mean that as more of one good is substituted, its value in terms of the other good declines.

A budget constraint is represented by a budget line which shows the combinations of consumption baskets that are attainable at a given level of income and a given set of prices. The slope of the budget line is (minus) the ratio of the prices of the two goods.

Changes in income and prices can be represented by changing the budget line. A change in income is represented by a parallel shift of the budget line. A price change is represented by moving the intercept of the good whose price has changed; this changes the slope of the budget line.

A consumer maximizes satisfaction when at a point where an indifference curve is tangent to the budget line. This insures that the highest attainable indifference curve has been reached. At this point, the value which the consumer places on the goods (the marginal rate of substitution) is equal to (minus) the ratio of their prices. The slope of the budget line is equal to the slope of the indifference curve.

Price-consumption curves graphically demonstrate how consumption patterns change as prices change. Income-consumption curves show how the consumption of each good changes with changes in income.

When price changes, there are income and substitution effects. The substitution effect is a result of the change in relative prices. The income effect comes about because real income changes as prices change.

New Terms

indifference curve analysis
indifference set
indifference curve
indifference map
marginal rate of substitution
principle of diminishing marginal rates of
   substitution
budget constraint

budget line
tangency solution
income-consumption curve
price-consumption curve
substitution effect
income effect
proportional income tax

Questions for Discussion

1 What does it mean to say that you are "indifferent" between two choices?

2 If the tuition at your college or university were doubled, what income and substitution effects would you experience?

3 Show the effects of a 20 percent increase in the price of all goods (x and y). Then show the effect of a 20 percent decrease in income. Is there any difference? Can inflation be viewed as a tax on income?

4 Why does it take more and more of an abundant good to compensate for the loss of one unit of a good that is becoming scarcer?

Suggestions for Further Reading

Ferguson, C. E., and S. Charles Maurice. *Economic Analysis*. Homewood, Ill.: Richard D. Irwin, 1978, Chapters 3 and 4.

Kamerschen, David R., and Lloyd M. Valentine. *Intermediate Microeconomic Theory*. Cincinnati: South-Western Publishing Co., 1977, Chapters 5 and 6.

CHAPTER 7

THE ECONOMICS OF PRODUCTION

LEARNING OBJECTIVES

After studying the materials found in this chapter, you should be able to do the following:

1 List the advantages and disadvantages of the various forms of business organization.

2 Calculate the least-cost method of production to determine economic efficiency.

3 Define
    (a) explicit and implicit cost,
    (b) normal and economic profit.

4 Use a production function to
    (a) define increasing and diminishing returns,
    (b) define economies and diseconomies of scale,
    (c) calculate cost when given the prices of the inputs.

5 Use the definition of $TC = TFC + TVC$ to calculate

    (a) ATC,
    (b) AFC,
    (c) AVC,
    (d) MC.

6 Diagram TC, TVC, TFC, ATC, AVC, AFC, $LRATC$, and MC.

7 List the sources of economies of scale and diseconomies of scale.

8 Determine the profit-maximizing level of production using
    (a) total revenue and total cost,
    (b) marginal revenue and marginal cost.

9 Calculate the present value of a stream of income using a present value table.

This chapter sets the stage for examining the behavior of firms. Before we can analyze firms in their activities as sellers of products in different types of markets, it is necessary to understand firms as purchasers of factors of production and to analyze their activities as producers of commodities. The firm buys *factors of production* (the terms "factors of production" and "inputs" are used as synonyms) and attempts to transform them into marketable outputs. This chapter examines that transformation, which we shall call *production*. It is especially important that this chapter be grasped clearly because it provides the foundation for the next four chapters.

THE FIRM

The *business firm* is organized by an entrepreneur or group of entrepreneurs to combine inputs of raw materials, capital, labor services, and organizational technology to produce outputs of goods and services. Firms are parts of industries. There are many ways to define an *industry*, but, in general, what economists have in mind as an industry is a group of firms producing similar or related products. For example, we may refer to the "automobile industry." We might include just the "big four" — General Motors, Ford, Chrysler, and American Motors. Or we might extend the coverage to include all foreign makers and all small domestic producers. We might also include all firms which supply parts, materials, and services to the direct producers or to automobile consumers. There are no absolute rules on how to define a particular industry. The definition will usually depend on our purpose or the particular problem or issue we wish to study.

In the United States, firms are organized primarily in one of three ways. These are legal, not economic, categories, and they differ mainly as to the legal liability of the owners. There are some interesting economic questions which arise because of the differences in treatment under the law, but these need not concern us at this point.

Sole Proprietorships

In the *sole proprietorship* form of enterprise, no legal distinction is made between the owner and the firm. The financial and thus the real resources of the firm are limited to those of the individual owner and what can be borrowed from friends or financial institutions. Thus, the profits and losses also accrue strictly to that same individual. Success of the firm is success of the owner; bankruptcy of the firm is bankruptcy of the owner. This intimate relationship usually means a constant involvement of the owner with the affairs of the firm. The incentives for hard work and diligence in decision-making are powerful.

Compared to the other forms of business enterprise, a proprietorship can come into or go out of business very easily. In certain lines of business, government approval is required, as licenses or permits may be needed, but typically the single proprietor starts and ends a business activity by simply doing so. Sole proprietorships account for more than 75 percent of the number of business firms in the United States. Most farmers, many professionals such as doctors, lawyers, and consultants, and many small firms, especially in retailing, are sole proprietorships. Although dominant in numbers, sole proprietorships account for only about 10 percent of annual business sales.

Partnerships

Partnerships are similar to sole proprietorships except that they have more than one owner. There are more resources available to a partnership than if only one of the persons formed the firm. This is true of personal resources as well as financial resources. Each partner brings to the relationship his or her special skills, knowledge, energy, and decision-making powers. Offsetting these advantages are the inevitable frictions that arise in operating the firm. Partners have to agree on the proportions of ownership owned by each partner, which may be dictated by the amounts of funds contributed, the amounts of work, or the amounts of other kinds of value contributed (such as ideas or patents). Joint rights and responsibilities have to be agreed upon. The partners share in any profits but are also legally liable together for any debts incurred by the enterprise.

The disadvantages of the partnership arrangement apparently outweigh the advantages since something less than 10 percent of the business organizations and only around 5 percent of annual business sales in the United States are accounted for by this form of business. As with sole proprietorships, the firms organized as partnerships tend to be quite small and are typically found in professional services — medicine, law, consulting, and some financial services. Until quite recently, most brokerage firms were partnerships.

Corporations

The dominant form of business organization in the United States, measured in any way except the absolute number, is the *corporate* form. *Corporations* account for slightly less than 15 percent of business firms but about 85 percent of annual business sales.

A corporation is a more formal and complex organization than the others we have described. The owners are the *stockholders*. Their numbers may run into the hundreds of thousands, although some corporations have only a few stockholders. The stockholders vote, according to the number of shares held, for a *board of directors*, who in turn appoint the officers of the corporation who manage the corporation along the guidelines set by the charter of incorporation and the directors.

One of the strengths of the corporate form is the relative ease of acquiring capital, either by issuing additional shares of **stock**, which are certificates demonstrating ownership in the corporation, by borrowing through the issuance of **bonds**, which are interest-earning certificates issued by the corporation, or by borrowing directly by loans from banks or other financial agencies.

The attractiveness of the corporation as a form of organization stems from the fact that the stockholders of the corporation are the legal owners and have rights to the profits, but their legal liability is very limited. This *limited liability* aspect is the critical advantage of the corporate form of business. In fact, in many countries corporations are referred to as limited liability companies and often have the letters *Ltd*. after the name of the firm to stress this feature to anyone who might deal with the enterprise. The letters *Inc*. after the name of a firm in the United States denote the same thing. A stockholder cannot be sued for failure of the corporation to pay its debts; only the corporation can be sued. Thus, the corporation, defined in law as a "legal person" in its own right, can go bankrupt without causing the owners to go bankrupt. Of course, if individuals have most of their wealth in the stock of one corporation, they might go bankrupt if that corporation goes bankrupt because the stock would no longer have any value. A second and very important attraction of corporate organization is the ease of transferring ownership. Ownership rights can be transferred through the sale of stocks, and markets (stock exchanges) have evolved to facilitate the transfer. The costs of transfer of ownership are for this reason significantly lower for corporations than for partnerships or single proprietorships.

These three different types of ownership may cause the managers of the firms to behave in different ways. For instance, an owner-manager of a single proprietorship may make decisions that are different from those of the hired manager of a large corporation. For now, we will ignore these differences and assume that firms, however they are organized, are organized for only one purpose, and that single purpose is to increase the wealth of the owners. To do this, firms try to maximize their profits. This assumption of profit maximization allows us to develop a powerful predictive theory about the economic effects of different market structures. Later, in Chapter 9, we will discuss some nonprofit motivations the firm or its managers might have.

ECONOMIC EFFICIENCY

The entrepreneur must combine the factors of production efficiently if the firm is to maximize profits. To do this, entrepreneurs must often decide between competing ways of producing a given output. Suppose, for example, South-Western Publishing Company, in deciding how to produce this book, were faced with the alternatives listed in Table 7-1. The production engineer has told the production chief that 100,000 copies of

TABLE 7-1   Alternative Ways to Produce 100,000 Copies of This Book

	Capital (Machines) Used	Labor (Worker/Years)	Land (Acres)	Output
Method A	5	5	1	100,000
Method B	4	10	1	100,000
Method C	3	15	1	100,000
Method D	2	25	1	100,000

Price of:

Capital Services $30,000 per Machine
Labor Services $ 4,000 per Worker/Year
Land Services $10,000 per Acre

Cost of:

Method A = $150,000 + 20,000 + 10,000 = $180,000
       B = $120,000 + 40,000 + 10,000 = $170,000
       C = $ 90,000 + 60,000 + 10,000 = $160,000
       D = $ 60,000 + 100,000 + 10,000 = $170,000

this book could be produced in any of four ways. The engineer has determined the alternative ways to produce the book, and it is now up to the entrepreneur to decide how to actually produce the books. The entrepreneur must have a decision rule in order to select a production alternative. Here is where profit maximization comes into play. Without profit maximization as a goal, the entrepreneur would have to choose on some other basis — perhaps on a physical-units basis. The method that would minimize the inputs in a physical sense would be method A, which uses the fewest inputs. This method of choosing is based on **technical efficiency**. A drawback of this method is that it compares physical units of machines, acres of land, and worker/years of labor. To make any sense of such a rule, there would need to be some further rule. For example, the entrepreneur might be told, "Conserve on machines this year." The entrepreneur would then choose method D of production.

Such rules might be needed in a command-type economy, such as the Soviet Union. A market system, however, puts the inputs into dollar terms and lets the entrepreneur choose the least-cost method of producing. The least-cost method is based on **economic efficiency**. The least-cost method, or the economically efficient method, would always be chosen by the entrepreneur because of the assumption of attempted profit maximization. In Table 7-1 the entrepreneur would choose method C to produce the books. Regardless of the price of the books, method *C* maximizes profits (or minimizes losses) because costs are minimized.

OPPORTUNITY COST ONCE AGAIN

We just saw how the entrepreneur attempts to minimize costs to achieve economic efficiency. But we need to be very careful how we define cost. Costs of the inputs are the value of those inputs to the firm expressed in terms of their *opportunity cost*. Back in Chapter 1, you were introduced to the concept of opportunity cost, and now you will need to apply it with a vengeance. This can be a problem because you are not used to thinking in terms of opportunity cost. You are more used to thinking in terms of *explicit cost*. Explicit costs are bookeeping costs or money outlays. We will not ignore explicit costs, but we want to include *implicit costs*. Implicit costs are those costs implied by the alternatives given up. In sum, when we talk of costs, we include all of the opportunity costs, not just the part that is explicit.

Some examples can help make this clearer. Suppose you have the alternative of working two hours overtime at $10 an hour or going to a concert that costs $5 to attend. The *cost* of attending the concert is the $5 ticket plus the $20 you could have earned working overtime. Attending the concert will cost you $25. In December, 1976, Jimmy Connors failed to show up at the Grand Prix Masters Tennis Tournament in Houston. If he had shown up and played in the tournament, he would automatically have received $60,000 for his third-place finish in the year-long Grand Prix standings. Connors chose to stay away and "rest," and did not receive the $60,000. The *cost* of that rest was $60,000 plus the amount he spent while resting.[1]

Let's return to the example of Suzy Sizzle's lemonade stand which we used in Chapter 2. In Chapter 2, we developed supply curves for Suzy's lemonade stand. Now let's look at her financial statements. Table 7-2 presents the financial picture as a bookkeeper would prepare it. Only the explicit costs of doing business are considered. Suzy pays $2,800 for materials, $3,000 to her father for rent, and $4,000 to her only employee, herself. Considering explicit costs only, she shows a "profit" of $5,200.

Now let's consider the problem the way an economist would. Let's say that Suzy could have re-rented the land, for which she paid her father $3,000, to her uncle Billy for $5,000. In addition, she could have worked serving beer in her uncle's bar for $7,200 rather than the $4,000 she paid herself for serving lemonade. Since the opportunity cost of the land is $5,000 and the opportunity cost of her labor is $7,200, these are the

---

[1]This example also illustrates the income and substitution effects we discussed in the previous chapter. As Connors makes more money playing tennis, the cost of resting increases and he will rest less. On the other hand, as he wins more, his income goes up and he can afford to rest more. The amount of tennis he decides to play will depend on which of the two effects is stronger.

Opportunity Cost

Opportunity cost pervades all economic calculations. Every activity has an opportunity cost, because the decision to undertake one activity precludes the undertaking of another.

Recently, Professor Charles A. Lave of the University of California, Irvine, applied this basic economic concept in a study of the 55 MPH speed limit.[1] Lave examined statistics that showed that the cost of wasted travel time is enormous per life saved or energy saved by driving at 55 MPH rather than at 65 MPH. Let's examine the opportunity cost of driving at 55 MPH and compare it to the benefits. Studies show that commuters value their travel time at 42 percent of their hourly wage. If we calculate the time it takes to drive the same distance at 55 MPH instead of 65 MPH, and value the increased travel time at the 42 percent of commuters' hourly wages, we find that a 55 MPH speed limit costs about $6 billion in travel time per year. The government tells us that a 55 MPH speed limit saves 4,500 lives per year. Therefore, it costs about $1.3 million per life saved. In addition, we save roughly 1 to 2 percent of our gasoline. This is a trivial amount of savings and one which could be duplicated or exceeded by proper maintenance of air in our tires. So the primary benefit is in lives saved.

In his article, Lave reports on some other costs of saving lives. He reports that putting a smoke detector in every home would cost about $50,000 per life saved, kidney dialysis machines save lives for about $30,000 per life, mobile cardiac care units cost about $2,000 per life saved, and highway improvements cost between $20,000 and $100,000 per life saved. The conclusion is pretty obvious: Driving 55 MPH is a very costly way of saving lives. No wonder it is so unpopular! It is a good example of the government's forcing people to purchase a commodity, in this case safety, which the public views as too costly.

If you don't think a 55 MPH speed limit is too costly, what about a 45 MPH limit, or a 35 MPH limit? A 5 MPH speed limit would virtually insure no deaths from automobile accidents. Do you think a 5 MPH speed limit is a reasonable opportunity cost to insure no highway deaths? Probably not. So you see, it's a decision at the margin concerning what you think the proper trade-off between costs and benefits for safety happens to be. As Lave points out, the cost of saving one life by moving from 65 MPH to 55 MPH is 102 person-years of extra travel time per year.

---

[1]Charles A. Lave, "The Costs of Going 55," *Newsweek* (October 23, 1978).

**TABLE 7-2   Suzy Sizzle's Profit and Loss Statement:
Explicit Costs Only**

Total Revenue from Sales:	$15,000
Less Cost of:	
Cups	500
Sugar	1,000
Lemons	1,100
Water	200
Land	3,000
Suzy's Salary	4,000
	9,800
Bookkeeping Profit	$ 5,200

amounts that should be used in the calculation of her financial statement. Table 7-3, column A, shows these costs, and we see that Suzy has
made zero economic profit. This is not necessarily bad. By earning zero
profits, Suzy has at least earned her opportunity cost, which means that
her resources could not have been better used elsewhere and so are optimally employed. By saying that these resources are optimally employed,
we mean Suzy could not do anything else with these inputs that would
earn a greater rate of return.

**TABLE 7-3   Suzy Sizzle's Profit and Loss Statement:
Explicit and Implicit Costs**

	A	B	C
Total Revenue from Sales:	$15,000	$15,000	$15,000
Less Cost of:			
Cups	500	500	500
Sugar	1,000	1,000	1,000
Lemons	1,100	1,100	1,100
Water	200	200	200
Land	5,000	5,000	5,000
Suzy's Salary	7,200	15,000	5,000
Economic Profit	$ 0	$-7,800	$ 2,200

Now let's change the example slightly. Instead of working for her uncle and earning $7,200, let's assume she can earn $15,000 as a model for a major magazine. The opportunity cost for Suzy's labor is now $15,000. As we see in Table 7-3, column *B*, the lemonade firm now shows a profit of −$7,800, that is, a loss of $7,800. In this case, Suzy is not meeting her opportunity cost and should thus leave the lemonade business, rent her land to her uncle Billy, and work for the magazine. Very different results are obtained from those in Table 7-2. The book-keeper's assessment, which only considers explicit costs, has Suzy making a "profit" of $5,200. The economist's assessment, which considers opportunity costs, shows a loss of $7,800 and has Suzy closing her business to work for a magazine.

Let's change the example once more. Suppose Suzy's best alternative is to pick lettuce for her brother Jack and earn $5,000. As Table 7-3, column *C*, shows, the lemonade stand now earns an economic profit of $2,200. This *economic profit* is a return above explicit and implicit costs. It is extra; that is, it is not needed to keep resources in this industry. Of course, Suzy likes making this economic profit — in fact, other entrepreneurs would also like to earn more than their opportunity cost. It is inevitable, then, that additional resources in the form of more lemonade stands will move into this industry in an attempt to earn some of these economic profits. Those who enter the market will be those whose opportunity costs are lowest.

ECONOMIC COST AND NORMAL PROFIT

The concepts of cost and profit which we have just introduced are important and will be used throughout this book. The opportunity cost of capital and entrepreneurship is referred to as *normal profit*. A normal profit represents the rate of return that is necessary to keep capital in an industry. Say, for example, a normal rate of return is 12 percent. We would say that a firm earning a 12 percent rate of return is earning zero profits because its capital could earn 12 percent elsewhere. The concept of normal profit is relevant in utility pricing. If an electric utility is not granted a price increase and the rate of return on capital falls below the normal rate of return, capital will leave the industry because it can earn its opportunity cost elsewhere.[2]

Our definition of costs is important because we predict behavior from it. When economic profits are positive, we predict that firms will enter an industry; when negative, that firms will leave; and when zero, that firms will remain. Profits, then, signal movements into or out of an industry. If a firm isn't earning normal, or average, profits in the industry it presently produces in, the resources of this firm will flow to an industry where

---

[2]We will return to this problem in greater detail in Chapter 12.

average, or normal, returns can be earned. If more than average, or normal, returns are earned in an industry, resources will be attracted to it.

We now turn to three production relationships. First, we will discuss the relationship between inputs and outputs, or the production function. Next, we will show how output changes when inputs are varied. Finally, we will discuss how costs of production are related to levels of output.

PRODUCTION FUNCTIONS IN THE SHORT AND LONG RUN

A *production function* is a description of the amounts of output expected to be forthcoming from various combinations of input usage. It is usually expressed in tabular or graphic form, but it can also be shown by a mathematical formula. The production function describes a technical or technological relationship. The input combinations and their corresponding output quantities, which make up the production function, are determined by engineers, agronomists, chemists, and other technical experts. Only the best input combinations are included. For example, it might be that an output of 100 units of a commodity could be produced by 5 units of capital, 20 units of labor, and 2 units of land, or by 6 units of capital, 30 units of labor, and 3 units of land. Since the second combination is obviously inferior to the first, that method of production would be ignored. The production function is a reflection of the best technology available for a given level of output in the production process.

Usually, we are interested in only a portion of the production function. For instance, it is often convenient to ask what would happen to total production if all inputs were at a given, fixed level and only one was allowed to change in amount. Then we can speak of *fixed factors* and *variable factors*. Which factors are fixed and which are variable usually just depend on the problem we are studying, although in many cases it is natural to think of the land and the buildings of a firm as the fixed factors and labor as the variable factor. When we distinguish between fixed and variable factors, we are considering what is called the *short run*. In the *long run*, all factors are variable. *Short-run* decisions are those concerning the profit-maximizing use of the existing plant and equipment. The plant is used more intensively as the amount of variable factors, such as labor or additional machines, is increased. *Long-run* decisions are those concerning the selection of a plant size that will maximize profits.

These different time horizons may not correspond to time in the calendar sense. Some industries may be able to increase in size very rapidly. In addition, contractions in size may take longer than expansions since the only way to decrease the amount of fixed factors may be to use the plant and equipment until they wear out, or *depreciate*. In some cases contractions can occur more quickly, depending on whether the plant and equipment are adaptable for use in other industries. It is primarily for the convenience of analysis that we treat decisions as short-run and long-run decisions. You should keep in mind that these decisions are inherently related. Once a long-run decision to build a plant of a certain size is made, thereafter a whole series of short-run decisions are influenced because they must deal with this certain-size plant.

Increasing and Diminishing Returns

As we add more and more units of a particular variable factor to a given set of fixed factors, we at first obtain larger increments in output, but we eventually obtain smaller increments in output. This economic phenomenon is referred to as the *principle of increasing returns* and the *principle of diminishing returns*. It is plausible that returns are diminishing eventually because if it weren't true, all the wheat needed to feed the world could be produced on one acre of land (or in a flowerpot) by just adding more seed, more fertilizer, more water, and more labor to that acre of land. The principle of increasing returns says that at first, as inputs are added, the increase in output will be larger than the increase in the input. For example, inputs may be increased by 10 percent and output would rise by 12 percent. This is an increasing return. Eventually, however, diminishing returns take over.

The principle of diminishing returns is a fascinating and pervasive phenomenon. Nobody really knows why, but we never find the principle contradicted in our real-world observations. Why is it that a tree grows more slowly as it grows larger? Why do little pigs put on more weight from a given amount of corn than do big ones? Why is it more costly to add a floor to a twenty-story building than to a ten-story building? Why is it that adding water to parched soil yields remarkable results whereas adding the same amount of water to already moist soil may add very little to the crop? Why is it that when a firm adds a worker when the labor force is already large, the increase in output is less than when one is added at a time when the labor force is small? These are only a few of the thousands of examples that could be given of the principle of diminishing returns in action.

Note that diminishing returns is a short-run phenomenon. It says nothing about the long-run production function. It only says that if you add more and more variable input to a fixed factor, after a while the return will decline. Think of your own experience in studying for exams. The output is your score on a test and the variable factor is the time you spend studying. Assume you could get 55 percent without studying. One hour of studying boosts your score to 66 percent; two hours, to 75 percent; three hours, to 80 percent; four hours, to 84 percent; five hours, to 86 percent, and so on. You see that each additional variable input (hour spent studying) produces a smaller increment in output than the previous input. In this example, the first hour produced an improvement of 11 percent; the second hour, 9 percent; the third, 5 percent, and so on. We see a diminishing return to studying. It is up to you to decide when the return for an additional hour of studying is not worth the opportunity cost of that hour in terms of the other things you could be doing. So you see, even deciding how much to study is an exercise in rational economic calculus.

Marginal and Average Physical Product

In order to describe more precisely the changing relationship between inputs and outputs, economists use the concept of the *marginal physical product* (*MPP*) of the factors of production. The marginal physical product of labor, say, is the change in total output per unit change in the use of labor service. Formally,

$$MPP_L = \frac{\Delta TPP}{\Delta N}$$

where MPP_L is the marginal physical product of labor, ΔTPP is the change in the total physical product, and N is the change in the number of units of labor employed.

A firm employing 20 workers might have an output of 1,000 widgets, and if it increased the number of workers by 5, its output might increase by 100. In that event, the marginal physical product of labor would be $\frac{100 \text{ widgets}}{5 \text{ workers}}$ = 20 widgets per worker. Now, if one more additional worker were employed, output might increase by 15. This would be the MPP_L when $N = 26$.

The *average physical product* (*APP*) of the factors of production is simply the total physical product divided by the number of units of the factor (workers, in our example). Thus, when 1,000 widgets were produced employing 20 workers, the average physical product was 50. When 25 workers were employed and output was 1,100, the APP_L was 44, and since output was 1,115 when 26 workers were employed, the APP_L was 42.9.

A very important and basic relationship exists between average values and marginal values. Think of your grade point average. If your grade in this course (the marginal grade) is below your grade point average for all courses taken, your average will fall. If your grade in this course is above your grade point average, your average will rise. The same holds for every marginal-average relationship. If a basketball player's lifetime shooting percentage (average) is higher this week than last week, you know that in the intervening (marginal) games, the player has shot a higher than average percentage. If the average is rising, the marginal must be above average, or putting it the other way around, if the marginal is above average, it will pull the average up. If the average is falling, the marginal must be below the average.

COST IN THE SHORT RUN

The production function relates inputs to outputs. These inputs have prices and, therefore, represent costs to the firm. These prices are determined in factor markets and may or may not be affected by the firm itself. Given the prices of inputs and the production function, we can derive cost data for the firm. Although the derivation can be done formally, we will "derive" the costs in an impressionistic fashion and leave the formal derivation to more advanced texts and courses.

Costs Defined

Total cost (TC) is simply the total cost of producing different levels of output. A total cost profile for a hypothetical firm is given in column 4 of Table 7-4. Total cost is made up of two components, *total fixed cost* (TFC) and *total variable cost* (TVC). Total fixed cost is the cost of the fixed factors and they do not vary in the short run. These total fixed costs will, therefore, be the same regardless of whether the firm produces zero or any number of units of output. Total variable costs vary directly with output, increasing as more output is produced. This happens because more variable factors have to be purchased if more output is to be produced. Total fixed costs and total variable costs are represented by columns 2 and 3 in Table 7-4. Note we have said that $TFC + TVC = TC$. We assume that for every level of output, the firm chooses factor combinations that minimize the TVC associated with producing that level of output. Why should the firm pay a higher TVC than it has to? (Of course, the firm cannot decrease TFC in the short run we are considering.)

TABLE 7-4 **Cost of a Hypothetical Firm**

1 Output Per Week (Q)	2 Total Fixed Cost (TFC)	3 Total Variable Cost (TVC)	4 Total Cost (TC)	5 Average Fixed Cost (AFC)	6 Average Variable Cost (AVC)	7 Average Total Cost (AC)	8 Marginal Cost (MC)
0	60	0	60		0		0
1	60	40	100	60	40	100	40
2	60	76	136	30	38	68	36
3	60	108	168	20	36	56	32
4	60	140	200	15	35	50	32
5	60	175	235	12	35	47	35
6	60	216	276	10	36	46	41
7	60	262	322	$8^4/_7$	$37^3/_7$	46	46
8	60	312	372	$7^1/_2$	39	$46^1/_2$	50
9	60	369	429	$6^2/_3$	41	$47^2/_3$	57
10	60	430	490	6	43	49	61

Average total cost, hereafter designated AC, is the total cost of producing an output, divided by that output. Thus, $AC = \dfrac{TC}{Q}$. Likewise, *average fixed cost* (AFC) is total fixed cost divided by the number of units of output, and *average variable cost* (AVC) is the total variable cost divided by the number of units of output. AFC, AVC, and AC appear in columns 5, 6, and 7 of Table 7-4, respectively.

Marginal cost is the addition to (change in) total cost of producing one more (or one less) unit of output. More rigorously, $MC = \dfrac{\Delta TC}{\Delta Q} = \dfrac{\Delta TVC}{\Delta Q}$. This means that marginal costs are really marginal *variable* costs because there are no marginal fixed costs.

These cost measures are all mathematically interrelated, and you can make calculations to move from one to the other. As practice, be sure to work the problem in the study guide which gives you a table like Table 7-4 with blank cells. If you can fill in the blanks, you understand the relationship between the different measures of cost. All of these relationships are summarized in Table 7-5.

TABLE 7-5   Cost Measures Summarized

Total Cost = TC
Total Fixed Cost = TFC
Total Variable Cost = TVC
Average Total Cost = AC
Average Fixed Cost = AFC
Average Variable Cost = AVC
Marginal Cost = MC
$TC = TFC + TVC$
$TFC = TC - TVC$
$TVC = TC - TFC$
$AC = \dfrac{TC}{Q}$
$AC = AFC + AVC$
$AFC = \dfrac{TFC}{Q}$
$AFC = AC - AVC$
$AVC = \dfrac{TVC}{Q}$
$AVC = AC - AFC$
$MC = TC_{Q+1} - TC_Q$
$MC = \dfrac{\Delta TC}{\Delta Q} = \dfrac{\Delta TVC}{\Delta Q}$

Cost Curves

We can draw a series of cost curves for the production function described by the numerical data given in Table 7-4. The curves are drawn smoothly to better emphasize the relationship between the curves.[3]

The total fixed cost, total variable cost, and total cost curves are drawn in Figure 7-1. If you are confused as to how the curves are related, review Tables 7-4 and 7-5. The shape of the total cost curve and the total variable cost curve describes the shape of the production function. When the variable factor is increased, output increases and costs increase. If output increases more rapidly than the factor cost increases, total cost (as well as total variable cost) increases at a decreasing rate and returns are

FIGURE 7-1   **Total Cost Curves**

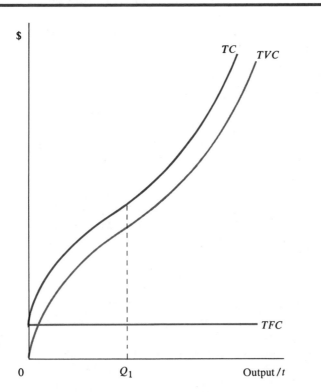

The shape of the total cost curve and total variable cost curve is a reflection of the shape of the production function. From zero output until an output of OQ_1, total cost and total variable cost increase at a decreasing rate. After output OQ_1, diminishing returns set in and these costs increase at an increasing rate.

---

[3]By drawing the curves smoothly, we are assuming that the gaps between the discrete points in Table 7-4 can be filled in with a continuous curve.

increasing. In Figure 7-1, this is what happens as output increases from zero to OQ_1. From OQ_1 to higher levels of output, output increases less rapidly than the factor cost increases, so total cost (along with total variable cost) increases at an increasing rate. The principle of diminishing returns is operating.

If this is not clear, consider this simple example. Suppose that a firm hires one more worker and output increases by ten units. The variable cost increases by the wage of that worker (for a given time period). Now, if it takes two workers to increase output by ten more units, total variable cost would increase by the wage rate times two. Clearly the cost has increased at an increasing rate.

Now, let's look at average costs within a production function. Figure 7-2 shows the *AFC, AVC, AC,* and *MC* curves of a hypothetical firm. The *AFC* curve declines continuously, getting closer and closer to the *x*-axis of the graph. This is because fixed costs are constant and average fixed cost is derived by dividing a constant cost amount by an ever-increasing quantity. The *AFC* thus becomes smaller and smaller as output increases.

AVC declines and then increases, as does *AC*. This *U*-shape represents at first increasing returns and then diminishing returns, as we discussed earlier. At first, returns to the fixed-size plant (we are looking at the short run) increase. This is represented by the output up to OQ_1 in Figure 7-2. OQ_1 in Figures 7-1 and 7-2 are the same. After OQ_1, returns to the variable factors decline. We have reached diminishing returns. In other words, increasing returns mean decreasing average costs and diminishing returns mean increasing average costs. The *AVC* and *AC* curves are *U*-shaped because of decreasing costs (increasing returns) for small levels of output and increasing costs (diminishing returns) at eventual higher levels of output.

The minimum point on the *AC* curve is referred to as the ***least-cost combination***. The least-cost combination is the lowest attainable per-unit cost for a given plant size. The least-cost combination in Figure 7-2 is point *A*. For a fixed plant size, it is impossible to produce at a lower per-unit cost than that represented by the least-cost combination.

It is very important to note that the *MC* curve intersects the *AC* and *AVC* curves at their lowest points, points *A* and *B* in Figure 7-2. This relates back to our earlier discussion of the average-marginal relationship. For the average curves to be declining, the marginal must be below the average, and in order for the average to be rising, the marginal must be above the average. This requires that the marginal and average be equal when the average curve is at its minimum point. If you don't see why this has to be the case, think back to the example of how your grade point average goes up or down depending on the grade in an added (marginal) course. Also, notice that when the marginal cost curve starts to rise, it is still below the average variable cost curve, and thus average

FIGURE 7-2   Marginal and Average Cost Curves

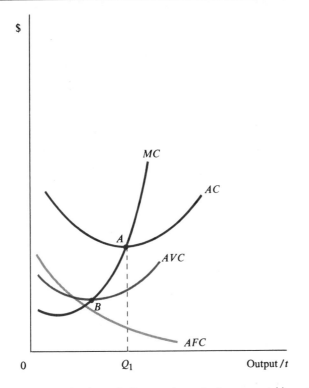

Average fixed cost declines continuously. Average variable cost declines, reaches a minimum, and then increases, as does average cost, resulting in a U-shaped cost curve. The marginal cost curve intersects the average variable cost and average cost curves at their minimum points.

variable cost is still falling. An average value falls as long as the marginal value is below it, regardless of whether the marginal value is falling or rising.

COST IN THE LONG RUN

In the long run, there are no fixed factors of production. As a result, there are no fixed costs. In the long run, all costs are variable. In fact, we define the long run as that period long enough to vary all inputs.

In essence, the long-run decision focuses on a determination of which size plant to build. Each plant size is represented by a short-run *AC* curve, so the long-run decision is the selection of the desired short-run cost curve. The decision will be based on the output the firm expects to produce. Figure 7-3 graphically illustrates this decision. Suppose that the technological factors (given by the production function) are such that only three plant sizes are feasible. These plants are represented by AC_1, AC_2, and AC_3 in Figure 7-3. The long-run decision of which short-run curve to be on would depend on the planned output of the firm. If output is to be less than OQ_1, then the plant represented by AC_1 should be built because it represents the plant size that will produce an output level between O and OQ_1 at the lowest attainable per-unit cost. Likewise, if outputs between OQ_1 and OQ_2 are planned, the plant represented by AC_2 should be built. If outputs greater than OQ_2 are planned, plant AC_3 should be built. In the long run, the average cost curve facing this firm is DEFGHIJ.

FIGURE 7-3   Alternative Plant Sizes

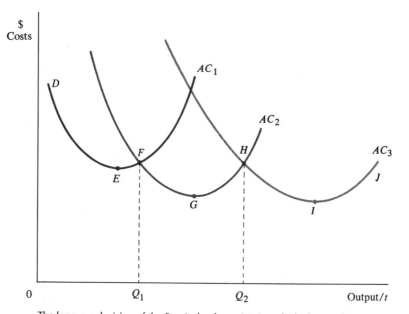

The long-run decision of the firm is the determination of which size plant to build. This decision is the selection of the desired short-run cost curve.

It is likely that more than three alternative plant sizes are available, and in the planning stage they would all be examined. Assume the firm faces all the alternative short-run curves as depicted in Figure 7-4. All the possible short-run curves are tangent to a curve that is sometimes referred to as a **planning curve**. It is called a planning curve because in the planning stage any point on the curve could be chosen by building a certain-size plant. Such a planning curve, more commonly called the *long-run average cost curve* (*LRAC*), is shown in Figure 7-4. The long-run average cost curve then represents the lowest attainable average cost of producing any given output. For example, if you knew you were going to produce exactly OQ output, plant size AC_4 would have the lowest average cost of doing so.

FIGURE 7-4   Long-Run Average Cost Curve

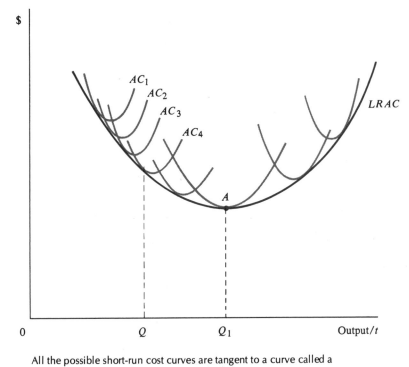

All the possible short-run cost curves are tangent to a curve called a planning curve. This planning curve is the long-run average cost curve and represents the lowest attainable average cost of producing any level of output. The optimal plant size would be found at point A, where the minimum point on a short-run average cost curve is tangent to the long-run average cost curve at its minimum point.

Only at point A on Figure 7-4, which represents an output of OQ_1 units, is there a tangency between the minimum point on the short-run average cost curve (the least-cost combination) and the minimum point on the *LRAC* curve. This point is referred to as the *optimal-size plant*. This is the optimal-size plant because it represents the short-run AC curve with the lowest possible attainable per-unit costs.

Economies and Diseconomies of Scale

The *LRAC* curve drawn in Figure 7-4 is *U*-shaped. This *U* shape means that, at first, as plant size and firm output increase, average costs fall. Increasing returns result from the firm becoming larger. After a certain point (point *A* on Figure 7-4), however, bigness starts becoming costly. As the plant continues to increase in size, average cost begins to rise. Economists refer to these returns and costs to increased plant size as ***economies and diseconomies of scale***. That is, as scale (plant size) increases, economies (savings) result. After a while, further growth results in diseconomies (costs).

It is easy to see how economies of scale result from a growth in plant size. As a firm increases its scale of operations, it can usually employ more specialized machinery and jobs can be more specialized. Equipment can be used more efficiently. By-products of the operation which might be uneconomical to recover, or exploit, in a small scale plant may become significant for a large operation. A large firm is often able to obtain quantity discounts and to purchase more precise amounts of intermediate products from other firms. Even political influence of economic value is more likely to accrue to a large rather than a small firm. These are just a few of the factors that account for the negative slope of the *LRAC* curve as the scale of plant increases.

Diseconomies of scale are perhaps harder to grasp, although anyone who has dealt with giant bureaucracies, public or private, will have seen evidence of them. Diseconomies result primarily from the fact that as an organization becomes very large, communication and coordination become more difficult and time-consuming, and control from the top diminishes. So when a firm has taken advantage of most of the gains to be achieved by growing larger, managerial inefficiencies set in and the *LRAC* curve turns upward with further growth.

Optimal-Size Plants in the Real World

Figure 7-4 depicted a smooth *LRAC* curve that had a single optimal-size plant corresponding to an output of OQ_1. If we look around in the real world, however, we see many different-size firms operating side by side in the same industry.

Economists have spent much time investigating economies of scale, and it appears that the range of actual *LRAC* curves is represented in Figures 7-5, 7-6, and 7-7. In Figure 7-5 we see economies of scale over a large range of output. This situation occurs in the steel and auto industries, where we see a few very large firms that seem to get larger and larger. The optimal-size plant in Figure 7-5 would be OQ_1, which conceivably might represent all the normal sales of the industry. In some industries a ***natural monopoly*** occurs because the economies of scale justify the existence of only one firm. Many public utilities, for instance,

FIGURE 7-5   Economies of Scale and a Few Very Large Plants

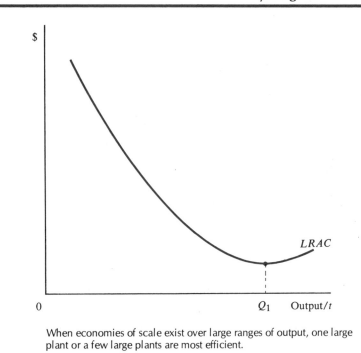

When economies of scale exist over large ranges of output, one large plant or a few large plants are most efficient.

in order to become large enough to be of optimal size, need to have all the sales in a market. (See Chapter 12 for a discussion of other causes of natural monopolies.)

In Figure 7-6 we see that a large number of different-size plants can be optimal. Distinctly different-size firms can all produce efficiently in the same industry at the same per-unit (or average) cost. In Figure 7-6 any firm producing an output between OQ_1 and OQ_2 would be efficient, and if the demand for the product was large enough to support many firms of this size, a very competitive situation would exist. This situation prevails in many industries.

In Figure 7-7 we see rapidly achievable economies of scale and then rapid diseconomies of scale. This would be the case when all the firms in an industry (where sales are large relative to OQ_1) are of a very similar size. The optimal-size plant in Figure 7-7 is, of course, OQ_1.

The concept of economies of scale is important. We observed that if the bigness of a firm is due to economies of scale, it is efficient to have production carried out by large firms. This is very important for antitrust policy because these large-scale firms may exert monopoly pricing powers. We will return to this problem in some detail in Chapter 12 when we examine some actual studies of economies of scale and monopoly power in selected industries.

FIGURE 7-6   **Many Optimal-Size Plants of Different Sizes**

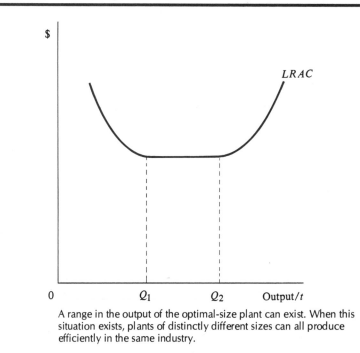

A range in the output of the optimal-size plant can exist. When this situation exists, plants of distinctly different sizes can all produce efficiently in the same industry.

FIGURE 7-7   **Many Optimal-Size Plants of Similar Sizes**

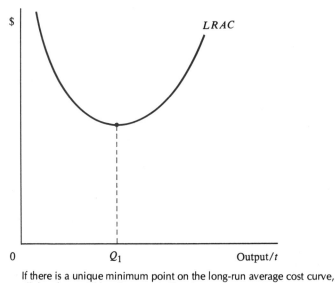

If there is a unique minimum point on the long-run average cost curve, all the plants will be of a very similar size.

PROFIT MAXIMIZATION

We will soon be ready to examine production and sales under different market structures, but first we must cover a few more preliminaries. First, we need to discuss profit maximization, and second, we need to examine choice over time.

We will assume that the firms we will examine in the next four chapters are all profit-maximizing firms. But what does profit maximization mean in terms of production decisions? It means that in the short run, the firm will attempt to choose the output that maximizes the difference between total revenue and total cost. **Total revenue** (TR) is the price an item sells for times the number of units sold. **Marginal revenue** (MR) is the addition to (or change in) total revenue from selling one more unit. Our operational rule for profit maximization, then, is to produce that output at which marginal revenue equals marginal cost ($MR = MC$). Notice that the directive to produce where $MR = MC$ is just another way of saying, Produce where total profit is at its maximum, or alternatively, Produce where total revenue exceeds total cost by the largest amount. These are simply different ways of saying the same thing. It happens that, generally, the $MR = MC$ rule is the most convenient one with which to work.

First, let us convince you that profit is maximized where $MR = MC$. Since MR is the change in total revenue per unit change in sales, if you add up all of the marginal revenues from zero to the current quantity (say OQ_1), you will get the total revenue at OQ_1. Likewise, if you add up all the marginal costs from zero output to the current output, you will get the total variable cost of the current output. Anytime MR is greater than MC, total revenue is increasing faster than total cost when output and sales are increased. This, in turn, means that profit is increasing (or losses are decreasing). If you decreased output when $MR > MC$, total revenue would decline more than total cost declines, so profit would fall. But if output were increased, total revenue would increase more than total cost would increase, and profit would increase.

On the other hand, if $MC > MR$, an increase in output and sales would cause total cost to increase more than the increase in total revenue, so profit would fall. But a decrease in output and sales would decrease costs more than revenues, so profit would increase, So far we have said that if $MR > MC$, expand production and sales, and if $MC > MR$, decrease production and sales. If $MR = MC$, it would be unprofitable to either increase or decrease production.

It is easy to see this on a graph. On Figure 7-8, the firm is a *price taker*, which means that the price is fixed as far as this firm is concerned. Thus, the total revenue curve in Figure 7-8, panel (a), is a straight line from the origin, and the MR curve in panel (b) is a horizontal line and is equal to the price of the product. The total cost curve is consistent with the law of diminishing returns after output OQ_2. (From zero output to OQ_2, the cost curve represents increasing returns and decreasing average

FIGURE 7-8   **Profit Maximization under Conditions of Pure Competition**

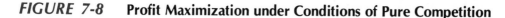

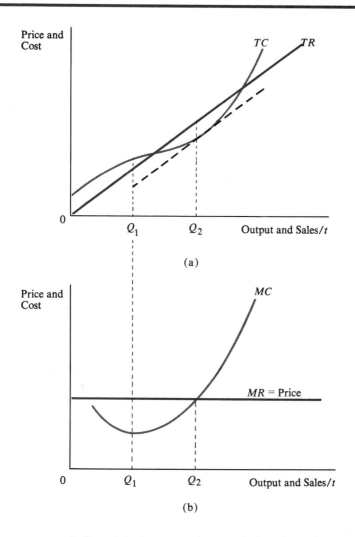

(a)

(b)

Profit maximization occurs where marginal cost is equal to marginal
revenue. The vertical distance between total revenue and total cost is
greatest [panel (a)] at the same level of output where marginal cost
equals marginal revenue [panel (b)].

costs.)

The vertical distance between TR and TC is greatest at output OQ_2,
and at that point the slopes of TR and TC are equal. Remembering that
the slope of TR is MR and the slope of TC is MC, it is clear that $MR =
MC$ at output OQ_2. This can be seen clearly in Figure 7-8, panel (b).
Note that if output were decreased from OQ_2, MC would fall below MR

and TR would fall less than TC, so profit would fall. If output increased from OQ_2, TC would increase more than TR and MC would be greater than MR, so again profit would fall. Profit is at a maximum at OQ_2.

This decision rule, to produce that output where marginal revenue equals marginal cost, will come up again and again in this and in other books on microeconomics, so it is important to make sure you understand it. There are certain modifications that will be made in some other contexts, such as monopoly, but it will always be true that a firm that maximizes profit will be operating at that point where $MR = MC$.

PRESENT VALUE

So far, our discussion of costs and the movement from the short run to the long run has been simplified in many ways in order to make it understandable. However, it is important to keep in mind that when the entrepreneur makes the decision of which plant to build, based on forecasted production, there is much uncertainty surrounding that decision. To make these forecasts, a great deal of information must be gathered and many factors must be considered.

When production decisions, or for that matter any economic decisions, are made, costs and revenues over a number of periods of time are affected. The decision maker needs a way of comparing revenues and costs in different time periods because a dollar cost or a dollar revenue today is not the same as a dollar cost or a dollar revenue next year or ten years from now.

In order to compare future dollars (costs or revenues) for different periods with present dollars, we calculate the **present value** of these future dollars. The present value of an item is its value after we *discount* it to the present period. **Discounting** is the name given to the technique of calculating present values. It works simply and has many important uses in daily life.

We live in a society where you can save (refrain from consumption) and receive interest as a reward for your saving. As a result, you are always better off delaying a payment of a fixed sum that you must make and speeding up a payment of a fixed sum you are to receive. For example, suppose you owe your friend $100 and your friend doesn't care when you pay off the debt within the next year. If the interest rate is 10 percent you could take $90.90, put it in the bank, and in one year pay off the $100 debt because you would receive back from the bank the $90.90 you deposited *plus* interest of $9.10. In other words, the present value (PV) of the $100 debt to be paid in one year at 10 percent interest is only $90.90. Conversely, if you were owed $100, you would want the money now so you could put the $100 in the bank and have $110 at the end of a year. Two principles emerge from this example of discounting. The first is: the higher the interest rate, the lower the present value. The second is: the longer the time period, the lower the present value.

The formula for calculating present value is $PV = \dfrac{V_t}{(1 + r)_t}$, where V_t is the value in year t, r is the interest rate, and t is the number of years. The formula is rarely used in calculations, however, as present value tables, like Table 7-6, are readily available. This table shows the present value of one dollar received in any future year up to 50 years at different interest rates. You can easily read the table to see, as in our previous example, that the present value of $100 for one year at a 10 percent interest rate is $90.90 (.909 × $100).

TABLE 7-6   Present Value of $1.00

Year	3%	4%	5%	6%	7%	8%	10%	12%	15%	20%	Year
1	.971	.962	.952	.943	.935	.926	.909	.893	.870	.833	1
2	.943	.925	.907	.890	.873	.857	.826	.797	.756	.694	2
3	.915	.890	.864	.839	.816	.794	.751	.711	.658	.578	3
4	.889	.855	.823	.792	.763	.735	.683	.636	.572	.482	4
5	.863	.823	.784	.747	.713	.681	.620	.567	.497	.402	5
6	.838	.790	.746	.705	.666	.630	.564	.507	.432	.335	6
7	.813	.760	.711	.665	.623	.583	.513	.452	.376	.279	7
8	.789	.731	.677	.627	.582	.540	.466	.404	.326	.233	8
9	.766	.703	.645	.591	.544	.500	.424	.360	.284	.194	9
10	.744	.676	.614	.558	.508	.463	.385	.322	.247	.162	10
11	.722	.650	.585	.526	.475	.429	.350	.287	.215	.134	11
12	.701	.625	.557	.497	.444	.397	.318	.257	.187	.112	12
13	.681	.601	.530	.468	.415	.368	.289	.229	.162	.0935	13
14	.661	.577	.505	.442	.388	.340	.263	.204	.141	.0779	14
15	.642	.555	.481	.417	.362	.315	.239	.183	.122	.0649	15
16	.623	.534	.458	.393	.339	.292	.217	.163	.107	.0541	16
17	.605	.513	.436	.371	.317	.270	.197	.146	.093	.0451	17
18	.587	.494	.416	.350	.296	.250	.179	.130	.0808	.0376	18
19	.570	.475	.396	.330	.277	.232	.163	.116	.0703	.0313	19
20	.554	.456	.377	.311	.258	.215	.148	.104	.0611	.0261	20
25	.478	.375	.295	.232	.184	.146	.0923	.0588	.0304	.0105	25
30	.412	.308	.231	.174	.131	.0994	.0573	.0334	.0151	.00421	30
40	.307	.208	.142	.0972	.067	.0460	.0221	.0107	.00373	.000680	40
50	.228	.141	.087	.0543	.034	.0213	.00852	.00346	.000922	.000109	50

Applications of Present Value

Applications of present value calculation surround you in your day-to-day life. Let's look at two examples.

Suppose that on your first job as an executive you are given the task of planning a new phase of operations for your boss. The engineer tells you the operation can be built in any of three ways and over a period of three years, but the firm's cash outlay will be spread out differently over the years. The alternatives are listed in Table 7-7. All alternatives are equal in the sense that they do not affect the operation of the project and have the same date of completion, and all payments are made at the end of the year. Which should you choose? Each plan costs $600. The only way to determine which alternative will maximize profit is to use present value analysis and discount the future dollar amounts. Using Table 7-6, we can calculate the present value of each amount in Table 7-7. The present values, using a 10 percent interest rate, are in parentheses in Table 7-7. We can then total the present value amounts to find the least-cost method of production, which turns out to be alternative C. Alternative C turns out to be 4 percent cheaper than alternative A and 9 percent cheaper than alternative B, meaning a substantial savings for the firm —and maybe a raise or promotion for you!

TABLE 7-7   **Present Value Example**
                 (10 percent interest rate)

Alternative	Cost in Year 1	Cost in Year 2	Cost in Year 3	Total Cost
A	$200 (181.80)	$200 (165.20)	$200 (150.20)	$600 ($PV$ = 497.20)
B	$400 (363.60)	$100 (82.60)	$100 (75.10)	$600 ($PV$ = 521.30)
C	$100 (90.90)	$100 (82.60)	$400 (300.40)	$600 ($PV$ = $473.90)

Now let's use present value analysis to understand the real value of professional athletes' reported high salaries. Several years ago, before the World Football League collapsed, it was reported in the newspapers that Joe Namath rejected a $4 million offer from the WFL's Chicago franchise. The particulars of the offer were reported in the papers and are presented in Table 7-8. The deal included a $500,000 bonus, a 3-year contract with a salary of $500,000 per year, and a 20-year $100,000-per-year pension. Using an 8 percent interest rate and assuming all payments are made in a lump sum at the end of the year (for computational convenience), the present values are calculated (from Table 7-6) and presented in Table 7-8. The present value of the $4 million offer is $2,770,200, or 31 percent less than it appears at face value. To be sure, $2.77 million is a lot of money, but it isn't $4 million. In other words, don't be fooled by large salaries to be paid in the future. Keep in mind that if you were

TABLE 7-8   Joe Namath's $4 Million Deal

Amount	When Due (Years from Now)	PV (8 Percent)
$500,000 (Bonus)	Now	$ 500,000
$500,000 (Salary)	1	463,000
$500,000 (Salary)	2	428,500
$500,000 (Salary)	3	397,000
$100,000 (Pension)	1	92,600
. .	2	85,700
. .	3	79,400
. .	4	73,500
. .	5	68,100
. .	6	63,000
. .	7	58,300
. .	8	54,000
. .	9	50,000
. .	10	46,300
. .	11	42,900
. .	12	39,700
. .	13	36,800
. .	14	34,000
. .	15	31,500
. .	16	29,200
. .	17	27,000
. .	18	25,000
. .	19	23,200
. .	20	21,500

Total Present Value of $4 Million Deal = $2,770,200

hired for a year's work at $1 million to be paid in 50 years, discounted at 10 percent, you would be earning only $8,520!

Summary

Firms are organized by entrepreneurs to produce outputs by combining inputs. The entrepreneur does this to maximize profits. While single proprietorships are the dominant form of organization by number, corporations account for about 85 percent of annual business sales in the United States.

Economic efficiency means selecting that combination of resources that minimizes the cost of producing a certain output. Economists calculate both implicit and explicit costs of production. Implicit costs are those costs implied by alternatives given up, and explicit costs are expenditure, or bookkeeping, costs.

When total costs (both implicit and explicit) are equal to total revenues, the economist says there is zero economic profit. This means the firm is covering all opportunity costs, including a normal return on capital. When costs exceed revenues, firms and resources will leave an industry in order to earn the opportunity cost associated with those resources.

A production function is the technical relationship between factors of production and outputs. In the short run, some factors are fixed. In the long run, all factors are variable.

In the short run, as variable factors are added to the fixed factor, the firm may experience increasing returns at low levels of output but eventually will incur diminishing returns at some higher levels of output. These increasing and diminishing returns account for the U shape of the short-run average cost curve. In the long run, the U shape of the long-run average cost curve is attributable to economies and diseconomies of large-scale production.

Cost curves are derived from the production function. An understanding of cost relationships is useful in predicting firm behavior and will be used extensively in the next few chapters.

Profit maximization means that an entrepreneur will produce that level of output that equates marginal cost and marginal revenue, thus insuring that total revenue exceeds total cost by the largest amount possible.

Present value calculations are techniques for making dollar amounts to be received or paid in the future comparable with dollar amounts in the present.

New Terms

factors of production
production
business firm
industry
sole proprietorship
partnership
corporation
stockholders
board of directors
stocks
bonds
limited liability
technical efficiency
economic efficiency
explicit cost
implicit cost
economic profit
normal profit
production function
fixed factors
variable factors
short run
long run

depreciate
principle of increasing returns
principle of diminishing returns
marginal physical product
average physical product
total fixed cost
total variable cost
total cost
average fixed cost
average variable cost
average total cost
marginal cost
least-cost combination
planning curve
long-run average cost curve
optimal-size plant
economies of scale
diseconomies of scale
natural monopoly
total revenue
marginal revenue
present value
discounting

Questions for Discussion

1 Why are cost curves normally *U*-shaped (both in the long and the short run)?
2 What is a normal profit? Why is it necessary for a firm to earn a normal profit?
3 The famous epigram of the Chicago School of Economics is: There is no such thing as a free lunch. What does this mean?
4. How does the short run differ from the long run? What would be the short run in farming? in the lemonade stand business? in electricity generation?
5 The President has asked us all to find ways to conserve fuel. How will the market work to bring this about using the motivation of profit maximization?
6 List as many things as you can think of that cause diseconomies of scale.
7 At what size do universities start experiencing diseconomies of scale? What does the existence of many different sizes of universities indicate about the optimal-size university?
8 Does a university have to reach a certain size to have an efficient (winning) sports program? How would you gather empirical evidence on this?
9 What is the difference between diminishing returns and diseconomies of scale?
10 If we were to change the assumption of profit maximization, how would we predict what output the firm would decide to produce? Do certain organizations that you have dealt with operate by motivations other than profit maximization? Name some.

Suggestions for Further Reading

Dean, Joel. "Opportunity Versus Outlay Costs." Reprinted in *Readings in Introductory Economics*, by John R. McKean and Ronald A. Wykstra. New York: Harper & Row, Publishers, 1971.

Kamerschen, David R., and Lloyd M. Valentine. *Intermediate Microeconomic Theory*. Cincinnati: South-Western Publishing Co., 1977, Chapters 8 and 10.

North, Douglas C., and Roger Leroy Miller. *The Economics of Public Issues*, 4th ed. New York: Harper & Row, Publishers, 1978.

CHAPTER 8

THE ECONOMICS OF PURE COMPETITION

LEARNING OBJECTIVES

After studying the materials found in this chapter, you should be able to do the following:

1 List the assumptions of pure competition.

2 Diagram the interaction of a representative firm and the total market.

3 Calculate profits, given information on TC and TR.

4 Calculate profits, given information on Q, MR, MC, AC, and Price.

5 Define the shutdown point in terms of

(a) Price and AVC,
(b) TFC and losses.

6 List the characteristics of a
(a) constant cost industry,
(b) increasing cost industry,
(c) decreasing cost industry.

7 List the rules for the firm-industry equilibrium system based on MC and MR.

Chapter 7 developed the principles of production and the general cost relationships that are derived from the production process. Any firm making production decisions will relate potential or forecasted revenues to these costs in determining output levels. However, the forecasted revenues will depend on the market conditions faced by the firm.

In the next four chapters we will look at four different abstractions, or models, and we will then refer to these different models as different *market structures*. The first model we will discuss is the model of *pure (or perfect) competition*. It is important to keep in mind that this is a theoretical model. It does not describe reality but rather allows the development of tools that indicate what would be produced if conditions were close to pure competition. In other words, the purely competitive model is the abstract ideal to which we will compare other market structures. This purely competitive model underlies the basic supply and demand model we used in Chapters 1–4.

CHARACTERISTICS OF PURE COMPETITION

We require five basic characteristics for the model of pure competition. In developing the theory, we assume these five characteristics exist in the market in which the firm is selling its product.

First, we assume that there are large numbers of sellers in the industry. We don't specify any particular number as being large, but say that a large number means there are so many sellers of the product that no sellers take into account how their production affects price. A wheat farmer would be an example of this. No single wheat farmer has any influence on the price of wheat. The farmer could sell the entire crop, or none of the crop, and as far as the farmer could tell, it wouldn't affect the price one bit. This is because the market is large relative to any single producer.

Second, we assume that there are large numbers of buyers. Again, large numbers mean that no one buyer affects the price in any perceptible way. In other words, no single purchaser has any *market power*.

Our third assumption is that purely competitive firms produce a homogeneous product. The product of one firm is no different from the products of other firms in the industry. Since this is the case, purchasers have no preference for one producer over another. If you are a miller and want to purchase wheat, you don't care if Farmer Jones or Farmer Smith produced the wheat — a bushel of number 1 winter wheat is a bushel of number 1 winter wheat!

Fourth, and very important, we assume that there is free entry into and free exit out of the industry. This means that if one firm wishes to go into business or if another firm wishes to cease production, it does so without governmental or any other kind of constraint. Keep this assumption in mind because it is one of the assumptions that is crucial in distinguishing pure competition from monopoly, which we will examine in the next chapter.

Last, we assume there is perfect knowledge and perfect mobility of resources. This assumption means that when economic profits exist, firms will find out about these profits and enter the industry. Of course, these two assumptions are even more unrealistic than the others. Resources are costly to move and information is costly to acquire. Still, the assumptions are valuable because the abstraction allows us to see the adjustments which take place in an ideal setting.

COMPETITIVE ADJUSTMENT IN THE SHORT RUN

Recall from Chapter 7 that a profit-maximizing firm always produces where marginal cost is equal to marginal revenue. (Return to that chapter and review if you are not clear as to why this is so.) Now that we know what costs look like (again from Chapter 7), we need to determine what the firm's marginal revenue looks like. Since the firm is small relative to the market, and its product is indistinguishable from the product of other firms, the purely competitive firm views itself as having no influence on market price. if the purely competitive firm wants to sell any of its output, it must sell at the market price. For this reason, some economists and some economics textbooks refer to the purely competitive firm as a **price taker**. The firm takes the market price as its selling price. If it sets a higher price, none of its output will be sold because buyers could purchase an identical product for the market price elsewhere. By the same token, it makes no sense to sell below market price because the firm can sell all it wants to sell at the established market price.

The market demand and supply curves and the firm's resultant demand curve are drawn in Figure 8-1. Market demand (D) and supply (S) curves are such that the market equilibrium price is OP_1. If the market is in equilibrium, the purely competitive firm can sell as much of the product as it wishes at price OP_1. From the firm's viewpoint, it faces a perfectly elastic demand curve at price OP_1.

Demand curves show price-quantity relationships and the **total revenue** of a firm is the price times the quantity sold ($TR = P \times Q$). **Average revenue** (AR) would then be $\frac{TR}{Q}$, which is also the price-quantity relationship we depict in a demand curve. Demand curves are thus average revenue (AR) curves. The firm's perfectly elastic demand curve in Figure 8-1 is, as a result, also a perfectly elastic AR curve. Average revenue is the revenue per unit sold, which in this case is the price of the product. **Marginal revenue** is the change in total revenue of selling one more or one fewer unit ($MR_n = TR_n - TR_{n-1}$). In Figure 8-1, the change in total revenue, if sales increase from x_1 to x_2 to x_3, etc., is $OP_1(Ox_1)$, $OP_1(Ox_2 - Ox_1)$, $OP_1(Ox_3 - Ox_x)$, etc., where each change in x is one unit of x. In other words, in the case of a perectly elastic demand curve, such as the firm's demand curve in Figure 8-1, $D = P = AR = MR$. The marginal revenue curve of a perfectly elastic demand curve is the same as the demand curve.

Frank H. Knight

Frank H. Knight (1885–1972)

Frank H. Knight was a major contributor to the development of the "Chicago School" of economics. The large numbers of present-day economists who were trained by Knight in the 1940s and 1950s are now imprinting Knight's economic thoughts on still more generations of future economists.

Knight studied at Milligan College in Tennessee and at the University of Tennessee. He later moved to Cornell University, where he received his Ph.D. in 1916. His first teaching post was at the University of Iowa, but he moved to the University of Chicago in 1927, where he remained a faculty member until 1955 and an active scholar-teacher until his death in 1972.

Knight has had a profound impact on economics through his writing, but even more through his students. This is largely because of the obscure nature of some of his published work. Some historians have remarked that one needed to have been one of Knight's students to really understand his writing. His work has become so central to economics that it is included in most beginning texts. Knight first formalized the assumptions of the model of pure competition that we covered in this chapter, and he first spelled out the functions of all economic systems that we discussed in Chapter 1.

Of all his publications, *Risk, Uncertainty and Profit* (1921) is the most famous. In this book, Knight makes a clear distinction between risk and uncertainty. The model of pure competition assumes perfect knowledge, thus insuring that no economic profit can exist. Knight showed that a slight relaxation of the assumption of perfect knowledge introduced uncertainty. Because of this uncertainty, profits can exist even in a competitive environment. This uncertainty is distinct from risk. Risk is uncertainty that can be measured and insured against. Uncertainty cannot be measured and, therefore, cannot be insured against.

FIGURE 8-1   Elastic Demand at Market Equilibrium

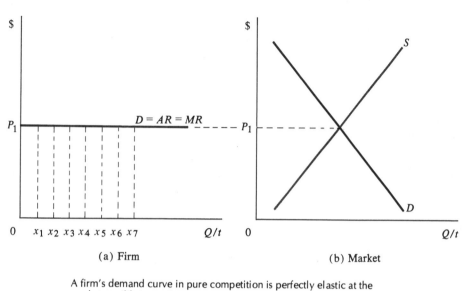

(a) Firm   (b) Market

A firm's demand curve in pure competition is perfectly elastic at the market equilibrium price.

Using marginal cost and marginal revenue, we can now determine how the firm will adjust its output in the short run. The market and *representative firm* are depicted in Figure 8-2. A *representative firm* is an average firm — one of the many firms in this market. In Figure 8-2, the firm's marginal cost curve is also drawn in. We see that the firm maximizes profits by producing Ox_1 when the price per unit is OP_1 because at Ox_1, $MR = MC$. Now assume the market demand increases to D_1. This causes the price to rise to OP_2 and the firm's demand curve, average revenue curve, and marginal revenue curve to change to D_1, AR_1, and MR_1, respectively. The firm responds by increasing its output to Ox_2, where $MR_1 = MC$. What we have seen in Figure 8-2 is that the firm's short-run marginal cost curve is the same as its **short-run supply curve**. As demand increased, the firm moved along its MC curve. Another increase in market demand would cause the firm to move further up its MC curve.

Profits, Losses, and Shutting Down

We have just seen how the firm adjusts in the short run to changes in market demand, but we don't yet know if the firm is making a profit or a loss and how large this profit or loss is. In order to determine profit or loss, we need to add the average cost curve to the graph. Also, in order to decide if the firm should continue to produce if losses are encountered, we need to add the average variable cost curve.

FIGURE 8-2   Profit Maximization

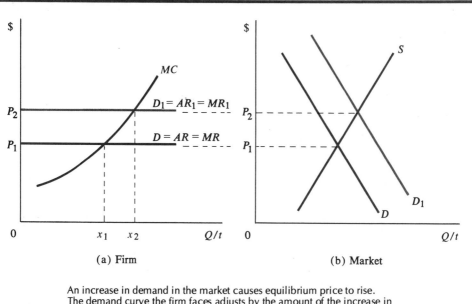

(a) Firm   (b) Market

An increase in demand in the market causes equilibrium price to rise.
The demand curve the firm faces adjusts by the amount of the increase in
equilibrium price. The firm increases its output to equate marginal cost
and marginal revenue. The adjustment process is such that the firm's
marginal cost curve is its short-run supply curve.

In Figure 8-3 the firm is maximizing profit by producing Ox_1 at price
OP_1 where $P = MR = MC$. The average cost of producing Ox_1 can be
seen to be x_1C on Figure 8-3. The total cost of producing Ox_1 is represented by the area of the rectangle OP_1Cx_1. The total revenue is also
OP_1Cx_1, so $TR = TC$. The firm is thus making zero economic profits. It
is meeting its opportunity costs. Remember that this includes *normal
profit*, which is the return on capital necessary to keep firms in the
industry.

If the firm's average cost curve is as drawn in Figure 8-4, the average
cost of producing Ox_1 would be x_1A. Total revenue is still OP_1 times
Ox_1, or the area OP_1Bx_1. Total cost is now $OCAx_1$. $TR > TC$, so there is
an economic profit equal to CP_1BA in Figure 8-4. Alternately, if the
average cost curve is represented by the one drawn in Figure 8-5, the
average cost of producing Ox_1 would be x_1A. Total revenue is OP_1Bx_1
and total cost is $OCAx_1$. In this case $TC > TR$, so losses are being
incurred. The loss is equal to P_1CAB in Figure 8-5.

Now an important question is whether the firm in Figure 8-5 should
continue to produce, and if so, for how long. After all, it is suffering a
loss, which means the factors could earn more in some other use. Opportunity costs are not being met. But keep in mind that this is the short
run, which means that some factors are fixed. These fixed factors represent the fixed costs and thus cannot be removed. Fixed costs must be

FIGURE 8-3   Firm Earning Zero Economic Profit

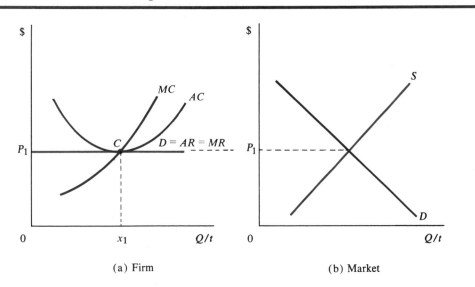

(a) Firm   (b) Market

The average cost curve can be used to determine if the firm is making an economic profit. If price (average revenue) is equal to average cost, the firm is making zero economic profit.

FIGURE 8-4   Firm Earning an Economic Profit

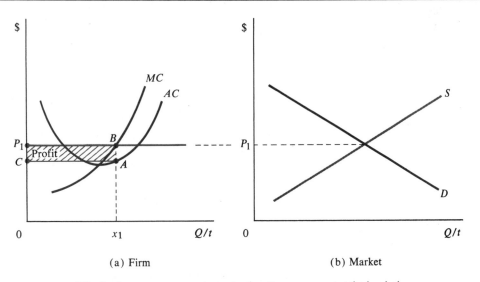

(a) Firm   (b) Market

If the firm's average revenue is greater than its average cost at the level of output being produced, the firm is making an economic profit.

FIGURE 8-5 Firm Suffering a Loss

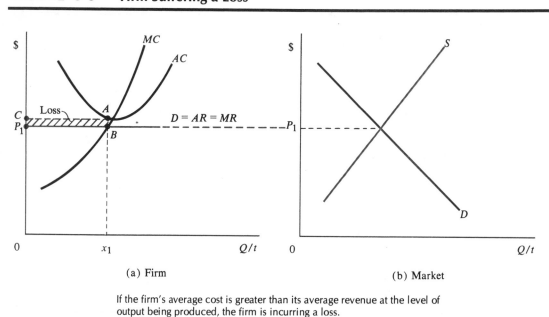

(a) Firm   (b) Market

If the firm's average cost is greater than its average revenue at the level of output being produced, the firm is incurring a loss.

paid in the short run even if production is ceased. We need, then, to include the AVC curve to determine the conditions under which the firm should cease production. A firm is depicted in Figure 8-6 with several equilibrium points represented. At a price of OP_1, which represents a marginal revenue of MR_1, the firm maximizes profits by producing Ox_1. At OP_1 the firm is thus making an economic profit because total revenue (OP_1 times Ox_1) is greater than total cost (x_1D times Ox_1). At price OP_2 $= MR_2$, the firm would produce Ox_2 and make zero economic profit because $TR(= OP_2Bx_2)$ is equal to $TC(= OP_2Bx_2)$. Examine carefully what happens when price falls to OP_3 and marginal revenue to MR_3. The profit-maximizing or loss-minimizing output is now Ox_3. At output Ox_3, losses are incurred because total revenue is now OP_3Sx_3 and total cost is $OCEx_3$. Losses are thus represented by the rectangle P_3CES. The question we need to answer is, Should the firm produce and incur this loss or should it cease production? Remember, if production is halted, fixed costs must still be paid. In Figure 8-6, if price is OP_3, the firm is earning a total revenue of OP_3Sx_3 and its total variable costs are OP_3Sx_3 ($TVC = AVC \cdot Q$). In other words, the firm is covering (exactly) its total variable costs and losing an amount equal to its total fixed costs. It must pay these fixed costs even if it shuts down, so at OP_3 the firm is indifferent about shutting down or continuing to produce, but if price fell lower than OP_3, the firm would shut down. It would make sense for it to shut down if price fell below OP_3 because shutting down would minimize

FIGURE 8-6   The Shutdown Point

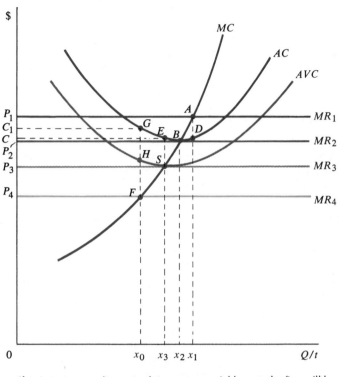

If average revenue is greater than average variable cost, the firm will be able to cover total variable costs and make a payment toward total fixed costs. If price falls below average variable costs, the firm will lose less money if it shuts down than if it continues to produce.

losses. By shutting down, only total fixed cost would be lost, instead of total fixed cost plus some portion of variable costs if it continued to produce. The minimum or low point on the AVC curve is thus called the **shutdown point** because if price (MR) falls below the minimum point on AVC, it pays the firm to cease production.

Consider price $OP_4 = MR_4$ on Figure 8-6. Our $MC = MR$ rule tells us that at OP_4 the firm should produce output Ox_0. However, at Ox_0 the firm is losing $P_4C_1GF (=OP_4Fx_0 - OC_1Gx_0)$. Total revenue of OP_4Fx_0 does not cover the AVC of x_0, which is x_0H times Ox_0. In other words, the firm is losing more than total fixed cost. It is making variable cost outlays it wouldn't have to make if it stopped production entirely. The firm would be better off to shut down and only incur its fixed costs. (We give a numerical example below.) Consider now our earlier statement that the firm's marginal cost curve represents its short-run supply curve; we see that this statement is not exactly correct. A firm's short-run supply curve is represented by its marginal cost curve *above* point S, the shutdown point. Below point S, the firm would produce no output, so we consider the marginal cost curve starting at the minimum point on the AVC curve to be the firm's supply curve.

To review, we should note that the minimum point on the AC curve is the least-cost combination, and the minimum point on the AVC curve is the shutdown point. The MC curve above the AVC is the purely competitive firm's supply curve. Also keep in mind that these are all short-run phenomena. We will trace the long-run adjustment later.

A Numerical Example

We can see the same short-run adjustments just discussed using a numerical example. Table 8-1 reproduces some of the cost data which we used in the last chapter in Table 7-4. We can assume that different market prices are the result of different market equilibrium situations, and we can then calculate the response the firm would make to these changes. In Table 8-1, six different market prices are assumed. When the market price is $61, we know that the demand and marginal revenue curves the firm faces are perfectly elastic at $61. The firm would then produce 10 units ($MR = MC = \$61$) and earn an economic profit of $120. This numerical example corresponds to the geometric example in Figure 8-4. At a market price of $46, the firm maximizes profit where $MR = MC = \$46$, which is at an output of 7 units. Since $TR = TC$ at 7 units, there is zero economic profit. This corresponds to Figure 8-3. When market price falls to $41, the firm reacts by decreasing its output to 6 units ($MR = MC = \$41$), and at 6 units it incurs a loss of $30. This corresponds to Figure 8-5. The firm will continue to produce in the short run until price falls below $35 because the minimum point on the AVC curve is at $35. To see why, examine the adjustment when market price falls to $32. At $32 the firm would produce 4 units, but if it does, it loses $72. ($TR = 4 \times \$32 = \$128$; $TC = 4 \times \$50 = \$200$; and $\$128 - \$200 = -\$72$.) If it shuts down, the firm loses only $60 in total fixed cost, as the total variable cost (TVC) would have been $140 if production had taken place. ($TVC = 4 \times \$35 = \$140$; $TFC = \$200 - \$140 = \$60$.) So it loses less if it ceases production. At any price less than $35, the firm will shut down.

The Market Supply Curve

We can now look at the interaction between supply and demand in the market in terms of the relationship between the firm's marginal cost curve and the market supply curve. We saw that the firm's marginal cost curve represents its output response to increased market prices. If we were to add all the individual supply curves, just as we did in Chapter 2, we would in effect have constructed the market or industry short-run supply curve. The market supply curve is simply the aggregate of all the firms' supply curves. The short-run market supply curve, then, is the aggregate of all the firms' marginal cost curves that lie above their average

TABLE 8-1   **Pricing Problem**

Output	AVC	AC	MC	TC
1	$40	$100	$40	$100
2	38	68	36	136
3	36	56	32	168
4	35	50	32	200
5	35	47	35	235
6	36	46	41	276
7	$37^3/_7$	46	46	322
8	39	46½	50	372
9	41	47⅔	57	429
10	43	49	61	490

Market Price (MR)	Firm's Output (equate MR with MC)	TR	Firm's Profit
$61	10	$610	$120
50	8	400	28
46	7	322	0
41	6	246	−30
35	5	175	−60
32	4	128	−72

variable cost curves. As time is extended to the long run, more firms can enter an industry as a response to economic profits or leave in response to losses. The market supply curve will shift to the right because it is now made up of more individual firm supply curves. Conversely, as firms leave an industry due to losses, the market, or industry, supply curve will shift to the left, representing a decrease in supply. This time the decrease is due to the fact that there are fewer individual firm supply curves to be summed.

COMPETITIVE ADJUSTMENT IN THE LONG RUN

To trace the adjustment process when firms have time to adjust the fixed factors, thus allowing new firms to enter the industry, consider the example in Figure 8-7. The solid D_1 and S_1 lines in Figure 8-7, panel (b), show the industry in equilibrium. The industry is in equilibrium when there are no economic forces working that would cause it to expand or contract. In Figure 8-7, panel (a), equilibrium prevails because the representative, or average, firm is making zero economic profit at price OP_1 and

FIGURE 8-7   **Adjustment to an Increase in Demand**

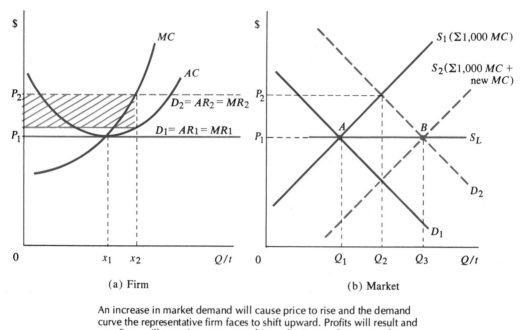

(a) Firm   (b) Market

An increase in market demand will cause price to rise and the demand
curve the representative firm faces to shift upward. Profits will result and
new firms will enter in response to this profit. As new firms enter the
industry, the market supply curve shifts to the right, causing price to fall
to the point at which the representative firm is again earning zero
economic profit.

output Ox_1. Let's assume this representative firm is one of 1,000 identical firms, so the market supply curve (S_1) in Figure 8-7, panel (b), is the summation of 1,000 MC curves (above the AVC curve). Since these firms are making zero economic profits at price OP_1, the industry is in equilibrium with an industry output of OQ_1 and each firm producing Ox_1, where $1,000 \cdot (Ox_1) = OQ_1$. Now let's suppose there is an increase in market demand to D_2. This increase, let's say, is brought about by an increase in real income and the good under consideration is a normal good. When market demand shifts to D_2, market price rises to OP_2 and the demand curve facing the firm rises to be perfectly elastic at price OP_2. The firm's new demand curve is represented by D_2, AR_2, MR_2. These changes are all represented by dashed lines. The firm's initial (short-run) response is to increase its output to Ox_2 because $MR_2 = MC$ at output Ox_2. Thus, the initial increase in consumption in the market (from OQ_1 to OQ_2) is met by each of the 1,000 firms increasing their output from Ox_1 to Ox_2. Note, however, that each firm is now making an economic profit equal to the shaded area in Figure 8-7, panel (a). Profit, you recall, means that factors are earning more than their opportunity cost. This profit means the industry is out of equilibrium. Other firms are going to attempt to grab some of this profit. The existence of profit, then, is the signal for new firms to enter this industry.

Since we initially assumed that free entry and perfect knowledge are characteristics of pure competition, entrepreneurs will be aware of this profit and will enter the industry. As firms enter the industry, the market supply curve will shift, because it now is the summation of 1,000 MC curves plus the MC curves of the new entrant firms. In fact, firms will keep entering the industry until equilibrium (zero profit) is restored. In Figure 8-7, firms enter until the number of new firms is such that all profit has disappeared. If all firms have the same costs (that is, all firms are exactly like this representative firm) and if nothing happens to change these costs (in Figure 8-7 we assume that this is the case), equilibrium will be restored when the price has been reduced to OP_1, the original equilibrium price. If the new equilibrium price is OP_1, and industry output is OQ_3, each firm is producing Ox_1, and the summation of the firms' output (1,000 + the new number of firms times Ox_1) is equal to the industry output, which is OQ_3. If we connect the market equilibrium points, points A and B in Figure 8-7, we get the industry's long-run supply curve (S_L). This represents what occurs after all adjustments have had time to take place.

You can check your understanding of this adjustment process by going through the adjustments for a decrease in demand. Figure 8-8 illustrates this. The industry is initially in equilibrium at price OP_1 and output OQ_1. Firms are making zero profits and producing Ox_1 units of output. Something or someone, perhaps the government, says the product is dangerous to your health and this causes demand to decrease to D_2, represented by the dashed line in Figure 8-8, panel (b). Market price falls to OP_2 and industry output falls to OQ_2. Firms adjust their output to Ox_2 where $MC = MR_2$. At Ox_2, however, firms are incurring losses represented by the crosshatched area. (We are assuming OP_2 is above AVC, so the firm continues production.) The industry is now out of equilibrium. Just as profits were the signal for firms to enter, losses are the signal for firms to exit the industry. Entrepreneurs move their factors to the production of other commodities, seeking to earn their opportunity cost elsewhere. We assumed perfect knowledge, so the entrepreneurs will know where they can earn their opportunity cost. As firms leave the industry, the short-run market supply curve will shift, because it is now derived by adding up fewer firms' MC curves. Firms will leave the industry until those remaining firms have zero economic profits. This equilibrium is restored when the market supply curve shifts so as to restore a price of OP_1. Industry output is now OQ_3 with each of the 1,000 minus the exited firms producing Ox_1 units of output. As before, the long-run supply curve (S_L) can be found by connecting the industry's equilibrium points, which are represented by points A and B in Figure 8-8, panel (b).

The adjustment we traced in Figures 8-7 and 8-8 proceeded by assuming that factor prices and thus costs were unaffected by the quantity

FIGURE 8-8   Adjustment to a Decrease in Demand

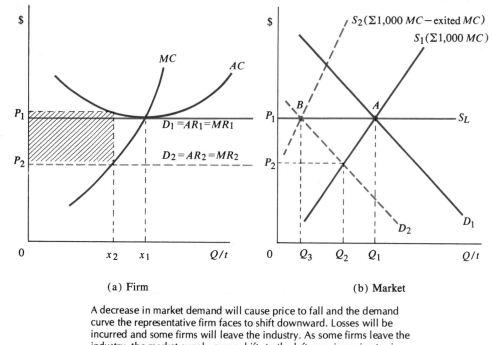

(a) Firm   (b) Market

A decrease in market demand will cause price to fall and the demand
curve the representative firm faces to shift downward. Losses will be
incurred and some firms will leave the industry. As some firms leave the
industry, the market supply curve shifts to the left, causing price to rise
until a remaining representative firm is earning zero economic profit.

of output the industry produced. This meant that as firms entered the
industry (Figure 8-7) or exited the industry (Figure 8-8), the prices of the
factors of production were not changed and as a result the cost curves
didn't change. When this is so, the industry is referred to as a *constant
cost industry*. In a constant cost industry, as more steel, labor, electricity, or whatever is purchased to increase output, the cost of those inputs
does not increase. This would probably be the case where the industry's
purchase of inputs is small relative to the market supply of these inputs.
If the industry's use of inputs is small relative to the market supply, the
increased demand for inputs would not increase the price of these same
inputs. For example, take the citizens' band radio industry. If profits exist
and firms enter, these firms will demand more inputs. They will demand
more steel, more labor, more transistors, etc. If all the CB-producing
firms have similar production functions and comprise an insignificant
amount of the consumption of these inputs, the increase in demand will
not cause the price of steel, labor, and transistors to rise.

Figures 8-7 and 8-8, then, represent contractions and expansions in
constant cost industries. The short-run response to a contraction in demand was a decrease in price. An expansion in demand produced a short-

run increase in price. The market adjustment, however, returned price to its original level with fewer firms in the case of the contraction and additional firms in the case of the expansion. The long-run supply curve in a constant cost industry is thus seen to be perfectly elastic, even though the short-run supply curve has a positive slope.

Increasing Cost Industries

Sometimes an expansion in industry output will cause costs to increase in the long run. In this case, as an industry expands output and demands more inputs, the increased demand will cause prices to rise in the input markets. For example, an increase in demand for wine causes new firms to enter the wine industry and to demand more grapes, grape pickers, land, and wine makers. If the increased demand causes the price of grapes, grape pickers, land, or wine makers to rise, the production costs of the firm will increase as a result of the increased demand for wine. Also, less efficient factors and firms will be drawn into the industry. This is the case in an *increasing cost industry*.

Figure 8-9 illustrates the long-run adjustment process in an increasing cost industry. The industry is originally in equilibrium at price OP_1 and output OQ_1. Each firm is producing Ox_1. Market demand increases to D_2 and, as a result, market price rises to OP_2. The firm now faces a demand which is perfectly elastic at OP_2. The firm's demand is now represented by $D_2 = AR_2 = MR_2$. The firm's short-run response is to increase output to Ox_2, where $MC_1 = MR_2$. Industry's output is now OQ_2. At this increased output, two things will happen. First, new firms will enter the industry because of the economic profits that now exist. Second, costs are rising as a result of the increased demand for inputs. This rise in cost is represented by the upward shift to MC_2 and AC_2 in Figure 8-9, panel (a). This upward shift of MC and AC assumes all costs are increased proportionately. In most cases this would not be exactly true, as some inputs (the scarcer ones) would rise faster in price, but the illustration is clearer if we assume all factor prices rise proportionately, and this assumption does not seriously affect the analysis. Firms, as consumers of inputs, are likely to be a significant influence in some input markets and insignificant in others. In our previous example, as the demand for wine increased and firms entered the industry, there may have been no effect on the price of land but a significant effect on the salaries of wine makers. It is also possible that firms less able to produce the good in question will be attracted to the industry. In this case, a representative firm would have higher costs, indicating less efficient production.

The net result of the increased number of firms and increasing costs is a rightward shift in the short-run market supply curve. The supply curve shifts to the right because there are more firms' MC curves to add up, but it will not shift as far as before because costs have risen for every

FIGURE 8-9   Adjustment in an Increasing Cost Industry

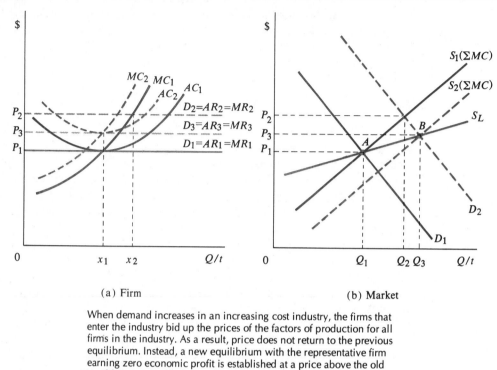

(a) Firm   (b) Market

When demand increases in an increasing cost industry, the firms that enter the industry bid up the prices of the factors of production for all firms in the industry. As a result, price does not return to the previous equilibrium. Instead, a new equilibrium with the representative firm earning zero economic profit is established at a price above the old equilibrium price but below the initial increase in price.

firm. A new short-run market supply curve will be created when equilibrium is reached at price OP_3 where firms are no longer making profits. Industry output is now OQ_3 and each firm is producing Ox_1 where $MR_3 = MC_2$.

As before, we can find the long-run supply curve by connecting the industry's equilibrium points. Connecting points A and B in Figure 8-9, panel (b), produces a long-run supply curve (S_L) with a positive slope, indicating an increasing cost industry. We will leave it to you to diagram the adjustment process reflecting a decrease in demand for an increasing cost industry.

Decreasing Cost Industries

To complete the analysis, we must examine a *decreasing cost industry*. In a decreasing cost industry, expansion in industry output causes input prices to fall, and as a result costs decrease. A real-world example is hard to come up with. In a decreasing cost industry, as more firms enter the industry, causing the demand for inputs to increase, input prices fall. This implies that there are economies of scale in an industry that is supplying an input to the industry under examination. For example, as more electricity is demanded, more efficient generators are built and the price of this input falls.

Figure 8-10 demonstrates this adjustment process. The market equilibrium price, OP_1, is given by the intersection of the market demand and supply curves, D_1 and S_1. The firm is in equilibrium producing Ox_1 at price OP_1. Now suppose there is an increase in the price of a substitute good. This means that demand for the good in question increases to D_2. The short-run response is for price to rise to OP_2.[1] This changes the firm's demand curve to D_2, AR_2, MR_2. The representative firm responds by increasing its output to Ox_2 where $MR_2 = MC_1$. Profits now exist and new firms will enter this industry. As new firms enter, two things happen. First, the market supply curve will shift to the right, increasing, because it is now composed of more MC curves. Second, as industry output increases, costs fall. In Figure 8-10, panel (a), the decrease in costs is assumed to be a proportional decrease in the cost of all inputs. Again, this assumption is not realistic, but it simplifies the graph. If costs decrease with industry expansion, it is more likely that this decrease would be a result of a decrease in the price of a major input rather than a proportional decrease in the price of all inputs. The decrease in costs for the representative firm is shown in Figure 8-10, panel (a), as a shift from AC_1 to AC_2 and from MC_1 to MC_2.

The decrease in cost and increase in supply causes price to fall. A new equilibrium at a price such as OP_3 will be reached. At OP_3 the representative firm faces demand curve D_3, AR_3, MR_3. Equilibrium is reached at output Ox_1 where $MC_2 = MR_3$. No economic profits exist.

As before, we can now connect the equilibrium points in the market. These points are represented by points A and B. The long-run industry supply curve is represented by the S_L curve in Figure 8-10, panel (b). The curve has a negative slope. This would mean that an increase in market demand would eventually lead to a new equilibrium at lower product prices. Decreasing cost industries thus have negatively sloped long-run supply curves. (The short-run supply curves are still positively sloped since they are the aggregate of firms' MC curves.) Industries with decreasing costs are very unlikely but theoretically conceivable. We leave diagramming the adjustment process for a decrease in demand to your understanding of the adjustment process in decreasing cost industries.

EQUILIBRIUM: SO WHAT?

The model of pure competition is such that the firm and industry are driven to equilibrium at zero economic profit. Herein lies the appeal of

---

[1] If you need to review why the change in the price of a substitute good causes demand to change, return to Chapter 2, pages 31 to 32.

FIGURE 8-10   Adjustment in a Decreasing Cost Industry

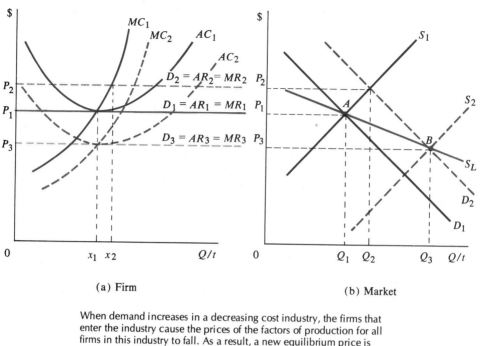

(a) Firm

(b) Market

When demand increases in a decreasing cost industry, the firms that
enter the industry cause the prices of the factors of production for all
firms in this industry to fall. As a result, a new equilibrium price is
established that is below the initial equilibrium price.

pure competition as a standard against which to judge other market
structures. Economists view this equilibrium as an ideal, a social optimum. In equilibrium, resources are optimally allocated among competing uses. Figure 8-11 shows a firm in equilibrium. At equilibrium, price
(P) is equal to average cost (AC) and also is equal to marginal cost
(MC).

First, consider $P = MC$. This means that *allocative efficiency* is
being met, or that the resources of the firm are being allocated exactly as
consumers wish. It means that firms are expanding production exactly to
the level desired by consumers. If $P > MC$, it would mean that the firm
was not putting enough resources into the production of the good in
question. Consumers would be willing to pay more than it costs to produce another unit of the good. If $P < MC$, too many resources are being
devoted to the production of the good. Consumers would not be willing
to pay as much as it costs to produce another unit of the good. In other
words, where $P = MC$, the "correct" amount of resources is being devoted to producing the good.

Second, consider $P = AC$. This means that firms are only earning
normal profits. There is no incentive for firms to enter or leave the
industry.

FIGURE 8-11   **Equilibrium Condition**

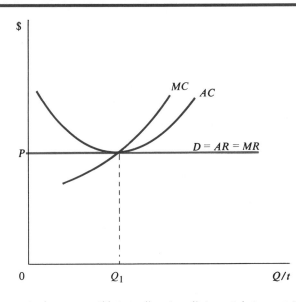

In short-run equilibrium, allocative efficiency is being met. This means that the resources of the firm are being allocated as consumers wish.

Third, consider $MC = AC$. This means that AC is at minimum, and therefore the firm is at the least-cost combination. This means that the variable resources are being combined as efficiently as is technically possible.

In the long run, the short-run average cost curve (AC) will also be tangent to the long-run average cost curve at its minimum point, $AC = LRAC$, as in Figure 8-12. This means that all firms are at the technically efficient size and are also combining variable resources efficiently. The firms are at the least-cost combination and at the optimal plant size. All firms must be technically efficient or they will be driven from the market by incurred losses. If any one firm is more efficient than normal, or more efficient than the representative firm, it will be able to make an economic profit even though the other firms don't.

At equilibrium, then, we have $P = AC = MC = LRAC = LRMC$. The purely competitive model is thus the ideal of efficiency that we will hold the other market structures up to for comparison.

PROFITS: THE DRIVING FORCE

It is important to note the role of profits in the purely competitive model. Profits serve as the signal for firms to move in and out of an industry. When profits exist, entrepreneurs rush in to attempt to capture them and the industry is forced to equilibrium. Likewise, when losses are present,

FIGURE 8-12   **Long-Run Equilibrium**

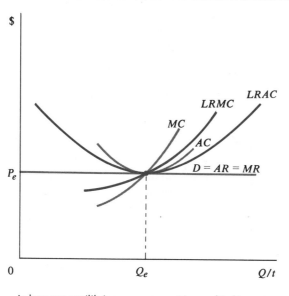

In long-run equilibrium, average cost is equal to long-run average cost. This means that all firms are at the technically efficient size and are also combining variable resources efficiently.

firms leave to earn higher returns elsewhere. Equilibrium is forced by the profit-seeking nature of firms. In equilibrium, we have efficiency. It is not because of some altruistic behavior on the part of the entrepreneur that the firm is efficient; rather, the entrepreneur is assumed to be a profit maximizer interested solely in individual self-interest, and this brings about efficiency. In the competitive model, self-interest and the quest for profits produce the efficiency that benefits consumers. The firm is not striving for efficiency but for profits.

EXAMPLES OF PURE COMPETITION

Perhaps the closest we can come to the model of pure competition in the U.S. economy are the markets for various agricultural products. In these markets there are large numbers of buyers and sellers and there is a homogeneous product. This homogeneity is reflected in the fact that there are no brand names associated with most farm products. In addition, there is relatively free entry into and exit out of the industry. Anyone with capital, or the ability to borrow capital, can enter the agriculture industry. There are very few, if any, educational requirements, in the sense of having a degree or passing a test, and little in the way of licenses, inspection codes, or officials who must be bribed. So, if you don't like thinking in abstract terms all the time, you can use agriculture as an

Adam Smith

Radio Times Hulton Picture Library

Adam Smith (1723–1790)

Adam Smith is considered by most historians to be the father of economics. Smith provided the basis for economics as a discipline by bringing together in one volume, *The Wealth of Nations*, a systematic treatment of all aspects of economic activity.

Adam Smith was born in Kirkcaldy, Scotland, in 1723. His father died before he was born. Smith was educated at the University of Glasgow and later at Oxford University. After leaving Oxford, he returned to a professorship at the University of Glasgow.

Smith may be the archetype of the absent-minded professor. He is described in many books as being given "to fits of abstraction." These fits of abstraction manifested themselves in strange behavior, such as when he once brewed a pot of bread and butter and later called it the worst tea he had ever tasted! On one occasion, he became so involved in a discussion he fell into a tanning pit.

Smith wrote only two books. The first, *The Theory of Moral Sentiments* (1759), attracted immediate attention and made Smith a famous philosopher. The second, *The Wealth of Nations* (1776), serves as the cornerstone of the classical school of economics. Every economist for the next 100 years was influenced in some way by Adam Smith. Many, like David Ricardo (see page 355), were drawn by Smith's writing to the study of economics.

A key idea in the *Wealth of Nations* is that a natural harmony, or an "invisible hand," exists in the world. According to Smith, competition promotes the common good because it forces each individual economic actor to pursue his or her own self-interest. This idea is reflected in the model of pure competition developed in this chapter. Smith's ideas are at the heart of the classical liberal approach to economics. He saw the role of government as very limited. He expected government to provide for the national defense, provide and regulate a money supply, and protect property rights; i.e., supply a system of laws. In Smith's view of the world, any other activity of the government impinges upon the freedom of the citizens of that country.

industry and a wheat farm as a firm to illustrate our theory of pure competition. Of course the example is not perfect because resources tend to be immobile in agriculture and our model assumes relatively mobile resources. Agriculture, is however, a very useful example of pure competition.

The model of pure competition is not meant to be a perfect description of reality. Nor in every case is it the ideal state that we should be striving to reach. In certain industries it may be too costly to bring about the necessary conditions to make that industry purely competitive, in which case we would accept less than the ideal. The model of pure competition is a tool for the economist. The economist can compare the real-world situation to the hypothetical world of pure competition to determine what would be the case if pure competition existed. In this sense, pure competition is a benchmark, or yardstick, by which analysts can measure the costs of other market structures.

Summary

Pure competition is characterized by large numbers of buyers and sellers, homogeneous products, ease of entry into and exit from the industry, and perfect knowledge and mobility of resources. The firm in a purely competitive market faces a perfectly elastic demand curve at the price determined by equilibrium in the market. The firm's short-run supply curve is its short-run marginal cost curve above the minimum point on the average variable cost curve, known as the shutdown point.

Long-run adjustments to changes in market demand are dependent on the cost characteristics of the industry under consideration. Since entry is easy, firms will enter as long as profits are present. As a result, economic profits brought about by an increase in demand will bring about new entry. The new equilibrium position will depend on whether the industry is characterized by constant, increasing, or decreasing costs. The slope of the long-run supply curve will also depend on these different cost situations.

In equilibrium, $P = AC = MC = LRAC = LRMC$. This is the efficiency ideal that we hold other market structures up to for comparison.

Profits are the force that drives the model to efficiency. The firm is not seeking efficiency but profits. This search for profits produces the efficiency which characterizes the model of pure competition.

New Terms

market structures	representative firm
pure competition	short-run supply curve
market power	shutdown point
price taker	constant cost industry
total revenue	increasing cost industry
average revenue	decreasing cost industry
marginal revenue	allocative efficiency

Questions for Discussion

1 Show how the long-run market supply curve will be brought about by short-run supply adjustments in an increasing cost industry.
2 Diagram a situation showing a market in equilibrium and a representative firm. Then show a decrease in market demand. Trace through the short-run and long-run adjustment, assuming this is a decreasing cost industry.
3 "If the price of wheat doesn't rise, farmers will lose money and the long-run price will be even higher." Discuss this often-heard argument.
4 Why does profit maximization bring about efficiency?
5 What situations cause long-run supply curves to be positively sloped?
6 Explain in your own words why you might keep producing in the short run even if you were incurring a loss.
7 What does it mean to say that in pure competition long-run equilibrium means that $P = AC = MC = LRAC = LRMC$?

Suggestions for Further Reading

Kamerschen, David R., and Lloyd M. Valentine. *Intermediate Microeconomic Theory*. Cincinnati: South-Western Publishing Co., 1977, Chapters 11 and 12.
Leftwich, Richard H. *The Price System & Resource Allocation*, 6th ed. Hinsdale, Ill.: Dryden Press, 1976, Chapter 9.
Stigler, George J. *The Theory of Price*, 3d ed. New York: Macmillan Publishing Co., 1966, Chapter 10.

THE ECONOMICS OF PURE MONOPOLY

LEARNING OBJECTIVES

After studying the materials found in this chapter, you should be able to do the following:

1 Define pure monopoly.

2 Calculate and diagram average revenue and marginal revenue, given data on price and output.

3 Label sections of a downward-sloping demand curve according to elasticity, given information on MR.

4 Diagram a monopolistic firm in terms of AR, MR, MC, and AC making
  (a) an economic profit,
  (b) a loss,
  (c) an economic profit of zero.

5 List natural and artificial barriers to entry into an industry.

6 Define the misallocation of resource by a monopolist in terms of P, AC, and MC.

7 Show that a monopolist does not have a supply curve.

8 Define two types of price discrimination.

9 Define and illustrate consumer surplus.

10 Discuss the alternative theories to profit maximization.

11 Define
  (a) dumping,
  (b) local monopoly,
  (c) natural monopoly.

Pure monopoly is at the other end of the market continuum from pure competiton. The word ***monopoly*** is derived from the Greek words *mono* for "one" and *poly* for "seller." Monopoly is thus the market structure in which the firm is a single seller of a product that has no close substitutes. It is necessary that there be no close substitutes to insure that there is only one firm in the industry. If a close substitute product exists, the firm is not a single seller.

It is important to keep in mind that pure monopoly is a theoretical model and as with pure competition, real-world examples are almost nonexistent. The theory is still useful, however. Like pure competition, the model of pure monopoly affords us another tool to examine real-world situations. The definition of a pure monopoly as a single seller of a product with no close substitutes establishes conditions which make finding examples quite difficult, but there are many firms that have some of the same economic effects as pure monopoly. We say these firms have ***monopoly power***. (Technically these firms are called *oligopolies*, and we will examine oligopoly in detail in Chapter 11.)

Perhaps the best example of monopoly in U.S. history is the Aluminum Company of America prior to World War II, which was then the only aluminum producer in the United States. But even this example contradicts our model to some extent because aluminum does have some close substitutes. For example, beer can be put into bottles, steel cans, or even wooden kegs; golf clubs can be made with steel or even wooden shafts; and not long ago the top tennis players got along with wooden racquets. So, before we worry too much about finding a *real* monopoly, let's analyze adjustment under monopoly and then compare the allocation of resources under pure monopoly to those under pure competition.

DEMAND AND MARGINAL REVENUE

In the last chapter we saw that the purely competitive firm faced a perfectly elastic demand curve and as a result price and marginal revenue were equal. However, a monopolistic firm faces the *market* demand curve because the firm is the single seller and is, therefore, the industry. This is a very important distinction because market demand curves have negative slopes. Since the demand curve has a negative slope, the marginal revenue curve is going to lie below the demand curve, which is, as we saw before, the average revenue curve. The commonsense reason for the relationship of the demand and marginal revenue curves or the fact that the marginal revenue curve lies below the average revenue curve is that the monopolist must lower price in order to sell more units of output. This is because the monopolist faces a negatively sloped demand curve. Price reductions apply to *all* units of output the monopolist sells. Each additional unit sold thus adds to total revenue by the amount it sells for — its price — but takes away from total revenue by the reduction in price times the previous units sold, so this change in total revenue (which is equal to marginal revenue) must be less than price.

An arithmetic example is presented in Table 9-1. When three units are being sold, the total revenue is $186 (=3 × $62). In order to sell four units, the monopolist must reduce the price from $62 to $60. Total revenue will then increase by $60 because an additional unit is being sold for $60, but it will also decrease by $6 because the first three units now sell for $2 less each, or for $60 each rather than for $62. The net result is that the monopolist has added $54 (=$60 − $6) to total revenue by reducing the price from $62 to $60. Notice that MR is $54 and price (average revenue) is $60 for four units. MR has to lie below AR whenever there are previous units that suffer a price reduction.

TABLE 9-1   Demand and Marginal Revenue Relationships

Units Sold	Price (Average Revenue)	Total Revenue	Marginal Revenue
1	$64	$ 64	$64
2	63	126	62
3	62	186	60
4	60	240	54
5	58	290	50
6	56½	339	49
7	55	385	46
8	52	416	31
9	47	423	7
10	40	400	−23

This relationship can be seen graphically in Figure 9-1. You may remember that in Chapter 3 we discussed the relationship between elasticity and total revenue. We can now relate that discussion to marginal revenue and the monopolist. When a demand curve is inelastic, we saw that this meant that price decreases cause total revenue to decline. If total revenue is declining, it must mean that the additions to total revenue are negative, or that the MR is negative. This is graphically demonstrated in Figure 9-1. Price reductions below OP_1 will decrease total revenue because marginal revenue is negative. This corresponds to the inelastic portion of the curve. Conversely, a reduction in price from OP_2 to OP_1 would increase total revenue because the demand curve is elastic in this range.

Go back and read pages 56–60 in Chapter 3. In the problem presented there, we determined that the monopoly owner of a mineral spring with no cost of production would set price at the point where the price elasticity of demand was unitary. We can now see this same principle

FIGURE 9-1   **Demand and Marginal Revenue**

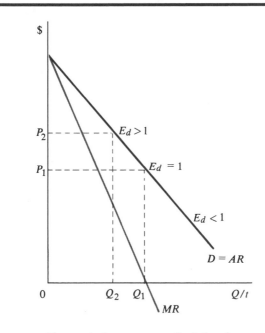

The marginal revenue curve lies below the average revenue curve in the case of a negatively sloped demand curve. In drawing the relationship between average and marginal revenue, the marginal revenue curve will intersect the x-axis exactly halfway between the origin and the point where the average revenue curve intersects the x-axis.

using our profit maximization rule of $MR = MC$. If costs are zero, the MC curve would be superimposed on the quantity or x-axis. In Figure 9-1, the monopolist would maximize by producing OQ_1 at price OP_1 where $MC = MR = O$. What is happening is that the mineral spring monopolist will increase sales of the product as long as marginal revenue is positive since it costs nothing more to produce another unit. You should note that this does not mean the mineral spring monopolist sells as much as possible, but rather sells the quantity which maximizes total revenue, which in this case happens to be the same as the quantity where profit is maximized, since costs are zero.

PRICE AND OUTPUT DECISIONS

The monopolist searches out the profit-maximizing price and output by equating marginal cost and marginal revenue. Whereas the purely competitive firm is a price taker, we say that the monopoly firm is a *price searcher*. A monopolist sets the profit-maximizing price, not the highest price. We can see this process graphically by looking at cost relationships under monopoly.

In Figure 9-2 we see a monopolist producing good x. The market demand is D_1, from which MR_1 is derived. The monopolist's AC curve and MC curve are also drawn in. The monopolist will maximize profit by producing Ox_1 units of x because at Ox_1, $MR_1 = MC$. If $MR > MC$ (that is, if output is less than Ox_1), the monopolist can increase profits by expanding output because additions to output add more to total revenue than to total cost. On the other hand, if $MR_1 < MC$ (that is, if output is greater than Ox_1), the monopolist would contract output because additions to output add more to total cost than to total revenue.

FIGURE 9-2   The Profit-Maximizing Position of a Pure Monopolist

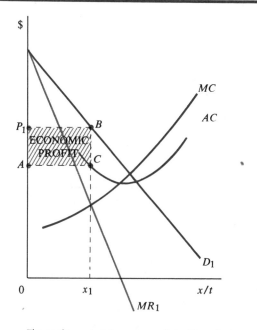

The profit-maximizing monopolist will produce output Ox_1, where MR_1 = MC. Since average cost is less than average revenue (price) for output Ox_1, the monopolist is making an economic profit.

At OP_1 and Ox_1, the monopolist is making an economic profit. The average revenue (price) is OP_1. OA is the average cost, so $OP_1 > OA$ and thus the monopolist is making a profit of $OP_1 - OA$ per unit, or a total profit of $(OP_1 - OA) \cdot Ox_1$. In Figure 9-2, total cost is represented by rectangle $OACx_1$ and total revenue is represented by rectangle OP_1Bx_1. TR minus TC equals profit, or rectangle AP_1BC. Since the costs depicted in the cost curves include both explicit and implicit costs, this profit means that the monopoly firm is making more than its opportunity cost, that is, more than is necessary to keep its resources employed in this industry.

We can see this same price and output determination using a numerical example. Table 9-2 combines the revenue data of Table 9-1 and the cost data of Table 7-4. We see that the monopolist would maximize profits at 7 units, where $MC = MR = \$46$. Price would be $55 because the demand curve (AR) tells us that 7 units will sell for $55 each. At a price of $55, total revenue is $385 (=7 × $55) and total cost is $322 (=$46 × 7), which means the monopolist is making a profit of $63 (=$385 − $322). If you don't believe this is maximum profit, construct an eighth column for Table 9-2 and call it profit. Calculate the profit at each level of output from 1–10 units and you will see it is maximized at 7 units because at 7 units, $MR = MC.$[1]

TABLE 9-2   Monopolist's Cost and Revenue Data

Output and Sales	Total Cost	Average Cost	Marginal Cost	Average Revenue	Total Revenue	Marginal Revenue
0	60	∞	0	0	0	0
1	100	100	40	64	64	64
2	136	68	36	63	126	62
3	168	56	32	62	186	60
4	200	50	32	60	240	54
5	235	47	35	58	290	50
6	276	46	41	56½	339	49
7	322	46	46	55	385	46
8	372	46½	50	52	416	31
9	429	47⅔	57	47	423	7
10	490	49	61	40	400	−23

Profits and New Entry

Other entrepreneurs will want some of the profits the monopolist is receiving. There will, as a result, be pressure from new firms entering the industry in order to cash in on some of these profits. But wait! A monopoly is a single seller producing a product for which there are no close substitutes, so if there is new entry, we no longer have monopoly. If a monopoly is to exist, there must be some forces at work to keep new

[1] If you undertake such a calculation, you will find that profit is $63 at an output of 6 units and at an output of 7 units. This result obtains from the fact that in numerical examples we use discrete data, or numbers, rather than functions. The principle is that profit maximization implies producing where $MC = MR$, but a unique point only exists when dealing with functions and using calculus. In this example the actual profit-maximizing output would be somewhere between 6 and 7 units of output.

firms from entering. Economists say there must be *barriers to entry*. Barriers to entry are natural or artificial obstacles that keep new firms from entering an industry.

A *natural* barrier to entry is economies of scale. If the long-run cost curves are such that an optimal-size plant occurs only when the firm is very large relative to the size of the market, it could be that there is room for only one cost-efficient firm in the industry. If there are significant economies of scale, one firm which gets bigger than any of the others will be able to undersell them. In such a case the bigger firm will cut price below its rivals and eventually become the only firm in the industry. When just one firm emerges in this way — and this happens in very few industries — the firm is called a *natural monopoly*. Public utilities fit this category. The government recognizes that these are natural monopolies and therefore regulates them. Difficulties in such regulation will be discussed in Chapter 12. As you might guess, the incidence of natural monopoly is very low. Some would argue that even public utilities are not natural monopolies. If the frequency of natural monopoly is low, then any monopoly power that exists in our economy must be due to artificial barriers.

An *artificial* barrier to entry is one which is contrived by the firm (or someone else) to keep others out. It doesn't take much imagination to come up with a list of such barriers. The least sophisticated, but perhaps the most effective, would be the use of violence. Say you have a monopoly on the illegal numbers racket in south Chicago. If a new entrepreneur ("family") moves in to reap some of these profits, you simply blow them away — very effective! This sort of tactic may sound preposterous, but business history contains many examples of such activity. The early history of oil exploration and drilling is one example where violence was sometimes used and private "armies" were often a must.

On a more civilized level, you may be able to erect artificial barriers that are legal, or at least quasi-legal. If you could capture ownership of all the raw materials in an industry, you could then control entry by not selling to potential new entrants. The classic example of this behavior is the Aluminum Company of America, which before World War II controlled almost all the known free-world sources of bauxite, the essential ore for the production of aluminum.

Another technique would be to get a patent on a process or machine that is vital in production. Patent rights give sole authority to use the process or machine to the holder of the patent. The problem with a patent is twofold. First, it expires after 17 years in the United States, and then everyone is entitled to use the idea. Second, to get a patent you must provide detailed plans on how the item is produced, and these plans are available to potential competitors at the Library of Congress. So it appears a patent is not a very effective entry barrier to anyone who is willing to risk a lawsuit brought by the offended patent holder (and patent holders don't always win their cases). You may have already thought of a good alternative to patents — secrecy. If you can keep your vital process secret, you can keep new firms out of your industry. So now you know why there is barbed wire around research and development offices, why you aren't told the formula for Pepsi Cola, and why corporate spying is big business.

The Government and Barriers to Entry

In the final analysis, it is very difficult to be a monopolist because it is very hard to keep new entrants out of your industry — unless you can get the government to help you. Consider the industries you regard as monopolies or near monopolies. Let's look briefly at two industries with significant market power, the steel industry and the airline industry.

Suppose that firms in the steel industry are earning economic profits. Firms that are producing steel in Europe see these profits being earned and gear up to export steel to the United States in order to earn some of these profits. In effect, these foreign steel firms are entering the U.S. industry. The domestic firms then appeal to Congress or the President to keep these firms out, to block their entry, and we may suppose *tariffs* or *quotas* are then put into effect. These tariffs or quotas serve as artificial barriers to entry by raising the price of foreign goods or prohibiting them outright.[2]

Next consider the airline industry. Suppose American Airlines is the only carrier flying between New York and Los Angeles. Other firms see profits being made and schedule flights between New York and Los Angeles. But wait! In order to offer commercial flights on such interstate routes, the service and the fares must be approved by the Civil Aeronautics Board (CAB). The artificial barrier to entry is the CAB. Entrepreneurs like Freddy Laker of Laker Airlines, who began the no-frills "Sky-Train" between London and New York in 1977 at less than half the fares then prevailing, are the enemies of monopolies because they try to break down entry barriers.

In both of these examples, the federal government supplied the artificial barrier to entry, but state and local governments also restrict entry and thereby insure protected market positions. Taxicab franchising and liquor licensing are just two examples. It should not be too surprising that many of the graft and payola cases in government have centered on the granting of monopoly privileges. A government official or agency protects a monopoly by keeping competitors out, and the monopolist is often willing to pay for this, either in campaign contributions, favors, or outright bribes such as direct cash payments, free vacations, or jobs for relatives.

When you examine industries that possess monopoly power, keep in mind that governments help monopolies exist by erecting barriers to entry. If the monopoly power persists for a long period of time, there is

---

[2]We will study tariffs and quotas in detail in Chapter 16.

very likely some explicit or implicit government support of that monopoly. This is because monopoly profits are a very powerful and attractive force, and new entry is very difficult for the firm alone to block. As a result, monopolies usually try to enlist governmental support of one kind or another.

RESOURCE ALLOCATION WITH MONOPOLY

No entrepreneur likes to sell in a purely competitive industry. A firm that is able to use its power to create a successful monopoly is rewarded with profits. (This ability to use power in markets is stressed in marketing and management courses — hence there are no marketing courses for wheat farmers!) Obviously monopoly can be good for the monopolist. But as we are about to see, monopoly can be bad for society.

To see what's so bad about monopoly, let's examine Figure 9-3. First, suppose that Figure 9-3 represents a purely competitive market. The market demand curve is that faced by the numerous sellers and the MC curve is the summation of all the individual firm marginal cost curves. The competitive price and output would be OP_c and OQ_c. Now, suppose that the industry is monopolized by one firm that has bought up all the individual competitive firms and that this doesn't change any of the cost curves. The monopoly firm, then, would face the same cost conditions that the aggregate competitive firms faced. The *market* supply curve would represent the monopolist's marginal cost curve, because it would be the summation of the purchased firms' marginal cost curves. Likewise, the monopoly firm faces the *market* demand curve and its corresponding marginal revenue curve. The monopoly firm will produce OQ_m at price OP_m. It is thus a very simple matter to contrast pure monopoly to pure competition. The monopolist produces a smaller output ($OQ_m < OQ_c$) and charges a higher price ($OP_m > OP_c$), than does the purely competitive firm. This is possible because the monopolist excludes entry into the industry. Since the monopolist excludes entry, consumers are not getting the "correct" amounts of those goods that are produced by monopolized industries. Monopoly restricts output. This is the classical argument against monopoly.

The monopolistic output and price, then, represent monopoly misallocation, with monopoly having the same cost conditions as the aggregate of the competitive firms. You should note that the misallocation of monopoly might even be worse if, in buying up the individual firms, the monopoly introduced diseconomies of organization. This would be represented by an upward shifting of the cost curves in Figure 9-3.

We can learn more about this misallocation of resources by examining Figure 9-4. The monopoly is in equilibrium producing OQ_1 at a price of OP_1. Monopoly profits are represented by rectangle CP_1AB. Let's examine closely what is going on at this equilibrium. First, price OP_1 is not equal to AC (average cost), which is OC per unit; that is, $P > AC$.

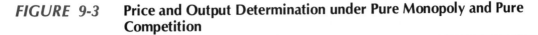

FIGURE 9-3   **Price and Output Determination under Pure Monopoly and Pure Competition**

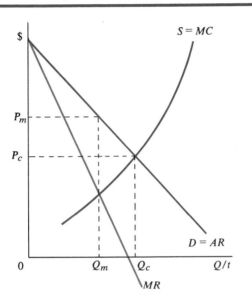

The monopolist, equating marginal cost and marginal revenue, produces output OQ_m at price OP_m. If this same industry were competitive, the price would be OP_c and output would be OQ_c.

This means that economic profits are being earned. Second, $P > MC$, which means the value consumers place on the item (P_1) exceeds the opportunity cost of producing more units (MC). This means, from a welfare point of view, that more should be produced, but the monopolist prohibits that from happening by restricting entry. Third, average cost at output OQ_1 is not equal to marginal cost at OQ_1, as $AC > MC$. This means that OQ_1 is not being produced at the least-cost combination of factors. That could happen only at output OQ_2. The monopolist is not forced to be fully efficient, although the firm does produce its actual output for the lowest cost possible. You can easily see, then, what we mean by saying that monopoly misallocates resources.

THE MONOPOLIST'S SUPPLY CURVE?

A monopoly firm does not have a supply curve in the same sense that a purely competitive firm's marginal cost curve can be viewed as its supply curve. A supply curve shows how much output will be supplied at any price, but a monopolist sets the price, so it doesn't make sense to ask how much will be supplied at various prices. For a monopoly, the profit-maximizing output where MC is equal to MR will depend on how the demand curve shifts. Consider Figure 9-5. When demand is D_1, the

FIGURE 9-4   **Monopoly Misallocation of Resources**

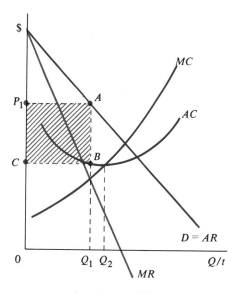

A monopoly misallocates resources because price is greater than marginal cost. This means the value consumers place on the item exceeds the opportunity cost of producing more units.

monopolist produces OQ_1 at price OP_1. If demand increases and becomes more elastic, shifting to D_2, output increases to OQ_2 and price falls to OP_2. In this case, a supply curve could be formed by joining points A and B. But there is no way we can predict, without knowing the exact nature of the shift in demand, what the monopolist will do. In this sense, then, the monopolist has no supply curve. The predictive powers of the economist are therefore considerably more limited in an analysis of monopoly. We can no longer say, *ceteris paribus*, an increase in demand will cause price to rise. In Figure 9-5, the increase in demand caused price to fall.

MONOPOLY, PROFITS, AND PRICE

Monopoly is not a license to make profits. If the U.S. government granted you an absolute monopoly in the sale and manufacture of Conestoga wagons, or if the Israeli government granted you the sole right to sell bacon in Tel Aviv, or if the Mormon church made you the coffee monopolist in Salt Lake City, or if you had a monopoly in the sale and manufacture of Edsels, you might lose money. High costs and/or insufficient demand for the product of a monopolist may cause the monopolist to lose money. The plight of the Penn Central Railroad is perhaps the

FIGURE 9-5   A Monopolist's Lack of a Supply Curve

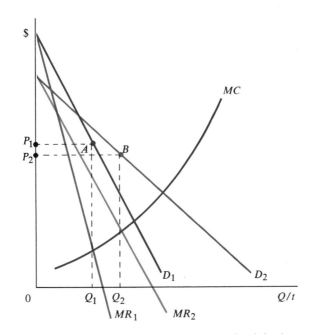

When the demand curve facing the monopolist shifts, the
profit-maximizing position will shift, so we can't predict output or price
unless we know the exact nature of the shift in demand. In this sense, the
monopolist has no supply curve.

best recent case in point. Still, there is a common misconception among
students and the public that a monopoly situation guarantees profits.

Figure 9-6 graphs a monopoly suffering a loss. The monopoly is producing OQ_1 and charging the profit-maximizing price of OP_1. Average
costs of producing OQ_1 are OC per unit. As a result, the monopolist is
incurring losses equal to rectangle P_1CAB. Since the demand curve is
below the average cost curve, there is no way of avoiding losses. The
next question of course is, Will the monopolist continue to produce? If
price is above AVC, as is the case in Figure 9-6, the monopolist will be
better off in the short run to continue rather than stop production. In the
long run, if demand does not increase, the monopoly will go out of business. This is because the presence of losses indicates that the factors are
not earning their opportunity cost. The factors will move or be moved to
more productive uses.

Consider the case of the Penn Central Railroad. It clearly had monopoly power because it had sole authority (granted by the government)
to provide rail transportation between different east coast cities. However, costs rose (as the price of capital and labor increased); at the same

FIGURE 9-6   **A Monopoly Suffering Losses**

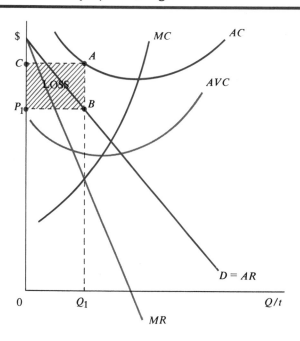

The monopolist might suffer losses in the short run. If average cost
exceeds average revenue, the monopolist is suffering a loss.

time demand declined because of competing modes of transportation.
Eventually, losses were incurred. The market was signaling that the factors of production were more valuable elsewhere. In this case, what happened? The government granted subsidies to make up the losses. This
raises an interesting question: Should government subsidize (certain)
monopolies that are incurring losses? If so, how do you decide which to
subsidize? Should we subsidize the steel companies by helping them
keep out less expensive foreign steel? The government recently granted a
direct subsidy to Penn Central, but refused to give a direct subsidy to
Lockheed.

Just as monopolists can suffer losses, it is also possible that a monopoly might only earn normal profits. Figure 9-7 illustrates. The monopoly
is producing OQ_1 and charges OP_1. TR is equal to TC, rectangle
OP_1AQ_1. In this instance, the monopoly is earning its opportunity cost
and there will be no incentive for other firms to enter this industry or for
this firm to leave the industry. $P = AC$, which means that producers are
not earning economic profits. It still is the case, however, that $P > MC$,
indicating that more units should be produced.

So we see, then, monopolies don't have a license to make profits. In
fact, they can often incur losses and go out of business. Also, monopolists do not charge the highest price possible. Remember the mineral

FIGURE 9-7   A Monopoly Earning Normal Profits

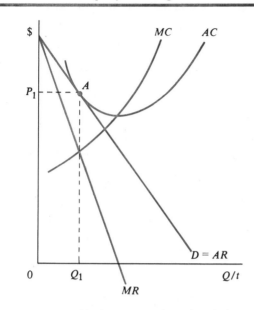

It is possible that a monopoly might only earn normal profits. In this instance, there is no incentive for other firms to enter the industry, and there is no need for barriers to entry.

spring example? Monopolists charge the *profit-maximizing* price, and this price will depend on the demand conditions (and costs, of course) in that industry.

MONOPOLY IN THE LONG RUN

The monopolist, unlike the purely competitive firm, can continue to earn economic profits in the long run. As long as the entry barriers remain, economic profits can be maintained. Long-run maintenance of entry barriers is very difficult, however, because the economic profits will bring about new firms and processes to compete for any economic profits that exist. In principle, then, even with government help the power of any single monopoly is likely to decline in the very long run. In the railroad example, entrepreneurs will be attracted by the profits existing in transportation and trucks, buses, private cars, barges, and planes (if they are permitted to compete) will decrease the demand curve for rail transportation.

PRICE DISCRIMINATION

In analyzing monopoly behavior, we have assumed that the monopolist charges the same price to all consumers and the same price for all units sold to a particular consumer. If, on the other hand, the monopolist is able to charge different consumers different prices, or a particular consumer different prices depending on the quantity purchased, we say the monopolist is able to practice *price discrimination*. First we will examine a monopolist practicing price discrimination with one consumer, and then we will examine the case where price discrimination means different prices for different consumers.

Consider the demand curve for a single consumer or group of homogeneous consumers in Figure 9-8. At price OP_1, the individual will consume OQ_1 units of the good. You will remember from our discussion of utility-maximizing behavior in Chapter 5 that the marginal utility of the last unit purchased is equal to the price of the unit. That means that the marginal utility of each previous unit purchased was greater than price OP_1. The consumer would have been willing to pay higher prices for these previous units, so at the market price of OP_1, the consumer receives a bonus in terms of utility. The total purchase is worth more to the consumer than the total amount (price times quantity) that is paid. This extra utility gained is called *consumer surplus* and is represented by the shaded area in Figure 9-8.

A monopoly producer might be able to deal separately with the consumer for each unit purchased. In terms of Figure 9-9, the monopolist

FIGURE 9-8   Consumer Surplus

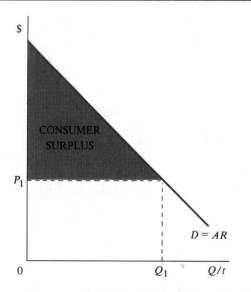

Consumer surplus is the difference between the total utility received from the purchase of a product and the total revenue generated by the product. It exists because the marginal utility of each previous unit purchased was greater than price OP_1.

could say, "You may buy OQ_1 units for OP_1, $OQ_2 - OQ_1$ units for OP_2, $OQ_3 - OQ_2$ units for OP_3, and $OQ_4 - OQ_3$ units for OP_4." By doing this, the monopolist has extracted most of the consumer surplus and converted it into revenue for the firm. Compare the shaded area in Figure 9-9 to the shaded area in Figure 9-8. Both represent consumer surplus. In Figure 9-9, by charging different prices for different amounts of consumption, the monopolist has expropriated much of the consumer surplus. It is theoretically possible for the monopolist to get all of this consumer surplus by perfectly discriminating in differential prices for each unit.

FIGURE 9-9   A Discriminating Monopolist

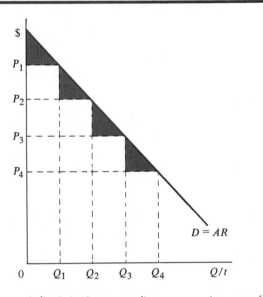

A discriminating monopolist can expropriate most of the consumer surplus by charging different prices for different amounts of consumption.

A second type of price discrimination which isn't as advantageous to the monopoly but which is more feasible occurs when a monopolist can separate markets and charge different prices to different consumers or groups of consumers. If the monopoly can separate the markets and prevent resale, it can price discriminate by adjusting for the different demand elasticities in the two markets. The monopolist does this by equating marginal revenue to total marginal cost in each submarket. If marginal revenue is not equal to marginal cost in each submarket, a switching of sales between markets would increase total revenue.

Price Discrimination in Practice

In practice, we very seldom see the first type of price discrimination. It requires the seller to have the power to separate sales on a unit-by-unit basis. We do see some crude approximations, such as "artichokes 40¢, two for 65¢," but this is hardly very close to Figure 9-9. The second type of price discrimination is more common. It only requires that the seller be able to separate markets according to the elasticity of demand in these different markets. Examples of such price discrimination abound. Bookstores offer lower prices to professors than to students; airlines charge lower fares for students than for nonstudents; university athletic departments offer lower priced tickets to students and faculty than to "townies"; medical doctors charge different patients different fees for the same service (less to poor students than professors, but more to rich students). Consider plane fares. If you fly to Europe and can stay for 14–21 days, the fare is cheaper than if you stay for less than 14 days. If you stay for 21–48 days, flights are even cheaper. Why? Which class of consumers of air transportation have the most inelastic demand? Business people, of course, who tend to travel on tight schedules and have bosses who don't want them playing in France for 14 days!

It should be clear, even from your personal experience, that if you are going to practice price discrimination, two conditions are necessary. First, you must be able to separate consumers into groups that have different demand elasticities. These groups need to be economically identifiable (if it costs too much to identify the groups, discrimination might not pay) and must have different demand elasticities. So when we, as economists, talk about price discrimination, we're not talking about creed, color, or sex, unless certain creeds, colors, or sexes tend to have different demand elasticities for certain products. In our example of air fares, you can separate the classes of consumers by length of stay. Business people seldom travel to a destination for more than a few days; rarely do they travel for more than 14 days.

The second major requirement for price discrimination is that the monopolist *must* prevent the resale of goods or the movement of customers between markets. Consider the case of charging different prices to different classes of consumers for a football game. It only works if you prohibit the lower priced customers from reselling. If you don't, you are no longer a monopolist in the sale to the higher priced market. Is it any wonder that the athletic department requires you to show your picture I.D. card *and* your ticket at the gate? The higher priced ticket holders are only required to present their tickets. You might have guessed that price discrimination works well where resale is very difficult. Did you ever try to resell a flu shot or an appendectomy? Medical doctors are very successful in practicing price discrimination because they have easily recognizable submarkets with different elasticities (by income category) *and* because resale is almost always ruled out. Little wonder that Dr. David Reuben, the doctor who told you all you ever wanted to know about sex-ual problems, when asked to explain his pricing policy, replied, "I have an infinitely sliding scale. Everyone should pay, but nobody can pay more than he can afford. So I charge some patients five dollars an hour and others one hundred."[3]

Is Price Discrimination Bad?

Price discrimination does have a positive side effect in that it will usually cause output under monopoly to increase. We saw earlier in this chapter that monopoly is undesirable because it restricts output. If a monopoly can, however, sell output one unit at a time, output will be pushed to the point where $P = MC$. This is just common sense, because the single monopolist restricts output in order to keep price from falling. If price will only fall on the increments in output (not other units), production will be pushed to the point where $P = MC$. This is the same solution as obtains in pure competition. The difference, of course, is that the profits accrue to the monopolist. Price discrimination turns consumer surplus into monopoly profits. This means monopolists are wealthier and consumers are worse off. It is important to note that this is a transfer of wealth and doesn't change any of the other good or bad effects of the monopolist.

On another level, many people believe price discrimination is unfair or immoral because it means different people pay different amounts for the very same product. Why should an airplane ticket be cheaper because someone is a tourist rather than a business traveler? Why should professors get their books and pens for lower prices than students? Why should students pay less for a football ticket than nonstudents?

Interestingly, it is sometimes the group that benefits from price discrimination that complains. Price discrimination is common in international trade because the separation of national markets is often easy to maintain. Tariffs and transportation costs can help prevent resale. When firms in a country sell in a foreign market at a lower price than they do at home, they are engaging in price discrimination. Demand in the foreign country is more elastic than domestic demand, so the foreign monopolist sells to foreigners at a lower price than at home. The U.S. Treasury calls this practice *dumping*. Dumping occurs, for example, when the Japanese sell televisions in the United States at a lower price than they sell the same sets at home. The odd thing is that dumping has an unfavorable connotation. When the Japanese dump televisions in the United States, the U.S. government takes action against Japan. This is curious because Japanese firms are giving U.S. consumers a better deal than Japanese consumers. Complaining about the lower price is a little like writing to the school paper to say that you don't like the fact that you can get tickets

---

[3]Reported in the *Chicago Sun-Times*, June 23, 1974, and cited in James V. Koch, *Microeconomic Theory and Applications* (Boston: Little, Brown and Co., 1976), p. 233.

to the big game for one-third the price that the "townies" pay. Seen from another angle, however, dumping is an objectionable practice: You can understand that domestic manufacturers of TV sets don't particularly approve of the lower priced products offered by foreign competitors.[4]

SOME OTHER "COSTS" OF MONOPOLY

There are some other costs associated with monopoly that are often ignored. These are the inconveniences and rudeness often associated with monopolies, particularly the regulated monopolies. Consider the telephone company. Students at some colleges are required to place a $100 deposit plus wait three weeks at the beginning of the year before telephone service is begun. Can you imagine such treatment from a firm where there are close substitutes? The reason the telephone company is able to get away with this is that most of us don't consider the mails, or cans connected with waxed string, a good substitute for telephone service.

WHO RUNS THE FIRM? ALTERNATIVES TO PROFIT MAXIMIZATION

We have consistently assumed in this chapter and in Chapter 8 that firms are profit maximizers. This assumption allowed us to predict how the firm would adjust in the two distinct market structures of pure competition and pure monopoly.

The profit-maximizing assumption might have seemed reasonable for firms such as wheat farms when we were concerned with competitive firms, but what happens when we move into the realm of monopoly power and giant firms run by professional managers? We saw in Chapter 7 that corporations account for about 85 percent of the annual business sales in the United States. Yet corporations are run by hired managers, not owners. Managers might operate by some principle other than profit maximization. This proposition is sometimes referred to as the *hypothesis of the separation of ownership and control* and simply means that managers who control corporations may behave differently than would owner-managers. This different behavior would result only if the managers have different goals *and* owners can't control managers.

The hypothesis that behavior deviates from the profit-maximization assumption of economic theory is based on organizational theory which

---

[4]There may be some other reasons for objecting to dumping. The government may fear that the Japanese are selling below cost to drive U.S. firms out of business in an attempt to corner the market on televisions. Or the Treasury may fear Japan is transmitting macroeconomic disturbances to the U.S. by weakening the U.S. television industry. But the bottom line is that we are objecting to someone selling us goods too cheaply.

you have probably studied if you have taken a course in social psychology or management. The hypothesis assumes that management will follow standard procedures even if these procedures result in lower profits. Managers of big business are seen as bureaucrats who react conservatively to avoid mistakes and to cover their liability, much as managers in the military, the federal bureaucracy, or any large organization do. Those who argue that a firm does not maximize profits offer several competing hypotheses to the standard profit-maximization hypothesis. Let's look briefly at some of these hypotheses.

The *satisficing hypothesis* argues that the management of a firm does not seek maximum profits but rather certain target levels of output and profits that are satisfactory to the ownership interests. Unfortunately, in order to perform empirical tests of this hypothesis to determine its validity, it would be necessary to specify what a firm's target happens to be; otherwise any result that is found would be consistent with satisficing behavior. The proponents of the satisficing hypothesis have not as yet accomplished this specification. As a result, the predictive value of the hypothesis is very low.

Another alternative hypothesis has been suggested by Professor William Baumol of Princeton University. Baumol argues that given some numerical level of profits, the managers' primary goal is to increase the *sales* of the firm. In essence, Baumol is saying that managers are rewarded by stockholders, according to the relative size of their firm in the market, for any increase in their percentage share of the market, say from 15 to 20 percent. This is called the *constrained sales maximization hypothesis*. The implication of this hypothesis is that monopoly might not be as bad as we concluded earlier. If sales rather than profits are the primary goal of a monopoly, the firm will lower prices and increase output. The lower prices and increased output will insure that the misallocation of resources will not be as bad as we had predicted with profit maximization.

A rejoinder to these competing hypotheses is the *long-run profit maximization hypothesis*. Following this hypothesis, if the firm maximizes sales, it is doing so because this will lead to higher profits in the long run. Likewise, if the firm is concerned with social responsibility and philanthropic or altruistic projects, the long-run profits of the firm may be maximized by consolidating its goodwill. The problem with this hypothesis is that unless we specify a distinct time period, almost any behavior would be consistent with long-run profit maximization. The theory then becomes a cataloging exercise rather than a theory; there is no way to refute such a theory because it is consistent with everything and therefore can predict or explain nothing.

If monopoly firms substitute other goals for profit maximization, one goal that might be substituted is religious or racial discrimination. In other words, they may sacrifice some profits in order to sell to or hire the type of people with whom they identify. A very interesting test of this

Herbert Simon

Photograph courtesy of the Public Relations Department of Carnegie-Mellon University

Herbert Simon (1916–   )

Herbert Simon was born in Milwaukee, Wisconsin, and educated at the University of Chicago. Professor Simon has held teaching positions at the University of California, the Illinois Institute of Technology, and the University of Pittsburgh. He is presently at Carnegie-Mellon University.

Simon has never held a teaching post as an economist. Instead, he has held professorships in political science, administration, psychology, and information sciences. He is thus an economist in the broadest sense of the word, like the early classical economists.

In awarding the 1978 Nobel Prize in Economics to Simon, the Royal Swedish Academy paid particular attention to his work, which we discuss in this chapter, concerning the development of alternatives to profit maximization. The committee made the following statement in its official announcement:

> In his epoch-making book *Administrative Behavior* (1947), and in a number of subsequent works, he described the company as an adaptive system of physical, personal and social components that are held together by a network of intercommunications and by the willingness of its members to cooperate and to strive towards a common goal. What is new in Simon's ideas is, most of all, that he rejects the assumption made in classic theory of the firm of an omnisciently, rational, profit-maximizing entrepreneur.[1]

Professor Simon has had an important impact on more academic disciplines than any of the other Nobel prizewinners in economics. His work in management science and public administration is credited with bringing scientific approaches to the "art" of management. Professor Simon is perhaps the best example of the economic theorist who has made a major impact on business and public administration.

---

[1]"The Nobel Memorial Prize in Economics," *The Scandinavian Journal of Economics*, Vol. 81, No. 1 (1979), pp. 72–73.

hypothesis was conducted several years ago by Professor Armen Alchian of UCLA and the late Professor Rubin Kessel of the University of Chicago. They examined the employment of Jewish and non-Jewish graduates of the Harvard Business School according to the market structures in which they were employed. In the years examined, 36 percent of the graduates were Jewish. Comparing the employment of these Harvard MBAs in monopolized and relatively competitive industries, they discovered that the monopolized category was 18 percent Jewish and the competitive category was 41 percent Jewish.[5] This evidence is consistent with the hypothesis that monopoly power makes discrimination against minorities easier (less costly) and points to yet another cost of monopoly power.

Before we go too far afield developing a list of behavioral hypotheses about firm behavior, we need to think back to our discussion of what theory is and what it does. Theory abstracts from the real world by concentrating on the important aspects or effects of a phenomenon. If profit maximization is a reasonably valid assumption about firm behavior, it will yield reasonably accurate predictions about firm behavior. The profit-maximization assumption is a cornerstone of many hypotheses that have been empirically tested and found to be valid. Alternative assumptions have yet to be as rigorously tested.

EXAMPLES OF MONOPOLY

We have pointed out that there are no examples of pure monopoly in the real world. Our theoretical definition prohibits this. There are, however, firms with monopoly power, and we can use the monopoly model to explain the behavior of and to predict economic outcomes for these firms. Public utilities, for example, are considered natural monopolies (and are regulated as a result). State trading monopolies, that are set up by some nations to engage in international trade, are also monopolistic. They have been demonstrated to practice price discrimination by selling to different countries at different prices. *Local monopolies* are another form of real-world monopoly. If you grew up in a small, remote town, there may have been only one movie theater or perhaps only one grocery store. A firm in such a situation is a local monopoly because the close substitutes are costly in that you must travel to reach them. In all of these real-world examples of monopoly, we can use the model of pure monopoly to examine the effects of monopoly power.

Summary

Pure monopoly is the market situation in which there is a single seller of a product with no close substitutes. The monopoly firm faces a negatively

---

[5]A. A. Alchian and R. A. Kessel, "Competition, Monopoly, and the Pursuit of Money," in H. G. Lewis, *et al.*, *Aspects of Labor Economics* (Princeton, N. J.: Princeton University Press, 1962).

sloped demand curve and a marginal revenue curve that lies below that demand curve. The monopolist maximizes profits by producing the output at which $MC = MR$ and sets the price at which exactly that output can be sold. Since price is often greater than average cost in the monopoly case, economic profits often exist.

The monopolist is sometimes able to erect barriers to entry which allow profits to exist in the long run. These barriers are very difficult to maintain and, as a result, monopolists often appeal to the government for help in maintaining entry barriers.

Monopolies produce a lower output at a higher price than do competitive firms. At equilibrium, the monopoly firm is producing at a level of output where $P \neq AC \neq MC$. Monopoly power is not, however, a guarantee of profits. Some monopolies go out of business because of persistent losses and others make only normal profits.

A monopoly can increase its revenues if it practices price discrimination. For price discrimination to be successful, the monopolist must have customers with different demand elasticities and they must be separated and prohibited from reselling the product.

The satisficing hypothesis and the sales maximization hypothesis are both derived from the idea of the separation of ownership and control. They argue that hired managers, as opposed to owner-managers, attempt to maximize sales or meet *satisfactory* profit targets rather than maximize profits.

Although no examples of *pure* monopoly exist, the model of pure monopoly is useful in analyzing monopoly power.

New Terms

monopoly
monopoly power
price searcher
barriers to entry
natural monopoly
tariffs
quotas
price discrimination

consumer surplus
dumping
separation of ownership and control
satisficing
constrained sales maximization
long-run profit maximization
local monopoly

Questions for Discussion

1 Explain in your own words why marginal revenue is less than average revenue under conditions of monopoly.

2 Should business firms be socially responsible? Respond to the argument that they should maximize profits and leave social responsibility to elected and appointed officials.

3 List as many barriers to entry as you can. Which are the most effective?

4 Why will a monopolist never attempt to produce in the inelastic portion of the demand curve?

5 Suppose you are hired as an economic adviser to a monopoly drug company. Can you think of ways in which it can increase its monopoly profit?

6 Should government subsidize monopolies that are losing money in order to keep them in business?

Suggestions for Further Reading

Baumol, William J. *Business Behavior, Value and Growth*, rev. ed. New York: Harcourt, Brace & World, 1967.

Mansfield, Edwin (ed.). *Monopoly Power and Economic Performance*, rev. ed. New York: W. W. Norton & Co., 1968.

Mason, Edward S. "Corporation," *International Encyclopedia of the Social Sciences*, edited by David L. Sills, Vol. 3. New York: Macmillan Publishing Co., 1968.

Sherman, Roger. *The Economics of Industry*. Boston: Little, Brown and Co., 1973, Chapter 9.

CHAPTER 10

THE ECONOMICS OF MONOPOLISTIC COMPETITION

LEARNING OBJECTIVES

After studying the materials found in this chapter, you should be able to do the following:

1 Define monopolistic competition.

2 List the characteristics of the model of monopolistic competition.

3 List the parts of the market structures continuum.

4 Diagram a representative firm in monopolistic competition making
   (a) an economic profit,
   (b) a loss,
   (c) an economic profit of zero.

5 Diagram the long-run equilibrium in monopolistic competition compared to such an equilibrium in pure competition.

6 Define
   (a) excess capacity,
   (b) product differentiation.

7 Define the relationships between
   (a) excess capacity and product differentiation,
   (b) product differentiation and elasticity of demand.

In the last two chapters we have developed the two polar ends of a theoretical spectrum of market structures. At one extreme we have pure monopoly and at the other we have pure competition. Figure 10-1 illustrates these polar cases. There are no perfect, theoretically correct real-world examples of either polar case, but for many years all real-world industry structures were analyzed by appealing to these two polar cases. In the 1930s all this changed and theories were developed that filled in the continuum in Figure 10-1. We call the space between these two poles *imperfect competition*. We can further divide imperfect competition into *monopolistic competition*, which we will analyze in this chapter, and *oligopoly*, which we leave to the next chapter.

The development of monopolistic competition is usually associated with Edward Chamberlin and Joan Robinson. Chamberlin, who died in 1967, was a Harvard professor and published a book in 1933 entitled *The Theory of Monopolistic Competition*. Joan Robinson published *The Economics of Imperfect Competition*, also in 1933. Robinson was only 30 years old when this classic was published and she is still a professor at Cambridge University in England. These two books presented the basics of monopolistic competition.

FIGURE 10-1   Market Structures Continuum

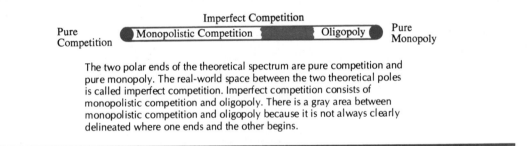

The two polar ends of the theoretical spectrum are pure competition and pure monopoly. The real-world space between the two theoretical poles is called imperfect competition. Imperfect competition consists of monopolistic competition and oligopoly. There is a gray area between monopolistic competition and oligopoly because it is not always clearly delineated where one ends and the other begins.

CHARACTERISTICS OF MONOPOLISTIC COMPETITION

In developing the model of monopolistic competition, we assume that the industry is composed of a large number of sellers. Each of these sellers produces a product that is *differentiated*, which means that the products of these firms have either real or imagined identifiable characteristics that are different from each other. All that this means is that there is a difference in the product of one firm when compared to others. This differentiation can take many forms. It might be that the salespeople are nicer, that the packaging is prettier, that the credit terms are better, or that the service is faster. It could even be that a famous person is associated with the product, such as Joe Namath promoting a popcorn popper that he uses or the panty hose that he wears, or Joe DiMaggio endorsing

Joan Robinson and Edward Chamberlin

Photograph by Ramsay & Muspratt, Cambridge

Joan Robinson (1903–   )

Victor Jorgensen-Scope for Fortune Magazine

Edward Chamberlin (1899–1967)

Joan Robinson and **Edward Chamberlin** are given joint credit for developing the theory of monopolistic competition. Chamberlin published his *Theory of Monopolistic Competition* (1933) six months before Robinson published *The Economics of Imperfect Competition* (1933). Chamberlin in later years was preoccupied with trying to differentiate his ideas from Robinson's. Robinson is reported to have commented on Chamberlin's anguish over her receiving joint credit by saying at one point, "I'm sorry I ruined his life."

Chamberlin was born in the state of Washington, but attended high school in Iowa, where he was an all-around student and a successful athlete. He later attended the University of Iowa, where he met Frank Knight (see the biography on page 183). He then went to the University of Michigan to study and ultimately received his Ph.D. at Harvard. He taught at Harvard until his death.

Joan Robinson developed her ideas quite independently of Chamberlin (they did not know of each other) while a junior faculty member at Cambridge University. After the appearance of her path-breaking book, Robinson expanded her interests and research over a wide range of economic policy issues. Still a very active economist and social critic, Robinson is an outspoken foe of the market system. Her more recent antimarket publications include *An Essay on Marxian Economics* (1956), *Economic Philosophy* (1962), and *Freedom and Necessity* (1970).

Both Professor Robinson and Professor Chamberlin have had a significant impact on economics, but their careers were strikingly different. Chamberlin's career was characterized by a single pursuit: the development of the theory of monopolistic competition. Few great economists have applied themselves to so singular a purpose and yet achieved fame. Perhaps this singleness of purpose in part explains Chamberlin's pain at having to share his fame with Robinson. Unlike Chamberlin, Robinson's interests have been wide ranging. After contributing to micro theory, she worked with Keynes and helped to develop macroeconomics. Subsequently, she became a fiery social critic with varied interests. It is likely that she views her work on monopolistic competition as important but in no way the dominant part of her contribution to economic analysis.

a coffee pot. It is important to note that a product is differentiated if consumers view it as different. Chemists tell us that aspirin is aspirin, that there is no difference between the brands. Yet if consumers view the brands as different, we have product differentiation.

In monopolistic competition, we have an industry characterized by a large number of firms, each producing a differentiated product. A third and very important assumption we make is that entry into this industry is relatively easy. New firms can enter the industry and start producing products that are similar to those already being produced. In his original description of monopolistic competition, Chamberlin called the market for a good that was differentiated but had a large number of close substitutes a **product group**. Chamberlin characterized monopolistic competition as the large group case where there was rivalry between many firms in a product class.

You will probably recognize monopolistic competition as the market structure of most firms that you are familiar with since retail firms often fit this description. Monopolistic competition is generally what most people think of when they think of competition. Pure competition, with its required product homogeneity, simply does not fit commercial reality, where people are madly trying to make their products different.

SHORT-RUN ADJUSTMENT

Analysis of the short-run position of the monopolistically competitive firm is remarkably similar to the analysis of the purely competitive firm. In Figure 10-2 we have a firm's demand curve. We start the analysis by depicting a representative firm rather than depicting the market and then deriving the demand curve faced by a representative firm as we did with pure competition. This is necessary because, with product differentiation, each firm faces its own separate demand curve. The firm's demand curve in Figure 10-2 is negatively sloped, unlike the perfectly elastic demand curve of the purely competitive firm. This slope is caused by the differentiated nature of the product the firm is producing. If the product's price is raised, the firm will not lose all of its customers because some will prefer this product to those of competing firms. Likewise, if price is lowered, the firm will gain customers, but some customers will be loyal to the products produced by other firms. It's easy to see that the elasticity of the demand curve is a measure of the degree of differentiation within the industry. If the goods are only slightly differentiated, they are then close substitutes and each firm's demand curve will be very elastic. If the differentiation is significant, the curve will be relatively inelastic, indicating that the firm could more easily raise price without losing many customers. Its customers are more loyal. Think of the aspirin example. If some people are willing to pay more for Bayer than for Brand X aspirin because they think it is different, the makers of Bayer will be able to raise

FIGURE 10-2   **Short-Run Profits in Monopolistic Competition**

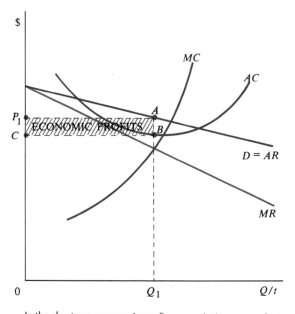

In the short run, economic profits can exist in monopolistic competition.
These profits will cause new firms to enter the industry.

price without losing a large number of customers. The more people are
convinced that the products are different, the greater the degree of price
autonomy. Thus, the Bayer people will be limited in their price autonomy by the amount of differentiation they are able to create. At some
price, too few people will be willing to pay for the differentiation. In
other words, some people may be willing to pay 10¢ more for Bayer, but
as price is raised higher, more and more people will shift to other brands.

Figure 10-2 has a negative slope, indicating product differentiation,
but the curve is very elastic, indicating that there are many good substitutes. Since the curve is negatively sloped, the marginal revenue curve
will lie below the demand (average revenue) curve for the same reasons it
did in the case of pure monopoly. The firm will, of course, maximize
profits at price OP_1 and output OQ_1, where marginal revenue is equal to
marginal cost. The representative firm in Figure 10-2 is earning economic profits because average revenue, OP_1, exceeds average cost, OC.
Total revenue is represented by rectangle OP_1AQ_1 and total cost is represented by rectangle $OCBQ_1$. Total profits are thus shown by the shaded
rectangle CP_1AB.

LONG-RUN ADJUSTMENT

What about long-run equilibrium in monopolistically competitive industries? In Figure 10-2, we saw a short-run equilibrium with economic profits. This signals profit-seeking entrepreneurs to enter this industry. Since we assumed that entry into monopolistically competitive industries is relatively easy, new firms will enter the industry. As firms enter the industry, the demand curve that any single representative firm faces will shift to the left because the new firms will be attracting customers away from firms already in the industry. This is what happens in an area when a new retail grocery store opens. It draws customers away from the existing firms. The demand curve will continue to shift to the left as new firms enter, and new firms will enter as long as economic profits are to be made. Long-run equilibrium thus must occur at the zero economic profit (or normal profit) number of firms. Such an equilibrium is depicted in Figure 10-3. Price is OP_1 and output is OQ_1. Total revenue and total cost are represented by rectangle OP_1AQ_1. There are no economic profits being earned and no additional new firms will attempt to enter this industry.

FIGURE 10-3   Long-Run Equilibrium in Monopolistic Competition

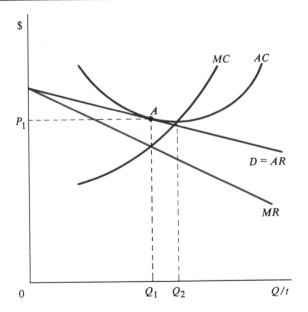

Since entry into monopolistically competitive industries is relatively easy, there can be no long-run profits. Firms will enter until the existing firms are earning only normal profits.

Of course, too many firms might enter the industry in the mistaken anticipation of economic profits. If this happened, losses would be realized and firms would leave the industry as the long-run adjustment proceeded. In Figure 10-4, a monopolistically competitive firm making losses of P_1CBA is shown. Firms would respond by leaving the industry, which would cause the demand curves faced by the remaining firms to increase (shift to the right) until the equilibrium shown in Figure 10-3 is restored. The long-run adjustment process thus produces a situation in which zero economic profits exist.

FIGURE 10-4   Short-Run Losses in Monopolistic Competition

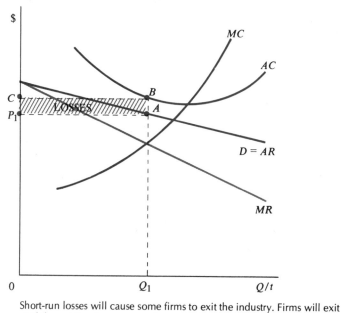

Short-run losses will cause some firms to exit the industry. Firms will exit until the existing firms are earning normal profits, as in Figure 10-3.

EXCESS CAPACITY

The adjustment process we have just examined causes the firm to choose an output which produces an underutilization of existing plant size. This underutilization is called *excess capacity* and is depicted in Figure 10-3. The profit maximization output was seen to be OQ_1, where $MR = MC$. This is not, however, the output that would have resulted under pure competition because under pure competition the firm is producing at the least-cost combination. The least-cost combination is where average cost is at a minimum and is the socially optimal output because it represents maximum attainable efficiency. This efficient output is represented by OQ_2 in Figure 10-3. In other words, in long-run equilibrium, the monopolistically competitive firm produces less than the efficient capacity of the firm. Economists call this excess capacity.

Is this excess capacity a bad thing? To answer this, it is necessary to understand what causes it. The firm is producing less than the socially ideal output because it maximizes profits by producing this lower output. This comes about because the demand curve is downward sloping. We can see this by examining Figure 10-5. Begin with demand curve D_1. The monopolistically competitive firm would produce OQ_1 at price OP_1. Now make the demand curve more elastic by rotating it, as in Figure 10-5. As the demand curve becomes more and more elastic and finally perfectly elastic, like D_2, the output would increase to the socially efficient output OQ_2 and price would fall to OP_2. The excess capacity is thus easily seen to be a result of the negative slope in the demand curve. This negative slope, you recall, is a result of the product differentiation. The excess capacity, therefore, results from product differentiation.

FIGURE 10-5   Excess Capacity

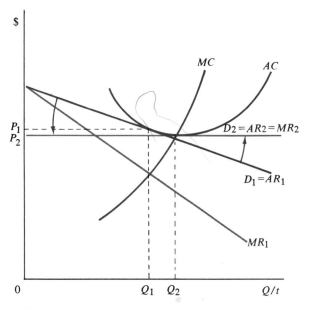

Excess capacity results from the negative slope of the demand curve. As the demand curve becomes more elastic, the excess capacity diminishes and disappears when the curve becomes perfectly elastic. The slope, and therefore the excess capacity, is a result of product differentiation.

It might be argued that this excess capacity is a good thing because consumers willingly accept the extra cost it implies in return for the differentiation that results.[1] It would indeed be a very boring world without product differentiation. We might all be wearing khaki-colored shirts, for example. How should we evaluate this argument? The major problem lies in separating desired from undesired product differentiation. If a consumer is faced with considerable product differentiation, but little price competition, the consumer is not able to choose whether or not to pay extra to get the differentiated product. This doesn't seem to be too important a problem when there are many firms, however, as in monopolistic competition. Consider aspirin again for an example. If the only products in the industry were produced by Bayer, Anacin, Tylenol, and Bufferin, the consumer really would not have a low-price choice, since these firms compete almost exclusively by advertising rather than by lowering prices. But the consumer does have a choice of lower priced aspirin brands. So in choosing Bayer over Brand X, we can say that the consumer voluntarily chooses the product differentiation. In this case, product differentiation seems to be a good thing because the consumer is maximizing individual utility by choosing. If, on the other hand, there are no options for lower priced products and the consumer must choose among those products that compete only through advertising, then the consumer may not have a choice about bearing the cost of the differentiation except, of course, by doing without the good altogether.

PRODUCT DIFFERENTIATION AND ADVERTISING

The firm in monopolistic competition will try to differentiate its product because this shifts its demand curve to the right *and* makes it more inelastic by developing consumer loyalty. This means that it will advertise as well as make changes in color, style, quality, and so on. This advertising can inform consumers of higher quality or it can develop brand loyalty, either of which creates differentiation. Competing with rivals through advertising, style changes, color changes, and the like is referred to as *non-price competition*.

If a firm, by effective use of non-price competition, can successfully differentiate its product so that other firms' products do not seem to compete, the firm can earn economic profits in the long run. Such a firm has in essence turned its share of the monopolistically competitive market into a mini-monopoly.

Consider McDonald's as an example. Fast food preparation is a monopolistically competitive industry. There are large numbers of firms and entry is relatively easy. If a firm is able to so successfully differentiate its product that consumers don't consider the products of other firms as close substitutes, the firm is then able to earn long-run profits because it

---

[1]In fact, Professor Chamberlin argued this himself.

can keep would-be competitors out of its segment of the industry. For example, McDonald's can't keep firms out of the hamburger market, but it can keep firms out of the McDonald's hamburger market — if everyone believes there's nothing like a Big Mac!

It is easy to determine how successful a firm is at this type of differentiation by examining its prices relative to its competitors' prices. You may take your brother or sister to McDonald's if a Big Mac is $.15 more than the competition, but would you if it is $.55 more or $1.15 more? There is some price at which the other products will become good substitutes. That price is a measure of the effectiveness of the product differentiation. It may be that a Big Mac is worth more to you because it has a higher quality or it may be that it is worth more only because McDonald's has a very successful advertising and public relations program. The point is that it doesn't matter what causes the differentiation; the economic impact is that McDonald's can earn an economic profit in the long run.

RESOURCE ALLOCATION IN MONOPOLISTIC COMPETITION

Our theory of monopolistic competition has several implications for the allocation of resources that are different from the social ideal developed in pure competition. First, at the zero economic profit, long-run equilibrium, there will be excess capacity. This means that price will be greater than marginal cost. So, consumers are paying only the average costs of production, but these costs are higher than the most efficient level of production would produce.

Second, if costs are the same under pure competition and monopolistic competition, prices will be higher in monopolistic competition. Third, firms in monopolistic competition will provide a wider variety of styles, colors, qualities, and brands. This, of course, is related to the differentiation and excess capacity which caused average costs to be higher.

Fourth, there will be advertising and other forms of non-price competition. This is not necessarily bad; to the extent that it adds to satisfaction and as long as the product is voluntarily purchased, it can be viewed as a good thing. Some social critics view any advertising that does more than convey information as a bad thing. As economists, we would argue that it is a bad thing only if people don't have options to consume alternative goods.

MONOPOLISTIC COMPETITION: HAVE WE LEARNED ANYTHING NEW?

The theory that we have presented in this chapter has been the focus of much debate by economists. This debate has sometimes been referred to as "Chamberlin vs. the Chicago School."[2] Economists at Chicago, and notably Professor George Stigler, have argued that the theory of monopolistic competition doesn't offer any additional insights or predictions that the model of pure competition hasn't already offered. This goes back to our earlier discussion in Chapter 1 of the role of theory. Stigler would admit that monopolistic competition is more descriptive of the real world than pure competition, but he would contend that this does not make it more useful. Stigler would argue that usefulness as a description of the real world is not important. The crucial question is whether or not the model of monopolistic competition offers different insights or more correct predictions than the model of pure competition. Professor Stigler would argue that it does not offer either.

It would be a mistake to make too much of this controversy. It may be acceptable for academic economists to argue over such matters; after all, academic careers have been based on such arguments. For the purposes of this course, the model of monopolistic competition is useful, and most economists view it as useful. The general usefulness of the model lies in its attempt to fill in and enrich the gap between pure competition and monopoly. The way in which we view non-price competition, the way we analyze advertising, and the way we view the costs of product differentiation owe much to the development of the model of monopolistic competition. So, even if we could get by with only the tool of pure competition, the model of monopolistic competition enriches the analysis.

Summary

The model of monopolistic competition is the market situation characterized by many producers of a heterogeneous product. The model was developed by Edward Chamberlin and Joan Robinson, in part because of dissatisfaction with the unrealistic assumptions of pure competition.

Key assumptions in the model of monopolistic competition are large numbers of producers, product differentiation, and relative ease of entry. This means that economic profits can exist in the short run, but entry of new firms will insure a long-run equilibrium with zero economic profits unless product differentiation is successful. Because of product differentiation, a firm at equilibrium produces less than the socially optimal output. This underproduction is referred to as excess capacity. The "extra" cost caused by this excess capacity is the cost of product differentiation.

Monopolistically competitive firms produce a smaller output at a higher price than firms with the same costs engaged in pure competition. Although it is true that consumers pay only the opportunity costs of production at long-

---

[2]See G. Chris Archibald, "Chamberlin versus Chicago," *Review of Economic Studies* (October, 1961), pp. 1–28.

run equilibrium, these costs are not at their minimum. Marginal cost is not equal to average cost in long-run equilibrium.

Controversy surrounds the model of monopolistic competition regarding its usefulness. Some economists argue that no new insights (different from those of pure competition) can be derived from the model. In general, however, most economists feel that the model adds richness to the theory of the firm.

New Terms

imperfect competition
monopolistic competition
differentiated product

product group
excess capacity
non-price competition

Questions for Discussion

1 Is advertising wasteful?
2 Firms in monopolistic competition only earn normal profits in the long run unless they can successfully convince consumers that their product is really different. List as many examples of product differentiation as you can. Do you think the differences are real, imagined, or created?

Does product differentiation make any economic difference?
3 Do you think the model of monopolistic competition is a useful tool for economic analysis? Why?
4 What is excess capacity? Is it a good or bad thing?

Suggestions for Further Reading

Chamberlin, Edward H. *The Theory of Monopolistic Competition*. Cambridge, Mass.: Harvard University Press, 1933.
Robinson, Joan. *The Economics of Imperfect Competition*. London: Macmillan & Co., 1933.
Stigler, George J. *Five Lectures on Economic Problems*. New York: The Macmillan Co., 1949.

CHAPTER 11

THE ECONOMICS OF OLIGOPOLY

LEARNING OBJECTIVES

After studying the materials found in this chapter, you should be able to do the following:

1 Define
   (a) oligopoly,
   (b) pure oligopoly,
   (c) differentiated oligopoly,
   (d) Class I oligopoly,
   (e) Class II oligopoly,
   (f) Class III oligopoly.

2 List the characteristics of a cartel and what is necessary to assure that a cartel will not break up.

3 Diagram
   (a) price leadership with a dominant firm and competitive fringe firms,
   (b) the kinked demand curve theory of oligopoly.

At approximately the same time that Professors Chamberlin and Robinson were developing the concept of monopolistic competition, the German economist Heinrich von Stackelberg published a book entitled *Market Structure and Equilibrium* (1934), which discussed the idea of interdependence between firms and formed the basis of the model of oligopoly. **Oligopoly**, the other form of imperfect competition, is the market structure in which there are *few firms*. "Oligopoly" comes from the Greek words for "few" and "sellers." The scarcity of sellers is the key to firm behavior in oligopoly. In oligopoly the firms realize that their small number produces mutual interdependence among them. A firm will, as a result, forecast or expect a certain response from its rivals to any price or output decision that it might initiate.

Because of this mutual interdependence, it is very difficult to develop models that predict the output and pricing behavior of oligopolistic firms. What economists have developed is a categorization of different types of oligopoly behavior. This categorization often includes heavy doses of descriptive economics, which stress institutional factors. In this chapter we will present a standard description of the types of oligopoly behavior and present examples of that oligopoly behavior.

TYPES OF PRODUCTS PRODUCED BY OLIGOPOLIES

Oligopolies produce a range of products from homogeneous to differentiated, and oligopolistic industries are sometimes categorized by the type of product they produce. An oligopoly which produces a homogeneous product is referred to as a **pure oligopoly**. The distinction is important because pure oligopolies will be characterized as having a single price for the output of all the firms. An example of a pure oligopoly would be the cement industry. As a consumer, you would be indifferent to which firm produced the sack of cement you purchase.

As opposed to a pure oligopoly, a **differentiated oligopoly** produces goods that are different. The auto industry would be a good example. In differentiated oligopolies we get **price clusters**, which are groupings of prices for similar but not homogeneous products. The price differentials in these clusters will depend on the amount of product differentiation. The more differentiated the products, the greater the price divergence. Tight price clusters indicate very little differentiation.

OLIGOPOLY COLLUSIVENESS

Perhaps the most useful classification tool for analyzing oligopolies is the system of definitions proposed by Professor Fritz Machlup, who is retired from Princeton University and now teaches at New York University.[1] Professor Machlup divides oligopoly behavior into three classes.

---

[1]Fritz Machlup, *The Economics of Sellers' Competition* (Baltimore: Johns Hopkins Press, 1952).

The class breakdown is based on the degree of communication, coordination, and collusion among the new firms. **Communication** refers to the ability of the firms to signal their intentions to each other. **Coordination** refers to the firms' ability to relate their production decisions to the other firms in the industry, and **collusion** refers to agreements between the firms in an industry to set a certain price or to share a market.

It should be obvious that the ability to communicate, coordinate (organize), and collude will depend on the number of firms. As the number of firms increases, the cost of keeping communication open will increase. This point will be stressed as we proceed. In Machlup's scheme, **Class I oligopolies** are characterized by independent action. The firms are both unorganized and uncollusive. **Class II oligopolies** are characterized by perfect joint action. These firms are both organized and collusive. **Class III oligopolies** are those that have imperfect joint action. They are unorganized, but still collusive. We will start by examining Class II, next we will take up Class III oligopolies, and then we will turn to Class I oligopolies.

Class II Oligopolies

Organized, collusive oligopolies are *cartels*. *Cartels* are groups of independent firms which agree not to compete. Perfect cartels are able to behave as a monopoly behaves. In striving for joint profit maximization, it is necessary for the cartel to set prices, outputs, and marketing areas. However, the cartel can't always set these variables so that each individual firm in the cartel is maximizing its own profits. Examine Figure 11-1 to see this more clearly. In Figure 11-1 we have two firms, A and B, in a cartel which produces a homogeneous product. The marginal cost curves of each firm are MC_A and MC_B, respectively. MC_T is the horizontal summation of MC_A and MC_B. The cartel would maximize profits, behaving exactly as a monopoly, by producing OQ_C at price OP_C because $MR = MC_T$ at OP_C and OQ_C. Now the centralized cartel must enforce this solution by requiring firms A and B to produce OQ_A and OQ_B, respectively. The difficulty is that each firm is not at its individual profit-maximizing output. If each firm could view one half of the market as its own, represented by demand curve d in Figure 11-1, the profit-maximizing outputs would be where $MC_A = mr$ and $MC_B = mr$.[2] Firm A would produce OQ_a and firm B would produce OQ_b.

In short, the profit-maximizing goal of the cartel is not necessarily consistent with the profit-maximizing goals of each individual cartel member. In the example in Figure 11-1, firm A would prefer to produce *more* at a *higher* price and firm B would prefer to produce *less* at a *lower* price. The example here points out the most important problem faced by cartels. The problem is that joint cartel profit maximization and individ-

---

[2]Remember that $MR = 1/2D$. (See pages 187–189 and Figure 9-1 in Chapter 9.)

ual firm profit maximization are often in conflict. As a result, a cartel-type organization is very unstable.

FIGURE 11-1 Cartel Profit Maximization

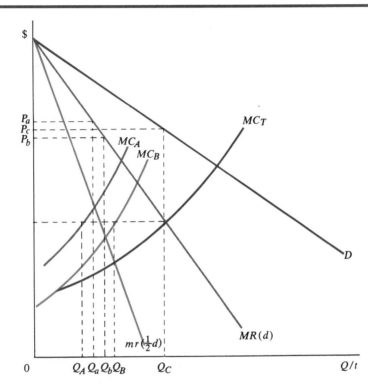

Joint profit maximization by the two firms would occur where $MC_T = MR$. This would establish a price of OP_C and output of OQ_C. The cartel must now force output OQ_A and OQ_B from firms A and B, respectively. The cartel must force this behavior because individual profit maximization, assuming each firm could view one half of the market, represented by demand curve (d), as its own, would establish a price of OP_a and output OQ_a for firm A and a price of OP_b and output OQ_b for firm B. The cartel must force firm A to reduce its production and firm B to expand its production relative to their individual maximizing output.

Perhaps the greatest danger a cartel faces is that members find it in their own self-interest to cheat or to *chisel* on the cartel. If, for example, a cartel agrees on a set price, such as OP_C in the previous example, individual members may attempt to give secret price cuts and capture more of the market. If either firm A or firm B believes the other is untrustworthy, they will have more of an incentive to chisel. As the number of firms increases, it becomes increasingly likely that individual firms will become suspicious of their fellow cartel members.

Some Examples of Cartels. You may be familiar with the case of Icelandic Airlines. International airline companies have a cartel called IATA (International Air Transport Association), pronounced *eye-ata*. Icelandic refused to join IATA and set fares below the cartel price, and this decision greatly increased its share of the market. Before 1978 Icelandic offered the only low-cost air fare to Europe. In retaliation, many countries refused to grant Icelandic landing privileges.

The history of cartels is not impressive because they have usually held together for only short periods of time, primarily because of chiseling. In the few cases where cartels have had some long-term success, we usually find government participation. Once governments are involved, it becomes more difficult to chisel because government can police and penalize this bad behavior. The amount of chiseling, it should be clear, is closely related to the number of firms comprising a cartel. The fewer the firms, the more closely the cartel will be able to monitor behavior to determine if a firm is chiseling.

Other factors can help cartels control the problem of firm chiseling. For example, if the number of buyers is small and if the prices are widely publicized, the cartel members will not worry so much about one of their own members chiseling. Also, if the cartel is successful in acting as a monopoly and earning higher than normal profits, it must create barriers to entry; otherwise, new firms that might potentially compete with the cartel will enter the market. Let's briefly examine a few cartel-type organizations to see what elements affected their success or failure.

Organized, collusive activity in private industry in the United States has usually been invalidated by the courts. However, General Electric and Westinghouse engaged in secret conspiracies in the late 1950s to act as a cartel. They decided on a scheme that allowed them to rotate on submitting low bids on government contracts where the job was awarded to the low bidder. The most famous scheme depended on the phases of the moon. At every phase of the moon (every two weeks), the firm designated to be the low bidder would gain the right to that contract by the other firm's submitting an uncompetitive, high bid. This plan worked well because there were only two firms dealing with one buyer, the federal government. Each firm would know if the other was cheating because the bids would be made public. In this case the government was helping the cartel overcome the chiseling problem.

At the other end of the spectrum of firm numbers is an attempt at cartel formation known as the National Farm Organization (NFO). In 1967 and 1968, the NFO attempted to act as a producer cartel. In two separate actions — one to raise milk prices and the other to raise beef prices — the NFO tried withholding actions. In order to raise prices, cartel members would dump milk and keep cattle away from the market. The farm industry for milk and beef production is composed of large numbers of firms, and the NFO cartel consisted of about 10 percent of these firms. If the NFO members were successful in raising prices, the

nonmembers who continued to produce and sell would be the net beneficiaries and would react by expanding output in response to these higher
prices. Additionally, as prices would begin to rise, there would be tremendous pressure to chisel on the withholding action. In fact, the chiselers would benefit much more than the members who refused to chisel.
The realization of this fact resulted in violence. Cattle scales were blown
up. Withholding farmers sat down in the roads to keep chiselers from
taking their products to market. Some chiselers even resorted to taking
cows to market in house trailers to avoid detection. The lesson is clear. A
cartel with many members will find it very difficult to be successful.

Cartels are much more common in Europe than they are in the
United States. In Europe cartels are permitted and often encouraged by
governments. In Nazi Germany all the major industries operated as cartels, and in present-day Western Europe the Common Market Commission is actively promoting cartels in steel, textiles, and shipbuilding.

As we shall see in Chapter 12, cartels are, with one exception, illegal
in the United States. The one exception, based upon the Webb-
Pomerene Act of 1918, is the formation of cartels for the purpose of
foreign trade. These Webb-Pomerene cartels have not been successful in
raising prices, primarily because of the large number of firms in the par-
ticipating industries.[3]

OPEC — *Unparalleled Success Story*. Without question the most
successful cartel in recent years is the Organization of Petroleum Export-
ing Countries, known as OPEC. In the 1950s international oil companies controlled a major portion of the world's oil supply. These companies, although often attacked for acting as a cartel, frequently engaged in
active price competition. In fact, in an attempt to stop such price competition, the Arab governments, along with a few non-Arab governments,
formed OPEC in 1960. At first OPEC enjoyed little success. But this
changed in 1973, as the Arab-Israeli war heated up and the Arab countries came together. As of January 1, 1973, the price of oil was $2.12 per
barrel. Of this $2.12, $1.52 went to the governments involved. By January
1, 1974, the price was $7.61 with $7.01 going to the governments. By
January, 1975, the price was about $10.50. The most influential member
of the cartel was Saudi Arabia, the major producer.[4]

How did this cartel, which had been in existence since 1960 and
which had few members, come to flex its muscles in 1973? At that time,
importing governments helped by posting prices and dealing with the
OPEC governments in open forums where the individual members could
be less fearful of chiseling. More important, however, Saudi Arabia was

---

[3]For more on these failures, see Ryan C. Amacher, Richard J. Sweeney, and Robert D.
Tollison, "A Note on the Webb-Pomerene Law and the Webb-Cartels," *The Antitrust Bul-
letin* (Summer, 1978).

[4]For more data on these prices, see *International Economic Report of the President*
(Washington: U.S. Government Printing Office, February, 1974), pp. 110–111.

willing to cut back its production of oil to allow other members to sell all they wanted to produce at the high prices set by the cartel.[5]

How stable is OPEC? It is more stable than many observers first believed and more stable than most other cartels. We predicted earlier, however, that successful cartels will meet with two problems. First, there is chiseling. Within OPEC there has been a considerable amount of chiseling, and the real price of oil is now much lower than the 1975 high of $10.50 per barrel. To be sure, the price of oil is significantly higher than it was prior to 1973, but it is much lower than the 1975 price. Chiseling has weakened OPEC's ability to maintain the real price of oil during the rapid inflation of the late 1970s. This chiseling is increasing as increased cutbacks in production are needed to maintain the high price. Table 11-1 shows how substantial some of these cutbacks have been.

TABLE 11-1   **Changing Production of OPEC Member Countries, 1973–1975**

	Average for September, 1973 (Thousands of Bbl. Daily)	Average for September, 1975 (Thousands of Bbl. Daily)	Percent Change
Qatar	608	280	−53.9%
Venezuela	3,387	2,320	−31.5
Kuwait	3,520	2,700	−23.3
Libya	2,286	1,790	−21.7
Algeria	1,100	900	−18.2
Nigeria	2,100	1,920	− 8.6
Saudi Arabia	8,574	8,410	− 1.9
Ecuador	210	190	− 1.0
Indonesia	1,402	1,390	− 0.9
Iran	5,793	6,100	+ 5.3
United Arab Emirates	1,654	1,870	+13.1
Iraq	2,167	2,500	+15.4
Gabon	155	200	+29.0

Source: *Business Week* (January 26, 1976), p. 91.

The second problem a successful cartel faces is new entry. Large amounts of new oil are coming on stream from Mexico, the North Sea, and elsewhere. In addition, other sources of energy, such as solar and nuclear, that were uneconomical when oil was $2.00 per barrel, are now

---

[5]An interesting side issue is that much public criticism was leveled on the oil companies rather than the OPEC members. This is odd because the cartel profits are not going to the oil companies but to the governments of the OPEC member countries.

economical at the current high price of oil. This new entry has been slow to develop, but the future should prove more difficult for OPEC as new firms producing oil and other competing products enter and challenge the cartel's cohesiveness. OPEC, however, has the great advantage of being run by governments, with each government having the power to police and coerce within its own borders.

Class III Oligopolies

Class III oligopolies practice unorganized, collusive activity. Such *tacit collusion* is a much weaker form of collusion than that of Class II oligopolies or cartels. It is weaker because all the incentives to chisel are still present, but organized techniques to guard against chiseling are not present. The type of behavior associated with unorganized, collusive oligopolies is found in U.S. industry because Class II oligopolies are clearly illegal under U.S. antitrust laws. Class III oligopolies' behavior can in part be viewed as an attempt to form Class II cartels while avoiding antitrust laws. Collusion in Class III oligopolies usually takes the form of gentlemen's agreements to behave in certain ways. Often these agreements arise informally, without any need for clear-cut organization. The most common form of tacit, informal agreement is based on some form of price leadership.

Price Leadership. Price Leadership is the practice of industry pricing in which other firms typically follow the initiative of one firm, the price leader. The firm which is the price leader is typically the *dominant firm*, or largest firm, but it can be the *low-cost* firm, which may not be the largest firm in the industry. Price leadership is most effective where firms are few and have clearly similar products (e.g., the auto, cigarette, and steel industries). It helps if the demand for the product is price inelastic since this will further discourage price cutting. When the demand curve for the industry is perfectly inelastic, a firm that chisels on price will gain sales only at the expense of other firms because a lower price will not bring about additional sales for the industry. Thus, the conflict between firms will be sharper than if demand showed some response to price cuts.

Dominant Firm. In price leadership by the dominant firm, the largest firm which controls a significant share of the market sets a profit-maximizing price and the other firms divide up the market at that same price. The other firms, known as the *competitive fringe* firms, act much like firms in price competition. This can be seen by examining Figure 11-2. The market demand curve for the product is represented by D_m. The marginal cost curve of the dominant firm is MC_d and the summation of all the other fringe firms' marginal cost curves is MC_f. The fringe firms will make production decisions as price takers and will always produce where price is equal to marginal cost. MC_f can thus be viewed as a supply curve. The demand curve the dominant firm faces can then be derived by horizontally subtracting the amount supplied by the fringe (MC_f) firms from

FIGURE 11-2   **Dominant Firm with Competitive Fringe Firms**

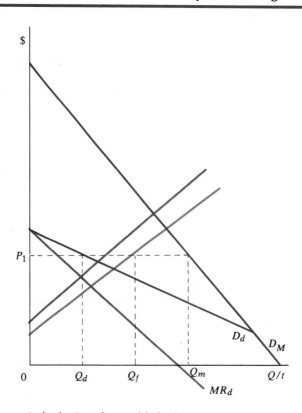

In the dominant firm model, the dominant firm views a part of the
market, D_d, as its own. D_d is determined by subtracting the competitive
fringe supply curve, MC_f, from the market demand, D_m. The dominant
firm then produces where marginal cost is equal to marginal revenue,
setting price OP_1 and producing OQ_d units. The fringe firms then face a
perfectly elastic demand at OP_1, thus producing OQ_f units where $MR = MC_f$.

the market demand curve. This subtraction gives the dominant firm's
demand curve, D_d, and its marginal revenue curve, MR_d. The dominant
firm will now set a profit-maximizing price and output of OP_1 and OQ_d.
Once price OP_1 is determined, the fringe firms view this price much as
competitive firms view the market price. The fringe firms will, therefore,
produce OQ_f units at the market price OP_1 because for them $OP_1 = MR$,
and they will, of course, produce where $MR = MC_f$. The production of
the dominant firm (OQ_d) and of the fringe firms (OQ_f) satisfies the market demand of OQ_m at price OP_1.

This model of price leadership is applicable to the oil industry,
where there is a small group of dominant firms and a large number of
small, fringe firms. Dominant firm price leadership also appears to pre-
vail in the aluminum, petroleum, and cigarette industries.

Historical Price Leadership. In a few cases, particularly in mature industries, it is possible for a firm to emerge as the price leader because it is convenient for the other firms in the industry to follow the leader and thus coordinate their pricing. This type of price leadership is no different than cartel behavior in intent. Its intent is exactly that of collusion — to achieve industry-wide profit maximization. Historical price leadership, however, is unorganized and thus not illegal in the United States. This type of price leadership is rampant in U.S. oligopolies. General Motors is the recognized price leader in autos, U.S. Steel in steel, and DuPont in chemicals. It is limited to mature or older oligopolies because it takes time for the firms to trust one another and follow the leader.

Successful Price Leadership. In order to be successful — that is, in order to raise industry profit levels — price leadership must produce a type of cartel but avoid legal sanctions. This means walking a tightrope because, as the tacit collusion embodied in price leadership becomes successful, the incentive to chisel increases. As a result, most "successful" price leadership situations that are not the dominant firm type occur in industries in which there are only a few firms. The record of such tacit collusion shows that such industries are characterized by rigid prices (they don't change often), and the price changes, when they occur, are generally small. Such industries are usually those that blame price increases on rising costs and that can punish firms who do not follow the price increase. The steel and auto industries are two examples. In these industries, potential chiselers know they cannot easily get away with not following the price leader.

Class I Oligopolies

Unorganized, uncollusive oligopolies are characterized by independent action. These oligopolists practice profit maximization independently but are affected by the action and response of their rivals; each tries to anticipate the response of its rivals and then takes the predicted response into account when making decisions. Economists tried to develop a model for this behavior in the early 1800s, and in 1838 A. Augustin Cournot (1801–1877) published a theory of duopoly (two firms). Cournot was an engineer, applied mathematician, and a high-level administrator in the French school system. His work in economics was highly original, and he is considered to be one of the founders of mathematical economics. His theory and the theories that followed up to the post-World War II period, while interesting to the theorist, are unsatisfactory for our purposes because they assume that the rival firm will not react to the action of the firm under investigation. The post-World War II developments in oligopoly theory rest heavily on mathematical game theory. Game theory is a relatively new field of mathematics and one which can provide insights into oligopolistic behavior. In game theory, "players" try to reach an "optimal" position through "strategic" behavior that takes into account the anticipated moves of other players. Game theory describes very accurately how oligopolists behave.[6]

The Kinked Demand Curve. One explanation of pricing in oligopoly was formulated by Dr. Paul Sweezy, who was a Stanford University professor and is now editor of *Monthly Review*. Sweezy formulated a model which explained the "fact" that prices in oligopolistic industries tend to be less flexible (meaning that they don't change very often) than prices in other market structures. The model develops a demand curve with a ***kink*** because firms come to believe that if they cut prices, their rivals will follow the price cut and as a result the price cut will not produce much of an increase in sales. A price increase, on the other hand, will not be followed and will therefore result in a significant loss of sales to the firm raising its price. As a result, a price once reached (Sweezy said nothing of how or why the original price came about) tends to remain in effect for long periods.

You can see the effect of a kink in the demand curve by examining Figure 11-3. A kink in the demand curve, D, comes about at point A (or at price OP) because the other oligopoly firms will match any price decrease, making the demand curve below point A relatively inelastic; the firm won't increase sales very much by decreasing price. Any increase in price above OP will have the opposite effect. Competing firms will not match the increase and, as a result, the demand curve above point A will be relatively elastic. Given this kink in the demand curve, the corresponding marginal revenue curve, MR, will be discontinuous, meaning it has a break in it, from B to C in Figure 11-3. This break allows a large fluctuation in marginal cost, from B to C, with no effect on the profit-maximizing price, OP, or output, OQ. For example, marginal cost could change from MC to MC_1 with no effect on price and output. Sweezy used this result to explain why prices were so rigid in oligopoly.

Sweezy's theory has been devastatingly attacked by Professor George Stigler of the University of Chicago. Stigler attacks the theory on both theoretical and empirical grounds.[7] The most telling empirical point is that he finds oligopoly prices to be *less* rigid than monopoly prices. This is one of those areas where there is an ongoing debate between theorists and empiricists.

Non-Price Competition. You should keep in mind that oligopolists compete in other dimensions than just the price dimension. In formulating models, economists tend to treat goods as homogeneous and view competition as occurring primarily through price adjustments. In the real world, however, competition can also take other forms. Firms can change the quality, color, texture, design, size, advertising, and a host of

---

[6]If you are interested in learning more about game theory, see John von Neumann and Osker Morgenstern, *The Theory of Games and Economic Behavior* (Princeton, N.J.: Princeton University Press, 1949). Von Neumann was the originator of game theory.

[7]See George J. Stigler, "The Kinky Oligopoly Demand Curve and Rigid Prices," *Journal of Political Economy* (October, 1947), pp. 432–449.

Public Info/U. of Chicago

Photo by Sam Sweezy

George Stigler (1911–   )

Paul Sweezy (1910–   )

George Stigler and Paul Sweezy

George Stigler and *Paul Sweezy* represent polar extremes in economic analysis. Both have written extensively in the field of industrial organization, but the similarities end there.

George Stigler is the personification of the "Chicago School" of free enterprise capitalism. He received a B.B.A. degree from the University of Washington, an M.B.A from Northwestern University, and a Ph.D. from the University of Chicago in 1938. Paul Sweezy is an American Marxist. He was awarded a B.A. degree, and a Ph.D. in economics from Harvard University in 1937.

Both economists are coeditors of prestigious journals that are at opposite ends of the ideological spectrum. Stigler is coeditor of the *Journal of Political Economy* and Sweezy is coeditor of the *Monthly Review*. Stigler's views are best delineated in *The Theory of Price* (1966) and *Organization of Industry* (1968). Sweezy's views can be found in *The Dynamics of U.S. Capitalism* (1972), *Introduction to Socialism* (1968), and *Modern Capitalism and Other Essays* (1972).

Stigler and Sweezy have clashed over Sweezy's development of the kinked demand curve. Sweezy formulated a model which explained the "fact" that prices in oligopolistic industries are more stable than prices in other market structures. This model has been devastatingly attacked by Stigler, who argues that Sweezy's theory is wrong and that his observation that prices in oligopoly are more stable than in other market structures does not stand up to empirical verification.

233

FIGURE 11-3   The Kinked Demand Curve

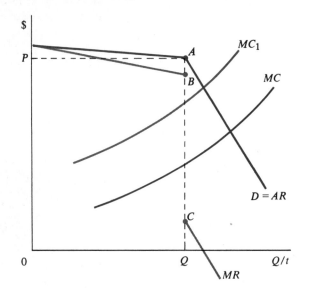

In the kinked demand curve model, the firm faces a kinked demand curve, D, because prices above OP will not be matched while prices below OP will be matched. The kink creates a discontinuity in the marginal revenue curve, which causes the price to be very rigid at the kink (OP).

other attributes of a product. An oligopolistic firm may resort to this type of non-price competition in an attempt to increase its market share.[8] This non-price competition does not mean that our model is invalid because we can apply the model to these other types of competition. For example, a firm contemplating a new advertising program will need to consider whether the program will increase its market share or instead prompt a rival to undertake a similar program. In the first instance, the program may be worthwhile. In the second, it would probably only increase costs without creating a larger market share. Thus, even with non-price competition, oligopoly firms are interdependent and need to consider the reactions of rivals.

THE IMPORTANCE OF ENTRY

You will recall that in pure competition entry was free, and in monopolistic competition entry was relatively easy. This contrasted with monopoly, where entry was blocked if the monopoly were to persist and

---

[8]Sometimes quality changes act as inverse price changes. For example, if the price of a candy bar remains at twenty-five cents but the amount of chocolate or almonds has been decreased, this is equivalent to a increase in price. Oligopolists often engage in this kind of disguised price cutting because it seems to provoke less response from rivals.

Rick Stafford, Harvard University News

**John Kenneth Galbraith
(1908–)**

John Kenneth Galbraith

John Kenneth Galbraith is perhaps the most well-known contemporary critic who happens to be an economist. His fame in the public's eye results from his attempt to write economics in clear English. However, economists as a group are not very sympathetic to his economic analysis. Their reservations stem from the fact that Galbraith criticizes in sweeping generalities. His arguments are almost never stated in precise, testable hypotheses. As a result, it is almost impossible for Galbraith to present evidence for his arguments. In a stinging review of Galbraith, Professor Robert Solow of M.I.T. argues that economists are "little thinkers" while Galbraith is a "big thinker." Solow then went on to illustrate his criticism of Galbraith by referring to

> . . . the old story of the couple who had achieved an agreeable division of labor. She made the unimportant decisions: What job he should take, where they should live, how to bring up the children. He made the important decisions: What to do about Jerusalem, who should be admitted to the United Nations, how to deal with crime on the streets.[1]

John Kenneth Galbraith was born in Canada and received a B.S. degree from the University of Toronto. He received a Ph.D. in agricultural economics at the University of California, Berkeley, in 1934. Galbraith went immediately to Harvard as an instructor, where he has been ever since. Galbraith, unlike most economists, is very politically active. He has been chairperson of the Americans for Democratic Action and was an early and outspoken critic of the Vietnam War. President John Kennedy, who knew Galbraith from his student days at Harvard, appointed Galbraith ambassador to India.

Galbraith has written a large number of books on both economic and noneconomic matters. The most important economics books are *American Capitalism: The Concept of Countervailing Power* (1956), *The Affluent Society* (1958), and *The New Industrial State* (1967). These books and Galbraith's other works on economics all have a common theme, which has come to be referred to as *Galbraithian economics*. This theme is that monopoly is the dominant force in the American economy and that these monopolies control and manipulate input prices, demand, and governmental policy. The control of the economy is now in the hands of a technostructure rather than the entrepreneur of conventional economic theory. Galbraith also argues that workers are generally exploited by these giant firms.

---

[1] Robert Solow, "Son of Affluence," *Public Interest* (Fall, 1967), p. 100.

235

maintain monopoly profits in the long run. In oligopoly, whether there are as few as two firms or as many as a dozen, conditions of entry again play an important role. Regardless of the class of oligopoly, if economic profits are to exist in the long run, it is necessary that the oligopolistic firms prohibit new entry. With new entry, profit-maximization techniques will tend to reduce these profits even if there are just a few firms. A second important point is that potential entry makes cartel formation much more difficult. Why go to the trouble and cost of organizing a cartel if economic profits will be eaten up by new entry? It is thus incumbent on cartels or would-be cartels to control entry. Consider the following examples.

First, let's examine the experience in an oligopolistic industry where entry was easily accomplished. Immediately after World War II, Milton Reynolds formed Reynolds International Pen Company with an investment of $26,000.[9] He was a monopoly producer of ballpoint pens protected by a patent. The pens were marketed by Gimbles department store in New York City and sold for $12.50 each. The first day of sales, Gimbles sold 10,000 pens and by early 1946 Reynolds had earned more than $3 million in net accounting profits. Clearly, above-normal profits were being earned. New entry was fierce. Macy's department store imported a pen to compete with the one Reynolds sold at Gimbles. Eversharp and Sheaffer announced plans to compete. Two totally new pen companies announced products in total disregard of the patent. In October, 1946, the new entry was such that Reynolds had reduced his price from $12.50 to $3.85. Two months later, in December, 1946, about 100 firms were producing ballpoint pens, some priced as low as $2.98. Another two months later, in February, 1947, Gimbles was selling pens produced by another company at $.98. By mid-1948 ballpoint pens were selling for $.39 and by 1951 prices were as low as $.25. In 1975 ballpoint pens were selling at prices starting at $.11.

This experience is a phenomenal one. In a 16-month period, prices fell 1,275.51 percent! This decline was purely the result of price competition from new entry. If Reynolds or a cartel of Reynolds, Sheaffer, Eversharp and others could have in some way prevented this new entry, prices would presumably have stayed much higher.

Contrast this experience with the case of the U.S. airline industry, where entry has been reasonably well blocked by a few firms. The CAB (Civil Aeronautics Board) has acted as an agent in cartelizing the airline industry. In order to fly between states — that is, in interstate commerce — an airline must receive permission of the CAB. To fly within a state, or intrastate, no such permission is required. The CAB thus restricts entry into the interstate industry. The result is a higher price than would exist without CAB regulation. We can see this by comparing in-

---

[9]For a detailed account of this experience, see Richard G. Lipsey and Peter O. Steiner, *Economics* (4th ed.; New York: Harper & Row, Publishers, 1975), pp. 320–321.

trastate and interstate rates. Theodore Keeler, a Berkeley economist, has done this.[10] He found that before 1978, without CAB regulation, the price of airline travel would have been between 20 and 95 percent lower, depending upon the route examined. When deregulation (of sorts) came in 1978, fares on some routes fell significantly.[11] The interesting question is why doesn't the CAB deregulate even more? One would think that entrepreneurs would be eager to compete for these passengers. The answer is, of course, that some entrepreneurs would, but the CAB doesn't deregulate because certain members of the industry favor the regulation and others (especially new firms) don't.

The domestic airlines tend to favor the CAB because it makes life easy for them by keeping out new entry and enforcing their cartel. To see this more clearly, examine the reprinted version of a recent lobbying pamphlet distributed by Western Airlines (pages 238–241). It was made available at ticket counters to convince passengers of the need for continued regulation. When you read it, note that most of the arguments talk about competition and new entry in a very derogatory way. Why do you think Western Airlines views competition and new entry in such a negative way? How do you suppose Milton Reynolds felt about the competition that reduced the price of his pens from $12.50 to $.11? Most arguments made with respect to the airline industry hold with equal force for the pen industry. You can imagine how the presidents of TWA and Pan American feel about Freddy Laker of Laker Airlines, who wants to fly his Skytrain between New York and Los Angeles at reduced rates as he does now between New York and London!

The most recent challenge to regulation is coming in the trucking industry. The Interstate Commerce Commission (ICC), the President, and Senator Kennedy's Senate Antitrust Subcommittee are all proceeding with deregulation plans. True to form, large trucking firms are fighting the proposals. Trucking executives, just like airline executives, are arguing that deregulation is not in the public interest.

As we have seen, the restriction of entry by a monopolist or an oligopolist is very difficult in the long run. Entrepreneurs sensing profit will find ways to compete. As a result, it is almost impossible to keep long-run profits above normal rates unless one gets the government to aid in blocking entry. In other words, government sometimes gives would-be cartels aid, and we find the interesting phenomenon of some firms liking regulation. These big firms may talk about free enterprise, but in fact they prefer the regulation. The presidents of the major domestic airlines have historically been opposed to reform and deregulation of their industry through reduction of CAB powers.

---

[10]Theodore Keeler, "Airline Regulation and Market Performance," *Bell Journal of Economics* (Autumn, 1972).

[11]To the surprise of many in the airline industry, revenues and profits zoomed. What does this say about the elasticity of demand? What implications might you draw about marginal costs?

Should the Airline Industry be Deregulated?

"Deregulate the U.S. airline industry," some highly-placed political forces are saying. They claim this would bring in new, innovative airlines, and bring about lower fares. Bills have been introduced, therefore, and are being considered in Congress now which would dramatically change our nation's airlines.

What would this "deregulation" mean to users of air service, to communities large and small, and to the taxpayers, as well as to the airlines and their personnel?

These questions are so vital and the issues so potentially damaging that the employees of Western Airlines, America's oldest and consequently most experienced airline, have studied the proposed legislation in detail. They have prepared this brochure in hopes of informing other airline personnel and the public of the facts before it is too late for them to take action and prevent deregulation from dismantling the finest air transportation system the world has ever known.

Q What do the pending bills on deregulation propose to do?

A The bills' sponsors want to bring more competition into the industry, which they represent would bring about lower air fares and better service. While the Civil Aeronautics Board would be maintained, it would be required to encourage the development of new airlines, and to encourage additional competition in established markets, whether or not those markets required additional service. The CAB's authority in determining reasonable fare structures would be almost removed, as carriers would be allowed to set fares which did not cover all their costs or raise fares without any justification required.

Q Would such deregulation bring lower air fares?

A A "rate war" might reduce fares for a short time on a few major routes as new carriers

238

enter potentially lucrative markets. But it must be remembered that deregulation will not alter the cost of providing air transportation. Under deregulation, the price of jet fuel will not go down; the wages of skilled and experienced airline personnel needed for a dependable operation will not be less; airports will not lower their landing fees; other suppliers of goods and services will not reduce their charges. These hard economic facts will catch up with the new carriers as well, for as in any other business air transportation in the long run must be priced to cover the cost of producing it. Under the predatory pricing of a rate war, the financially weaker airlines will either be driven out of the market or out of business, and the remaining carriers could then set fares at whatever the traffic will bear.

Q Are air fares excessive now?

A No, air fares are not excessive by any standard. As compared with the price of other goods and services, for example, the average U.S. airline fare has gone up less than 30 per cent between 1950 and 1976. During that same period the Consumer Price Index increased 120 per cent. Moreover, U.S. airlines fares are the lowest in the world. The coach fare (without the benefit of various discounts) between Salt Lake City and Chicago is 8.7 cents per mile. For that same distance of 1254 miles, the air coach fare in Canada is 15.4 cents per mile, in Australia it's 13.0 cents per mile, and in Europe 26.4 cents per mile. Our own company, Western Airlines, pioneered air coach service along the Pacific Coast in 1949, and today offers a wide variety of economy, commuter, off-peak, excursion, tour-basing, group, and charter fares.

Q Would deregulation result in more competition?

A Only for a time and only on heavily traveled routes. Excessive competition on these routes as additional carriers entered the market, with the price wars that ensued, would ultimately drive out some airlines and probably result in less competition than there was originally. Smaller markets would get little or no additional competition as carriers serving them would have to concentrate their forces against the "cream-skimming" operations on more lucrative routes. This could also result in reduction of service in the smaller markets.

Q Would small cities continue to have air transportation?

A With deregulation many would not, unless taxpayers subsidized it. The major U.S. carriers went off public subsidy for serving small cities more than 20 years ago. At present, service by major airlines to smaller cities is based on the same public service philosophy under which telephones are provided. The telephone companies utilize the profits of their entire system to provide the best possible service at affordable rates to all customers, no matter where they are. Airlines are also public utilities and common carriers, and follow this same policy. Without the security of today's system of certificates of public convenience and necessity (or licenses), and faced with the necessity to concentrate on meeting intensified competition on their more profitable, high-volume routes, airlines would be compelled to abandon or reduce service to many smaller communities. Either the passenger, mail, and air freight services essential to such communities will be disrupted, or the nation's taxpayers will find themselves footing the bill.

Q Would deregulation result in greater efficiency?

A It's difficult to imagine. U.S. airlines have been very innovative with respect to efficient operation, new services, and promotional tariffs, to a degree unmatched

239

in other industries. The sophistication of their equipment and the huge capital required for aircraft fleets have demanded that they keep ever alert to modern technology. Under deregulation, additional airlines and airplanes at the already crowded major airports would cause serious problems rather than create greater efficiency. This would even be wasteful of precious fuel supplies. And the carefully-developed national network of airline routes would be torn apart. Airline customers and communities alike would be facing the uncertainties of a guessing game as to service and rates.

Q Would deregulation impair the ability of airlines to work together to provide better service?

A Yes. For industry teamwork, deregulation would be a giant step backward. It would wipe out decades of progress during which systematic interline procedures were developed. These procedures today are directly related to customer convenience in being able to call one airline reservations center to obtain schedules and fares and book space on all carriers; to buy one ticket covering a trip on several airlines and check baggage which is automatically transferred. Cargo shippers benefit from the same inter-carrier cooperation. Under deregulation, the whole working structure of interline relationships would come under a cloud, because the proposed legislation would remove the anti-trust immunities which have been provided so that this public transportation system could function as an integrated national network. Deregulation would require that literally thousands of interline agreements be reviewed and revised.

Q How would deregulation affect the passenger?

A Rate wars on major routes, leading to the offering of tickets at less than cost, would force the removal of in-flight and ground service features and conveniences that airlines could no longer afford. Schedules would be adjusted to get more equipment utilization at marginal times, frequency of flights would diminish, and seat configuration would be high-density. Service to and from many smaller communities would be considerably reduced or eliminated unless taxpayer-subsidized.

Q How would deregulation affect users of postal service and airfreight?

A Under the proposals, mail and freight could be carried on charters as well as scheduled flights, so on the surface it would appear initially to benefit users of these cargo services. However, these added flights might prove temporary and they would not be going into all the variety of cities that scheduled airlines serve today. Remember, about eight out of ten first class intercity letters go by air now and this has been made possible by the fact that airlines serve so many cities at such reasonable cost. Contract, subsidized mail flights would probably be required for many of the small cities. This would be a step back to the very beginning of the airline industry, for contract mail service was where the U.S. airlines started.

Q How would it affect the travel agent?

A The entire commission structure that compensates travel agents for the sale of airline tickets and tours, and all the Air Transport Association rules and resolutions that guide the complex working relationship between the airlines and the travel agents, would be scrapped by deregulation. Instead of a businesslike and uniform industry approach, each airline would be required to negotiate separate agreements on commissions and operating practices with 13,000 individual U.S. travel agencies. In 1976 these agencies produced more than $7 billion in airline revenues for which they earned nearly $600 million in commissions (at no added cost to the public). The continued functioning of this huge sales force under deregulation would become chaotic.

Q How would it affect career airline personnel?

A The airline customer today enjoys the benefit and security of years of training and experience offered by the nation's 300,000 airline professionals. No U.S. airline any longer "flies by the seat of its pants." New carriers entering the industry would have relatively inexperienced personnel starting at the bottom of the wage ladder. This would be the one area of operating costs where they would have an initial ability to reduce fares. But as a result of the rate wars that would rage in an atmosphere of unrestrained competition, there would be fewer airlines surviving and there would be fewer employees in the industry.

Q Is the airline industry against "free enterprise"?

A Not at all. But we see the airlines as public utilities — just like the telephone and electric company or radio/television stations. They are all vital public services. It is essential to the users of these systems that their reliability of operation and fairness of rates not be left to chance. It is just as important that the airlines' obligation to provide adequate service continue to be a statutory mandate. Those factors are assured for the nation's air transportation network by the present regulatory structure. There is certainly room for improvement in its rate-setting and rule-making procedures, but this can be accomplished within the framework of the present statute. The latter has worked remarkably well in fostering the development of the world's greatest air transportation system.

Source: Adapted from *Should the Airline Industry be Deregulated?*, a pamphlet prepared by the "Support Our Service" Committee of Western Airlines Employees. While the position espoused in this brochure also was embraced by Western Airlines at the time the brochure was printed, the company's position subsequently changed to support a modified version of the proposed legislation.

MARKET STRUCTURES IN REVIEW

This chapter concludes our discussion of the four market structures in the theory of the firm. Table 11-2 gives a summary of some of the important variables that differentiate the market structures we have examined. The key to understanding the theory of the firm is a solid understanding of monopoly and pure competition. Oligopoly and monopolistic competition expand the theories of monopoly and pure competition, and in effect demonstrate that we can generalize from the pure models to the real-world situations we encounter.

TABLE 11-2   Summary of Market Structures

Market Type	Number of Firms	Product Differentiation	Control Over Price	Amount of Non-Price Competition	Examples
Pure Competition	Large numbers	Homogeneous product	None	None	Agriculture is reasonably close
Monopolistic Competition	Many	Slightly differentiated	Some	Advertising and product differentiation	Retail trade and service industry
Oligopoly	Few	Homogeneous *or* differentiated product	Some to considerable (it depends)	Advertising and product differentiation	Autos, steel
Monopoly	One	Unique product (no close substitutes)	Considerable	Public relations	Utilities (aluminum before 1945)

Summary

Oligopoly is the market structure in which there are only a few firms producing goods that are either homogeneous or differentiated. Because there are so few firms, they are interdependent and they take this interdependence into account in their economic decision making.

Oligopolies can be broken down into three classes. Class I oligopolies are characterized by independent action. Class II oligopolies are cartels. Class III oligopolies have imperfect joint action.

Cartels will be threatened by chiseling behavior on the part of individual members of the cartel. The larger the number of firms in the cartel, the harder it will be for the cartel to hold together. Successful cartels have historically used governments to help police the cartel. Price leadership is common in Class III cartels. Price leadership can be by a dominant firm or by a historical leader in mature industries. Oligopolies are characterized by extensive use of non-price competition.

Conditions of entry are important in oligopoly, just as they are in monopoly. Successful cartels or successful price leaders will raise profits above normal levels. This will attract new firms. If these above-normal profits are to be maintained, the oligopoly must keep these new firms out of the industry.

New Terms

oligopoly
pure oligopoly
differentiated oligopoly
price clusters
communication
coordination
collusion
Class I oligopoly
Class II oligopoly

Class III oligopoly
cartel
chiseling
tacit collusion
price leadership
dominant firm
competitive fringe
kinked demand curve

Questions for Discussion

1 When OPEC meets at its regularly scheduled meetings (usually at very posh resorts), why can't it just set a high price and let all the individual members sell as much as they want at this high price?

2 Is the NCAA (National Collegiate Athletic Association) a cartel? How do some universities (firms) chisel on the cartel? Why do they do this?

3 Explain how the expectation of new entry would limit cartel formation.

4 Name as many forms of non-price competition as you can. Do firms take the response of other firms into account when they plan new types of non-price competition?

5 Would government policies that require firms to report their sales by quantity and price make it easier or harder for Class III oligopolies?

6 How is Class I oligopoly different from monopolistic competition?

Suggestions for Further Reading

Boulding, Kenneth E. *Economic Analysis*. New York: Harper & Brothers, 1955, Chapter 22.

Kamerschen, David R., and Lloyd M. Valentine. *Intermediate Microeconomic Theory*. Cincinnati: South-Western Publishing Co., 1977, Chapter 15.

Machlup, Fritz. *The Economics of Seller's Competition*. Baltimore: Johns Hopkins Press, 1952.

Markham, Jesse W. "The Nature and Significance of Price Leadership." *American Economic Review* (December, 1951).

CHAPTER 12

THE ECONOMICS OF AMERICAN INDUSTRY

LEARNING OBJECTIVES

After studying the materials found in this chapter, you should be able to do the following:

1 Define an industry using the SIC system.

2 Give examples of the arbitrary nature of the definition of an industry.

3 Identify the characteristics of the structure of an industry.

4 Calculate the concentration ratio within an industry.

5 Use concentration ratios as an index of monopoly power.

6 Compare the results of studies of the relationship between concentration and

    (a) prices,
    (b) profits.

7 Show on a diagram the regulation of monopoly power through
    (a) price regulation,
    (b) taxation.

8 Identify and discuss the major antitrust laws in the history of antitrust legislation.

9 List the pros and cons of proposed new legislation designed to control monopoly power.

In the preceding chapters we examined four theoretically distinct types of market structures. In this chapter, we will apply these theories to the real world and examine the extent of monopoly power in American industry. To do this, we need to first determine what constitutes an industry. We can then attempt to determine whether a particular industry is monopolistic and what elements contribute to this monopoly power. Only then can we examine public policy options to address any monopoly power that might exist. This chapter, then, will take you into empirical *industry studies* to develop a real-world appreciation of the monopoly problem. As a separate subfield of economics, this area of investigation is sometimes referred to as *industrial organization*.

Once it is determined that an industry possesses monopoly power, it may be desirable to control or mitigate the worst aspects of that monopoly power. The monopoly power could be destroyed through antitrust action, the monopoly profits could be taxed away, or the monopoly could be regulated and thus forced to behave in some prescribed fashion. Or it might even be better to do nothing about the monopoly power. This chapter will examine the theory and practice of regulation and then the development and record of U.S. antitrust laws. It will conclude with an assessment of the record of both regulation and antitrust policy.

WHAT IS AN INDUSTRY?

We have up to this point been using the term industry without carefully defining what an industry is. In general, an *industry* is a group of firms producing the same, or at least similar, products. The difficulty with this definition centers on the degree of dissimilarity allowed before the two products are thought of as being produced in different industries. Consider the container industry. Are firms producing glass bottles and aluminum cans similar enough to be included in the same industry? How about including firms making paper cups or even pewter mugs in this industry? Most consumers regard pewter mugs and paper cups as quite different. If you are willing to pay more money for a pewter mug than for a paper cup, you show that you regard them as being distinct products. What about a plastic Ronald McDonald glass? Is it closer to a paper cup or a pewter mug? We raise these questions not because we plan to show you how to obtain a correct answer but rather to demonstrate that whatever answer we reach, it will be arbitrary to some degree and therefore some people, even some economists, may disagree with a particular definition.

The problem is even more difficult if we consider that some multiproduct firms produce a variety of goods that might be included in different industries. In which industry should we put a firm that produces coffee in addition to soap and cake mixes? Informed judgments and somewhat aributary definitions are necessary in order to move from the world of theory into the real world of industry studies.

There is a standard set of data available from the United States Census Bureau where these judgments have already been made. The data are a little more manageable than if each economist made individual judgments and, as a result, industry studies are comparable. The Census Bureau collects and classifies data according to the **Standard Industrial Classification (SIC) system**.[1] The SIC system divides the economy into about 400 four-digit industries. These four-digit groups can then be aggregated into three-digit or two-digit groups, or disaggregated into five-digit (or even seven-digit) product classes. Table 12-1 presents an example of how a product becomes more specific as the industry group is disaggregated. The purpose of such a system is to organize groups of processes, products, and materials into a workable, consistent classification. This SIC system is the basis for studies we will be referring to in the remainder of this chapter.

One of the principles developed in Chapter 3, cross elasticity of demand, could be useful in determining whether products belong to the same industry or different industries. We saw that if the coefficient of the cross elasticity of demand between two products is positive, the goods are substitutes.[2] Goods that are close substitutes would have a positive and very high cross elasticity of demand coefficient. If we could agree on a cross elasticity coefficient that would represent goods from the same industry, again an arbitrary decision, we could then use this figure in a very mechanical fashion to define an industry.

TABLE 12-1   **Sample SIC Codes**

Code Number		Designation	Name
Two-digit	20	Major Industry Group	Food & Kindred Products
Three-digit	201	Industry Group	Meat Products
Four-digit	2011	Industry	Meat Packing Plants
Five-digit	20111	Product Class	Fresh Beef

Source: U.S. Bureau of the Budget, *Standard Industrial Classification Manual* (Washington: U.S. Government Printing Office, 1967).

INDUSTRY STRUCTURE

Once we have overcome the hurdle of defining an industry, we can then determine its market structure. As we saw earlier, this structure will depend critically on a number of elements in that particular industry. Of these elements, degrees of concentration and conditions of entry are

---

[1]See U.S. Bureau of the Budget, *Standard Industrial Classification Manual* (Washington: U.S. Government Printing Office, 1967).

[2]$E_{x,y} = \dfrac{\text{percentage change in quantity demanded of good } x}{\text{percentage change in price of good } y}$. See Chapter 3, pp. 66–67.

especially important. Concentration and entry, of course, interact in such a way that entry barriers make for a more concentrated industry, but for the moment, let's consider them separately.

Loosely speaking, concentration refers to the extent to which a certain number of firms dominates sales in a given market. Measures of concentration have for many years been a primary tool of industry studies. The *concentration ratio* permits the economist to prepare an index of the relative degree of concentration in an oligopolistic market. To calculate a concentration ratio, the economist uses the SIC codes we just discussed and calculates the percentage of an industry's total sales accounted for by a certain number of firms.[3] For example, a four-firm concentration ratio would calculate the percentage of sales in an industry accounted for by the largest four firms. It is possible to calculate concentration ratios for the largest firm, the three largest firms, the eight largest firms, and so on. Most studies have employed four-firm ratios. Table 12-2 gives concentration ratios for a few selected industries.

TABLE 12-2   Concentration Ratios — Selected Industries

Product	Number of Firms	Concentration Ratio (Sales of Domestically Produced Goods)
Automobiles	4	100%
Telephone Service	4	98%
Chewing Gum	4	97%
Tennis Balls	2	100%
Detergents	3	86%
Soft Drinks	4	65%
Canned Soups	2	90%
Disposable Diapers	4	99%
Sanitary Napkins	2	95%
Air Travel	3	61%
Plywood	4	30%
Wood Furniture	4	14%
Concrete Block and Brick	4	5%

Source: Federal Trade Commission, *The Wall Street Journal, Financial World, Standard and Poor's,* and industry sources (various issues).

It could be argued that the percentage of sales is not the best measure of concentration in an industry. You might instead want to calculate concentration ratios using percentage of assets, percentage of employees, or

_____

[3]Prelaw students might anticipate a strategy for defense in antitrust cases. The defense would, of course, prefer to have concentration ratios calculated on the basis of the most general category possible in order to insure that any one firm has a small share of the sales in the industry. We will discuss this in greater detail later in the chapter.

value of shipments. The various measures of concentration are all statistically highly correlated, however, so it really isn't that crucial which type of ratio you select.

As we discussed earlier, the more concentrated an industry, the more likely it is that there will be a recognized mutual interdependence that leads to joint action of either a collusive or uncollusive nature. When a four-firm concentration ratio exceeds 40–50 percent, the degree of this interdependence is likely to be very high.

Entry is the second element affecting the market structure. Entry conditions have an important effect on concentration. If entry barriers exist and the industry is highly concentrated, it is more likely that joint action can be exploited to earn monopoly profits. We saw earlier that cartels are very unstable and that profits will strongly attract new firms into the industry, but if concentration is high and entry is blocked, the existing firms will in all likelihood be able to exploit their strong market position.

It is important, then, to consider the elements of concentration and entry together. Concentration produces the recognized interdependence that works to make cooperative behavior worthwhile, and entry determines the scope for such cooperative behavior.

CONCENTRATION AND ITS GROWTH OVER TIME

At first glance, it seems that the number of concentrated, oligopolistic industries in the U.S. economy is high. But just how concentrated is U.S. industry really? And does concentration make any difference? In other words, would you as a consumer be better off if U.S. industry were generally less concentrated and hence perhaps more competitive? Given the difficulty of defining industries and the fact that any classification scheme requires arbitrary judgments, it is not surprising that studies have reached widely differing conclusions on the degree and trend of concentration in U.S. industry. The studies can be divided roughly into three groups.

One group of studies, which investigated trends in concentration in the first half of the twentieth century, concluded that there had been a pronounced increase in industrial concentration in the United States. This group of studies is associated with and represented by the work of Gardiner Means, who looked at the assets of the 200 largest nonfinancial corporations. Means found (see Group I Studies in Table 12-3) that between 1909 and 1933 the percentage of total assets controlled by the 200 largest nonfinancial corporations increased from 33.3 percent to 54.8 percent.[4]

---

[4]Studies by Gardiner C. Means and by Norman R. Collins and Lee E. Preston are representative of such studies. Reference citations to these studies and the others discussed can be found in Table 12-3.

TABLE 12-3   Trends in Concentration

GROUP I STUDIES

1. Total Assets of All Nonfinancial Corporations: 200 Largest Corporations (Less Taxable Investments; Percent of Total)

1909	1929	1930	1931	1932	1933
33.3	47.9	54.3	55.5	54.8	54.8

2. Total Assets of All Manufacturing, Mining, and Distribution Corporations: 100 Largest Corporations (Percent of Total)

1909	1919	1929	1935	1948	1958
17.7	16.6	25.5	28.0	26.7	29.8

3. Total Net Income of All Nonfinancial Corporations: 200 Largest Corporations (Percent of Total)

1920	1921	1922	1923	1924
33.4	37.6	32.2	32.8	36.0

1925	1926	1927	1928	1929
37.1	40.0	38.4	40.0	43.2

GROUP II STUDY

4. Distribution of National Income by Type of Productive Organization

	1939	1958
Effectively Monopolistic	20.43	15.88
Workably Competitive	59.09	62.02
Governmental	20.16	21.52

GROUP III STUDIES

5. Total Manufacturing Assets: 200 Largest Manufacturing Concerns (Percent of Total)

1929	1933	1937	1941	1948
45.8	49.5	49.1	45.1	46.3

1950	1952	1954	1956	1958
46.1	47.7	50.4	52.8	55.2

Continued on page 250

TABLE 12-3   (continued)

1960	1962	1964	1966	1968
55.2	55.1	55.8	56.1	60.4

6. Value Added by Manufacture: 200 Largest Manufacturers (Percent of Total)

1947	1954	1958	1962	1963	1966	1967
30	37	38	40	41	42	42

Source: 1. Gardiner Means, National Resources Committee, *The Structure of the American Economy* (Washington: U.S. Government Printing Office, 1939), Part 1, p. 107.
2. Norman R. Collins and Lee E. Preston, "The Size Structure of the Largest Industrial Firms," *American Economic Review* (December, 1961).
3. Adeolf A. Berle and Gardiner C. Means, *The Modern Corporation and Private Property* (New York: Macmillan Co., 1933).
4. G. Warren Nutter and Henry A. Einhorn, *Enterprise Monopoly in the United States: 1899–1958* (New York: Columbia University Press, 1969), pp. 56–57.
5. Bureau of the Census, Department of Commerce, "Concentration Ratios in Manufacturing, 1967," *Special Reports,* 1970.
6. Federal Trade Commission Staff, *Economic Report on Corporate Mergers*, 1969, p. 173.

The studies that found increased concentration were challenged by G. Warren Nutter, who argued that between 1901 and 1937 industrial concentration declined in the United States. Nutter's studies were attacked on the grounds that they depended crucially on benchmark figures from 1899, which he took as a starting point, and that these early figures were suspect because of the poor data that existed then. Later, Nutter's figures were updated and extended by Henry A. Einhorn. Einhorn used Nutter's figures for 1939 as a benchmark and sought to determine if concentration had changed between 1939 and 1958. He divided production in the economy, as Nutter had earlier, into three structures: (1) monopolistic, (2) workably competitive, and (3) governmental. He then, like Nutter, sought to determine if the share of production originating in each of the three structures had changed. Einhorn concluded (see Group II Study in Table 12-3) that between 1939 and 1958 roughly three fifths of national income was generated by the workably competitive structure. The monopolistic sector declined only slightly and the governmental sector increased slightly. The conclusion of the Nutter-Einhorn research is that market concentration in the twentieth century has been surprisingly stable.

Two later governmental studies represent the third group of studies in Table 12-3. This third group of studies seems to indicate that concentration has increased very slightly in the 1950s and 1960s.

Table 12-3 summarizes the results of these three different sets of studies. Can we draw any conclusions from these seemingly conflicting studies? At one extreme in the debate we have the position that the level of monopoly power has been stable, und that monopolized production amounts to 15–20 percent of national income. At the other end of the debate we have the position that concentration in American industry increased dramatically in the early part of this century and, since World War II, has also increased but at a much slower pace than in the early 1900s. Regardless of whose data and technique you are most convinced by, it is significant that the most optimistic figures argue that only about 60 percent of U.S. production can be judged as originating in workably competitive industries.

A second thing to keep in mind is that these measures of concentration are all aggregate measures. They may understate the degree of monopoly power in American industry because they ignore or understate the power of local and regional monopolies. The beer industry is a good example. In 1970 the four-firm concentration ratio for beer sales was roughly 40 percent on a national level. However, in some regions the concentration ratio was much higher, approaching 75–80 percent. Thus, the national figures might lead some to conclude that the industry is workably competitive, whereas the regional figures seem to suggest that the industry consists of a series of regional monopolies. One possible way out of the difficulty of agreeing on the measures of economic concentration is to ask whether concentration is really very important.

CONCENTRATION AND PERFORMANCE

We have been discussing concentration and ways to determine the degree of concentration in an industry. Lurking in the background of this discussion is the implicit presumption that concentration, *per se*, is undesirable. This dislike of concentration has become commonplace among industrial organization economists. The reason is that the industrial organization economist typically sees a sequence of events running from (a) the structure of the industry to (b) the behavior of firms in that industry and then to (c) the performance of the industry itself. According to this line of thought, a highly concentrated structure will produce the antisocial behavior we attributed to monopoly in Chapter 9. The industrial organization economist, therefore, examines the structure of an industry to determine how the public welfare might be improved. This general structure-conduct-performance chain has been termed the **Market Concentration Doctrine**.

The Market Concentration Doctrine holds that the degree of concentration is a reliable index of monopoly power. Strict application of this doctrine might lead policymakers to suggest antitrust action or some other form of control when concentration ratios reach a certain level.

Before examining policy action against monopoly, let us first examine the premises behind this doctrine.

Administered Prices

Those who support the doctrine base their arguments primarily on two empirical points. The first is that prices are more rigid (less flexible) in concentrated industries, and the second is that profit rates and concentration are positively correlated. Supporters of this doctrine believe that both rigid prices and higher profit rates reflect the monopoly power associated with high degrees of concentration.

The lack of price flexibility in concentrated industries was first found by Gardiner Means, and his findings are described in a now famous monograph.[5] He argued, looking at data from 1926–1933, that price movements in different industries varied in frequency. In some industries prices changed very often, and in others prices tended to be constant for relatively long periods of time. He labeled the prices that were relatively rigid, or changed only infrequently, as *administered prices*. Later he demonstrated that these administered prices were related to the degree of concentration in the industry.[6]

This early work by Means has had a significant influence on discussions of public policy toward industry. As might be expected with so significant a study, it was subjected to close scrutiny. As is usually the case with empirical work, both the data and methodology used by both sides in the debate have been criticized. Competing researchers claimed that Means's study suffered because his data were gathered from reports submitted by industry to the Bureau of Labor Statistics. Since firms reported at different intervals, his reported price flexibility (or inflexibility) might simply reflect a different frequency of reporting.[7] Other researchers claimed that the Bureau of Labor Statistics' data were composed of prices *asked* by firms and the relevant data are prices *paid* by consumers.[8] Since oligopolists often want to hide their price cuts from their competitors, they often grant buyers secret cuts on posted prices. For this reason, the discrepancies between prices asked and prices paid might be significant.

Even though this question of administered prices has been scrutinized by economists for some time, we do not yet have a scientific conclusion. The standard "classroom fare" or "textbook knowledge" is that

---

[5]Gardiner Means, *Industrial Prices and Their Relative Inflexibility*, Senate Document 13, 74th Congress, 1st Session (January 17, 1935).

[6]National Resources Committee, *The Structure of the American Economy* (Washington: U.S. Government Printing Office, 1939).

[7]U.S. Congress, Joint Economic Committee, *Government Price Statistics*. Hearings before the Subcommittee on Economic Statistics of the Joint Economic Committee, 87th Congress, 1st Session (1961).

[8]George J. Stigler and James K. Kindahl, *The Behavior of Industrial Prices* (New York: National Bureau of Economic Research, 1970).

there is a loose association between concentration and price inflexibility. This conventional wisdom has become part of public policy debates, but the economist, *qua* scientist, would be hard put to prove this relationship.

Concentration and Profit Levels

The second element of the Concentration Doctrine is that profits and concentration ratios are positively correlated. The theoretical basis for this premise lies in the greater ability, which we examined in preceding chapters, for firms to behave collusively, the smaller the number of firms. The empirical link between concentration and profits begins with the work of Joe Bain.[9] Bain found, although he had some reservations, that his hypothesis that profit rates and concentration ratios were positively correlated was confirmed for a sample of 42 manufacturing industries. Bain found that when the concentration ratio exceeded 70 percent, there was a significant increase in average profit rates. Economist George Stigler, on the other hand, conducting similar research, found there was no clear-cut relationship between concentration ratios and profit rates.[10] In his study, Stigler defined an industry as concentrated if the four-firm concentration ratio for the value of output exceeded 60 percent. Other studies examining the same hypothesis concluded that there is a weak, but positive, relationship between concentration and profit rates.[11]

Recently there has been some debate about this tendency for profits to be higher in concentrated industries. President Johnson's Task Force on Antitrust Policy concluded that such a correlation exists.

> The adverse effects of persistent concentration on output and price find some confirmation in various studies that have been made of return on capital in major industries. These studies have found a close association between high levels of concentration and persistently high rates of return on capital. ... It is the persistence of high profits over extended time periods and over whole industries rather than in individual firms that suggest artificial restraints on output and the absence of fully effective competition. The correlation of evidence of this kind with very high levels of concentration appears to be significant.[12]

This conclusion has been challenged by the University of Chicago's Yale Brozen and others.[13] Brozen recalculated many of the older studies

---

[9]Joe S. Bain, "Relation of Profit-Rate to Industry Concentration: American Manufacturing, 1936–1940," *Quarterly Journal of Economics* (August, 1951).

[10]George J. Stigler, *Capital and Rates of Return in Manufacturing* (Princeton, N.J.: Princeton University Press, 1963).

[11]For a review of these studies, see Harold Demsetz, *The Market Concentration Doctrine* (Washington: American Enterprise Institute for Public Policy Research, 1975).

[12]White House Task Force on Antitrust Policy, *Role of the Giant Corporation* (1967), p. 883.

[13]Yale Brozen, "The Antitrust Task Force Deconcentration Recommendation," *Journal of Law and Economics* (October, 1970), pp. 279–292.

using data from later time periods. He found that with the passage of time there was a tendency for rates of profit in concentrated industries to converge with those of less concentrated industries. Rates of profit increased in the industries that previously had below-average profit levels and decreased in the industries with above-average profit levels. Other economists have pointed out that there are numerous hypotheses that are consistent with the data and that care should be taken before policy is based on any one hypothesis. Thus the concentration-profit hypothesis, like the concentration-price rigidity hypothesis, has been subject to challenge.

The Market Concentration Doctrine, then, is challenged on two of its most important tenets. There appears to be, at least, debatable evidence to contradict the conventional wisdom that concentration ratios are a good measure of monopoly behavior. Why is this important? It is important because much of present policy discussion concerning the reformulation of antitrust law uses market concentration as a guide. If concentration is illegal, *per se*, in part because concentration is taken as an indicator of monopoly behavior, many industries may be restructured by the courts simply because they are concentrated. If, instead, these industries are concentrated because there are economies of scale, antitrust activity would introduce inefficiencies into the economy.

In short, the Market Concentration Doctrine has become the conventional wisdom of policymakers. The challenges to this conventional wisdom, however, are significant enough that the doctrine should be examined closely. It is particularly important that economists reach a scientific consensus on this important issue before policymakers take public action to restructure American industry based on the Market Concentration Doctrine.

REGULATION OF MONOPOLY — THEORY

We have seen that monopoly power is present in the American economy, and we have seen that from the point of view of an optimal allocation of resources, monopoly is a bad thing. Society may decide that it is best to regulate a monopoly. Two common ways to do this are price regulation and taxation.

Consider the monopoly represented by Figure 12-1. The monopoly is maximizing its profits by producing OQ_1 at price OP_1. Let us assume that the government wants to force the firm to produce the same amount that would be produced if this were a purely competitive market, that is, to produce where the marginal cost curve intersects the demand curve. If the government would set a price ceiling of OP_2, the monopoly would react by producing OQ_2 units of output, because the demand curve that the monopoly faces is now represented by line P_2AD. The firm, as always, produces where $MC = MR$ and MR up to point A is equal to line P_2A because demand is perfectly elastic for segment P_2A. The setting of

FIGURE 12-1   Marginal Cost Pricing

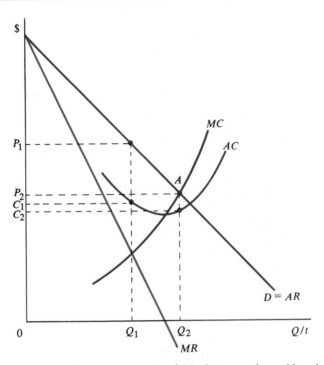

If the regulator imposes a price of OP_2, the monopoly would produce
OQ_2 units of output. Per-unit profits decrease from C_1P_1 to C_2P_2.

such a price ceiling is sometimes called **marginal cost pricing**. Note
that by regulating this monopoly, per-unit profits decrease from $C_1 P_1$ to
$C_2 P_2$. You may be thinking, why not lower the price below OP_2 because
every decrease in price between OP_1 and OP_2 will increase output and
lower price? The problem is that for output levels greater than OQ_2,
every unit produced costs society more than it is willing to pay $(MC > P)$,
so this is just as bad in its own way as monopoly behavior when $MC < P$
and the cost of an extra unit is less than society is willing to pay.

Consider Figure 12-2. The profit-maximizing monopolist is producing OQ_1 at price OP_1. The monopolist is receiving C_1P_1 profit per unit.
Now impose a regulated price of OP_2 on the monopolist. At OP_2 it appears the monopolist would increase output to OQ_2. But note, at price
OP_2 and output OQ_2 the monopolist would lose $C_2 P_2$ per unit sold. Price
is below average cost so the monopolist would leave the industry. In
other words, the optimal output from society's viewpoint is now where
$MC = AR$, but this output forces losses on the monopolist. This output
could, however, be produced if the government would make up the loss,
P_2C_2AB, in Figure 12-2. The monopolist would then produce the

FIGURE 12-2 Marginal Cost Pricing and Losses

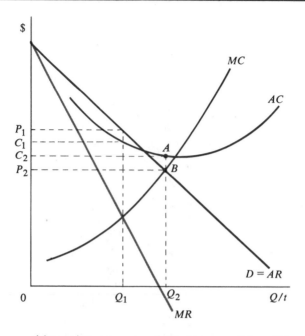

If the regulator sets a price of OP_2, the monopolist would lose C_2P_2 per unit of output sold. The monopolist would thus only produce if the regulator subsidizes the monopolist.

desired output, OQ_2, at price OP_2. The problem with this solution is that if the government subsidizes the industry out of general tax revenues, it is transferring income from taxpayers to the consumers of the good. Most people (except consumers of the particular good) would view such a transfer as an inequitable redistribution of income. The trick, then, for the would-be price regulator, is to set price equal to MC at the point where the MC curve intersects the demand curve, but only if price is equal to or greater than average cost for that level of output.

Now let's see how effective taxation is in regulating monopoly power. Suppose we impose a license fee on our monopolist in Figure 12-3. Before the tax, the monopoly, as before, is producing OQ_1 at price OP_1. The monopolist is earning profits of C_1P_1 per unit. If we charge the monopolist a fee for the right to do business, this fee is not related to the level of output, so it represents an increase in the firm's fixed cost. The AC curve thus shifts up by the amount of the fee to AC_1. The monopolist still maximizes profits by producing OQ_1 at price OP_1, but profits have been reduced to C_2P_1 per unit. Note that it is possible to set the tax or fee so as to capture all the monopoly profit. Such a tax shifts average cost to AC_2 in Figure 12-3.

FIGURE 12-3   **Taxing the Monopoly**

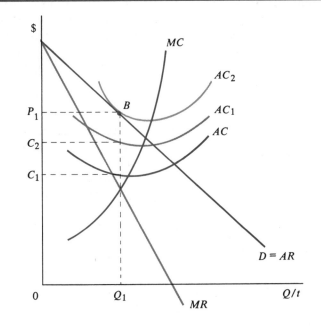

A license fee on the monopolist will be viewed as a fixed cost and will
increase average cost but not marginal cost. In this way, the monopoly
profit can be taxed away with no effect on output.

Although there are practical difficulties with both of these methods
of regulating monopoly, they have quite different effects on the industry.
Price regulation can cause the monopolist to produce the purely competitive output. Taxation, on the other hand, leaves price and output unchanged. A tax simply captures the monopoly profit for the public
coffers. It should be clear, then, that from the viewpoint of the allocation
of resources, price regulation is preferred because it increases output and
lowers price. The tax only corrects for the effect of monopoly on the
distribution of income.

REGULATION OF MONOPOLY — PRACTICE

We saw in Chapter 11 that attempts at regulation often increase the
power of oligopolies as the regulatory bodies are "captured" by the industry. There is, however, an additional problem that is relevant to the
previous discussion of setting prices to regulate monopoly output. This
problem centers on the fact that regulators may not be able to determine
marginal costs and must, therefore, turn to the alternative of regulating

the price based on average cost information. The usual practice is to allow a markup on average cost. This is referred to as *cost-plus pricing*. This type of regulation creates some distortions. If the monopolist is allowed to charge a price of, say, 6 percent above average cost, we have lessened the incentive of the firm to minimize cost, although the firm does have some incentive not to let costs get too far out of hand because the price is still constrained by consumer demand.

Perhaps the best example of this form of behavior is in our present regulatory environment for the utilities' industries — electricity, gas, water, and so forth. Since utilities are considered natural monopolies, they are regulated "for the public interest." Such regulation is on an average cost-plus markup basis. This markup is often called a *fair rate of return*. As a result, utilities have less real incentive to cut costs than do profit-oriented firms, which directly increase profits by any reduction in costs.

Try a little experiment to test this conclusion. Contrast the facilities of your local telephone and electric utility to those of a profit-oriented business in your community. If the proposition holds that regulated industries are less cost conscious, you would expect the regulated firm to have much nicer facilities since they need pay less attention to costs. Compare the facilities used by the executives of the two groups in your community.

Some communities have recently been involved in discussions of whether or not utilities should be able to advertise their product. The side against such advertising argues that it simply raises average costs and results in higher prices to consumers. Our analysis supports this argument. Interestingly, our self-interest model of individual behavior would predict that a certain group in the community would support utility advertising. Any guesses? Of course, it would be the news media. The news media have strongly supported utility advertising, often on the grounds of insuring free speech.

Regulation can not only make a firm less cost conscious, but it can also raise the actual cost of doing business. The attendant costs of compliance and noncompliance could mean that less is produced at higher prices because costs are higher. In this sense regulation is counterproductive to the goal of making monopolies produce a larger output.

Regulation, then, is at best a very tricky exercise and is often counterproductive. An alternative to regulation is to attempt to make monopolistic industries more competitive. This is the goal of our antitrust laws.

U.S. ANTITRUST LAWS

Around the turn of the century in the United States, there was a substantial increase in the growth of large business organizations. Legal arrangements such as *trusts*, which were legal organizations set up to control the stock of other companies through boards of trustees, and *holding companies*, which were single firms set up for the sole purpose of owning and thus controlling other firms, were established. These organizations enabled the *robber barons*, as they have been called by economic historians, to control and coordinate the activities of many previously independent firms. At first, this new form of business was viewed as a natural outgrowth of the Industrial Revolution in the United States. *Social Darwinism* — a popular social theory at the time — justified such behavior. Social Darwinism applied Charles Darwin's theory of the evolution of the species, often summed up (and simplified) as a belief in the survival of the fittest, to business enterprise. Under that view stronger firms were justified in getting bigger by "gobbling up" the smaller ones.

Eventually the public began to view some of these arrangements with suspicion. One of the earliest organized groups to vigorously oppose the trust movement, and one with which you are probably familiar from courses in American history, was the *National Grange*. The Grange began in 1867 as the Patrons of Husbandry and was opposed to trusts, in particular the railroad trust. The railroad trust was opposed by the Grange because of the high monopoly prices it set and also because it was able to practice price discrimination in the hauling of agricultural produce.[14]

As a result of the Grange and other similar populist political movements against trusts, several states enacted antitrust statutes that regulated businesses chartered in the state. These state statutes failed because corporations were able to seek out less restrictive states in which to seek charters. Two of the more hospitable states were New Jersey and Delaware. Eventually the antitrust sentiment became so widespread and intense that by 1888 both national political parties had an antitrust plank in their presidential platform.

In 1890 Congress passed the *Sherman Antitrust Act*. The Sherman Act had two major provisions. Section 1 of the act declared every contract, combination, or conspiracy in restraint of trade to be illegal. Section 2 made it illegal to monopolize or attempt to monopolize.[15] The language of the law is strong, but it is also vague, and the courts took years to determine its scope. We shall trace some of the important decisions, but first we will examine other antitrust laws.

The *Clayton Act*, passed in 1914, made illegal certain business practices that would lead to monopoly. It prohibited a company from acquiring the stock of a competing company if such an acquisition would

---

[14]See Chapter 9, pp. 199–204, for a review of the concept of price discrimination.

[15]Section 1: Every contract, combination in the form of trust or otherwise, or conspiracy, in restraint of trade or commerce among the several States, or with foreign nations, is declared to be illegal. ... Section 2: Every person who shall monopolize, or attempt to monopolize, or combine or conspire with any other person or persons, to monopolize any part of the trade or commerce among the several States, or with foreign nations, shall be deemed guilty of a misdemeanor. ... (Sherman Antitrust Act, Sec. 1, 26 stat. 209 [1890]).

"substantially lessen competition."[16] The act also prohibited tying contracts and price discrimination. *Tying contracts* are agreements between
producers and retailers whereby a retailer must agree to handle certain
items as a prerequisite to handling other items. The Clayton Act, though
it prohibited stock acquisition, was circumvented because it did not prohibit asset acquisition. The *Celler-Kefauver Antimerger Act*, passed in
1950, made it illegal in certain circumstances for a firm to merge with
another by purchasing its assets and thereby strengthened the Clayton
Act.

In 1914, along with the Clayton Act, Congress passed the *Federal
Trade Commission Act*. This act set up the Federal Trade Commission
(FTC) to police "unfair" industrial practices. Initially, the FTC had
many powers, but the Supreme Court, in 1919, denied it the power to
issue cease and desist orders without judicial review. In recent years, the
FTC has worked closely with the Justice Department in antitrust
matters.

The History of Antitrust Enforcement

As mentioned earlier, it took some time for the courts to determine
the scope of the Sherman Act. In particular, the term "in restraint of
trade" needed a legal definition. Of course, if we applied a strict economic definition, any firm with monopoly power, that is, power to restrict
output or to increase price, would be guilty of restraint of trade. The
courts, in two famous 1911 cases against Standard Oil and American
Tobacco, enunciated the *rule of reason*. The rule of reason said that
monopolies that behaved well were not illegal. In effect, the Supreme
Court defined — some might say rewrote — the Sherman Act to make
only "unreasonable" restraints of trade illegal. The test of reasonable-
ness was itself difficult to define. The court held that the existence of
competitors was sufficient to demonstrate reasonable behavior. In 1920
U.S. Steel, despite its dominance in the steel industry, was found not to
be an unreasonable monopoly. The court stated that the law does not
make mere size an offense.

In 1945, after 13 years of litigation, this rule of reason was changed.
Judge Learned Hand ruled in a case against Alcoa Aluminum that size
itself *was* enough to prove the exercise of monopoly power. The change
was so fundamental that commentators later referred to the ruling as the
"new Sherman Act." The Alcoa case was based on estimates of market
power and structural aspects of the industry. In such cases, the way in
which an industry is defined is extremely significant and in fact to a large
degree determines defense and prosecution strategies. As you might
guess, the defense would prefer the industry to be broadly defined, both
geographically and by the number of products included, since such a

[16]For a publication covering the technical details of all these laws, see J. G. Van Cise,
Understanding the Antitrust Laws (New York: Practicing Law Institute, 1973).

definition tends to reduce the importance of any one firm in any particular industry. These few cases, which we have mentioned, trace major changes in the application of antitrust law and also demonstrate the importance of the way the court has changed in its attitude toward the market power of large-scale enterprise.

Another significant change has taken place much more recently. The Sherman Act provides that private parties who are victims of monopoly under Sections 1 and 2 are entitled to sue for *treble damages*. In other words, if a firm is convicted under the Sherman Act, individuals can recover three times the damages they have sustained. This provision was intended to stimulate private suits by firms or individuals who had been victims of price discrimination, but historically it was of very little practical importance. Recently, however, consumer groups have become very active on this front and have brought many recent "class action" suits under the provisions of the antitrust laws. Consumer groups bring action on behalf of the entire "class" of consumers, and treble damages in these cases could be very large.

The point that there have been very few antitrust cases brought by damaged firms or individuals raises an important question — who brings most antitrust cases? The answer lies in the political process. The courts, as we have seen, have made some significant changes in enforcement, but the courts only rule on cases brought before them. The decision on whether to bring a case or not rests largely with the Antitrust Division of the Department of Justice. This decision is made by a presidential appointee, the Assistant Attorney General for Antitrust. Antitrust policy will therefore reflect the desires of the president. Theodore Roosevelt campaigned as the great "trust-buster." He, in fact, set up the Antitrust Division and his administration brought the first cases against industry. As we saw earlier, this trend was nipped by the Supreme Court and the rule of reason. Franklin Roosevelt's first term saw virtually no activity on the antitrust scene. To the contrary, in the early Depression years of the first Roosevelt administration, the government actually fostered anticompetitive practices through the *National Recovery Administration (NRA)*. The NRA tried to set up cartels in virtually every industry, but they were eventually declared unconstitutional. In 1937 the inaction of the Roosevelt administration changed. Thurman Arnold, the Assistant Attorney General for Antitrust, vigorously brought antitrust cases, including the Alcoa case, which ultimately reversed the rule of reason.

In recent years, as before, antitrust activity has reflected presidential appointees' and, therefore, presidential desires. Both the Eisenhower and Kennedy administrations pursued active antitrust programs. President Johnson's administration represented, perhaps because of the diversion caused by the Vietnam War, a retreat from vigorous antitrust policy. President Nixon's first appointee, Richard McLaren, vigorously worked to prohibit conglomerate mergers. McLaren ultimately resigned because of political interference by Nixon politicos in the International Telephone and Telegraph case. The interference clearly demonstrated that antitrust prosecution is very much a political decision. Thomas E. Kauper, who served as President Ford's Assistant Attorney General for Antitrust, pursued an active antitrust policy. He launched a major case against AT&T and tripled the number of price-fixing cases filed. He was also instrumental in changing the law to make price fixing a felony instead of a misdemeanor as it had been under the Sherman Act. Kauper, however, also resigned in a political cloud. President Carter appointed John Shenefield as his Assistant Attorney General for Antitrust. Shenefield promised at his confirmation hearings to make an antitrust impact on the concentration of power. Shenefield also promised to attack the notion of **shared monopoly**, in which very few firms control an industry, and to speed up the litigation process so cases would not drag on for dozens of years. It is still too early to judge the results, but you should watch the press for news of cases being brought.

It is sometimes argued that in periods of economic slump, politicians are not eager to interfere with the system. Likewise, when the economy is performing well, there are incentives not to tamper. Whatever the economic conditions, there is much room for political influence peddling. All of this considered, we might conclude that we shouldn't expect antitrust policy to be extremely effective. Let us turn now to the evidence to see if such a conclusion is warranted.

The Record of Antitrust Enforcement

Economists and lawyers have begun to statistically analyze the case-bringing activity of the Antitrust Division of the Justice Department. The first such study was conducted by Richard Posner and published in 1970.[17] Posner's study offers some statistical evidence concerning some of the propositions we have examined.

Posner found that from 1890, the time of the Sherman Act, to 1969, 1,551 cases were brought by the Justice Department. He found that this activity by the Justice Department does not appear to have been a function of the economic activity in the country. The hypothesis that antitrust activity increased during economic contractions was not supported. You remember, however, that antitrust activity can also be initiated by the Federal Trade Commission (FTC) and even by private citizens. Posner found that contrary to popular belief, the statistics do not bear out the contention that antimonopoly activity of the FTC has increased over time. The number of cases brought by private citizens has increased continuously and significantly since 1949. In the period 1965–1969, 3,136 such cases were initiated as compared to only 399 from 1945 to 1949.

Antitrust enforcement has also been stepped up by the states. This in part has resulted from a bill signed into law by President Ford in Sep-

---

[17]Richard A. Posner, "A Statistical Study of Antitrust Enforcement," *Journal of Law and Economics* (October, 1970).

tember, 1976. This law allows state attorneys general to sue suspected price fixers for treble damages on behalf of citizens. Politics enters here also. State attorneys general are often campaigning for reelection or for higher office. They will bring suits for publicity value but will be careful to avoid suits against powerful groups whom they need to count on in future elections. Watch such cases in your state. They are often brought against out-of-state firms. This creates good publicity, but doesn't damage in-state business support for the attorney general who aspires to higher office.

Other statistics show that although the antitrust cases are usually very protracted, with many lasting as long as five and six years, the success rate of the claimant in Justice Department cases is very high. This success rate is much lower in FTC and private cases. Even with high success rates, the problem is far from solved because remedies, the decisions the court imposes, have been far from successful in terms of restoring competition. In civil cases, the remedy has often taken the form of regulation. If we view the goal of antitrust as restoring competition, regulation is in fact an admission that competition cannot be restored. This and the additional problems that regulation introduces make the imposition of regulation a very inadequate remedy. On the criminal side, the decisions are notoriously weak. Not until the late 1950s was the first person sentenced to jail for price fixing. In 1960 seven more executives were sentenced to jail. In the few cases where sentences have been imposed, the terms have been very short. In addition, the fines levied have been too small to have much of a deterrent effect. In the post-Watergate environment, we have heard more rhetoric about bigger fines and tougher prison terms for white-collar crimes, but it is still too early to tell if this sentiment will affect antitrust decisions.

Posner's study has spawned some attempts to examine the determinants of antitrust activity. Posner himself pointed out that antitrust activity did not seem to be related to economic conditions in the country. He also examined the influence of politics by looking at the party affiliation of the president. He found that the political party in the White House does not seem to affect the number of cases initiated. This, of course, does not mean that politics does not affect the Justice Department's antitrust decisions, only that political interference has not, on average, been too different with one party or the other holding the presidency.

More recently, three economists have attempted to statistically examine the economics that seem important in antitrust activity.[18] They found that the case-bringing decisions of the Justice Department seem to be positively correlated to the size of the industry as measured by sales. Other variables which may more closely represent monopoly power, such as profit rates on sales and concentration, seem to play a less important role in explaining Justice Department case bringing.

---

[18]William F. Long, Richard Schramm, and Robert Tollison, "Economic Determinants of Antitrust Activity," *Journal of Law and Economics* (October, 1973).

The actual record of antitrust activity does not present an encouraging picture. We have seen that even though there is a reasonable success rate for cases brought, the litigation is a long process and civil remedies seldom restore competition. Moreover, the criminal sanctions have been applied with so little vigor that they probably have very little deterrent effect.

Reform of Antitrust Law

There have been some recent studies and reports concerning legislation to rewrite the antitrust law. This legislation was submitted to Congress yearly between 1972 and 1976 by the late Senator Philip Hart of Michigan. A group of senators plans to resubmit the bill in Senator Hart's name. The bill, the *Industrial Reorganization Act*, seeks to codify into law the structural position that size, *per se*, should be illegal. We discussed this structuralist position earlier in this chapter. One of the bill's primary goals is to remove the decision to seek antitrust action from the political arena.

Senator Hart's bill is divided into three titles. Title I makes the possession of monopoly power, *per se*, illegal. Title II sets up an Industrial Reorganization Commission whose function is to prosecute violations of Title I. This commission would be an independent agency whose head would be appointed for seven and one-half years by the president with approval of Congress. The essential difference between this agency and the present antitrust division is that the commission would have no discretion on whether or not to bring cases. If the commission were to find that a firm meets the requirements of Title I, it must report the case. Title III of the bill sets up a special industrial reorganization court to hear the cases and to restore "effective competition."

Title I addresses the problems we have been considering. It clearly states that monopoly power is illegal and establishes a definition of monopoly power.

There shall be a rebuttable presumption that monopoly is possessed —
1 by any corporation if the average rate of return on net worth after taxes is in excess of 15 percentum over a period of five consecutive years out of the most recent seven years preceding the filing of the complaint, or
2 if there has been no substantial price competition among two or more corporations in any line of commerce in any section of the country for a period of three consecutive years out of the most recent five years preceding the filing of the complaint, or
3 if any four or fewer corporations account for 50 percentum (or more) of sales in any line of commerce in any section of the country in any year out of the most recent three years preceding the filing of the complaint.[19]

---

[19]Senate Bill, S. 3832 (1972).

Obviously provisions 1 and 3 are the meat of the bill, since it would be hard to prove the charges under provision 2. An application of provision 3 would mean, for example, that prosecution would be brought in almost all the industries listed in Table 12-2. The bill represents the codification of the Market Concentration structure-conduct-performance hypothesis in industrial organizations. The bill, perhaps because it would have such a huge impact on the structure of American industry, has been criticized severely.[20]

Perhaps the strongest challenge to Senator Hart's bill comes from economists who argue that size or concentration is not a proxy for monopoly power. These studies, which we examined earlier, conclude that the Market Concentration Doctrine does not hold up to empirical verification and that the cost advantage of large firms relative to small firms is greater; that is, there are significant economies of scale which explain the concentration. Such studies indicate that Senator Hart's bill would introduce inefficiencies into U.S. industry by not allowing firms to reach the optimal level of production if such a level exceeded the bill's provisions.[21] Also, strict adherence to the 15 percent profit rate might restrict entrepreneurial activity in risky ventures. Why should an entrepreneur bear risk if the firm is limited in the potential future reward that can be captured from bearing this risk? Fifteen percent sounds like a lot, but at times in recent years, banks have charged more than 12 percent interest to their best customers. This line of reasoning obviously conflicts with that of other economists who argue that there are good economic reasons for trying to do something about concentration.

On the practical side, you may have already anticipated the legal problems the bill raises. Each case would center on determining a legal definition of what constitutes a "section of the country" or a "line of commerce" (see provision 3 of Title I). Our discussion of the SIC codes indicates that there might be substantial disagreement over these definitions. For example, if you defined a line of commerce as selling beer and a section of the country as the Southwest, Coors would probably be in violation of the bill. On the other hand, if you defined the line of commerce as selling alcoholic beverages, or selling liquid refreshment, and the section of the country as the United States, Coors would clearly not be in violation.

In all, Senator Hart's bill may have the potential to profoundly affect the present structure of American industry. We saw in both this chapter and the previous chapter on oligopoly that there is serious disagreement among economists on the possible effects of such a bill. The debate will probably continue and will probably receive more publicity in the press over the next few years.

---

[20]For a discussion of the bill, see Hearings before the Subcommittee on Antitrust and Monopoly, *The Industrial Reorganization Act*, 93rd Congress (Washington, 1973).

[21]The bill does provide for an escape clause that exempts firms if the market power is due solely to valid patents or if divestiture would result in the loss of substantial economies of scale.

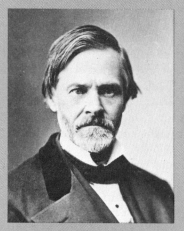

John Sherman (1823–1900)

Henry Clayton (1857–1929)

John Sherman, Henry Clayton, Estes Kefauver, and Philip Hart

John Sherman, Henry Clayton, Estes Kefauver, and *Philip Hart* were all U.S. politicians who played a large role in shaping U.S. antitrust policy.

John Sherman was a highly respected Republican Senator from Ohio. In 1888 he almost became the Republican nominee for president instead of Benjamin Harrison. Sherman worked hard for the passage of the first antitrust bill. The questions Congress debated concerning antitrust legislation were fundamental questions. Congress was concerned about the constitutionality of an antitrust bill and about the way in which the law could be enforced. Much debate was focused on how to define violations of the law. A bill was finally written in 1890 by the Judiciary Committee of the Senate and named for Senator Sherman to lend it prestige. In 1897 President McKinley named Sherman his Secretary of State.

The Clayton Act grew out of political unrest in Congress over dislike of the rule of reason coupled with the reformist tendencies of the Wilson administration. Passed in 1914 and named for Congressman Henry Clayton, the Clayton Act was more concerned with monopolistic behavior and much less with intended behavior. The Clayton Act made specific business practices illegal. Henry Clayton, who was a Democratic Congressman from Alabama from 1896 to 1914, was largely responsible for the act which bears his name.

The Bettmann Archive, Inc.

Estes Kefauver (1903–1963)

Bachrach Photographers

Philip Hart (1912–1976)

Estes Kefauver, a Democratic Congressman and later a Senator from Tennessee, was an active and outspoken foe of monopoly. In 1950 he was largely responsible for passage of the Celler-Kefauver Antimerger Act, which amended the Clayton Act to prohibit companies from purchasing the *assets* of competing companies. This closed a loophole in the Clayton Act, which had prohibited only the purchase of the *stock* of competing companies. Kefauver worked hard for antitrust laws because he believed monopoly was a threat to small business, which he saw as the foundation of American communities. In 1950 *Time* chose Kefauver as one of the "Senate's most valuable ten." In 1952 Kefauver ran against President Truman for the Democratic nomination for president. He won a stunning victory in New Hampshire, and Truman announced that he would not be a candidate two weeks later. Largely because of Truman's antagonism toward Kefauver, Adlai Stevenson eventually won the nomination. In 1956 Kefauver ran for vice-president on the Stevenson ticket.

Senator Philip Hart was the latest in this line of politicians who were primarily concerned with antitrust. Hart became chairperson of the Senate's antitrust committee after Kefauver's death. Hart was much more academic than Kefauver, and the Hart hearings produced volumes of very academic testimony. Hart proposed the Industrial Reorganization Act before his death in 1976.

267

ALTERNATIVES FOR CONTROLLING INDUSTRY

We have seen that there is a substantial amount of monopoly power, or at least concentration, in American industry. In Chapter 9, we explained theoretically why monopoly power is detrimental from society's point of view. Unfortunately our discussion of ways to control monopoly or to restore competition through antitrust enforcement has indicated that it is both difficult to control monopoly and that antitrust action has not produced the desired results. What, then, are the alternatives?

First, let's consider the one obvious justification for monopoly power — economies of scale. Is the claim of those against the Hart Bill, that it would produce inefficiencies, justified? There have been several empirical studies by economists that have attempted to measure the degree of concentration and relate this concentration to scale economies.[22] Table 12-4 summarizes part of one of these studies. As Table 12-4 indicates, there appears to be more concentration than is justified by economies of scale in production. This is calculated by assuming that all four firms in the four-firm concentration ratio are the same size. The actual size can then be compared to the efficient size. Thus there could be some deconcentration without introducing inefficiencies. Note that five of the ten industries in Table 12-4 would fall into the category deemed illegal under Senator Hart's bill (a concentration ratio of 50 percent or more). The interesting fact is that three of the five that would be prosecuted are not those that are the most "oversized," having the highest ratio of firm size to efficient size. In fact, in the tractor industry deconcentration might come dangerously close to creating less than optimal-size firms. So again we must be careful in designing hard and fast rules for deconcentration.

There does, however, seem to be at least one policy action which, if vigorously followed, could increase competitive pressures without endangering the efficiency produced by economies of scale. This policy action takes us back to our earlier discussion of industrial concentration and the threat of new entry. If policy could actually support new entry by actively dismantling *artificial* barriers to entry, competitive pressure would increase. In many cases the threat of new entry alone would be sufficient to alter the behavior of existing oligopolistic industries. We saw in Chapters 9 and 11 that these artificial barriers are both privately and publicly imposed. Vigorous enforcement of present antitrust law should be sufficient to remove private entry barriers. Deregulation in the airline industry, for example, is necessary in many cases to remove the governmentally sanctioned and imposed barriers. Removal of these barriers would cause market forces to introduce competitive pressure and this would not require the drastic action implied by courtroom interference and restructuring.

---

[22]See Roger Sherman and Robert Tollison, "Public Policy Toward Oligopoly: Dissolution and Scale Economies," *Antitrust Law and Economics Review* (Summer, 1971), for a review of several of these studies.

TABLE 12-4   **Economies of Scale and Concentration**

Industry	Efficient Size as a Percentage of Industry Sales	Four-Firm Concentration Ratio	Ratio of Firm Size to Efficient Size[1]
Tractors	12.5%	72%	1.44
Flat Glass	10.0%	91%	2.27
Chewing Gum	6.7%	87%	3.25
Soap	3.9%	88%	5.64
Beer	2.3%	28%	3.05
Steel	1.8%	54%	7.49
Petroleum Refining	1.8%	33%	4.58
Flour	1.0%	39%	9.76
Cement	0.9%	32%	8.89
Shoes	0.3%	29%	24.20

Source: Adapted from H. Michael Mann, "Seller Concentration, Barriers to Entry, and Ratio of Return in Thirty Industries," *Review of Economics and Statistics* (August, 1966).
[1]This ratio is found by dividing the four-firm concentration ratio by four and then dividing that number by the efficient size as a percentage of industry sales.

Summary

Industries are defined by SIC codes which are prepared by the Department of Commerce. These SIC codes can be used to prepare concentration ratios which are used to measure the degree to which markets are concentrated.

This chapter has presented a picture of the present state of empirical work by industrial organization economists. There is scientific disagreement on a number of important issues. Studies conflict on the trend in concentration in American industry. Some researchers have found increased trends in concentration and others claim to have found the concentration level in American industry to be quite stable. An even more important debate has emerged over the Market Concentration Doctrine. It is important because many economists have long held that the structure of an industry determines its ultimate performance. If this is true, it would imply that concentrated industries should be restructured. We found, however, that there is a good deal of debate concerning the degree to which concentration leads to higher profit rates and more rigid prices. Although most economists still accept the Market Concentration Doctrine, there may be enough competing evidence to warrant more study before we make policy based on the doctrine.

Regulation of monopoly leads to cost-plus pricing, which destroys cost-minimizing incentives. Taxation of monopoly does not destroy these incentives, but it does not change the monopoly price and output.

U.S. antitrust law began with the Sherman Antitrust Act in 1890. The Sherman Act and succeeding laws have been applied with varying vigor and success over their history. The record of antitrust enforcement is not too impressive. The litigation takes a long time and relief rarely restores competition. Politics plays an important role in antitrust activity.

Reform of the antitrust laws has been proposed. This reform could have a significant impact on U.S. industry and therefore needs to be carefully studied.

New Terms

industry studies
industrial organization
Standard Industrial Classification (SIC) system
concentration ratio
Market Concentration Doctrine
administered prices
marginal cost pricing
cost-plus pricing
fair rate of return
trusts
holding companies
robber barons

Social Darwinism
Sherman Antitrust Act
Clayton Act
tying contracts
Celler-Kefauver Antimerger Act
Federal Trade Commission Act
rule of reason
treble damages
National Recovery Administration (NRA)
shared monopoly
Industrial Reorganization Act

Questions for Discussion

1 Should profits be used as a measure of monopoly power? Should concentration be used as a measure of monopoly power? Discuss the wisdom of using either or both.
2 What would happen in a regulated industry if price were set so that the firm does not earn a normal rate of return?
3 If all prices in an industry are identical, is this evidence of an antitrust violation?
4 Do concentration ratios tell you anything meaningful about change in a particular industry?

Suggestions for Further Reading

Bilas, Richard A. *Microeconomic Theory*, 2d ed. New York: McGraw-Hill Book Co., 1971.
Blair, John M. *Economic Concentration: Structure, Behavior, & Public Policy*. New York: Harcourt Brace Jovanovich, 1972.
Caves, Richard. *American Industry: Structure, Conduct & Performance*, 3d ed. Englewood Cliffs, N.J.: Prentice-Hall, 1972.
Demsetz, Harold. *The Market Concentration Doctrine: An Examination of Evidence & a Discussion of Policy*. Washington: American Enterprise Institute for Public Policy Research, 1973.
MacAvoy, Paul W. (ed.). *Crisis of Regulatory Commissions*. New York: W. W. Norton and Co., 1970.
Scherer, Frederick M. *Industrial Pricing*. New York: Rand McNally & Co., 1970.
Sherman, Roger. *The Economics of Industry*, new ed. Boston: Little, Brown & Co., 1974.
Sherman, Roger, and Robert Tollison. "Public Policy Toward Oligopoly: Dissolution and Scale Economies." *Antitrust Law and Economics Review* (Summer, 1971).

CHAPTER 13

THE ECONOMICS OF FACTOR MARKETS

LEARNING OBJECTIVES

After studying the materials found in this chapter, you should be able to do the following:

1 Define
   (a) product market,
   (b) factor market.

2 List and give examples of the three characteristics of the demand for a factor of production, including
   (a) derived demand,
   (b) joint interdependence,
   (c) technologically determined demand.

3 Define and show the calculation necessary for
   (a) marginal physical product,
   (b) value of the marginal physical product,
   (c) marginal revenue product,
   (d) marginal resource cost.

4 State the profit-maximizing rule for a firm hiring a resource in terms of MRP and MRC.

5 Use a factor market diagram including VMP, MRP, D (demand for the factor), MRC, and S (supply of the factor) to illustrate the differences when there is
   (a) pure competition vs. monopoly in the product market,
   (b) pure competition vs. monopsony in the factor market.

6 Define monopsonistic exploitation in terms of a competitive wage vs. a monopsonistic wage.

7 List the factors which help explain the income of a resource owner.

8 Define
   (a) economic rent,
   (b) single tax,
   (c) crowding out.

The distribution of income in a market economy depends on the prices of the factors of production and on the distribution of the ownership of the various factors. In most discussions you're likely to come across, much more attention is given to the ultimate distribution of income than to the reasons for this distribution. This chapter discusses factor markets and explains why the distribution of income is what it is. In Chapter 15 we will discuss action that can be taken if society doesn't like the distribution of income that is produced by the market process. The following discussion is a theoretical explanation of how and why incomes are determined in a market system. We will be examining marginal productivity theory, which was first put forward by John Bates Clark in a book entitled the *Distribution of Wealth* published in 1899. Actually, Clark was not the first to explain most of the ideas, but he was the first to put them down in a clear and consistent fashion. Clark made his mark at a very young age and to this day the American Economic Association presents the John Bates Clark award to economists under the age of 40 who make significant contributions to economic theory.

THE DEMAND FOR FACTORS

The demand for factors is, of course, similar to other types of demand that we have studied. In previous chapters we discussed *product markets*, in which firms or individuals sell the goods and services they produce. We looked at markets in which producers sold to consumers. Now we want to examine *factor markets*, which are the markets in which firms buy factor inputs — the services of land, labor, and capital — from individuals who are supplying these factor inputs. We are, then, looking at markets in which individual owners of factors are selling services to producers. We can go far in understanding these factor markets by using the same tools we developed to study product markets. There are, however, some differences between factor markets and product markets, and we will concentrate on these differences.

The demand for a factor of production has three features that make it somewhat different from the demand for a product. The first is that it is a *derived demand*. A firm only demands labor because the labor can be used to produce goods which consumers are demanding. The demand for labor is thus derived from the demand for the product it produces. If there were no consumer demands for milk, there would be no demand for milkers, milking machines, or good dairy cattle grazing land. This holds true for all factors. They are only valuable to a firm if they help produce products that consumers value.

The second feature of the demand for factors is that the demand is *jointly interdependent*. In other words, the amount of one factor that is demanded will depend on the amounts of other factors a firm plans to use. The amount of labor a firm demands depends on the amount of land and capital that will be used with the labor.

John Bates Clark

Brown Brothers

**John Bates Clark
(1847–1938)**

John Bates Clark was the first American-born economist to achieve an international reputation as an economic theorist. He was a reformer and activist who helped form the American Economic Association, later becoming its third president.

Clark was born and raised in Providence, Rhode Island. He graduated from Amherst College in 1872. He gave up the idea of divinity school and instead studied economics from 1872 to 1875 at the University of Heidelberg and the University of Zurich. Upon his return to the United States, Clark taught political economy at Carleton College and then moved to Smith College, Amherst, Johns Hopkins, and finally to Columbia, where he taught political science from 1895 to 1923. After 1911 he became very active in pacifist causes and was the first director of the Carnegie Endowment for International Peace.

Clark's interests in economic theory reflect the times in which he lived. The American industrial revolution caused Clark to examine problems of production and distribution. Clark overcame his normative, reformist tendencies and instead concentrated on developing a positive theory based on the competition of rational, self-interested people, as illustrated in his book *The Distribution of Wealth* (1899). This was a radical change from Clark's earlier work, *The Philosophy of Wealth* (1887), in which he attacked the "hedonistic" assumptions of the classical economists. His influence on later economists is in large part due to the analytical tools that he developed.

John Bates Clark's status in the American economics profession is recognized in the awarding of a John Bates Clark prize by the American Economic Association. This prize is awarded every two years to the economist under the age of 40 who has made a significant contribution to economic theory. The list of 16 winners reads like a who's who of the American economics profession.

The third major feature is that the demand for a factor is in part *technologically determined*. That is, the demand will depend on techniques of production and on technological progress. We speak in terms of a *production function*. The production function tells how much of one factor is needed to produce a certain level of output, given a certain technique of production and the other factors of production used. It is the job of the engineer to help the entrepreneur understand the substitutions that can be made within this production function.

You will see these basic elements unfold as we examine *marginal productivity theory*. As we proceed we shall follow John Bates Clark's precedent by developing the theory using labor as an example. The theory holds for all factors of production, but most interest centers on labor and the returns to labor. At the end of the chapter we shall discuss factor markets other than labor markets.

THE DEMAND FOR LABOR

You remember that a demand curve graphically depicts the relationship between price and quantity demanded. A demand curve for labor will tell how much labor will be employed at various wage rates. If we want to develop a theory about the market demand for labor, we start by finding how much labor a firm will employ at various wage rates. Then we aggregate the results across firms in a way very similar to the way we found the market demand for a product in Chapter 2.

The Demand for Labor under Perfect Competition in Product and Factor Markets

We shall begin by looking at a firm that is selling its product in a perfectly competitive product market and buying its labor in a perfectly competitive labor market. This means that the firm will take the price of its product *and* the price of labor as given. The firm views itself as having no effect on product prices or on wage rates. We need next to determine the value of labor to the firm. Suppose the production function is such that, as we vary the amount of labor employed, *ceteris paribus*, the changes in the amount of total product initially become larger and larger but then become smaller and smaller. This demonstrates the principle of diminishing marginal productivity, which we discussed in Chapter 7 when we looked at costs. As we employ more labor with all the other factors in fixed proportions, the additional amounts of output per additional unit of labor will eventually decline. If this were not the case, we could theoretically grow the entire world's supply of wheat on one acre of land just by employing more workers, and we could do this without having average costs rise. Suppose we hold constant the quantities of the other factors, land and capital, and determine how the firm's output is related to the quantity of labor it uses.

The amount of *total physical product* for a hypothetical firm is given in column 2 of Table 13-1. Note that this output depends on the technical relationship found in the production function. Once we know the total product, we can determine how much extra product is produced when labor inputs are added; i.e., the *marginal physical product* (MPP_L) of that unit of labor. It is the marginal physical product because the output is in physical units; e.g., number of autos, pounds of coal, and so on. We can now evaluate this change in physical output to see what it is worth to the firm. To put a value on the output, we simply multiply the amount of the product by the price the firm can sell it for. This produces what we call the *value of the marginal physical product of labor* (VMP_L); it appears in column 6 of Table 13-1. The VMP_L is a measure of the value that each unit of labor adds to the firm's product. The *marginal revenue product of labor* (MRP_L) is the amount that each unit of labor adds to the firm's total revenue. It is found in column 7 of Table 13-1. You will note that in pure competition in the product market, the $VMP_L = MRP_L$. This is because the product price remains constant. The firm can produce and sell as much as it wants at the market-determined price, which is $2 in this example. In other words, when the firm faces a given price, marginal revenue is exactly equal to price, as we saw in Chapter 8.

TABLE 13-1   **The Demand for Labor in Purely Competitive Product Markets**

(1) Units of Labor	(2) Total Physical Product	(3) Marginal Physical Product (MPP_L)	(4) Product Price	(5) Value of the Physical Product = Total Revenue	(6) Value of the Marginal Physical Product (VMP_L)	(7) Marginal Revenue Product (MRP_L)
1	10	10	$2	$20	$20	$20
2	18	8	2	36	16	16
3	24	6	2	48	12	12
4	28	4	2	56	8	8
5	30	2	2	60	4	4

We can plot the VMP_L and the MRP_L on a graph, as in Figure 13-1. The MRP_L is the firm's demand curve for labor. If we know the price of labor, we will be able to determine how much labor the firm will purchase. We began by assuming this firm was in a purely competitive factor market. This means the firm can purchase labor at the market wage

FIGURE 13-1   The Demand for Labor in Purely Competitive Product Markets

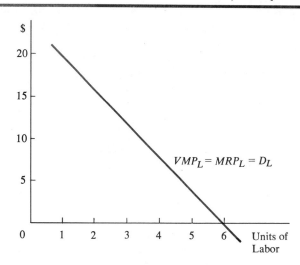

The marginal revenue product of labor curve is the firm's demand curve
for labor. When the firm's product market is purely competitive, the
marginal revenue product and the value of the marginal product are
identical.

(OP_w) with no effect on the wage. We see this in Figure 13-2. The market demand for labor (D_L) is the aggregate of all the individual firms'
MRP_L curves, since each MRP_L curve indicates the amount of labor each
particular firm will hire at any given wage rate. The market supply curve
of labor (S_L) is the aggregate of all the individual supply curves, showing
how much each worker is willing to work at different wage rates. The
equilibrium price OP_w is the wage rate. The firm can now purchase as
much labor as it wishes at OP_w. The supply curve the firm faces is thus
perfectly elastic at OP_w. This is represented by S_f in Figure 13-2. If the
supply curve the firm faces is perfectly elastic, the cost of each additional
unit of labor is the same, or constant. We refer to the cost of each additional unit of a resource (in this case, labor) as the **marginal resource
cost (MRC)**. For a firm in a perfectly competitive labor market, the marginal resource cost of labor, MRC_L, is the same as the supply curve. A
profit-maximizing firm will employ or purchase a resource until $MRP =
MRC$. This makes sense because if a factor adds more to revenue than to
cost (if $MRP > MRC$), it would be profitable for the firm to purchase
more units of the factor. However, if the factor adds more to cost than to
revenue (if $MRP < MRC$), the firm should purchase fewer units. In our
labor example, the firm will hire laborers (Figure 13-2) until the amount
they add to total cost (MRC_L) is exactly equal to the amount they add to
revenue (MRP_L). In Figure 13-2, the firm would employ Ox_1 units of

FIGURE 13-2   Perfectly Competitive Labor Market

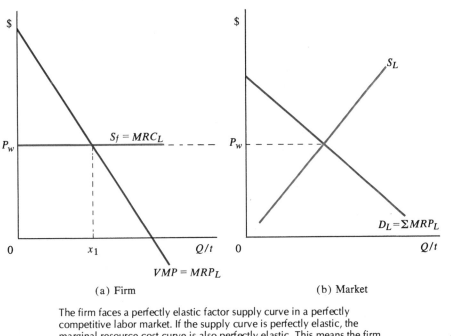

(a) Firm   (b) Market

The firm faces a perfectly elastic factor supply curve in a perfectly competitive labor market. If the supply curve is perfectly elastic, the marginal resource cost curve is also perfectly elastic. This means the firm can purchase as much labor as it wants at the market-determined wage rate.

labor at wage rate OP_w. In terms of our numerical example in Table 13-1, the firm would employ four units of labor if the market wage was $8 per unit. If the market wage was $4 per unit, five units of labor would be employed.

The Demand for Labor under Monopoly in Product Markets and Pure Competition in Factor Markets

The only thing we now want to change in our example is the assumption that the firm under consideration is a firm with monopoly power in product markets, rather than a firm selling its product in pure competition. This means that the product price will fall as the firm sells more units of its product. A numerical example is presented in Table 13-2. The difference between this and our first example is that product price (column 4) declines as the firm produces and sells more product. VMP_L and MRP_L are calculated in the same manner as before. VMP_L is simply the valuation of the labor's marginal physical product, so $VMP_L =$

TABLE 13-2   **The Demand for Labor in Purely Competitive Product Markets**

(1) Units of Labor	(2) Total Physical Product	(3) Marginal Physical Product (MPP_L)	(4) Product Price	(5) Value of the Physical Product = Total Revenue	(6) Value of the Marginal Physical Product (VMP_L)	(7) Marginal Revenue Product (MRP_L)
1	10	10	$10	$100	$100	$100
2	18	8	9	162	72	62
3	24	6	8	192	48	30
4	28	4	7	196	28	4
5	30	2	6	180	12	−16

$MPP_L \cdot P$ (column 3 times column 4). MRP_L is found by multiplying the MPP_L by marginal revenue. MRP_L is shown in column 7. Note that now $VMP_L > MRP_L$. This is because under monopoly, product price is greater than marginal revenue.

We have graphed both a VMP_L curve and an MRP_L curve in Figure 13-3. The MRP_L curve is again the firm's demand curve for labor. This firm, like the previous firm, will employ labor until $MRP_L = MRC_L$. Although the firm is selling its product in a monopolistic product market, it is purchasing labor in a competitive labor market. The firm is thus faced with the situation diagramed in Figure 13-4. The market demand curve is, as before, found by summing the MRP_L curves for all firms purchasing this type of labor. The market supply (S_L) depends on individual desires of workers. The market-determined wage is OP_w. This firm can purchase as much labor as it desires at OP_w, so the supply curve facing it, S_f, is perfectly elastic at OP_w. Since S_f is perfectly elastic, MRC_L is also perfectly elastic. The firm maximizes profits where $MRC_L = MRP_L$, so the firm hires Ox_1 units of labor. You will note from Figure 13-4 that the monopolist pays OP_w, the market wage. The fact that $MRP_L < VMP_L$ does not mean the monopolist exploits labor by paying too little — the monopolist has to pay the market wage just like any other employer in this market. Instead, it means that the monopolist employs fewer laborers than similar competitive firms would employ. You remember from Chapter 9 that the monopolist restricts output to keep price high. The analog of this in the factor market is that the monopolist restricts inputs in order to restrict output. If this were a competitive firm rather than a monopolist, it would want to be on the VMP_L curve (which would then also be the MRP_L curve) and hire Ox_2 workers.

FIGURE 13-3   The Demand for Labor with Monopoly in Product Markets

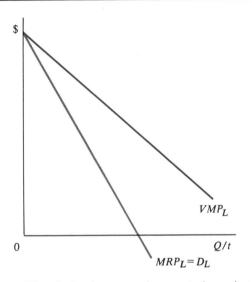

When the firm has monopoly power in the product market, the MRP_L curve will lie below the VMP_L curve. This is because under monopoly, product price is greater than marginal revenue.

Monopsony

We have looked at competitive and monopolistic firms demanding labor in competitive labor markets, but now we want to consider the case where there is market power in the labor markets. We have assumed to this point that the purchasing firm had no effect on wage rates. But what if the firm does affect wage rates, so that as the firm hires more labor, the wage rate rises? We refer to such a firm as having ***monopsony*** power. The word "monopsony" comes from the Greek words meaning "one purchaser." Just as pure monopoly is the case of a single seller of a product, pure monopsony is the case of a single purchaser of a particular factor.

Let's consider first the case of pure monopsony. We will begin by assuming a firm's MRP_L curve is known to us, as in Figure 13-5. It doesn't matter if this firm is selling its product in a competitive market or a monopolistic market, although it's hard to imagine a monopsonist without some degree of monopoly power in the product market. We also know the market supply curve of labor to this firm, S_L. Table 13-3 provides a numerical example of the monopsony supply curve to further your understanding of Figure 13-5. The market supply curve, S_L, is the supply curve the firm faces because the firm is the market for this class of labor by the definition of monopsony. If this were a competitive market, a wage rate of OP_c and output of OQ_c would have resulted. However, since the firm faces the upward-sloping supply curve, S_L, the marginal resource cost curve for labor (MRC_L) lies above the S_L curve, as in Figure

FIGURE 13-4   **A Monopolistic Firm Facing a Perfectly Competitive Labor Market**

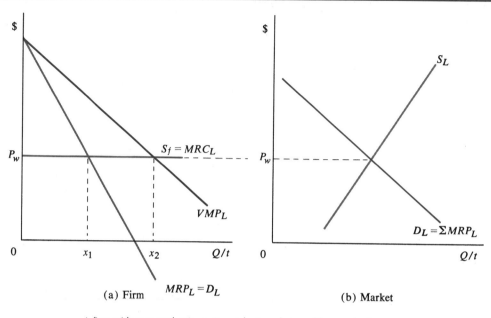

(a) Firm $MRP_L = D_L$ (b) Market

A firm with monopoly power in product markets and in a perfectly
competitive labor market will face a perfectly elastic supply curve. The
firm will hire units of labor until the marginal revenue product of labor is
equal to the marginal resource cost of labor.

13-5. To see why this is the case, refer to Table 13-3. The supply curve
is, of course, the graphical representation of columns 1 and 2. Since the
curve is upward sloping, the firm must pay a higher wage rate as it hires
more labor. As a result, total wage expenses (column 3) increase. The
amount that each additional unit hired adds to wage expenses is the marginal wage expense, or what we generally have been calling the marginal
resource cost.[1] You can see by comparing columns 2 and 4 that the curve
representing column 4 will lie above the supply curve, as shown in Figure 13-5. The firm, as before, maximizes profits where $MRP_L = MRC_L$.
This would be at point A on Figure 13-5. So the firm employs OQ_m units
of labor. But what is the wage rate? Remember the supply curve tells you
what has to be paid to hire OQ_m units of labor. So the firm will pay OP_m.
Note that $OP_m < OP_c$, so the monopsonist is paying a lower wage than
would have been paid in a competitive labor market. We refer to this
situation as ***monopsonistic exploitation*** because labor is receiving less
than a competitive wage. This does not mean that workers are forced to
work at wage rates below what they are willing to work for. Rather, the
monopsonist simply restricts input as the monopolist restricts output.

---

[1]Some other books call this the marginal factor cost.

FIGURE 13-5 Monopsony

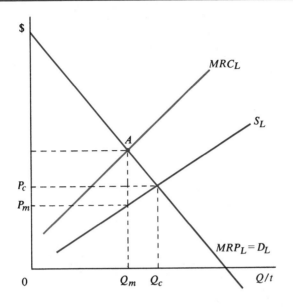

The monopsony firm faces the market supply curve for labor. Since this curve has a positive slope, the marginal resource cost curve lies above it. The monopsonist thus hires OQ_m units of labor at a wage rate of OP_m.

TABLE 13-3 Monopsony in Labor Markets

(1) Units of Labor	(2) Wage Rate	(3) Wage Expense	(4) Marginal Wage Expense (MRC_L)
1	$ 5	$ 5	$ 5
2	6	12	7
3	7	21	9
4	8	32	11
5	9	45	13
6	10	60	15
7	11	77	17
8	12	96	19
9	13	117	21
10	14	140	23

Monopsony in the Real World. Are there any real-world examples of pure labor monopsony? No, because all labor has some alternative employment. Pure monopsony, like pure monopoly, is a theoretical extreme. There are, however, real-world examples of monopsony power. You are probably familiar with the song about the miner who owes his soul to the company store. This song was written about mining companies and how they dominate as the major employer in certain areas. A large university in a small town would be a good example of monopsony power. If you compared university secretarial salaries for similar-sized schools in different-sized cities, hence varying the size of the labor pool, you would find that where the university dominates, the labor pool salaries would be lower. Why? Monopsony power, of course.

Perhaps the best example of monopsony in our present economy exists in professional sports. Congress has granted sports leagues exemptions from obeying the antitrust laws which we discussed in Chapter 12. This allows the leagues to hire as monopsonists by drafting and maintaining their control through reserve clauses.[2] As a result, wage rates will be lower than if the teams competed for players on an open or at least freer market. Even when there were only two competing leagues, such as the NFL and AFL in football and the NBA and ABA in basketball, salaries were relatively much higher than they are now. A few of you may remember when Joe Namath signed for what seemed like an astronomical salary. A study of the economics of baseball found empirical evidence of this monopsonistic exploitation. In 1964, Gerald Scully found the *MRP* of "star" pitchers to be $405,300 and their salary to be only $66,800.[3] Think about the case of "Dr. J.," Julius Irving, the basketball player. True, he receives a very high salary, but consider what he adds to the league in terms of marginal revenue. He fills up the arena for practically every game he plays.[4] His salary is surely under his *MRP*.

Except for these special cases, where we have buyers of very specialized labor skills, there are few instances of significant monopsony power. In general, this is because transportation and communication in U.S. labor markets have increased labor mobility, and with increased labor mobility there is decreased monopsony power. If the miner is aware of job possibilities in other areas and in other jobs, the mine will be forced to pay a competitive wage. Indeed, if only a small percentage of miners are willing to pull up stakes, the mine will be forced to pay competitive wages. This is because we don't need complete labor mobility; it's enough to have mobility only at the margin.

---

[2]Reserve clauses have and are being challenged. Players can now play out their options, thus reducing the monopsony power of the owners.

[3]G. W. Scully, "Pay and Performance in Major League Baseball," *American Economic Review* (December, 1964).

[4]*Sports Illustrated* reported that the Milwaukee Bucks realized an additional $700,000 profit during Kareem Abdul-Jabbar's first season. His salary was $250,000. So you can see, Abdul-Jabbar's $MRP_L > MRC_L$.

Monopsony Power and Minimum Wages. We saw in Chapter 4 that minimum wages are price floors set above the market clearing price and, as such, cause surpluses, or unemployment, in these markets. This is not correct 100 percent of the time because a minimum wage that is set in a monopsonistic market can cause employment to increase. Consider the monopsony market in Figure 13-6. The monopsonist would employ OQ_m units of labor at wage rate OP_m. Now suppose a minimum wage of OP_{m1} is imposed. The market supply curve is replaced by a horizontal line at OP_{m1}, the imposed minimum wage. In effect, the monopsonist is forced to accept the minimum wage. The market supply curve is now represented by the line $P_{m1} AS_L$. The marginal resource cost for labor, MRC_L, is now the same, or $P_{m1} A$. This is because the supply curve is perfectly elastic in the range $P_{m1}A$. At a wage rate of OP_{m1}, OQ_{m1} would be employed. If the minimum wage selected is OP_{m2} instead of OP_{m1}, the supply curve the firm faces is $P_{m2} BS_L$. The firm would face perfectly elastic supply and MRC curves in the relevant range. The firm would in this case employ OQ_m units of labor at wage rate OP_{m2}. You can see that if the minimum wage that is imposed lies between OP_m and OP_{m2}, it will result in more employment at a higher wage rate.

FIGURE 13-6   Monopsony and Minimum Wages

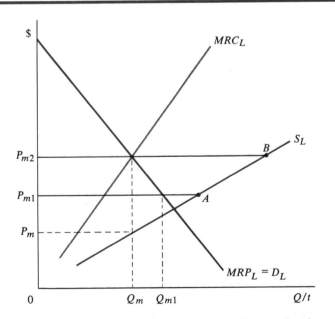

A minimum wage of OP_{m2} in a monopsonistic labor market changes the market supply curve from S_L to $P_{m2}BS_L$. The marginal resource cost curve is the same as the supply curve along $P_{m2}B$, the perfectly elastic portion.

What we have just analyzed is an exception to the case where minimum wages have antisocial effects. Be careful, though; this result only holds when there is monopsony power in the labor market, and monopsony is very hard to find except in certain very highly skilled situations, such as with basketball players. Most empirical studies of the effects of minimum wages show that the monopsony model is not important except, of course, as a special case in textbooks.[5]

MARKET COMBINATIONS

We have developed a set of combinations in product and factor markets that you can apply in considering market situations. There can be competition or monopoly in product markets and competition or monopsony in factor markets. The possibilities, when combined, are presented in Table 13-4. If we wanted to, we could even expand this list by making further refinements. Just as oligopoly in the product market can be viewed as real-world monopoly, *oligopsony* (few buyers) in the factor market can be viewed as real-world monopoly. Similarly, *monopsonistic competition* might be viewed as real-world perfect competition in factor markets. Making these refinements ("complications") would expand Table 13-4 to what we have in Table 13-5. It is not clear that such an expansion is worthwhile in terms of insights, but it does allow you to complete the classification of product and factor markets.

TABLE 13-4   **Market Combinations**

Product Market	Factor Market
Competition	Competition
Competition	Monopsony
Monopoly	Competition
Monopoly	Monopsony

CHANGES IN FACTOR DEMAND

We have developed the demand curve for labor and determined how the firm decides on the amount of labor to hire. Now we shall return to our earlier discussion of the differences in factor and product demands to determine what causes factor demand to increase or decrease.

---

[5]See Jack Hirshleifer, *Price Theory and Applications* (Englewood Cliffs, N.J.: Prentice-Hall, Inc., 1976), pp. 374–377, for a review of these empirical studies.

TABLE 13-5   **Market Combinations Expanded**

Product Market	Factor Market
Pure Competition	Pure Competition
Pure Competition	Monopsonistic Competition
Pure Competition	Oligopsony
Pure Competition	Monopsony
Monopolistic Competition	Pure Competition
Monopolistic Competition	Monopsonistic Competition
Monopolistic Competition	Oligopsony
Monopolistic Competition	Monopsony
Oligopoly	Pure Competition
Oligopoly	Monosponistic Competition
Oligopoly	Oligopsony
Oligopoly	Monopsony
Monopoly	Pure Competition
Monopoly	Monopsonistic Competition
Monopoly	Oligopsony
Monopoly	Monopsony

We said that the demand for labor is a derived demand. It is derived from the demand for the product it is used to produce. To see this more clearly, return to Table 13-1 and Table 13-2, which show the situations for a competitive and monopolistic firm, respectively. Suppose there is an increase in demand in the product market, with the market demand curve shifting parallel to the right. This would cause the product price to increase for the competitive firm and the demand curve to shift to the right for the monopolistic firm. The figures in column 4 in both tables would be larger. This would mean that the MRP_L for the competitive firm, column 7 in Table 13-1, would increase by the amount of the increase in product price. In most cases, this increase in demand would also cause the monopolist's MRP_L to increase compared to the figures shown in Table 13-2.[6] This would cause the MRP_L curve to shift outward for either kind of firm, representing an increase in the demand for labor. In a competitive labor market, this would result in each firm's wanting to hire more labor at the existing wage rate. This in turn would cause the market demand for labor to increase and thus would raise the wage rate. The amount by which the market wage increases will depend on how large

_____

[6]We can create cases where the demand facing the monopolist increases at every price, but marginal revenue and hence marginal revenue product actually falls, so that the demand for labor falls.

this industry is relative to the labor market. If the industry is small, there may be only an imperceptible increase in wages; but if it is large, the wage rate could rise significantly. In a monopsonistic market, the result would be an increase in wages and an increase in employment.[7]

A second important feature of factor demand is that the demands for different factors are mutually interdependent. Refer again to Table 13-1 and Table 13-2. Suppose the capital stock of the firm is now doubled. If labor and capital used together are complementary in the sense that an increase in capital makes labor more productive (and we assume they are), each unit of labor will now have a larger total physical product. This will show up in Table 13-1 and Table 13-2 as increases in the figures in column 2. This will cause the MPP_L to increase, which will cause the MRP_L to increase. What has happened is that the MRP_L has shifted outward, signifying that the demand for labor has increased. This is what is meant by complementarity; an increase in one factor raises the MRP of the other.

Increased productivity resulting from an increased capital stock can have several effects. Consider first what happens if the capital stock expands in one firm but has no industry-wide effects. This would cause the firm's demand curve (MRP_L) to increase (shift to the right) in Figures 13-2 and 13-4 without any (noticeable) effect on the aggregate demand curve because the firm is trivial in size relative to the industry. The result would be that the firm would employ more units of labor at the market-determined price. Alternatively, consider the effect of an industry-wide increase in the capital stock. All firms in the industry have an increase in capital, causing their MRP_L curves to increase. The aggregate curve also increases. The result is that more labor is employed at a higher wage rate. Such a situation is graphically depicted in Figure 13-7. Initially we are at equilibrium with the firm employing Ox_1 units of labor at the market wage of OP_w. The industry is employing OQ_1 units of labor. Now let's have an industry-wide increase in capital. The firm's MRP_L curve shifts to MRP_{L1}. Since all the firms in the industry have experienced this increase in MRP_L, the aggregate curve will also increase, as from D_L to D_{L1} in Figure 13-7. This causes the market wage to rise to OP_{w1}. As a result, the supply curve that the individual firm faces shifts from S_f to S_{f1}. The firm now will employ Ox_2 units of labor at wage rate OP_{w1}. Industry employment has risen from OQ_1 to OQ_2. The important point to understand in this scenario is that the response of the firm to more capital was to hire more workers at higher wages. This was because the increase in the stock of capital increased the marginal productivity of the workers. The demand for the factors, labor and capital, can thus be seen to be interdependent.

---

[7]You should work through the geometry of such increases.

FIGURE 13-7   An Industry-Wide Increase in Capital

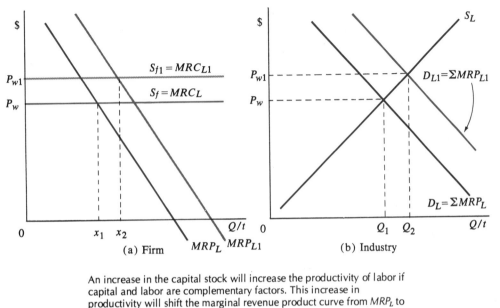

An increase in the capital stock will increase the productivity of labor if
capital and labor are complementary factors. This increase in
productivity will shift the marginal revenue product curve from MRP_L to
MRP_{L1} and the market demand for labor from D_L to D_{L1}.

MARGINAL PRODUCTIVITY AND INCOME

This analysis has served to point up an important conclusion of marginal
productivity theory. That is, in a competitive factor market, the productivity of the factor determines its price. In turn, the productivity depends
on the inherent productive qualities of the factors and the quantity of the
factor employed. Labor will receive higher wages the more productive it
is. Since wages determine incomes of laborers, more productive laborers
will have higher incomes. Laborers that are less productive will have
lower incomes. John Bates Clark, the original expositor of this theory,
held that it presented a morally correct outcome of economic activity.
Whether or not it is morally correct is not the province of economic
theory. Theory is positive and says nothing concerning whether the income distribution which results is a "good" one. Rather, the theory indicates that if markets for factors are competitive, factors will receive returns based on each factor's productivity. If we don't like the outcome,
we can then work to change it through political markets (this will be
discussed in Chapter 15), but theory does indicate that output will be
maximized in societies where factors are paid according to their marginal
products.

OTHER FACTORS OF PRODUCTION

So far in this chapter we have used labor to exposit the marginal productivity theory of factor markets. There are, of course, other factors of production which generate income for their owners. Most of the points we have made will hold for these other factors. Firms demand the services of land and capital because land and capital are productive, the demand being derived from the demand for the product that they help produce. It would be a waste of your time to repeat the analogy between labor and the other factors, so instead we will discuss differences in these other factor markets. In turn we shall examine rent and interest, the payments to the ownership of the services of land and capital.

Land and Rent

The property income that has generated the most political interest in the United States is rent. To begin, we must define the concepts of land and rent. To the British economists of the 1700s and 1800s, *land* was the input in the productive process that was fixed by nature. Such things as cultivatable acreage, water, oil, coal, etc., would all qualify as land. Now if something is in fixed supply, its supply curve is perfectly inelastic, as in Figure 13-8. If the supply is perfectly inelastic, the price is going to be a *demand-determined price*. In Figure 13-8, if the demand is D_0, the price is zero. As the demand increases to D_1, D_2, and D_3, the price rises to OP_1, OP_2, and OP_3, respectively. We call these prices *rent*. We must, however, be careful with this term, which is defined as the payment for the productive services of the land. It is not the price of the land. The price of the land would be the capitalized value of the expected flow of these payments. Refer back to Chapter 7 if you have forgotten how to use interest rates to capitalize the value of a stream of payments.

The idea of rent can be generalized to apply to any factor, and here is where students sometimes go wrong. *Economic rent* is technically a payment greater than the amount necessary to bring the factor into productive use. In other words, in Figure 13-8, all the payments to land are rent because the amount OQ_1 is fixed and the payments don't bring any more land into existence. This idea is distinct from the labor market supply curve in Figure 13-2, where higher wage rates increase the quantity of labor supplied, and the marginal workers entering the market do so only at the higher wage rate. The essential difference between labor and land in this regard is that humans have alternatives to work, such as leisure, which has utility. When land is not producing, it has no utility.

The concept of economic rent is important because it is a surplus being paid to the owner of the factor of production. This surplus could be taken away with no change in economic activity. For example, suppose running back Tony Dorsett's skills are such that he has only two work alternatives: being a bartender and earning $15,000 per year or

FIGURE 13-8   The Supply of Land

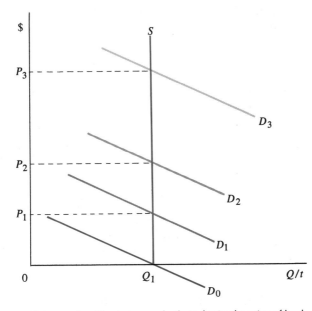

If the supply of land were perfectly inelastic, the price of land would be demand determined.

being a running back and earning $500,000 per year. Under such circumstances, he is earning economic rent. If the two occupations are equally attractive to him, he could be paid $15,001 and he would remain a football player.[8] We could then tax away $484,999 of his salary and he would not change his behavior. An idea similar to this was suggested by Henry George as a way to raise money to conduct governmental activity.

The Single Tax. In 1879 Henry George (1839–1897) wrote a book entitled *Progress and Poverty*, which suggested a ***single tax*** on land. George's book was very widely read and he may even be the best-known American economist of all time (if we measured this by the percentage of the population familiar with the book). George ran for mayor of New York City on the idea of his single tax and came very close to winning. He argued that the return to land was a *surplus* of unearned income and should be taxed away by the government. The proposal rested on two basic presumptions. First, the rent was unearned, and landowners were receiving the return simply because they held good land. If you think about this, it has political appeal. Why should someone get rich just because his or her grandfather happened to stake a claim on a piece of land

---

[8]Competition for players among NFL teams has kept Dorsett's salary above $15,001.

Henry George

Henry George (1839–1897)

Henry George may have been the most widely read economist of all time. George's book *Progress and Poverty* (1879) was a best seller — it sold millions of copies. If measured by sales as a percentage of the population, George's book would be the most popular economics book of all time.

Henry George was born in Philadelphia in a lower middle-class environment. He had almost no formal education and went to sea at age 14. He ended up in San Francisco and became a journalist. His interests in political economy were fueled by his experiences as a journalist. In California, George ran for the legislature but was defeated, in large part because of his strong opposition to state subsidies for railroads.

During this period, George was a devoted reader, and he turned his hand to writing books that combined economics and social commentary. Between 1870 and 1886 he published numerous books and articles, but *Progress and Poverty* brought him international fame. In it, George argued for a single tax on land because landowners contributed nothing to the productivity of land. Rising land values were explained by general economic growth and westward expansion. George's single tax rested on the proposition that such a tax would not change the allocation of land and, more importantly, that it was inequitable for landowners to get rich while nonlandowners remained poor. George argued that there was no reason that landowners should get rich by the simple economics of increased demand brought about by the westward expansion of the U.S. population. The increasing value of the land, George argued, was in no way determined or affected by the owners of the land. In this sense, George was arguing that the rising value of land was a "windfall" profit, much in the same way that President Carter argued that deregulation of oil creates "windfall" profits for holders of oil reserves.

George's book and his idea of a single tax made him immensely popular. In 1886 he re-entered politics. This time he ran as the Labor and Socialist parties' candidate for mayor of New York City. George was so popular that it took a major coalition of other parties to defeat him. He ran again in 1897, but died during the campaign.

that was located in a future population center? Second, the confiscation of this rent would not affect economic activity because the supply was perfectly inelastic. In other words, the tax wouldn't cause less land to be supplied, as an income tax causes less labor to be supplied.[9] George became a social reformer and argued that this land tax should be the only tax that government collects. His followers became known as the single taxers and some of them are still active today.[10]

The single tax movement died for political reasons (landowners are a strong political force), but also because of some severe theoretical problems. First, one could argue with the proposition that the quantity of land is fixed. Remember, when we draw a demand or a supply curve, we hold quality constant. It is therefore arguable that land can be improved in the quality dimension, thus increasing the quantity of land of a particular quality. Anyone who has seen agriculture in the Arizona or California deserts can attest to this fact. Increasing payments for land causes more land to be irrigated and increases the quantity supplied. If the return to land were taxed away, this incentive to improve land would be gone. Similarly, swamps can be drained and land can be reclaimed from the sea with dikes, as in the Netherlands. For example, several years ago there was a proposal to build a new airport near downtown Chicago. The idea was to build a dike in Lake Michigan, pump out the water, and build an airport on the lake bottom. Such projects would not even be contemplated if George's tax were operative.

Secondly, and even more fundamentally, rents serve a very important function even if they don't influence the quantity of land in existence. George argued that the rent the landowner receives plays no part in creating incentives for landowners to supply land. But the other side of the transaction is different. The payment made by the user of the land (the firm) rations the land between competing uses and insures that the land is put to its highest valued economic use. For example, suppose there is a choice acre of vacant land near your school. What should this land be used for — a McDonald's, a massage parlor, a church, or a dump? In a market system the decision will be determined by who is willing to pay the most. In other words, the market rations between competing uses for the land. If payments are not made, a universal planning system would have to be implemented to determine allocation among competing uses of the land.[11]

Thirdly, and perhaps most importantly, if government taxes rents, people will be discouraged from trying to earn them. The quest for these rents, however, is an important economic activity.

---

[9]To review the effects on the labor supply of an income tax, see pages 128–130.

[10]The economics department at the University of Missouri is one of their last enclaves.

[11]The perceptive reader will note that zoning commissions in part play this role in a mixed economy, and to the extent that they don't allow the most economic use of a piece of land, they are taxing the owner's right to the income from that land.

Capital and Interest

Firms demand capital because it is productive. We could derive a marginal revenue product curve for capital just as we did for labor. Such a curve is drawn in Figure 13-9. One difference you will note is that the demand for capital is expressed in dollars because it is in effect the price of money. It is important to realize that the demand for capital is not a demand for money itself, but rather a demand for physical capital. A demand for money can be used as a proxy, however, because the money is used to purchase the physical capital. In other words, money itself is not productive; the physical capital is productive.

FIGURE 13-9   The Demand for Capital

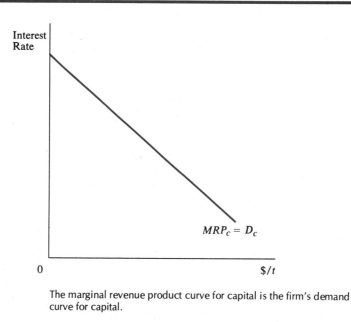

The marginal revenue product curve for capital is the firm's demand curve for capital.

It wouldn't work to put the price of money in terms of money, so the price of money is expressed as a percent per year, or the interest rate. Figure 13-9 tells us that at lower rates of interest there will be higher rates of capital formation by firms. You can see this more clearly by examining Figure 13-10, which shows the market and firm. The market we are talking about is often referred to as the market for loanable funds. The supply of loanable funds comes out of business savings and personal savings. Firms save out of profits in order to reinvest and individuals save in order to consume more in future periods. At higher interest rates people will save more because the present foregone consumption will allow

FIGURE 13-10 The Market for Loanable Funds

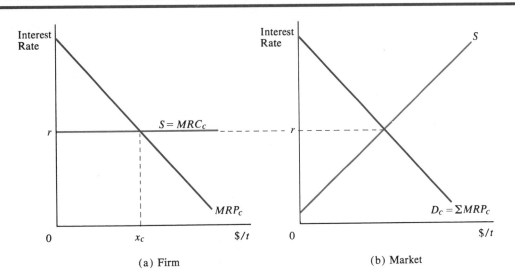

(a) Firm   (b) Market

The supply of capital to the firm is perfectly elastic at the interest rate set in the market for loanable funds. The firm then invests in capital until the marginal revenue product of capital is equal to the market rate of interest.

greater consumption in the future. As a result, we get a normal upward-sloping supply curve. In Figure 13-10, the market demand for capital is the summation of all the individual firm demand curves which are, of course, the marginal revenue product curves for capital. We then get a market rate of interest, Or, which determines, in a competitive capital market, the supply of capital available to a firm. The supply to the firm is perfectly elastic at the market rate of interest, which makes the marginal resource cost curve perfectly elastic. We can then determine the amount of capital formation for the firm, which in this case is Ox_c.

Crowding Out. The interest rate allocates loanable funds among competing firms and among competing uses exactly as the wage rate allocates labor services. If we expand on this idea a little we can see why some economists are so concerned with the federal deficit. Consider the fact that there are more than just business firms demanding loanable funds. There are two other important groups in this market for loanable funds. Consumers demand loanable funds to finance the portion of their consumption based on credit. They borrow to buy homes, furniture, automobiles, and more. The other demander of loanable funds is the government. At all levels, be it federal, state, or local, governments borrow loanable funds. The market for loanable funds is therefore composed of three important segments which might be represented as in Figure 13-11. The market for loanable funds is represented by a supply of S_L and a demand of D_L, which is the summation of the household demand for loanable funds, the business demand for loanable funds, and the governmental demand for loanable funds. The resulting interest rate is Or and a representative firm adds Ox units of capital to its capital stock.

FIGURE 13-11   Crowding Out

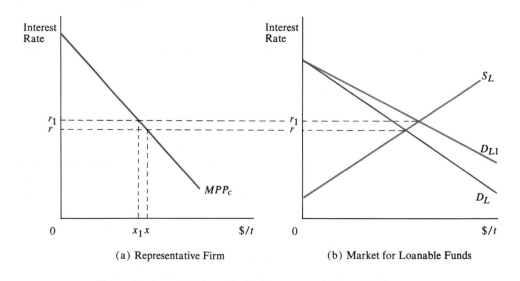

(a) Representative Firm   (b) Market for Loanable Funds

The market demand for loanable funds is composed of household, business, and governmental demands for funds. An increase in governmental borrowing will cause the market rate of interest to rise. The firm's response to this increased price of capital is to decrease the quantity demanded. We then say firms have been crowded out of capital markets.

Now watch what happens, *ceteris paribus*, when the government increases its borrowing. Government demand increases. This causes aggregate demand to increase to D_{L1}, which causes the interest rate to rise to Or_1. This means that the supply curve to the firm has shifted up by the amount of the increase from Or to Or_1. The net result is that the firm will decrease its investment from Ox to Ox_1. The government has crowded business (and households) out of capital markets. Interest rates allocate funds between the three uses, and when the government bids them up, households and business will get fewer of these funds.

Several political and business leaders, perhaps most notably William Simon, former Secretary of the Treasury, are very worried about such **crowding out**. Simon believes this crowding out is a very real burden of the federal deficit. He argues that the large amounts of borrowing cause the government to bid up the interest rate and compete investment funds away from business. When this happens, business does not grow as much as it would have and the productivity of the economy suffers. Remember the discussion above, of how increases in the capital stock raise the overall demand for labor. Crowding out would have the effect of keeping the demand for labor from growing as fast as it would have and as a result holds down the wages of workers.

Entrepreneurship and Profits

Profits are a residual. They are what's left for the entrepreneur after the land, labor, and capital have been paid. This is not to say that profits are not important; indeed, as we saw earlier, the quest for profits makes them the prime mover of a market economy. If profits above normal levels are earned, this will be the signal for firms to enter the industry, and if below-normal profits are earned, firms will leave the industry. In addition, potential profits are keys to innovative activity and risk taking. The entrepreneur takes chances, bets on the future, because of potential profits. Henry Ford installed the assembly line because he thought it would increase efficiency and lead to higher profits. He was profit motivated and this drove him to be innovative.

Thus, profits play a very important role. They are first and foremost the signal of the market system. Profits also generate the incentive to innovate and strive for greater efficiency.

THE DISTRIBUTION OF INCOME

This chapter has developed a theory which explains why the distribution of income is what it is. At its simplest level, the theory says that, given private property and competitive market conditions, a certain distribution of income will be produced. Labor will be paid according to its productivity, and the owners of capital and land will receive payments according to the productivity of the factors they own. Any event that causes the productivity of a factor to increase will increase the remuneration that factor receives.

This theory has received much criticism since it was first exposited by John Bates Clark, who was looking for a natural law to explain how the distribution of income was determined. The criticisms of the theory have almost all been on the grounds of *distributive justice*. Critics argue that such a market system of income distribution is unfair because the old, the sick, the young, and the blind, among others, will not receive a "fair" share since they are not productive or as productive as others. Another normative criticism of the theory rests on the premise that economic productivity, rather than social productivity, determines remuneration. A writer of sex novels earns more than a writer of poetry and some critics say this is also not "fair." You should recognize such criticisms for what they are: normative, ethical considerations, and not valid criticisms of the theory. Think back to our early discussion of the role of theory. A theory that is valuable provides a good explanation of some aspect of the real world. According to this test, marginal productivity theory stands up quite well.[12]

It is quite a different matter to be dissatisfied with the income distribution that exists in society and to argue that the government should take steps to change it. It is possible that such intervention might be very costly in terms of the goods and services given up. There are valid, normative arguments for governmental intervention in the market, and these we shall discuss in Chapter 15, but all of the consequences should also be understood.

Summary

The demand for a factor of production is a derived demand. It also depends on the amount of other factors used, as well as being technologically determined.

Labor is demanded by a firm because it is productive. The marginal revenue product curve is the firm's demand curve for labor. In a competitive labor market, the firm faces a perfectly elastic supply curve. When the supply curve is perfectly elastic, the marginal resource cost curve and the supply curve are the same. A monopoly firm in product markets uses less labor than a competitive industry would use. This results because the firm naturally restricts inputs in the process of restricting output.

A monopsony is the single purchaser of an input. Monopsony results in fewer units of labor being purchased at less than the perfectly competitive usage. Because the monopsonistic wage is below a competitive wage, we refer to the difference as monopsonistic exploitation. Improved market information and mobility of workers greatly reduce monopsony power.

Land is the factor of production that is in fixed supply. Rent is the return to this fixed factor. Economic rent is a payment above the amount necessary to attract an input. Henry George proposed a single tax on land. One important economic difficulty with this proposal is that if rents aren't paid, a planning authority would have to decide among competing uses of the land.

Capital, like the other factors, is demanded by firms because it is productive. The payment to capital is interest. As interest rates rise, the quantity of capital that the firm demands will decrease. In cases where the increase in the interest rate is a result of government action, we say that crowding out is taking place in capital markets.

Profits are a residual that entrepreneurs receive. Profits direct a market economy because they serve as the signal for firms to either enter or leave a particular industry.

---

[12]For a review of empirical studies, see David Kamerschen, "A reaffirmation of the Marginal Productivity Theory," *Rivista Internazionale Di Scienze Economiche E. Commerciali* (March, 1973).

Marginal productivity theory explains how the distribution of income is determined in a market economy. It says nothing about the normative appropriateness of this distribution.

New Terms

product markets
factor markets
derived demand
jointly interdependent demand
technologically determined demand
production function
marginal productivity theory
total physical product
marginal physical product (MPP)
value of the marginal physical product (VMP)
marginal revenue product (MRP)

marginal resource cost (MRC)
monopsony
monopsonistic exploitation
oligopsony
monopsonistic competition
demand-determined price
economic rent
single tax
crowding out
distributive justice

Questions for Discussion

1 What is economic rent? Have you ever earned economic rent? Would taxation of this rent have caused you to behave differently?

2 "Technology puts people out of work. Capital and labor compete for jobs and soon people won't be able to find jobs." Do you agree with this? Did the invention of the automobile put many blacksmiths out of work? Did the invention of modern supermarkets put home milk delivery out of business? Did home refrigerators put ice delivery people out of business? Were these "bad" or "good" things? Is it possible to think of a world where machines do

everything? Would you like to live in such a world? Would there still be scarcity?

3 The demand for accountants has skyrocketed in recent years and the salaries of accountants have increased significantly. Is the demand for accountants a derived demand? If so, from what?

4 Why are professional athletes against reserve clauses?

5 What does it mean to say profits are a residual?

6 Is there any similarity between the concept of economic rent and economic profit?

Suggestions for Further Reading

Neale, Walter C. "The Peculiar Economics of Professional Sports"; and Simon Rothenberg, "The Baseball Players' Labor Market." Both in *The Daily Economist*, edited by Harvey G. Johnson and Burton A. Weisbrod. Englewood Cliffs, N.J.: Prentice-Hall, Inc., 1973.
Stigler, George J. *The Theory of Price.* New York: Macmillan Co., 1966, Chapters 15, 16, and 17.

CHAPTER 14

THE ECONOMICS OF THE LABOR MOVEMENT

LEARNING OBJECTIVES

After studying the materials found in this chapter, you should be able to do the following:

1 List the economic goals of unions and the ways these goals might be achieved.

2 Define
- (a) exclusive union,
- (b) inclusive union,
- (c) featherbedding,
- (d) bilateral monopoly,
- (e) yellow-dog contract,
- (f) secondary boycott,
- (g) closed shop,
- (h) mediation,
- (i) arbitration,
- (j) union shop.

3 Diagram and analyze the economic effects of
- (a) an exclusive union,
- (b) an inclusive union,
- (c) bilateral monopoly.

4 List the major laws, organizations, dates, and leaders in the history of the labor movement.

After looking at factor markets in theory, we can now examine the effect that unions have on the factor markets for labor services. Unions in general have goals that are political as well as economic. American unions have concentrated on economic goals and have pursued objectives such as good salaries, job security, good pensions, and, of course, good jobs for union leaders. The most important goal has been to raise wages, and we will concentrate on the effects unions have had on the wage rate. We will begin with a theoretical look at unions to determine how they attempt to raise wages. We will then look at the empirical evidence of the success of unions in raising wages and discuss at whose expense these increased wages have come. Then we will take a look at the history of the labor movement in the United States.

THE ECONOMICS OF UNION GOALS

Unions have been formed for all sorts of reasons, many of which are social and political as well as economic. As we shall see later in this chapter, the only lasting American labor unions are those that have concentrated on economic goals. When we speak of economic goals, the bottom line, of course, is the real income of union members. It is largely correct, then, though somewhat of an oversimplification, to think of unions as existing to increase the wages of their members. Unions, of course, do pursue goals other than wage maximization. Unions have worked for shorter hours and better working conditions, to mention just two goals. These other goals all have the effect, *ceteris paribus*, of increasing the wage rate of workers. If wages are unchanged and working conditions have improved, the worker has received an increase in real income. In order to increase wage rates in a competitive labor market, such as the one shown in Figure 14-1, the union must do one of two things. It must either increase the demand for labor (such as to D_{L1}) or decrease the supply of labor (such as to S_U).

Increasing the demand for labor is a very difficult task for the union. Remember that D_{L1} in Figure 14-1 depends both on the demand for the product the labor produces and on the productivity of the labor. If the union is to increase the demand for labor, it must increase the demand for the product the firm produces. There have been some attempts at this. Unions have run programs to influence people to "buy union-made" and to decrease imports, thus attempting to increase the demand for domestically produced (union) products. Unions have encouraged educational training programs aimed at increasing productivity and thus increasing demand. The unions have also tried to get government to help by buying union-made goods and also by using macro policy.[1] All things considered, however, it is very difficult for unions to increase the demand for labor. In some instances, unions have had some success in forestalling

---

[1]The companion volume to this book goes into this in detail.

FIGURE 14-1   Union Goals — Raising the Wage Rate

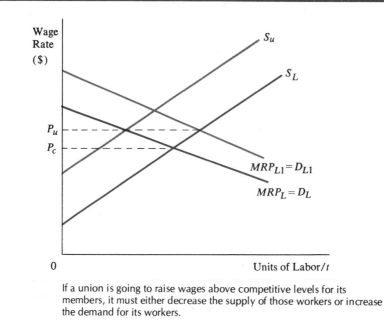

If a union is going to raise wages above competitive levels for its
members, it must either decrease the supply of those workers or increase
the demand for its workers.

reductions in jobs in declining or dying industries. A good example of
this is the practice of *featherbedding*, or insisting on required jobs that
management claims are unnecessary. A good example of featherbedding
is the case of railroad firemen. The advent of diesel and electric power
made the fireman obsolete, but unions were successful in maintaining
the job. However, even this type of activity may be of only short-run benefit because it speeds the decline of an already dying industry and ultimately weakens the union.

The conclusion we reach is that, because of the difficulties of changing demand, unions should work on the supply side of the market, attempting to shift the supply curve, such as from S_L to S_U in Figure 14-1.
Historically, many of the "social goals" of unions also have had the effect of restricting the supply of labor. Unions have sought to reduce immigration, limit child labor, encourage compulsory and early retirement,
and enforce a shorter work week. Whatever else you may think of these
goals, they all make economic sense for unions if the goal is to increase
the union wage rate.

TYPES OF UNIONS

In examining unions from a theoretical point of view, we can reduce the
different kinds of unions to two basic types, *exclusive* and *inclusive*. An
exclusive union derives its economic power from the fact that it ex-

cludes workers from the work force. Because of this exclusion, the wage rate is higher than it would be in the absence of the union organization. Figure 14-2 represents such a union. Supply curve S_C represents the competitive supply of labor and D_L represents the demand for labor. In the absence of any union organization, the wage rate would be OP_C, and OQ_C units of labor would be employed. The exclusive union attempts to exclude workers from the industry and thus shift the supply curve to S_U. If the union were to succeed in doing this, the wage rate for union workers would be OP_U and the number of labor units hired would be OQ_U.

FIGURE 14-2 An Exclusive Union

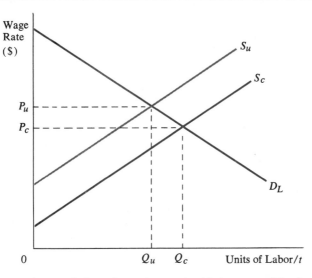

In an exclusive union, union membership is a precondition for employment. As a result, the union can exclude membership and decrease the supply of labor.

The key, then, to an exclusive union is that it restricts entry into the profession. Examples of exclusive unions are *craft unions*, which are unions comprised of skilled laborers such as plumbers and physicians. These unions are very often the type in which workers serve apprenticeships and internships in order to become members.

It should be obvious that a successful exclusive union is a very powerful force because the wage rate increase results directly from the exclusionary tactics. The union doesn't need to bargain, coerce, threaten to strike, and so forth. Its power to exclude competing workers is sufficient to cause the market wage to increase. The power of the union is difficult to challenge once the exclusion has been successful.

It should also be obvious that it is difficult to exclude workers from the union. When wages rise, there will be pressure from other workers to seek employment in these trades. This is a natural economic force and makes it necessary for the union to be able to control "licensure." In particular, many successful exclusive unions find it easier if they can get the government to help them exclude by requiring a worker to earn a license or permit to be a member of the trade. If the union can then gain control of this licensing function, it has an automatic way of excluding labor. This is one way in which plumbers, electricians, and medical doctors have maintained their union power.

The *inclusive union* attempts to organize all the workers in a particular industry. These inclusive unions are sometimes referred to as *industrial unions* and are represented by such unions as the Steelworkers, the Autoworkers, and the Teamsters. The goal of the inclusive union is to bring all workers in an industry into union membership and, as a result, present a strong bargaining position to management. Additionally, it is important that an industrial union organize all workers in that industry, or the nonunionized firms will be at a cost advantage and able to undersell union-organized firms. This will create incentive for unionized firms to try to break the union. As a result, such union organization has been most successful in oligopolistic markets where there are fewer firms in which the labor needs to be organized.

The inclusive union is represented by Figure 14-3. The competitive wage and employment are OP_C and OQ_C, respectively. The union organizes the industry and bargains a wage, OP_U. OP_U is in effect, then, a minimum wage in this industry and employment will be OQ_U. It should be clear that the ability of the inclusive union to raise wages depends on the strength of its bargaining stance, which will, of course, depend on its membership in the particular industry. It is important that an inclusive union have a significant membership in the particular industry in which it operates because its success depends on its ability to threaten the firms in that industry.

Bilateral Monopoly

The inclusive union has been most successful in industries which are very concentrated. The firms in these industries may possess monopsony power in labor markets. What we want to analyze here is a monopoly union selling to a monopsonistic purchaser of labor. Economists call this *bilateral monopoly*. The situation is depicted in Figure 14-4. In the absence of the union, the monopsony firm would employ OQ_M units of labor at a wage rate of OP_M. The competitive wage and employment would have been OP_C and OQ_C. The union, however, will press for a higher wage, say OP_U. The result of this process is *logically indeterminate*. That is, the model will not theoretically explain what the resulting wage will be. All we can say is that the wage will be between OP_M and

FIGURE 14-3   An Inclusive Union

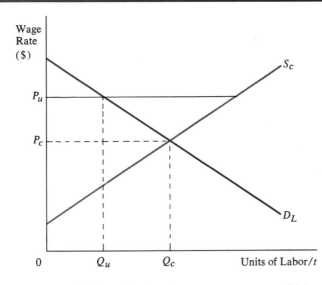

In an inclusive union the union attempts to organize all labor in the industry and then to bargain a wage. This bargained wage then works like a price floor (or minimum wage) in this labor market.

OP_U. Whether it is closer to OP_M or to OP_U depends on the relative bargaining strengths of the union and the monopsony firm. You should note that if the wage is anywhere between OP_M and OP_U, employment will rise with unionization. If, for example, the union is successful in bargaining a wage rate of OP_C (the competitive rate), employment would rise from OQ_M to OQ_C. You will note that this result is very similar to the effect of a minimum wage in a monopsonistic market, which we discussed in Chapter 13.

Do Unions Raise Wages?

Regardless of the power of a union, there will be constraints on the degree to which it can influence wages. There will always be competitive pressure from other labor inputs and substitution of other factor inputs for labor inputs. A good example would be a union organizing migrant workers. To compete with the union, the farmer substitutes machinery for labor. A second powerful constraint exists in the product market. If unions raise wages, costs rise and so prices rise. Consumers will react to the increased price and will shift consumption to nonunion products; the demand for union-made products and thus for union labor will then fall. These constraints are always present, and the union can do very little to offset them.

FIGURE 14-4   **Bilateral Monopoly**

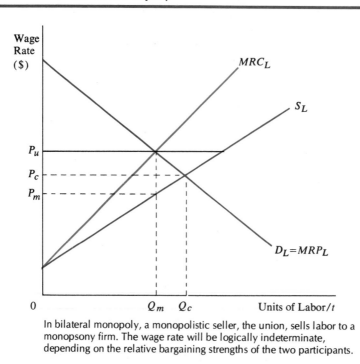

In bilateral monopoly, a monopolistic seller, the union, sells labor to a monopsony firm. The wage rate will be logically indeterminate, depending on the relative bargaining strengths of the two participants.

The question at hand, however, is, How successful have unions been in increasing the wages of their members? The path-breaking empirical study in this area was done by Professor H. Gregg Lewis, then of the University of Chicago and now of Duke University. He found that union workers with similar productivity characteristics received on average from 10 to 15 percent higher wages than nonunion workers.[2] The difficulty in this type of research is to separate wage differences based on productivity differences from those based solely on union power. Lewis based his study on data from the 1940s and 1950s. Later studies using Lewis's techniques and more recent data indicate that union salaries are 15 to 25 percent higher for similar productivity characteristics.[3] These same studies indicate that craft unions are more successful in raising wages than are inclusive unions.

If this is true, and most economists would agree with these results, where do these higher wages come from? Your first reaction may be that

---

[2]H. Gregg Lewis, *Unionism and Relative Wages in the United States* (Chicago: University of Chicago Press, 1963).

[3]See M. J. Boskin, "Unions and Relative Real Wages," *American Economic Review* (June, 1972); and P. M. Ryscavage, "Measuring Union-Nonunion Earnings Differences," *Monthly Labor Review* (December, 1974).

they come out of business profits, but can this be so? Let's reflect back on the theory we have developed in earlier chapters. Wages are a cost of production. If markets are characterized by competition (pure or monopolistic), the increased cost will result in higher prices because in the long run, with or without unions, the average firm will only be earning normal profits. If the firm possesses some monopoly power, the higher labor costs might reduce profits, but the increased costs will in part be passed forward in higher prices. Additionally, regardless of the firm's market structure, the increased costs of union-made products will cause the quantity demanded of their output to decrease (be less than it would have been without a union). The net result is that there are now more nonunion workers, and wage rates will fall in the nonunion work sector. The supply of nonunion workers increases as the supply of union workers decreases. This analysis indicates that the increased wages of union workers are paid by consumers in terms of higher prices for union-made goods *and* by nonunion workers in terms of lower salaries. Again, Professor Lewis has done empirical research in this area, and he concludes that nonunion salaries are 3 to 4 percent lower because of union-increased wages in the organized labor sector.[4]

Do Unions Cause Inflation?

We have just seen that unions cause wages to be higher in unionized industries and lower in the nonunion sector. We also saw that unions cause prices to be higher in unionized industries. But do unions cause inflation? The answer is *no!* Of course, unions bargain for higher wages and businesses raise prices in inflationary times, but these are responses to the inflation, not causes of the inflation. In fact, the empirical evidence indicates that union wages rise less rapidly during the early years of an inflation than nonunion wages.[5] This is because the unions were unaware in the early years of the inflation of how high the inflation would be and committed themselves to long-term contracts with wage increases less than the inflation rate. When these contracts expire, the unions try to make up for the inflation in their wage demands, and it sometimes appears as if they are responsible for the inflation, rather than the victims of it who are only trying to catch up.

There is one indirect way in which union activity can be inflationary. If unions are successful in raising wages above competitive levels in their sector of the economy, less employment in this sector results. If this unemployed labor is unable to find employment in the nonunion sector, unemployment rates will rise. If macro policymakers (the president and Congress) pursue an expansionary monetary and fiscal policy to reduce

---

[4]H. Gregg Lewis, *op. cit.*
[5]See Albert Rees, "Do Unions Cause Inflation?", *The Journal of Law and Economics* (October, 1959).

the unemployment rate, inflation might result. In this sense, then, unions place an inflationary bias into macro policy. Keep in mind, though, that unions, as well as businesses, do not cause inflation — government macro policymakers cause inflation through expansionary monetary and fiscal policy. These policymakers may blame unions and business, but don't be tricked. It probably is good politics for the president, the president's advisers, and Congress to try to shift the blame for inflation to business and unions, but microeconomics and macroeconomics tell us that this is not the case.

A SHORT HISTORY OF THE LABOR MOVEMENT

In the early 1900s the U.S. economy was shifting rapidly from a largely agrarian society to an industrial society. By 1910, employment in industry exceeded employment in agriculture. This industrial labor force grew rapidly, and labor organizers attempted to capitalize on this growth. In 1914, about 7 percent of the work force was unionized. Growth in the labor force and growth in unionization were accompanied by a rapidly rising real wage rate. The real wage rate advancement was largely attributable to rapid growth in technology and in the human capital of the wage earner. This was reflected in the fact that both union and nonunion labor made substantial wage advances during this period.

The Early Unsuccessful Years

To better understand the labor movement in the United States, it is worthwhile to view it in its historical perspective. In the early 1800s, the labor movement was unsuccessful in organizing significant numbers of workers and was limited to the eastern cities in the United States. During this period, the work day changed from a sunup to sundown situation to, for the most part, a 10-hour day. Interestingly, workers still spent 12 hours on the job, but received two 1-hour (mid-morning and mid-afternoon) breaks.

It became apparent by the mid-1800s that a national effort was necessary if unions were to be successful. This was because the transportation network was developing so successfully that local or regional gains by any union would be dissipated by competitive pressures from other geographic areas. In other words, if labor could successfully raise wages above free market equilibrium wage rates in any area, these gains would be short term, because "foreign labor" (labor from other regions of the country) would produce cheaper goods that could be shipped in via the rapidly growing, low-cost transportation network. The U.S. Constitution forbids any interference with interstate commerce, so regions or states could not place tariffs on the goods from other regions or states. This meant that all labor in the firms of a particular industry had to be organized if organization was to be successful.

The first successful attempt at organizing a national union was made by William H. Sylvis. Sylvis had been treasurer of the short-lived Iron Molders International Union and in 1867 founded the *National Labor Union*. The National Labor Union was deeply involved politically and espoused the eight-hour day, arbitration, and cooperatives, where union members owned the firms in which they worked. The union published a journal, *The Workingman's Advocate*, as a political voice. The union grew rapidly to a membership of 600,000, but rapidly fell apart after Sylvis' death in 1869. Organizers learned an important lesson from the experience of the National Labor Union. The political environment of the time was such that reform legislation was likely to be unsuccessful and as a result would not lead to much labor advancement.

In 1869, the *Knights of Labor* was organized by Uriah Stevens as a secret society. The secrecy was to protect members from reprisals by management. As might be expected, the secrecy led to much suspicion and bad public relations, and, as a result, was dropped in 1879. The Knights' greatest accomplishment was to win the first major strike in U.S. history. The Knights won a strike against the Wabash, Missouri-Kansas-Texas, and Missouri Pacific railroads, which were owned by Jay Gould, the personification of the capitalist "robber baron." But by the turn of the century, the Knights had become unimportant as a labor force. The reasons for its demise were important for future labor organizations. The Knights' philosophical goal for political reform was to abolish the wage system and replace it with worker cooperatives. It thus had reformist motivations rather than economic goals. These political reformist goals, coupled with some unsuccessful large strikes and some violent cases of sabotage, contributed to the union's failures.[6]

The *American Federation of Labor (AFL)* was founded in 1886 by Samuel Gompers (considered the father of the American labor movement).[7] It was the first *business union*, Gompers' description of unions that worked for economic goals for their members without wanting to change the business organization in which they worked, and it overcame many of the problems the earlier national unions had faced. Gompers was, above all, pragmatic and set a single goal of economic gains for his union members. Importantly, there were no leftist or social-reformist goals. Gompers thought it necessary that national labor leaders be supreme and have sole authority to call strikes and control membership dues. This principle has remained in the labor movement to the present

---

[6]The Knights of Labor were linked to the infamous Haymarket bomb-throwing incident in Chicago in which seven policemen were killed. Eight anarchists were arrested. One was a Knight and the local union refused to expel him because of his involvement. This caused many people to link the Knights with the most radical elements of the labor movement and was politically very costly to the labor movement in general, as well as to the Knights of Labor in particular.

[7]Technically, Gompers founded the Federation of Organized Trades and Labor Unions in 1881, which is regarded as the precursor of the American Federation of Labor.

Samuel Gompers

**Samuel Gompers
(1850–1924)**

Samuel Gompers is often called the father of the American labor movement. Gompers was born in a very poor ghetto of East London, England. He quit school after four years and was apprenticed to become a cigar-maker like his father. When he was 13 his family moved to the United States. His home was a two-room tenement next to a cattle slaughterhouse in New York's lower east side. He continued his career as a cigar-maker, leaving home at the age of 17 to get married. His wife and 14 children were to experience much misery and violence because of his devotion to the labor movement.

Gompers joined the Cigar Makers' International Union and aided in development of the local chapter. In 1874 he was elected president of the local. He was ousted seven years later by socialist opponents.

In December, 1886, Gompers helped found the American Federation of Labor (AFL) and became its first president. By 1904 membership had grown to nearly 2 million members. Much of the union's success was due to Gompers' abilities. Although in his younger days Gompers had been a radical, he realized that to succeed in America the labor movement had to shed its radical-socialist image. Gompers worked hard to overcome the bad publicity for organized labor generated by the management of large corporations and fed by the activities and radical-activist tactics of other unions, such as the International Workers of the World. Gompers joined the National Civic Federation, an association of wealthy, Eastern capitalists, editors, professional people, and some corporation officers. The National Civic Federation particularly emphasized that labor union strength did not undermine American business and that strong business was good for labor.

Perhaps the best evidence of Gompers' success was his acceptance by the political establishment. He proved that labor leaders were respectable members of the establishment, not communist radicals seeking to overthrow American capitalism. During World War I, President Wilson appointed Gompers to the advisory commission to the Council of National Defense and in 1919, at the Versailles Peace Conference, Gompers served as chairperson of the Commission of International Labor Legislation.

day. The Federation was primarily organized for the skilled worker and was an exclusive union movement.

Business and labor are not always at odds. In some cases union organization brings stability to an industry, and in other cases an oligopolistic industry may even use labor power to help monopolize the industry. Before the days of the United Mine Workers, mine operators had a very difficult time with labor, because mine workers were and are a very independent lot. The **United Mine Workers**, under the leadership of John L. Lewis, brought organization *and* discipline to labor. When Lewis ordered the miners back to work, they went back to work! In recent years the United Mine Workers' leadership has not had that sort of control and **wildcat strikes**, which are local strikes unauthorized by the national union, have been frequent. The point is that it is conceivable that management might not be hostile to union organization. In recent years, unions and management have often worked together to lobby for reduced pollution control legislation, to curb imports, and even recently to urge tax cuts for business.

Having briefly examined these early unions, we can now sketch the labor movement in a more general historical framework. Early progress, as we have seen, was not rapid. This can be attributed in large part to the massive immigration of the period. The early hostility of management toward organized labor was understandable, and attempts to break strikes and even labor organizations proved successful with a steady supply of young, healthy, eager, skilled, semiskilled, and unskilled workers streaming in from Europe.

World War I and the accompanying prosperity marked the beginning of success for American unions. Membership increased steadily during this period, and the image of unions started to improve. Much credit for this is due Gompers, who served on President Wilson's Advisory Commission of the National Council of Defense. Unions were, however, flexing their muscles during the war period, and there were many strikes in 1917. This was largely a reflection of the war-generated inflation and the effect this inflation had on longer term union contracts. In 1918 labor was successful in negotiating an eight-hour day and collective bargaining rights in exchange for a no-strike agreement. As a result, labor emerged from World War I stronger than it had ever been.

The postwar period brought increased inflation and more activity to increase wages via strikes. The **International Workers of the World (IWW)** organized the steelworkers, who were unskilled and thus not members of Gompers' Federation. The IWW had been associated with several socialists and was regarded as a radical movement. At this time, the Russian Revolution and the fear of a worldwide Bolshevik revolution gripped the United States. The IWW subsequently went on strike against U.S. Steel and lost. The breaking of the strike was a major victory for steel companies, who successfully branded the union leaders as socialists attempting to overthrow capitalism. The breaking of the U.S. Steel strike had more significance than one would normally attribute to a single strike. The union's failure, coupled with the depression of 1920–1922, broke what had been a steady rise in union prestige and membership.

The 1920s proved to be a bad time for the labor movement. The Republican presidents, Harding, Coolidge, and Hoover, were probusiness, and business was aggressively opposed to organized labor. The government sanctioned *yellow-dog contracts*, which were contracts in which the employee had to agree to refrain from union activity as a precondition of employment and which allowed the firm to discharge the worker for violation of the agreement. In addition, the courts reflected this attitude and were hostile to union activity. This hostility was primarily apparent in the ease with which management was able to receive court *injunctions* requiring labor to return to work. And a section of the Clayton Act (1914), which had been hailed by Samuel Gompers as the Magna Carta of labor because it limited the use of injunctions against labor, was declared unconstitutional.

Success and Power

These bad times for unions were swept away with the election of Franklin D. Roosevelt in 1932. Roosevelt campaigned as the friend of the worker, and the legislation proposed and passed during the Roosevelt terms established the bond between organized labor and the Democratic party which still exists today. The two key pieces of legislation were the *Norris-La Guardia Act* (1932) and the *Wagner Act* (1935). These pieces of legislation vastly strengthened unions and set the stage for their rapid development. Jointly, the two acts gave workers the right to organize and made illegal any interference with this right. Yellow-dog contracts were outlawed, and picket lines and *secondary boycotts*, which were union actions to stop one employer from doing business with another employer, were sanctioned. A secondary boycott is more powerful than a picket line because it involves actions against and pressures on third parties. In other words, a union not only boycotts a certain product or firm, which would be a *primary* boycott, but it also boycotts firms (and their products) who do business with the firm the union has an action against. Injunctions against unions and their activities were limited to "unlawful acts," and businesses were required to engage in collective bargaining and to "bargain in good faith." In addition, the Wagner Act established the *National Labor Relations Board (NLRB)*. The NLRB was empowered to investigate unfair labor practices and to determine legitimate bargaining agents for labor when there were competing unions. This act was challenged in the courts and declared to be constitutional by the Supreme Court. Under these laws, private-sector workers were given the right to organize without interference from management. In practice, if organizers can get 30 percent of the work force in a particular place of employment to sign authorization cards, the NLRB steps in and conducts a vote.

If the majority of workers support the union, the management of that company must recognize the union and bargain with it.

About this time, a very important debate was going on within the AFL concerning whether or not the AFL should undertake union organization in the mass-production industries. The AFL was primarily an organization of exclusive unions, but rapid labor growth had occurred in the mass-production industries such as steelworking, automobile manufacturing, and mining. The AFL decided not to promote unions in these industries and, as a result, a number of affiliated unions broke away in 1935 and formed the Committee for Industrial Organization. Shortly thereafter the name was changed to the *Congress of Industrial Organizations (CIO)*. John L. Lewis, the colorful, forceful head of the United Mine Workers, became the first president.

World War II and the 1950s

The wartime boom economy brought a number of serious strikes. The Wagner Act had given unions more legal power and the coffers of union treasuries were full. Unions flexed their muscles and a wave of strikes causing substantial work stoppages followed. The unions were successful in achieving sizable settlements. But public sympathy began to shift away from labor and, as a result, Congress passed the *Taft-Hartley Act* in 1947, which was designed to reverse some of the excesses fostered by the Wagner Act. President Truman vetoed the act, but Congress overrode the veto, reflecting the antiunion political atmosphere. The Taft-Hartley Act shifted several legal rights back to employers. *Closed shops*, where workers were forced to become union members before employment, were outlawed. Unions were required to bargain in good faith, and featherbedding and secondary boycotts were outlawed. In certain instances, the president was empowered to call 80-day "cooling-off" periods before strikes. During this 80-day period, *mediation* is attempted and the government appoints a fact-finding board. Mediation is simply third-party intervention into the strike. The mediator attempts to keep the parties together and talking by offering suggestions and clarifying issues. This is distinct from *arbitration*. In arbitration, a third party hears the arguments of both management and labor, studies their positions, and renders a decision. If the dispute has been submitted to *binding* arbitration, both parties must abide by that decision. Union leaders fought this bill as a "slave labor law" every step of the way, and union leaders continue to campaign to reverse some of its provisions. Despite the Taft-Hartley Act, however, unions have continued to show great strength, which is enhanced by careful and well-organized political activity.

In 1955, the American Federation of Labor and the Congress of Industrial Organizations merged to form the *AFL-CIO*. This gave the labor movement a more unified stance under the leadership of Walter Reuther and George Meany. The *Landrum-Griffin Act*, passed in 1959, was a response to further public concern over union power and practices. The Landrum-Griffin Act was decidedly antiunion and was based on the idea that union practices needed further curbing. The act made unions more democratic, restricted Communist party members and convicted felons from union leadership, and strengthened the Taft-Hartley Act by making picketing under certain circumstances illegal.

The 1960s to the Present

Recent years have seen a decline in the union membership share of the labor force, partly as a result of the fact that the economy is becoming more service oriented and less manufacturing oriented. Thirty years ago almost 40 percent of the American labor force was unionized. Today less than 25 percent is unionized. Some observers forecast that by 1990 relative union membership will be at the level it was before the wave of unionization in the mid-1930s. One notable exception has been a dramatic increase in the membership of public unions. The *American Federation of State, County, and Municipal Employees (AFSCME)* is a large and very rapidly growing union. Under the leadership of Jerry Wurf, AFSCME has been politically active. However, in 1977 the union lost its first major battle in a confrontation with Mayor Maynard Jackson of Atlanta. The union garbage workers' affiliate struck the city of Atlanta. Much as in 1920, when U.S. Steel broke the IWW, Mayor Jackson refused to bargain with the local AFSCME chapter and hired strikebreakers. Unemployment problems in the city aided the strikebreaking and the jobs were quickly filled. The immediate future should determine if the Atlanta strikebreaking is a minor setback for the public union movement or the first of a series of fatal blows. We should see much in the news in the coming months and years concerning this aspect of the labor movement.

Of course, the real-world operation of labor-management relations does not always run the way a review of the law would indicate. The NLRB is often slow to act and sometimes slow to rule in cases of unfair labor practices. The battleground of labor-management relations has shifted to the South where much of the new industrial growth in this country is taking place. It is also mainly in the South that *right-to-work laws* are found. Right-to-work laws allow people to hold jobs without belonging to unions. This outlaws *union shops*, where union membership is necessary for a worker to remain employed. A union shop law requires that all workers join within a certain period (usually 30 days) of employment. The union shop is allowed under federal law, but the federal law permits individual states to pass right-to-work laws. These laws obviously greatly undermine union power. We saw earlier in this chapter that inclusive unions must organize and present a unified front to be successful in bargaining with management. Right-to-work laws greatly undermine an inclusive union's ability to present this united front.

Jerry (Jerome) Wurf

**Jerry (Jerome) Wurf
(1919–   )**

Jerry (Jerome) Wurf is president of the American Federation of State, County and Municipal Employees (AFSCME). AFSCME is now the largest single union in the AFL-CIO federation and is also the fastest growing union in the country, adding about 1,000 members per week. This is a far cry from the early days of AFSCME. The union was formed in Wisconsin in the early 1930s and was chartered by the AFL in 1936. By 1955 the union had only 100,000 members, compared to the more than 1,000,000 members it now has. In large part, the phenomenal growth is due to two factors: (1) the large growth in public sector employment and (2), the organizing ability of Jerry Wurf. In 1964, Wurf won the presidency of AFSCME from Arnold Zander, the founder and president, who had hired him. After he won the presidency, Wurf began the job of building its membership. In these early years, he was often regarded as the *enfant terrible* of the labor movement. He was frequently at odds with George Meany, president of the AFL-CIO. Many of Wurf's fights with Meany have been over international politics. Wurf was an early opponent of the Vietnam War and served on the National Advisory Council of Amnesty International, U.S.A.

In many ways, Wurf's task is similar to that of Samuel Gompers, and there are some important parallels in their styles of leadership. Gompers had to develop membership in an era when public opinion was hostile to the labor movement. Wurf has had much the same problem in that, while the environment is no longer hostile to unions, it is often very hostile to public employee unions, at times even challenging labor's right to organize such workers. Gompers overcame many of these difficulties by supporting business and arguing for "safe and sane business unionism." His idea was that unions would prosper by supporting industry in many areas. Wurf takes much the same approach. He argues that the union members should fight for tax reform, which most public union officials abhor. Wurf anticipated Proposition 13 in California and told Californians they should work for tax reform. In this way, Wurf is following a strategy very similar to that of Gompers. He is arguing for positions that make state and local governments stronger, realizing that tax reforms that weaken local government also weaken his union.

In the months and years ahead, the public union movement will likely be at the center of the union movement and the center of public policy debates on public finance and tax reform issues. Jerry Wurf and AFSCME will likely be at the center of these debates.

There has been little in the way of new labor legislation since the Landrum-Griffin Act, except, of course, for frequent increases in the minimum wage. Labor has campaigned vigorously against some aspects of the Taft-Hartley Act, and these campaigns are worth watching. The two most important pieces of legislation that organized labor currently favors are (1) the repeal of right-to-work laws, and (2) the common situs picketing bill, which grants any union the right to picket an entire construction job even when the union represents only a small part of the labor used on the project. In late 1978, however, President Carter did sign the ***Humphrey-Hawkins Full Employment Bill*** into law. The original bill was highly praised by organized labor, but the bill that finally passed Congress is viewed by many labor leaders as meaningless. The bill sets national goals to reduce unemployment from its current level to 4 percent by 1983 and to cut inflation to 3 percent by 1983 and to zero by 1988. The bill defines full employment as the right of full opportunity for useful employment at fair rates of compensation for all individuals able and willing to work. The bill is regarded by labor as merely symbolic because it does not include any means to reach the goals specified, but rather leaves them all to future legislation.

President Carter has proposed a program of labor legislation that the unions view very favorably. The Carter Administration claims that its program is only a reform of the NLRB to make it more responsive. Secretary of Labor Ray Marshall (formerly an economics professor at the University of Texas) has argued that the Carter Administration only wants to perfect the implementation of the present law. The National Association of Manufacturers and the U.S. Chamber of Commerce view the bill quite differently and are opposed to the Carter plan. If you watch the news, you should see activity as organized labor tries to capitalize on the political support it gave in the 1976, 1978, and 1980 presidential and congressional elections.

The Broad Sweep

As the union movement developed in the United States, several motives for unionization were evident. These different motives are reflected in union goals. Some unions were ***welfare unions*** (the Knights of Labor) that had lofty ideals of social welfare and sought these goals by advocating an end to the wage system and the establishment of worker cooperatives. Other unions were ***revolutionary unions*** (the International Workers of the World) that sought changes in the social order. Still others were ***business unions*** (the American Federation of Labor) that eschewed social and political goals and sought only to better the economic status of their members. History indicates that it is this third type that has been successful and able to survive in the American economic system.

The movement and the struggles of these different types of unions fit into three clearly identifiable periods. The early period from the 1700s until 1930 might be called the *repression phase* because of the hostility of the courts. This was a difficult time for union organization and one in which the successes of unions were few and far between. The period from 1930 to 1947 might be termed the *encouragement phase*. Government support and key labor legislation greatly increased the power and prestige of unions. Unions reached their peak period of influence during this period. The period since 1947 and the Taft-Hartley Act would properly be labeled the *intervention stage*, in which the government has intervened and attempted to put big business and big labor on a more equal footing. It is altogether possible that we are now in a fourth stage where the basic underpinnings of the labor movement are in a state of flux.

Summary

In this chapter we have taken a look at unions and the labor movement in the United States. Our analysis of the ways in which unions attempt to raise wages led to the conclusion that exclusive unions are more likely to be successful than inclusive unions. The empirical evidence indicates that this is the case. The evidence also indicates that unions have been successful in raising wages and that this success comes at the expense of consumers and nonunion labor, not at the expense of business profits.

The question of whether or not (and if so, how) unions contribute to inflation is a volatile question. Politicians blame labor unions for inflation, but the evidence doesn't support this indictment.

The history of the labor movement is one of progression through phases. Early unions had reformist goals and were largely unsuccessful. When Samuel Gompers turned the American Federation of Labor toward strictly economic concerns, he was successful. It wasn't until 1932, however, and the election of President Franklin Roosevelt, that unions received active encouragement from government. Legislation in 1932 and 1935 greatly enhanced the power of unions. In 1947 and 1959 this power was diminished and management and labor were put on more equal footing.

In recent years union membership has declined except for growth in public employee unions. A new phase for the union movement may now be taking place and key legislation in the next few years will be important for the labor movement.

New Terms

featherbedding
exclusive union
craft unions
inclusive union
industrial unions

bilateral monopoly
logically indeterminate
National Labor Union
Knights of Labor
American Federation of Labor (AFL)

business union
United Mine Workers
wildcat strikes
International Workers of the World (IWW)
yellow-dog contracts
injunctions
Norris-La Guardia Act
Wagner Act
secondary boycotts
National Labor Relations Board (NLRB)
Congress of Industrial Organizations (CIO)
Taft-Hartley Act
closed shops
mediation

arbitration
AFL-CIO
Landrum-Griffin Act
American Federation of State, County, and
    Municipal Employees (AFSCME)
right-to-work laws
union shops
Humphrey-Hawkins Full Employment Bill
welfare unions
revolutionary unions
repression phase
encouragement phase
intervention stage

Questions for Discussion

1 Do unions raise wages? If so, at whose expense?
2 Do unions cause inflation?
3 Explain the differences between closed shops, union shops, and right-to-work laws.
4 Suppose that César Chavez is successful in organizing the grape pickers in California. What will be the likely effect on the price of California wine? What will be the likely effect in the number of grape pickers employed? Does the fact that the United States-Mexican border is rela- tively easy to cross, and hence the supply of undocumented workers is relatively elastic, have any impact on Chavez's organizing costs?
5 Has union strength in the North had any impact on business activity in the South?
6 Public unions are increasing in strength, yet many states forbid public unions from going on strike. Can you think of any reasons why this should be so? Is a police officer in Los Angeles any different than a bank guard in Los Angeles?

Suggestions for Further Reading

Dulles, Foster Rhea. *Labor in America: A History*. New York: Thomas Y. Crowell Co., 1966.
Kemmerer, Donald L., and C. Clyde Jones. *American Economic History*. New York: McGraw-Hill Book Co., 1959.

CHAPTER 15

THE ECONOMICS OF GOVERNMENTAL INTERVENTION

LEARNING OBJECTIVES

After studying the materials found in this chapter, you should be able to do the following:

1 Define
   (a) natural monopoly,
   (b) externality,
   (c) public good,
   (d) private good.

2 Diagram cases of
   (a) negative externalities,
   (b) positive externalities.

3 Give the details of the Coase theorem and the conditions under which it holds.

4 Define
   (a) egalitarianism,
   (b) free-riding behavior,
   (c) logrolling,

   (d) risk aversion,
   (e) utility interdependence.

5 List the advantages of a negative income tax as a tool to alter the distribution of income.

6 Use a Lorenz curve to show the relative distribution of income in a society.

7 Define
   (a) absolute poverty,
   (b) relative poverty.

8 List the major federal government programs designed to alter the distribution of income.

In previous chapters we have dealt principally with the operations of a market mechanism free of governmental involvement. When government activity was discussed, it was often shown to have a counterproductive effect on economic efficiency. We don't want to give the impression that economic activity undertaken by the government is necessarily always bad, however. In this chapter we will examine theoretical justifications for governmental activity on grounds of market failure. After examining instances where governmental activity is called for, we will examine how such activity has developed in the United States.

NATURAL MONOPOLY

As we saw in Chapter 9, there may be some industries in which economies of scale are such that it makes economic sense to have only one firm. The monopoly that results is called a natural monopoly because efficiency considerations dictate that there be only one firm. When natural monopoly exists, governmental control is justified to prevent the company from abusing its monopoly position. The most common response to this situation is for government to regulate the natural monopoly, and sometimes government ownership is instituted. You can refer to Chapter 12 to review the problems associated with regulation and government ownership.

EXTERNALITIES

Where there is interdependence among economic units, and when this interdependence is not reflected in market transactions, externalities may result. *Externalities* are costs or benefits that are imposed on economic units. These units are forced to bear the costs without compensation or are able to gain the benefits without paying for them. An example of an external cost would be air pollution. If you live near a steel mill, you are forced to breathe polluted air without being compensated for the fact that the mill is using the air to dump its debris.

Firms purchase inputs to produce goods and services. A steel mill will purchase iron ore, coal, electricity, and labor, among other inputs. It uses air in much the same way it uses labor or electricity. In the process of producing steel, it is using up clean air. It doesn't pay for this clean air. Instead, society pays, or, more correctly, the people who live in the area near the steel mill pay. They bear this cost in many ways. The area isn't pretty, as you know if you have driven through Gary, Indiana, recently. People cannot hang their clothes outside to dry. They must paint their houses every three years instead of every five years. There is even evidence that in some areas people may die sooner because they breathe bad air. All these are real costs and are borne by the people who live in the affected area.

The economic importance of this is that the firm doing the polluting avoids paying these costs. They are *external* to the firm using the production process, hence the term externality. It is quite simple to determine the theoretical effects of these externalities; it is more difficult to determine how to correct for them.

Let us assume we have a competitive industry that is generating a *negative* externality. Smoke, for example, is generally viewed as a negative externality.[1] Smoke causes damage, or what we could call **social costs**, to those in the general area. This situation is represented in Figure 15-1. The demand curve is the normal market-demand curve for the commodity. The supply curve is, of course, the summation of all the individual-firm marginal cost curves (above their average variable-cost curve). Equilibrium is reached at price OP_1 and output OQ_1. Now suppose we know what costs are generated by the externality and that these social costs are represented by the curve SC. They are zero at zero output, and we assume (to make the graph more simple) that they increase at a constant rate. If we add these social costs to the supply curve, we get the true supply curve, S_t. This curve is the summation of the extra social costs and the private costs embodied in the firms' marginal cost curves. The socially optimal level of production is no longer OQ_1 but the smaller OQ_2. Likewise, the efficient price is OP_2, which is higher than OP_1.

In commonsense terms, when we include the social costs of production, the good becomes more expensive. It wasn't that these costs weren't being borne before, but they weren't being borne by the producers of the commodity; instead, they were being paid by citizens in the area near the production. In failing to take into account the social costs, the firm is producing too much of the good and charging the consumer too low a price because the firm is not paying some of the costs of production. If the set of people who consume this good and the set of people who suffer the externality are different, a subsidy is taking place. The people who bear the externality are subsidizing the people who consume the good.

In the real world, this means that in those areas where significant externalities exist, the people who bear the externalities subsidize consumers of the product. The people who live in Gary, Indiana, pay costs that allow consumers of steel to pay lower prices for it. If steel producers had to pay for the externality, less steel would be produced, and it would be sold for a higher price. The general theoretical conclusion is that where negative externalities exist, the amount of production will not be optimal. Too much output will be produced at too low a price.

It is very important to understand that accounting for an externality such as pollution does not cause the amount of pollution to fall to zero. In the example in Figure 15-1, the costs associated with the externality fell from OC_1 to OC_2 after the social costs were added in, but some pollution and the costs associated with it continued.

---

[1] If you like to smoke, you might view smoke as a positive externality. But most people consider smoke a negative externality.

FIGURE 15-1   **Externalities and Market Equilibrium**

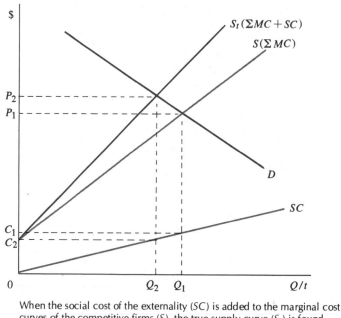

When the social cost of the externality (SC) is added to the marginal cost curves of the competitive firms (S), the true supply curve (S_t) is found. This true supply curve indicates that too much of the good is produced at too low a price unless the externality is taken into account.

Externality Internalization

In the jargon of economists, the trick is to ***internalize*** the externality. That simply means that the costs that are borne by society must be taken into account in production decisions. In terms of Figure 15-1, the firms have to bear the social costs SC, so that S_t becomes the supply curve. How can this be done? We must turn these social costs into production costs. It would be a simpler matter if we could easily determine what the social costs were. We can draw general cases, as in Figure 15-1, but in the real world it is very difficult to come up with a dollar value. What is the cost of x number of people dying a year earlier because of respiratory problems? Or how much is not being able to grow grass worth? If we could determine these costs, we could place a tax on the industry that would shift the supply curve to S_t. (Refer to Chapter 4 to recall how taxes shift supply curves.) The market solution would then result in a price of OP_2 and output of OQ_2.

We could also charge the firms for the amount of externalities they create. We could monitor each firm and charge for amounts on a monthly basis. It would be possible to put a meter on each smokestack and measure the pollutants. In such a way, firms could be charged for the air they use just as for the electricity or labor they use. This would cause costs to rise and move production toward the socially optimal level of output. The problem in this case is similar to the problem with taxation — how to come up with the "correct" charge per pollutant.

These difficulties notwithstanding, we have a legitimate case for government intervention in the market process. Markets, when there are externalities, don't produce socially optimal results, and it can be argued that government should step in to correct for the market imperfection. The question is, How should the government intervene?

The Coase Theorem and Small-Number Externalities. In an article that has had significant impact on the field of economics, Professor Ronald Coase of the University of Chicago has pointed out that where the number of affected parties is small, individual maximizing behavior will correct for the externality.[2] Coase demonstrates that if property rights are clearly defined, the affected individuals will take action to internalize the externality. Consider, as Coase did in his paper, that there are only two parties involved in a particular dispute, a wheat farmer and a cattle rancher. The externality is the damage done by the cattle roaming on unfenced land. As the rancher increases the size of the herd, the damage done by straying cattle will increase. To account for the externality, it is necessary to cause the rancher to take these costs into account, much as we discussed earlier and depicted in Figure 15-1. If government intervened, it would likely solve the problem by requiring the rancher to pay the farmer for the damage to the farmer's wheat. As a result, the rancher would restrict the number of cattle in the herd until marginal cost equaled marginal revenue (and the marginal cost includes the damage to the wheat, as we saw in Figure 15-1). Coase shows that even if government did not intervene, the same solution would be obtained. Consider Figure 15-2. D_c and MR_c represent the demand and marginal revenue of raising cattle. MC_c represents the marginal cost of raising cattle and SC_w represents the marginal social cost, or the damage of the externality (the damage to the wheat). Without internalization of the externality, the rancher would raise OQ_1 cattle per year, and the farmer would incur a dollar loss to the wheat crop of OW_1 for the last cow raised. Government intervention would require that, through some tax scheme or direct regulation, the rancher be forced to act on the joint $MC_c + SC_w$ curve and, as a result, the rancher would raise only OQ_2 cattle.

Now consider a Coase solution. All that is necessary is that property rights be defined and enforced. First assume that the farmer has the right *not* to have the wheat harmed. The rancher will then be forced to pay damages, as shown by the SC_w curve, and will add these to production costs. The rancher will then raise OQ_2 cattle. If the rancher has the right to let the cattle roam, the important question then is how much the

---

[2]See Ronald Coase, "The Problem of Social Cost," *Journal of Law and Economics* (October, 1960).

FIGURE 15-2   The Coase Theorem

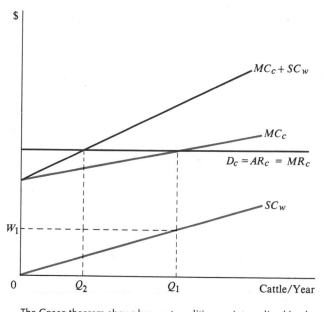

The Coase theorem shows how externalities are internalized by the
assignment of property rights. The social cost (SC_w) is automatically
embodied in the marginal-cost curve (MC_c) to form $MC_c + SC_w$, the true
cost of raising cattle. The optimal product, OQ_2, will result because a
bribe or payment equal to the social cost will automatically come about.

farmer will be willing to "bribe" the rancher to keep the cattle away. The
farmer will be willing to bribe the rancher an amount just slightly less
than the cost of the damage done by the cattle, because this makes them
both better off than allowing the cattle to damage the wheat. The farmer
would pay OW_1 for the last cow not to be raised. The rancher then must
include these bribes as opportunity costs, because if the cattle are raised
the bribe is foregone. When the foregone bribe is added to the marginal
cost curve, the rancher will raise OQ_2 cattle.

The result is that OQ_2 cattle will be raised regardless of who has the
property right, as long as the property right is defined and the numbers of
people involved are small. Small numbers are necessary because the
farmer and rancher must get together. Note that the Coase solution says
only that allocative results, or the number of cattle produced, will be the
same, whoever has the property rights. It says nothing about the distribution of income. The property right assignment does affect who is better
off. In one case the farmer's income is higher, in the other the rancher's
income is higher.

The importance of the *Coase theorem* is that it draws attention to
property-right assignments. Many of our current social problems result

from ill-defined or nonexistent property-right assignments. Consider, for example, the case of buffalo and cattle in the Old West. Why were buffalo almost wiped out while cattle thrived? The animals are very similar and roamed the same country. The answer is simple. Nobody owned the buffalo,[3] or rather, everyone had a right to shoot them. Consider air pollution as another example. If a copper mine dumped tailings on your yard, you would sue for damages or expect payment for the use of your land as a dump. Yet when this same mine dumps soot in your air, you are helpless because you don't own the air above your land.

Large-Number Externalities. Even if property rights are well defined, there may still be externality problems. If there are large numbers of people sustaining damages or large numbers of firms doing the damage, the results of the Coase theorem may not hold. It may be that the costs of organizing the involved parties prohibit the damaged individuals from suing for damages or organizing a bribe. The individuals damaged would have to mount a door-to-door campaign, advertise in newspapers, and arouse the group for joint action. If the damaging firms are hard to identify, the problem is even greater. In an area with severe air pollution, it would be necessary to determine how each of many firms contributes to this air pollution. It would be necessary to determine who should be sued (or bribed). Because the information and transaction costs increase rapidly as the number of parties increases, it is often argued that the Coase theorem cannot solve the market failure that externalities create.

Government Intervention Again

We are, in a sense, back to square one, needing government intervention to correct the externality. Usually government controls are direct controls, and such controls often lead to unfairness in their own right. Consider the case of the government requiring that all cars have a pollution device that costs $300. The salesperson who drives a lot, and as a result pollutes a great deal, pays very little on a per unit of pollution basis. The person who only drives once a week pays a great deal on a per unit of pollution basis.

In addition, government intervention affects the distribution of income. The incidence of programs can sometimes even impact disproportionately on the poor. For example, as auto prices rise because of pollution equipment, it impacts as a percentage of income much more heavily on the poor, since the poor spend a higher proportion of their income on cars than do the rich.

Since governmental intervention is not without costs, we need to be sure that externality costs are indeed worth worrying about. Sometimes

---

[3]For a discussion of how to protect eagles by assigning property rights to them, see Ryan C. Amacher, Robert D. Tolleson, and Thomas D. Willett, "The Economics of Fatal Mistakes: Fiscal Mechanisms for Preserving Endangered Predators," *Public Policy* (Summer, 1972).

even the government makes mistakes, and these mistakes inflict costs on the economy. Externalities have received much attention in recent years, and this attention may overstate the real costs. We have all seen gruesome pictures of oil spills and fish kills, yet this damage seems to be of an exceedingly short duration. This is not to say that such damage is insignificant. It is only to suggest that the costs of correcting for an externality may exceed the damage it causes, and we need to consider this before racing headlong into governmental regulation of externalities.

The federal government has usually responded to calls to control noxious externalities through regulation. These regulations impose costs on firms, and the regulatory bodies themselves spend large amounts of money. The costs imposed on firms are hard to estimate until the required action is taken. For example, the Council of Environmental Quality estimates that EPA (Environmental Protection Agency) regulations will cost the economy $40 billion in 1980. The manifestation of the growth of the regulatory bodies and the budgetary cost they impose can be seen in Table 15-1. From 1970 to 1975 the number of "economic" regulatory agencies grew 25 percent and their expenditures by 157 percent, while the number of "social" regulatory agencies grew 42 percent and their expenditures by 193 percent.

TABLE 15-1   Growth in Federal Regulation, 1970–1975

Year	Number of Major Federal "Economic" Regulatory Agencies	Number of Major "Social" Regulatory Agencies	Expenditures of Major "Economic" Regulatory Agencies (In Millions)	Expenditures of Major "Social" Regulatory Agencies (In Millions)
1970	8	12	$166.1	$1,449.3
1971	8	14	$196.8	$1,882.2
1972	8	14	$246.3	$2,247.5
1973	8	17	$198.7	$2,773.7
1974	9	17	$304.3	$3,860.1
1975	10	17	$427.6	$4,251.4
Percent Increase (1970–1975)	25	42	157	193

Source: William Lilley, III, and James C. Miller, III, "The New Social Regulation," *The Public Interest* (Spring, 1977).

Each individual call for externality regulation should be carefully considered. Some of these externalities may have already been corrected for by market mechanisms. For example, houses near airports sell for lower prices because of airport noise. The people who buy these houses are freely choosing to do so because the lower price compensates for the noise they must bear. To then change the law because these people don't like the noise would generate a windfall gain to these people. It is not surprising that these residents should lobby for such a change, but it cannot be justified economically. The problem is complicated, however, by the fact that some residents may have purchased their homes before the noise became bad. It might make sense to compensate these individuals.

What we have discovered is that negative externalities cause market solutions to diverge from optimality. We have also seen that government intervention has the potential to correct for these externalities. The government, however, does not intervene in a costless fashion, and we must determine if the costs of this intervention are preferred to the original externality cost.

PUBLIC GOODS

Public goods are those goods that generate external benefits, or *positive* externalities that are consumed by more than one person. Public goods are different from private goods in that it is very difficult to exclude people from consuming public goods. A pure public good would be a good that the whole country (or world) consumes automatically. A good (but not perfect) example at the national level would be national defense. A problem arises because people cannot be excluded from consuming the good, so they will try to consume the good without paying for it. Economists refer to this behavior as *free-riding behavior*. *Free riders* mask their true demands and indicate they don't want the good, or they only want a little of a good because they know once it is produced they can consume it without having to pay for it. When free-riding behavior is prevalent, less than the optimal level of production is attained.

This can be seen clearly by examining Figure 15-3. The demand curve D_P represents a normal demand curve that is based on the private benefits that consumers receive. Suppose the good is produced in a perfectly competitive industry, and the industry's supply curve and marginal cost curve of the good are represented by MC. The consumer or group of consumers will purchase OQ_1 units of the good at the competitive price OP_1. If, however, there are external benefits to others and if the paying consumers can't exclude the others, there are social benefits. In Figure 15-3, the demand curve that includes these social benefits is represented by D_{P+S}. The socially efficient level of consumption is no longer OQ_1 but instead is now OQ_2. As a result, we have another legitimate role for government. Government should grant a subsidy to the producing firms in an attempt to induce consumers to consume the socially desirable amount OQ_2. Government is necessary because the free riders can be forced to pay if taxes are levied on them. In terms of Figure 15-3, the government would have to grant a subsidy to producers equal to amount AB. At output OQ_2, consumers pay OP_3, suppliers receive OP_3 plus the subsidy AB, and this gives a price to suppliers of OP_2.

FIGURE 15-3   **External Benefits**

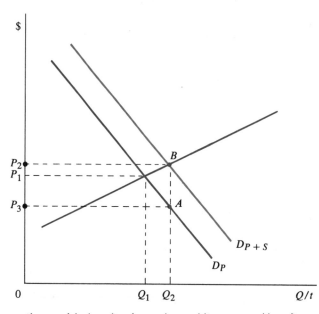

If some of the benefits of a good are public or external benefits,
consumers will be unwilling to pay for these benefits that spill over to
other consumers. As a result, the private demand curve (D_P) will
understate the true demand curve (D_{P+S}), which includes the public
benefits.

The theoretical justification for supplying public goods can now be
seen. Markets don't produce enough goods which have external or spill-
over benefits, so the government needs to intervene. For example, consider a city building an airport. The argument is that many of the benefits are external to the citizens in the locality. These citizens will build
too small an airport because they can't force "foreigners" to help pay for
the airport. The federal government can correct for this by taxing all
citizens and giving the locality a grant to build an airport of the correct
size.

Imperfections in the Political Process

Externalities and public goods, as we have seen, cause imperfections
in markets, and political responses arise to correct for these imperfections. But there are political imperfections as well as market imperfections. One of the best ways to uncover these imperfections is to see how
the supply of public goods is actually determined and to contrast that to
the way the political process works in theory. In theory, voters form a
group, or club, or level of government, and vote to supply themselves

with a public good. They do this through the political process to over-come the free-riding problem. The government can force all consumers of the good to pay and can thus insure that the correct amount is pro-duced. We need to examine how the desires of voters are translated into the provision of public goods in order to determine how well the political provision of such goods works in practice.

Public Goods and Governmental Budgets[4]

The size of federal government expenditures has grown rapidly in recent years. Table 15-2 depicts some of this growth, while Table 15-3 shows that an increasing share of state and local spending has consisted of *grants* to lower levels of government by the federal government. Much of this expenditure is for public goods provision, such as highways, air-ports, and education. We need, then, to see how well the political process is supplying public goods. There are several conflicting theories as to how well the political sector reacts to consumer demands. In order to reach an answer, however tentative, it is necessary to examine the sys-tematic forces that operate in the political sector.

There is no lack of disagreement among economists, as well as polit-ical scientists, as to whether the public sector in the United States is too large or too small, and there may even be a few who would argue that the present public-private mix is the correct one. While different individuals inevitably have different opinions based on their underlying preferences and economic, political, and social positions, one can nevertheless exam-ine the systematic forces at work in the U.S. political and economic sys-tems to determine if they bias the mix of public versus private spending from what the average voter-consumer desires.

Probably the most widely known discussion of the appropriate size of the public sector in the United States is given by John Kenneth Gal-braith in his book *The Affluent Society*. Galbraith has argued that there is a systematic imbalance in favor of the private sector and against the pub-lic sector, in part because of heavy advertising in the private sector. But it is possible to argue against Galbraith on the grounds that the public sector also advertises. Some of this advertising is concentrated on a few members of Congress and could be more effective than private-sector ad-vertising. In addition, many lobby groups tell the public that certain kinds of public spending are good.

Anthony Downs, a Chicago-based economic and political consultant, has arrived at a conclusion similar to Galbraith's; namely, that the gov-ernment budget in a two-party democracy tends systematically to be too small.[5] He has argued that democratic budgets are not expanded enough

---

[4]This section draws heavily from Ryan C. Amacher, Robert D. Tolleson, and Thomas D. Willett (eds.), "A Menu of Distributional Considerations," *The Economic Approach to Public Policy: Selected Readings* (New York: Cornell University Press, 1976).

[5]Anthony Downs, "Why the Government Budget is Too Small in a Democracy," *World Politics* (July, 1960).

TABLE 15-2   **Federal Government Expenditures as a Percentage of National Income**

Year	Defense Expenditures	Transfers	Other (Except Transfers and Defense)	Total
1929	0.8	1.1	10.2	12.1
1934	1.3	3.2	21.9	26.4
1938	1.7	3.5	19.3	24.5
1944	48.1	1.7	6.9	56.7
1949	6.2	5.5	13.8	25.5
1954	13.7	5.0	13.0	31.7
1959	11.5	6.4	14.7	32.6
1964	9.4	6.7	17.4	33.5
1969	9.9	8.2	18.8	36.9
1970	9.2	9.5	20.1	38.8
1971	8.2	10.5	20.7	39.4
1972	7.7	10.4	20.5	38.6
1973	6.9	10.7	20.2	37.8
1974	6.8	11.9	21.4	40.1
1975	6.9	14.0	22.6	43.5
1976	6.3	13.5	21.8	41.6

Source: G. Warren Nutter, *Growth of Government in the West* (Washington: American Enterprise Institute, 1978).

in certain directions when vote-maximizing parties compete for the support of utility-maximizing voters. The "correct" budget, by Downs' benchmark, is the budget which would emerge if political parties and voters had perfect information. This benchmark is clearly ethical in character (as Downs stresses), requiring the value judgment that democracy works well under conditions of perfect information. Following this guide, he argues that many potential benefits of governmental action will not be produced in a complex and interdependent democracy where parties must appeal to voters lacking perfect information. Such governmental benefits are remote and uncertain in nature; for example, the benefits of foreign aid expenditures in preventing a future war, or the potential benefits from safety, food, and drug regulation. Voters are simply (and rationally) not aware of the potential returns from governmental activity in such areas and would not recognize such benefits even if political parties invested in an advertising program to make them known. On the other side of the fiscal account, Downs argues that taxes, even indirect ones, are more accurately taken into account by voters than the remote benefits under realistic circumstances.

Professors James Buchanan and Gordon Tullock, both of Virginia Polytechnic Institute, have mounted arguments generally counter to

TABLE 15-3   U.S. Federal Grants as a Percentage of State and Local Spending

Year	Percent
1929	0.1
1940	9.7
1950	10.3
1960	12.1
1970	18.5
1975	23.9
1977	25.3

Source: *Survey of Current Business*, selected months.

those of Downs and Galbraith.[6] They arrived at this position by employing a methodology that is similar, but not identical, to the methodology used by Downs. Buchanan and Tullock argue that majority voting tends to result in overinvestment in the *specific* benefits projects, such as rivers and harbors, at the expense of *general* benefit items, such as defense. They adopted as a benchmark a voter's choice based on the voter's perceived personal costs from collective action. It is a similar benchmark to that of Downs in that it is an ethical criterion. Buchanan and Tullock point out that whether the budget is pushed too far in terms of specific or general benefits depends on the type of taxation that applies. The implication is that general benefit items suffer at the expense of specific benefit items. Under these conditions, the absolute budget size will be too large. What happens is simple to understand. Members of Congress have the power to give projects to their districts and win votes by helping their districts receive projects. Taxes go up by only a small amount due to any one project, but the citizens of an area receive much in benefits. With all members of Congress playing these games, we tend to produce too many projects. The representative from Arizona votes for a bridge in Kentucky in order to get the Kentucky representative to vote for a dam in Arizona. This vote trading is called *logrolling*.

Still other approaches to the question have yielded different conclusions. It has been suggested that budgets are too large because of the monopoly character of governmental agencies; that budgets become too large because bureaucrats have incentives to vote for and help politicians who promise still larger budgets because, as budgets grow, bureaucrats become more powerful and receive bigger raises; and that risk elements such as the possibility of war cause us to spend too much on military projects. The conclusions are often mixed, and the arguments concerning the appropriate size of the budget are surrounded by a great deal of confusion.

---

[6]James Buchanan and Gordon Tullock, *Calculus of Consent: Logical Foundations of Constitutional Democracy* (Ann Arbor: University of Michigan Press, 1962).

A very important point emerges from all this confusion. We have seen that the market breaks down with regard to public goods, but the political process also diverges from the theoretical ideal. What we need to determine is which of these two imperfect mechanisms does a better job of providing goods that are more or less public in nature. In some cases, such as national defense, it is likely the government. In others, such as tennis courts, it may well be the market process. It is not clear that we should always presume that market failure implies the need for governmental intervention. What we have suggested is that market failure and government failure are *both* possible in the real world.

INCOME DISTRIBUTION AS A PUBLIC GOOD

It could be argued that redistribution of income is a public good. Some members of the polity will "free ride" on private redistributive efforts, and, as a result, less than the optimal amount of redistribution of income will take place. This will happen because the free riders will think that there is no need to help the poor because others will give. The electorate, as a result, may decide to redistribute income and tax all citizens to achieve a better outcome than the market-produced outcome.

The need for this redistribution comes from the normative conclusion that we don't like the distribution of income the market produces. This distribution was discussed in detail in Chapter 13, and at that time we said that the theory only explained how the distribution came to be what it was, and that later we would examine how and why it could be changed. However, we need first to measure the distribution of income to determine just what we mean by an unsatisfactory distribution of income. Then we can examine governmental redistribution programs to see why they have or haven't worked.

Does the Market Produce Equitable Outcomes?

Assuming a perfectly competitive market for the factors of production (land, labor, capital, and entrepreneurship) and abstracting from the question of "unearned income," what determines the laissez-faire distribution of income, and is this a "just" or "equitable" solution? Economic theory gives as an unambiguous answer to the first of these two questions. The second is much more difficult to answer. In this discussion, the marginal productivity theory of income distribution, which we examined in detail in Chapter 13, will serve as a quite useful benchmark as we consider some additional *normative* and *positive* questions concerning the distribution of income. This marginal productivity theory is an important cornerstone of positive economics. It enables economists to analyze many problems concerning factor movements and changes in factor shares in the face of changed market conditions. As we shall see, many of the normative questions about income distribution arise because the market is not the only institution affecting the distribution of income in most societies. The discussion that follows will consider how other factors might affect the market-produced distribution of income in such a way as to make it unacceptable.

As we saw in Chapter 13, the return to the factors of production (rent, wages, interest, and profits), hence, the distribution of income, is determined by the supply of and demand for factors of different kinds and qualities. This functional distribution of income is treated in economic theory as a reflection of choices made by individuals in the marketplace. The demand for factors of production, including labor, is a demand derived from the demand for the good the factors are combined to produce. A factor's value is derived (thus, "derived demand") from what it produces. The differences in income that do exist are a result of a combination of influences, including differences in the productivity of factors and in the demand for the final products they produce.

This competitive market solution is at once both a reward to the value of the input and the value of the output of the productive unit (the firm). Given factor inputs of equal physical productivity, the highest reward will go the factor unit employed in the industry producing products most highly valued in the market. Conversely, labor inputs of different skills employed in the same industry will be rewarded with respect to their physical productivity, with the more productive factor receiving the greater remuneration at the margin. Additionally, the return to the factor will be affected by the physical productivity of the other factor units it is combined with and by the relative amounts of each factor employed. Thus, it is possible that factors of "equal quality" receive different remuneration when combined with different factors of production. A good example of this point is the return to the management of General Motors versus the return to the management of a small, hometown plant. The managers of General Motors receive a higher return for one reason — because they are combined with larger amounts of capital, making the value of these units of managerial decision-making higher.

An important aspect of this determination of income distribution is that it is associated with efficiency in resource allocation. *Ceteris paribus*, factors flow to those employments with the highest remuneration; that is, those in which their productivity is most highly valued. Such a system has value because it rewards productivity rather than some other ethical, nonmarket determination of factor remuneration. In freely operating markets, the return to factors of equal productivity will tend toward equality and, over time, factors will tend to transfer to their highest valued use.

The Role of Chance

The market-determined distribution of income may be unsatisfactory because there are substantial elements of chance associated with this distribution. Most economists view risk as an unattractive situation and one which individuals will avoid unless they can be compensated for assuming this risk. We say people have ***risk aversion***. An individual's future income is subject to a considerable degree of uncertainty. To a great extent this uncertainty may not be avoidable privately; hence, where most people are *risk-averters*, government programs of an ***egalitarian*** nature (programs aimed at creating a more equal distribution of income) affecting either the income distribution or the distribution of specific commodities, may appear. Thus, privately uninsurable risk may lead to income redistribution as a valid function of the state. Government may respond to such risks either by acting to reduce the risk itself or by implementing various types of insurance plans. In the former case, there are many examples of preventative public programs, such as public health and education programs, and programs designed to regulate product safety. In the latter case, institutions such as Social Security, unemployment insurance, progressive income taxation, and the stabilization policy you learned about in macroeconomics are examples of governmental policies that respond to some extent to risk-aversion among voters.

Should Distribution Be Completely Separated from Market Outcomes?

As we saw in Chapter 5, economists have been reluctant to make interpersonal comparisons of utility. This has somewhat restricted their analysis of distributional problems. The basic reason for this reluctance on the part of the economic scientist is that value judgments are necessary to judge alternative distributions of income, and to an economist, value judgments are not scientific data. However, various economists and philosophers have developed general distributional schemes which depend in one way or another on interpersonal comparisons.

For example, a utilitarian would argue that income should be distributed to maximize society's satisfaction. Of course, this would be a difficult criterion to agree upon since there is no scientific way to compare satisfaction. Operationally, it would be difficult, if not impossible, to obtain reliable measures of satisfaction since each individual would have a clear incentive to lie. As stated above, economists have long argued that there is simply no way to make interpersonal comparisons of satisfaction, even if there were a way to operationally measure individual satisfaction. For example, say we wish to tax a rich student $100 and redistribute the $100 to a poor teacher. It is impossible for us to conclude that the satisfaction the rich student gave up by consuming $100 less champagne is less than the satisfaction the poor teacher received by consuming $100 more of Coors beer.

Since general schemes such as "maximizing society's satisfaction" are both theoretically and operationally impossible to implement, it might make sense to distribute income on some computed egalitarian basis as an approximation of the desire to make income more equal.

Plato was explicit on such a rule. He argued that no one in society should be more than four times richer than the poorest member of society. Once such a normative decision to redistribute is made, the problem then becomes one of determining an operational basis. Again, economists have done little work in this area because of unwillingness to make the necessary value judgments.

A Negative Income Tax

Perhaps one operational rule that could be applied would be for everyone in a jurisdiction to be guaranteed at least some minimum income. This suggests that a guaranteed annual income is probably the best operational way to change the market-determined income distribution. Assuming that this idea is accepted, the problem is then to select what the minimum income should be. Again this has to be a strictly normative decision; economic theory can give us no clue as to what this level should be. The most workable approach would seem to be that of calculating a typical poverty-level budget at current prices.

Professor Milton Friedman has suggested a *negative income tax* to replace the costly, inefficient, and incentive-destroying "present grab-bag" system of redistribution.[7] A negative income tax is a transfer to people from the government, rather than a transfer to the government from citizens; hence the term negative income tax. A negative income tax has two components: an income guarantee and a negative tax rate. In Friedman's plan the basic income guarantee varies with family size. Let's say a family of four would have a guaranteed income of $3,000. The negative tax is, say, 50 percent. This means that for each dollar the family earns, it loses 50¢ of welfare payments. This is argued to be more conducive to work incentives because the family keeps part of its earned income rather than losing 100 percent in welfare reductions. Table 15-4 gives a hypothetical example for four families, assuming a $3,000 income guarantee and a 50 percent negative tax. The transfer received by a family is $3,000 minus 50 percent of any income earned that is less than $6,000. The amount of welfare that a family receives can be determined by the formula

$$T = IG - t_n (EI),$$

where T is the welfare payment, IG is the income guarantee, t_n is the negative tax rate, and EI is the earned income. At some point the family reaches the break-even point, which is the point at which no more income is transferred, and the family starts paying normal, positive taxes. With an income guarantee of $3,000 and a negative tax of 50 percent,

[7]See Milton Friedman, "The Case for the Negative Income Tax," *Republican Papers*, edited by M. R. Laird (New York: Praeger, 1968).

TABLE 15-4   A Negative Income Tax[1]

Family:	A	B	C	D
Earned Income	$ 0	$2,000	$4,000	$6,000
Transfer	3,000	2,000	1,000	0
Disposable Income	3,000	4,000	5,000	6,000
Increase in Income of $100	100	100	100	100
Earned Income Becomes	100	2,100	4,100	6,100
Tax Rate	(−50%)	(−50%)	(−50%)	Normal Tax Rate
Welfare Payment	2,950	1,950	950	0
Disposable Income	3,050	4,050	5,050	6,100
				(less normal tax on income over $6,000)

[1]Assumes a $3,000 guaranteed income and a 50 percent negative tax rate.

this break-even point would occur at $6,000. Table 15-4 represents a numerical example and shows how an additional $100 of income would benefit the welfare recipient.

The major benefits of the negative income tax system are easy to see. In the first place, it concentrates public funds on the poor rather than on a large welfare bureacracy through which funds must trickle down to those in need. It would therefore cost less for the same amount of redistribution because it is directed specifically at poverty, eliminating the need for intermediary agencies. And, instead of cutting off funds to those whose income is just above the poverty level, it provides aid to the near-poor as well. Perhaps most importantly, however, the negative income tax does not eliminate work incentives. Most present systems reduce transfers by 100 percent of any earned income; if a person on welfare earns $1,000, benefits fall by $1,000. A system that allows individuals to keep a portion of what they earn would be favorable to work incentives. Another argument for such a system is that it would greatly reduce the cost of administering welfare programs. Then the welfare bureaucracy could be largely dismantled and the function of redistribution carried out by the Internal Revenue Service. The negative income tax is an objective and impersonal vehicle, thus allowing recipients to maintain a sense of dignity, instead of forcing welfare recipients to deal with a bureaucracy that at times is arrogant and demeaning. Furthermore, many programs, such as minimum wage legislation and agricultural subsidies, are justified on distribution grounds. It might be possible to eliminate some of these if the negative tax system were operative.

As long as a negative income tax is not merely superimposed on the current system so that it does not become simply another "rag in the bag" but, instead, replaces all direct public-assistance programs, if not all welfare programs in general, it is considered by most authorities to possess a decided advantage over other welfare-reform proposals. The main obstacle to its adoption is the entrenched vested interests of the present welfare bureaucracy.

Should Strings Be Attached?

A question basic to discussions of income redistribution is, What should be redistributed? In other words, should general money grants such as a guaranteed income be given or should the redistribution be in the form of goods (in kind)? If money is redistributed, a related question is whether or not conditions should be attached to the transfer.

The argument that money should be given instead of certain goods is part of the argument that lump sum transfers of general purchasing power are the optimal form of transfer. A transfer of money allows more options and maximizes the freedom of the recipient; that is, it places the individual on the highest possible indifference curve. This is the traditional welfare analysis of transfers of money and is based solely on the idea of maximizing the utility of welfare recipients. It assumes we should transfer money and let the welfare recipients maximize their own well being.

Professor James Buchanan has argued that maximizing the utility of welfare recipients by allowing them freedom is not relevant; one should instead consider maximizing the freedom of the welfare donor. This implies money or in-kind transfers, depending on what the donor specifies. This argument applies if we are discussing negative externalities (such as the poor) or positive externalities (such as faculty members or citizens' groups deciding what is "best" for students to read).

The conditional granting of transfers is likely to be an important factor when the motivation for the transfer is *not* concern for the welfare of the recipient, per se. The motivation may stem from a distaste for a particularly noxious externality, or it may stem from a desire to influence behavior in a certain way. That is, it may stem from a desire to reduce the cost of policing against a certain action or a fear that unless some redistribution takes place the poor will become unruly. These are distinctly separate motivations, but they produce the same distributional response, and they both imply that it is the freedom of the donor that should be maximized. When these motivations are important to the donor, it is likely that strings will be attached to the transfer. Probably the best example of such conditional granting of transfers is the often-cited example of the welfare requirement that able-bodied males must be willing to accept work if offered. In effect, the argument here is that transfers to reduce specific externalities may be quite rational from the point of view of the donor-voter. This is supported in a positive sense by the observation of the large amounts of such specific transfers in practice.

Basic Needs

Many of the transfers that we observe are in-kind transfers of specific commodities; for example, the surplus-commodity food program and Salvation Army soup kitchens. Grants and transfers of this kind may result when the concerns of those initiating the transfer are aimed at what they consider "basic needs." The transfer is not so much based on the desire to reduce income inequality as on the desire to insure that basic needs, such as food and shelter, are provided. Professor James Tobin of Yale University has pointed out this distinction by referring to it as *specific egalitarianism*. Tobin feels that most economists are *general* egalitarians (to the extent they are egalitarian), because they recognize the inefficiencies introduced by in-kind transfers. The majority of the electorate, however, are *specific* egalitarians. They are concerned with ill-clothed and ill-fed people, not with poverty per se. If this observation is correct, one can expect most public transfers to be transfers in kind, or with strings attached.

Redistribution Through Jobs

An exception to the argument that recipients prefer the money transfer to the in-kind or strings-attached transfer is the argument that the poor do not want welfare, but rather, meaningful jobs. This is, in essence, a call for in-kind transfers in the form of jobs, sometimes publicly provided. This argument can often be added, in a subtle fashion, to arguments concerning monetary and fiscal policy. Labor leaders often argue in Washington that publicly provided jobs are needed to cushion the harshness of contractionary monetary and fiscal policy.

Redistribution to Special Interests

An interesting case of redistribution occurs when the recipients attempt to conceal the fact from themselves and others that a transfer is being made. This case constitutes back-door welfare; that is, transfers from the general public to special interest groups via some form of trade-restricting legislation. Arguments for such legislation, as you will see in Chapter 16, appear frequently in international trade literature, but arguments for tariffs and quotas are by no means the only arguments used by special interest groups for back-door welfare. An example of such an argument would be the mink-breeders' association arguing that they need protection from cheap mink being imported from Eastern Europe. In effect, the mink breeders are asking for an income transfer from consumers of mink. It is an income transfer because the tariff or quota will allow the price of mink to be higher than it would be in the absence of any import restrictions. This means the consumers of mink pelts, or people who buy mink coats, are transferring income to the mink producers. Some of you might think this is all right, because people who buy mink

coats are rich, but what if we change the example to say the people who
want the tariff are producers of cotton shirts, or beef, or shoes. The
transfer is well-camouflaged, and many industry leaders and producing
firms would strongly object to putting the protection argument in these
terms. Nevertheless, the protection represents a transfer to the protected
industry.

In fact, it might well be argued that every lobbyist in Washington is
really an entrepreneur for back-door welfare. In addition to promoting
these transfers, one could say that these lobbyists help produce unproductive entrepreneurial activity. An example here would be investment
in tax avoidance through the hiring of tax lawyers and accountants, the
employment of whom is solely undertaken to avoid taxes.

Private Versus Public Mechanisms for Redistributing Income

There are many ways that the types of general or specific transfers we
have been discussing can be carried out. The manner in which redistribution is accomplished can influence the type and amount of the ultimate transfer.

Private redistribution through charity takes place voluntarily. Such
transfers can spring from a variety of motivations, all linked to some form
of concern by an individual about other individuals in society. The analytical term for such concern is *utility interdependence*. Interdependence of utility functions exists for any one of a number of reasons, ranging from a sense of social justice to finding offensive the lifestyle of those
who are poor. The important point about such transfers is that they are
voluntary and hence may be presumed to be optimal in the sense that
both parties benefit. However, as we argued before, there is a problem
with relying upon private redistribution alone. If the income equality
achieved via private charity can be characterized as a public good, the
private charity might produce too little redistribution. This would happen because the individuals in a large group would recognize that they
do not have to contribute since others will. In large groups there is a
tendency to free ride in this way and, in practice, give very little to charity. The reason, as Professor Tullock has so aptly put it, is that the two
drives of consuming and helping the poor are in conflict. The result is
that people generally talk as if they are charitable but in practice demonstrate that they are not as charitable as they profess. Of course, if all
followed this strategy, there would be no private redistribution or at least
not enough redistribution. Such an argument provides a basis for collec-
tivizing the function of income redistribution. The person who gives to
others because of the personal satisfaction gained from the act does not
present a free-rider problem. However, if the personal gain the giver receives is seeing less poverty in the world, the act of others' giving diminishes the need to give, and the free-rider problem can arise.

An important variable in determining the amount of private redistribution is the size of the group in which the distribution takes place. If

we are dealing with a relatively small, homogeneous group of givers and receivers, the amount of private redistribution increases. This is observable in such groups as the Mormon Church and certain Amish sects. It is consistent with the view that the externalities associated with poverty are more significant (i.e., observable) the smaller the group size. Thus, one might predict that in a collective context, a small country with a relatively homogeneous population, such as Sweden, would likely practice more redistribution than a large "melting pot" country like the United States.

We have to this point been discussing the theory that those who are relatively rich use the state as a mechanism in transferring income to the poor. There is, however, another theory: that the poor use the state as a means of extracting transfers from the rich. This view is grounded on some empirical evidence, since the poor vote and the amount of redistribution does seem to be a function of the degree to which they vote.

Positive Theories of Income Redistribution

The preceding discussion has centered on a consideration of some basic motivations that lie behind various arguments for income redistribution. The result has been a conclusion that redistribution follows from any one of a number of benign and nonbenign motivations. There have been very few attempts to distill these arguments into a positive theory of income redistribution based on the usual self-interest models employed by economists. Two exceptions to this have been positive theories exposited by Professor George Stigler of the University of Chicago and Professor Gordon Tullock, who consider why people might try to redistribute to themselves rather than to others.

Stigler theorizes that the government will use its coercive power to extract resources which would not be forthcoming by voluntary agreement in the society. Any group that can gain control of the government machinery can then use this power to its own benefit. Stigler argues that the group that controls government is the middle class; hence, most public expenditures are made for the benefit of the middle class.

Along similar lines, Tullock argues that only a small portion of the massive amounts of government transfers go to the poor. He argues that in the nature of the voting process, resources will be taken from the rich, but it is not entirely clear how they will be distributed. Since the middle-income groups will be crucial in obtaining the authority needed to take resources from other members of society, he expects that money will flow from both ends of the income ladder toward the middle.

Both Tullock and Stigler argue that the state is used primarily for the taking of resources and that political power will be used to advance these ends. As a result, income distribution will in reality be a method by which the dominant political group, the middle class, extends its power. Both Tullock and Stigler present examples, such as farm policy, education, and so on, where examination of the incidence of the benefits supports this hypothesis. The lesson that should be drawn here is that the real reason for income redistribution and the expressed political intent are often quite different. Of course, these arguments are closely related to some of the arguments that were treated earlier. In fact, they are forms of special-interest redistribution or redistribution via bureaucracy. In the latter case, Tullock's contention that in most cases transfers do not reach the poor is particularly telling.

A Complex System

We have considered some of the normative and positive arguments concerning the distribution of income. As one would naturally expect, the discussion was complex. There are many ways of looking at the question of the distribution of income and obviously many trade-offs to be considered in determining an optimal or acceptable answer to the question of what is the proper distribution. Our approach has been only to sketch the relevant questions and trade-offs. We have followed this approach because the resolution of distribution questions is something that we cannot pronounce upon as economists. Rather, we hope that the discussion of distribution considerations that we have presented will be helpful in coming to grips with the basic trade-offs involved in understanding distribution policy, which by necessity can only be determined in the political arena.

MEASURING THE DISTRIBUTION OF INCOME

If we are going to design programs to redistribute income, we must first determine what the distribution of income is and identify the poor. A traditional way to measure the distribution of income is with a *Lorenz curve*. A Lorenz curve traces the cumulative percentage of income households receive, ranked from lowest to highest. In Figure 15-4 we have Lorenz curves for three hypothetical economies. A perfectly egalitarian society would have a Lorenz curve represented by Distribution *A*. If incomes were absolutely uniformly distributed, the lowest 10 percent of the households would have 10 percent of the income, the highest 20 percent would have 20 percent, and so on. When we get a distribution in which everyone does not have the same income, the Lorenz curve diverges from the 45-degree line of perfect equality. Distribution *B* in Figure 15-4 represents a less than perfectly egalitarian society. The greater the difference between the 45-degree line and the Lorenz curve, the greater the inequality in the cumulative distribution. In terms of Figure 15-4, Distribution *C* represents a more unequal distribution of income than Distribution *B*.

We can draw Lorenz curves for countries to compare them to the level of egalitarianism among other countries. If we did that, we would

FIGURE 15-4   Lorenz Curves

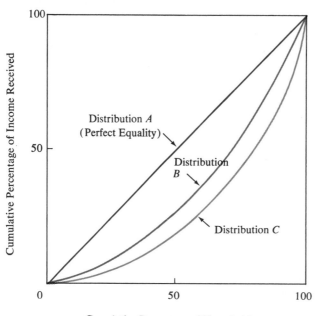

A Lorenz curve traces the cumulative percentage of income households
receive, ranked from lowest to highest. A perfectly egalitarian society
would have a Lorenz curve represented by Distribution A. Distributions
B and C represent more unequal distributions of income, respectively.

find Sweden's Lorenz curve to be closest to the 45-degree line, and the
countries in the underdeveloped world to be the most skewed from the
45-degree line. Another useful exercise is to examine how the distribution of income changes over time. The data in Table 15-5 allow us to
draw the Lorenz curves of Figure 15-5. Both the table and the figure
indicate that our society has become more egalitarian since 1929.

Lorenz curves tell us about the *relative* distribution of income. A
particular Lorenz curve might indicate that the lower 20 percent of the
households have only 5 percent of the income, but it doesn't say if this
income is high or low in an absolute sense. This 5 percent could be high
enough so that everyone is well fed, well housed, and well clothed. Being
in the lowest 5 percent in the U.S., for example, may be better than being
in the middle 5 percent of some other country.

The Absolute Level of Income

We need to somehow determine how much income, or perhaps more
appropriately, how little income, defines poverty in an economy. This is

TABLE 15-5 **Income Distribution in the United States, 1929–1976**

Family	Income Class	Percentage of Income				
		1929	1947	1960	1972	1976
Lowest	5th	3.5	5.1	4.8	5.4	5.4
Second	5th	9.0	11.8	12.2	11.9	11.8
Middle	5th	13.8	16.7	17.8	17.5	17.6
Fourth	5th	19.3	23.2	24.0	23.9	24.1
Highest	5th	54.4	43.3	41.3	41.4	41.1
Highest	5%	30.0	17.5	15.9	15.9	15.6

Source: *Statistical Abstract of the United States*, 1977 and previous issues.

FIGURE 15-5 **Income Distribution in the United States, 1929 and 1976**

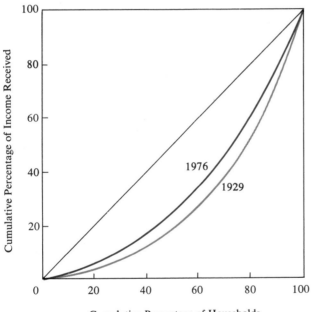

Plotting Lorenz curves for the United States for 1929 and 1976 shows that the distribution of income has become more equal.

hard to do because poverty is both an absolute and a relative concept. People who are relatively poor in one country may be well off by another country's standard, or in the same country in different decades or centuries. These problems notwithstanding, we need to attempt to measure poverty. The U.S. government makes such definitions and updates them from time to time. In 1976 an individual earning less than $2,884 per year and a family of four earning less than $5,818 per year were considered to be below the poverty level. These figures are, of course, much higher in 1980 due to the rapid inflation we have been having. Table 15-6 shows that in recent years, the number of people below the poverty level has decreased. The next relevant question is, Who are these poor? The answer, of course, is difficult to determine. The poor come from everywhere and from every age group. However, it may be possible to pinpoint certain social, geographic, and racial characteristics of the poor. Geographically, for example, the poor tend to live in the rural south and the northern cities. Table 15-7 points out some other important characteristics of people below the poverty line. If we take 11 percent as the standard, because 11 percent of all families fell below the poverty line in 1975, we can see that the incidence is higher than 11 percent for certain segments of the population. Nonwhites have a much higher incidence of poverty. Age is an important variable, with the young and old representing a sizable percentage of the group below the poverty level. Education is important, with high school and college graduates being under-represented. This, of course, makes good sense if we view education as investment in human capital and suggests that education is one way to deal with the problem of poverty. Marital status is important also; as you can see, widowers and divorced women who are heads of households have a high incidence of poverty.

TABLE 15-6   Percentage of Population Considered Poor

1959	22.4
1966	14.7
1972	11.9
1976	11.8

Source: U.S. Bureau of the Census and *Statistical Abstract of the United States*, 1977.

Nonwhite Poverty

The picture we have just painted is that to be nonwhite is to have a much higher incidence of poverty. Of course, a major reason for this is that the nonwhite population has a much higher representation of the characteristics associated with poverty listed in Table 15-7. Another reason is racial discrimination. Whatever the cause of this race-related poverty, the effects have not diminished in recent years despite programs to overcome nonwhite poverty. Table 15-8 shows that the nonwhite-white income differential has remained surprisingly stable throughout the 1970s. Perhaps the most hopeful sign is that the educational achieve-

TABLE 15-7   **Poverty Incidence — 1975**

Characteristic	Percentage Who Fall Below Poverty Line
All Families	11
Race	
White	10
Black	30
Spanish Surname	27
Age	
Children Under 18	16
White	13
Black	41
65 and Older	12
Employment Status	
Employed	5
Unemployed	21
Not in Labor Force	22
Education of Family Head	
Elementary	18
1–3 Years of High School	14
4 Years of High School	6
Some College	3
Marital Status	
Married — Spouse Present	8
Widowed	41
Divorced — Women (head of household)	33

Source: U.S. Bureau of the Census, *U.S. Census of Population*, 1976.

ment of nonwhites has been increasing significantly, and this achievement should translate into higher income levels. UCLA Professor Thomas Sowell, for example, has argued that the returns to education are much higher for minority individuals than they are for nonminority individuals.[8]

PROGRAMS TO REDISTRIBUTE INCOME

Regardless of how one feels about the theoretical arguments concerning whether or not redistribution should be publicly or privately provided, it

---

[8]See Thomas Sowell, *Race and Economics* (New York: David McKay Co., 1975).

Courtesy of Thomas Sowell

Thomas Sowell (1930–)

Thomas Sowell

Thomas Sowell is currently a professor of economics at U.C.L.A. He has a B.A. from Harvard, an M.A. from Columbia, and a Ph.D. in economics from the University of Chicago. Professor Sowell has used positive economic theory and analysis to examine some politically explosive problems of race and income distribution in the United States. These problems have often been examined only in a very normative fashion.

In one study, Professor Sowell examined the need for affirmative action employment plans in higher education. He demonstrated that the administration of affirmative action programs has run counter to the intent of the Civil Rights Act of 1964. The law rejected quotas and placed the burden of proving discrimination on the government. In reality, the burden of proof has been shifted to the employer. This has resulted in a tremendous increase in the costs of higher education. Sowell found in a statistical comparison that salaries of black academics with comparable training and credentials equaled or surpassed salaries of white academics before the application of the law in 1971. Sowell also statistically demonstrated that male-female career differentials are not the result of employer discrimination but are more likely explained by social mores that place family responsibilities disproportionately on women. This explanation suggests that government intervention aimed at reducing these differentials simply won't work.

In all his work, Sowell has applied the reasoned logic of economics to examine social policy questions of considerable interest. In doing so, he does not shy away from very sensitive questions of race and claims of discrimination. To examine Sowell's ideas and arguments, you should read his *Affirmative Action Reconsidered* (1975); *Black Education: Myths and Tragedies* (1970); and *Race and Economics* (1975).

TABLE 15-8   **Nonwhite-White Income Differentials**

Year	Mean Incomes of Nonwhites as a Percentage of Mean White Income
1964	56
1965	55
1966	60
1967	62
1968	63
1969	63
1970	64
1971	63
1972	60
1973	62
1974	65
1975	66

Source: U.S. Bureau of the Census, *Current Population Reports*, Series P-6, N. 114, 1976.

is unmistakably clear that redistribution of income has become a public activity. Table 15-9 shows that the public share of welfare has increased dramatically in recent years. The governmental programs are varied and have varied constituencies. Yet there is a basic philosophy that has run through the welfare program. This philosophy calls for jobs for those who are able to work, social insurance for the elderly and those temporarily unemployed, and direct assistance for children and the infirm.

Employment opportunities are provided through macroeconomic policies and programs. The Humphrey-Hawkins Bill, which has been a topic of heated debate in the late 1970s, further advocates this aspect of governmental responsibility by codifying into law the proposition that every American has a right to a job and that it is the government's responsibility to provide jobs as the employer of last resort.

TABLE 15-9   **Private and Public Share of Welfare**

Fiscal Year	Percent Private	Percent Public
1950	35.0	65.0
1955	50.0	50.0
1960	40.7	59.3
1965	32.6	67.4
1970	20.0	80.0
1975	12.2	87.8

Source: *Significant Features of Fiscal Federalism* (Washington: U.S. Government Printing Office, 1976).

Old Age, Survivors and Disability Insurance (Social Security) is the government's program to provide social insurance. The Social Security Act was passed in 1935 and pays retirement subsidies to the aged and to widows and children of workers who are covered under the law. Medicare and Medicaid are other examples of governmental social insurance. Unemployment benefits are also paid to those temporarily out of work.

Direct-assistance programs are designed to help the poor who are not covered by social insurance. The largest of such programs are the AFDC (Aid to Families with Dependent Children) and OAA (Old Age Assistance) programs. These programs are targeted to the categories with high incidences of poverty, as we saw in Table 15-7. In addition to these programs, there are many other direct-assistance programs such as food stamps, rent supplements, Head Start, and so on.

Problems in Governmental Transfers

There has been much recent frustration with the inability of governmental welfare programs to do much to alleviate poverty. Senator Daniel P. Moynihan, who was President Nixon's welfare adviser, believes the problem is that many of the governmental programs simply don't reach the poor. He says, "This money did not go to poor people, but to the new class of professionals who manage the programs."[9] This view of the system from someone who tried to change it fits very closely with the theories of Stigler and Tullock, which we discussed earlier in this chapter.

The inability of government programs to substantially affect poverty has led to a so-called welfare crisis. Many citizens are frustrated by what is perceived as a large group of welfare cheats and by the belief that, for many individuals, welfare has become a way of life. One reason for this view is that present welfare practices have had the effect of destroying work incentives and in some cases have even created incentives for family dissolution. AFDC is a case in point. Fathers have been known to leave home so the family could become eligible for AFDC payments. Work incentives are destroyed because an increase in earnings usually means an equivalent loss of welfare benefits. The negative income tax which we discussed in detail earlier in this chapter could help to overcome this problem.

The difficult policy decisions and conflicting social goals among which policymakers must choose are inescapable under a negative income tax program. But it is important to remember that virtually none of the major problems or objections to the negative income tax are limited only to this proposal. They are to be found in any welfare program, particularly with respect to the work-incentive question.

---

[9]*Newsweek* (November 7, 1977), p. 42.

The Department of Health, Education, and Welfare (HEW)

The Department of Health, Education, and Welfare

The Department of Health, Education, and Welfare (HEW) was established in April, 1953, by President Dwight D. Eisenhower. HEW is a large, bureaucratic organization that touches the life of every American citizen in one way or another. There are four operating agencies of HEW, each of which has a different area of interest. These agencies are the Office of Education, the Social Security Administration, the Social and Rehabilitation Service, and the Public Health Service. These four agencies have many subdepartments. For example, the Public Health Service consists of the National Institute of Health; the Food and Drug Administration; the Alcohol, Drug Abuse, and Mental Health Administration; the Center for Disease Control; the Health Resources Administration; and the Health Services Administration. In addition to this complicated array of departments and subdepartments, HEW is also responsible for three unique American educational institutions. HEW funding supports Howard University, established in 1867 to educate black Americans; Gallaudet, a college specifically established for the deaf; and the American Printing House for the Blind.

This brief description of the different agencies and responsibilities of HEW indicate that it must be an extremely difficult department to manage. Indeed, much criticism of the failure of social programs has been directed at the bureaucratic inability of HEW to accomplish its goals. President Carter has proposed a new Department of Education, which would be intended to streamline administration by partially reducing the responsibility of HEW. The Secretary of HEW opposed such a reorganization.

Social Security: A Case Study of Welfare Problems

The crisis in welfare reform is perhaps no better demonstrated than in the furor over Social Security and the increases in Social Security taxes. To begin, it must be made clear that Social Security is not a retirement program as we know private retirement programs to be. The government does not collect your payments and place them in a fund which it invests in order to pay you benefits when you retire.

Social Security is purely and simply a tax and transfer mechanism. It taxes current workers and transfers this money to retired workers. When the number of retired workers was small and the work force was large, this seemed like a very simple system. In recent years, however, the system has grown in complexity. In addition to providing benefits to retired workers, it pays benefits to dependents of retired workers, to surviving dependents of deceased workers, and to disabled workers and their dependents. Benefits to all these groups have grown dramatically in recent years and have lately even been indexed to the inflation rate. Additionally, the size of the retired population as a percentage of the work force is increasing. This means that fewer workers are paying taxes to support more retirees. The system works like a chain letter, and there are fewer and fewer people to send the letter to.

Who is responsible for this mess? The benefit increase is easy to pinpoint. Congress and the president have increased benefits significantly. In the past 20 years the average monthly benefit has increased from $62 to $225. These increases are politically popular and win votes. The increase in taxes to pay for these benefits is less popular. The furor in 1978 over the on-again-off-again Social Security tax package is a case in point.

Again we are reminded of the theories of Professors Stigler and Tullock. They predicted transfers would not reach the poor but would circulate among the nonpoor. This proposition receives some empirical support in the case of Social Security when those who must work to supplement their Social Security benefits suffer benefit reductions because of their earned income, while the individual who earns income from stocks, bonds, or other assets does not incur Social Security reductions.

Prospects for Reform

Welfare reform is, of course, high on the political agenda. The prospects for meaningful reform dim, however, when one examines the bureaucratic vested interests involved. We will have to wait to see how any of the various proposed welfare reforms fare in the political arena. Choosing between different welfare programs requires value judgments. Economic theory can help us analyze the effects of different programs, but it cannot tell us which is the "correct" reform. Such questions require political solutions.

Summary

This chapter has examined theoretical arguments for government intervention to correct for market failure. Externalities exist where there is interdependence between economic units and when this interdependence is not reflected in market transactions. As a result of externalities, competitive firms will produce too much output at too low a price. The government *may* be able to internalize the externalities and move the market closer to a social optimum. The Coase theorem suggests that, where few parties are affected by externalities, the government may not need to intervene.

The issue of public goods is another area where government intervention may be necessary. Public goods may be underproduced because problems of exclusion allow individuals to free ride on the provision of the goods. As a result, the government may need to provide for the goods out of general tax revenue if the correct amount is to be provided.

In both the externality case and the public good case it is necessary to weigh carefully the costs of government intervention. Although it is easy to show that markets do not always produce optimal outcomes, the government does not intervene in a costless manner. The choice is between two imperfect mechanisms, and we should be careful to be sure that the cost of the market failure is greater than the cost of the government intervention. One of the costs of government provision is providing the correct amount of public goods. Economists have different ideas about whether government produces too large or too small an amount of public goods.

It can be argued that one of the primary public goods that government produces is income redistribution. The motivations for income redistribution are many and varied, but we should begin from the presumption that the market produces a less than desirable distribution of income. The Lorenz curve is the most common technique for measuring the relative distribution of income in a society. But income distribution is an absolute as well as a relative concept. Varied measures of absolute levels of poverty and the social characteristics associated with this poverty are necessary to paint a picture of the level of poverty in America.

The American response to poverty has taken three distinct forms: to provide jobs, to provide social insurance, and to provide direct assistance to children and to those who are unable to work because of age or health reasons.

Actual governmental programs are beset by a number of problems, not the least of which is that very little money filters down to the most needy in our society. In addition, many welfare programs destroy work incentives and are very degrading. The negative income tax concept would overcome some of these undesirable characteristics.

New Terms

externalities   Coase theorem
social costs   public goods
internalize   free-riding behavior

logrolling   negative income tax
risk aversion   utility interdependence
egalitarian   Lorenz curve

Questions for Discussion

1 Should the government intervene in every case where an externality exists?

2 Is there air or water pollution near where you live? What should be done about it? Should the pollution be entirely done away with? How much more in taxes or higher prices for goods would you be willing to pay in order to have less pollution?

3 What factors determine wages? What causes some people with equal skills to receive different wages? Would a competitive economy reduce or increase these differentials?

4 Who is responsible for the fact that some people are poor? What would you do about it if you were in a position to take some action?

5 Do you think a negative income tax would solve the U.S. poverty problem? Why or why not?

6 Is a melody a public good? If so, why don't melodies have to be supplied by the government?

7 Is education a public good? If not, why should taxes help pay for the college education of some individuals?

Suggestions for Further Reading

Amacher, Ryan C., Robert D. Tolleson, and Thomas D. Willett. "Budget Size in a Democracy: A Review of the Arguments." *Public Finance Quarterly* (April, 1975).
—— (eds.). "A Menu of Distributional Considerations." *The Economic Approach to Public Policy: Selected Readings*. New York: Cornell University Press, 1976.
Oates, Wallace. *Fiscal Federalism*. New York: Harcourt Brace Jovanovich, Inc., 1972. Chapters 3 and 4.
Weil, Gordon L. *The Welfare Debate of 1978*. White Plains: The Institute for Socioeconomic Studies, 1978.

CHAPTER 16

THE ECONOMICS OF INTERNATIONAL TRANSACTIONS

LEARNING OBJECTIVES

After studying the materials found in this chapter, you should be able to do the following:

1 Contrast absolute advantage to comparative advantage.

2 Diagram the adjustment to a supply curve necessitated by a
    (a) quota,
    (b) tariff.

3 List the arguments used in favor of protectionism.

4 Outline the reasons why the arguments used in favor of protectionism are incorrect.

5 Define
    (a) clean floating,
    (b) dirty floating,
    (c) pegged exchange rates,
    (d) flexible exchange rates,
    (e) fixed but adjustable exchange rates,
    (f) tariffs,
    (g) quotas.

6 Diagram and explain intervention on the part of a government when either a price floor or a price ceiling is placed on an exchange market.

In this book we have talked about markets without any reference to the country where these markets are located. Households and firms have appeared in our models without any distinction between domestic markets and foreign markets. This was as it should be because a national border does not make the economics of the exchange any different. But when national borders do separate trading groups, there are considerations, often based on political motivations, that intervene and sometimes interfere with what would have been a simple economic transaction. In this chapter we will discuss why countries trade, and why they sometimes interfere in the free flow of trade. We will also discuss the simple economics of exchange rate movements.

WHY COUNTRIES ENGAGE IN FOREIGN TRADE

Countries engage in trade for the same reasons individual consumers do. In fact, in countries where private enterprise plays a role, most of a country's trades are made by individuals.

Trade Between Individuals

One evening, Freddy Foghorn trades two six-packs of Michelob to Suzy Sizzle for three six-packs of Bud. They do so because it looks like a good deal; both of them believe they'll be better off from the trade. Voluntary exchanges are mutually beneficial, or they wouldn't be entered into. It works the same way with nations if Freddy and Suzy are nationals of different countries.

Even with the simple example of Suzy and Freddy, there are problems of misinterpretation to clear up. First, Suzy may decide that while the deal looked good in advance, she's sorry afterwards. Trade is always based on *expected gains*, and we can sometimes be wrong in our estimates. But if we observe that Suzy and Freddy go on trading week after week, we have to believe that their estimates are pretty close to what actually happens and that they keep trading because both feel better off with trade than without.

Second, Freddy may feel that Suzy is getting the better deal even though both are better off with trade than without. Both of them gain from trade, but the *gains from trade* may not be evenly split in the eyes of one (or both) partners.

Third, before Suzy came on the scene, Freddy was trading with Jerry Jock. Suzy offers a better deal, so Freddy reduces his trade with Jerry, and Jerry feels injured by Suzy's "unfair" competition in trade. Of course, no one likes to fight competition, so it's easy to understand Jerry's feelings. It's still true, though, that all three of them are better off with some trade than they would be if they couldn't trade at all. As compared to the old days when only Jerry and Freddy traded, the new arrangement makes Suzy better off (otherwise she wouldn't trade), makes

Freddy better off (or he would be trading only with Jerry), and makes Jerry worse off — he wishes Suzy would get lost! However, Jerry is better off competing with Suzy than not trading at all.

Differences Between Nations and Individuals

Trade makes individuals better off or they wouldn't do it. International trade makes nations better off in the same way; they give up something they have for something they want more than what they give up. The problem is, while the nation as a whole is better off with trade, usually some individuals are worse off. Those who are hurt naturally don't like the trade that causes the damage and seek some protection from the government against this damage from foreign trade.

Economists say that countries are better off with free trade than with no trade, but we have to clarify what this means. After trade starts, some people will gain from it while some will lose. It would be possible to take funds from the gainers and give them to the losers until the losers are just compensated for their losses, and the gainers would still be better off. With this sort of compensation, nobody loses and some people gain, so it is clear that the people of the nation as a whole are better off. However, since this kind of compensation is seldom carried out, the losers can't be blamed for being upset.

The losers are people who are hurt by competition from imports. This is just like Jerry's competition with Suzy, only now Jerry can think of his competitor as a foreigner, and when foreigners are involved, it is easier to get the government to interfere in the process. The gainers are those who can buy more cheaply from abroad than at home or those who can sell their output abroad at a better price than they could at home. Consumers of goods generally gain, and so do the factors of production engaged in the export industries, as well as businesses that import raw materials or semifinished goods from abroad. In fact, these groups can generally gain enough to completely compensate those who suffer from import competition and still be ahead as compared to a no-trade situation.

Productivity as a Basis for Trade

So far, we have explained trade as simply being due to a natural desire to trade what you have for something you would prefer to have. It's important to have gone this far because we can see that if you are forbidden to trade, your level of satisfaction and number of options would both be reduced. But we have to ask why trade can boost satisfaction. What is it that makes you (and nations) willing to trade? That is, we want to go behind the desire to trade and ask what causes this desire.

In the early 1800s, David Ricardo and other economists offered an explanation of trade based on different levels of productivity of nations in different industries. Ricardo's example dealt with trade between England and Portugal. He considered two goods: wool, which England exported, and the port wine which Portugal exported.

Let us look at his example, supposing that each country has only one factor of production, labor. Table 16-1 shows that one English worker could produce either six bales of wool or three casks of port. In England, then, the opportunity cost of one more cask of port is two bales of wool. In Portugal, however, one worker can produce one bale of wool or one cask of port. Thus, in Portugal the opportunity cost of one more cask of port is one bale of wool. Or, to get one more bale of wool, the Portuguese must sacrifice one cask of port. Table 16-2 shows how the opportunity cost is determined for production in each country.

TABLE 16-1   Wool and Port Wine as Produced by England and Portugal

	One English Worker	One Portuguese Worker
Wool	6 bales	1 bale
Port	3 casks	1 cask

TABLE 16-2   Opportunity Costs of Production

England

6 bales of wool cost 3 casks of port, so
1 bale of wool costs ½ cask of port.
3 casks of port cost 6 bales of wool, so
1 cask of port costs 2 bales of wool.

Portugal

1 bale of wool costs 1 cask of port.
1 cask of port costs 1 bale of wool.

This is the perfect opportunity for a sharp entrepreneur. The entrepreneur could buy one cask of port in Portugal for one bale of wool. Thus, one bale of wool could be shipped to Portugal, traded for one cask of wine, which could be sold in England for two bales of wool. Thus, differences in prices in two countries which arise from differences in productivity can explain the motives for international trade.

David Ricardo

Brown Brothers

David Ricardo (1772–1823)

David Ricardo may have been the most influential of all the classical economists. Born in London to Dutch-Jewish parents, he entered his father's stockbrokerage firm at the age of 14. Seven years later he married a Quaker and became a Christian. He did this against the wishes of his family, and, as a result of their disapproval of his wife, he started his own business. By age 25 he had amassed a sizable fortune.

In 1799 while he was on vacation, Ricardo picked up a copy of Adam Smith's *Wealth of Nations* because he was bored. He was immediately attracted to economic theory by the power of Smith's analysis. Despite his lack of formal education, he quickly became a leading intellectual of his time. His experience is in contrast to almost all the other classical economists, who had pursued rigorous programs of formal education. In 1814 Ricardo retired to devote his time to political economy. In 1819 he became a member of Parliament and, with the help of James Mill (father of the great economist John Stuart Mill), founded the Political Economy Club of London. This club became the forum in which the classical economists discussed their ideas.

Ricardo was a prolific writer of letters and pamphlets intended to influence policy discussions on economic matters. His chief formal work, *On the Principles of Political Economy and Taxation*, was published in 1817. He is perhaps best remembered for his statements on the principles of comparative advantage and his support of free trade, which are only a part of his comprehensive work. In fact, much of his early interest in economics was generated by his interest in international trade and by his interest in showing the benefits of such trade. Ricardo also developed a labor theory of value which greatly impressed Karl Marx, who extended and radicalized Ricardo's theory.

Transferring one worker from the wine industry to the wool industry reduces port production by three casks in England but raises wool production by six bales, so the opportunity cost of two more bales is one cask, or the opportunity cost of one more cask is two bales. In Portugal, the opportunity cost of one more bale is one cask, and similarly one more cask will cost one bale.

Absolute Advantage Vs. Comparative Advantage

Look again at Table 16-1. It was designed to show that a worker in England is more productive in both industries than a worker in Portugal. How can Portuguese workers hope to compete? The answer lies in the difference between *absolute advantage* and *comparative advantage*.

In absolute terms, the English worker is at an advantage (more productive) compared to the Portugese worker in both industries. But notice that while an English worker is six times more productive than a Portuguese worker in the wool industry (producing six bales while the Portuguese worker can produce only one bale), the English worker is only three times more productive in the port industry (producing three casks while the Portuguese worker can produce only one cask). Thus, if we compare industries, the English worker is relatively more productive in the wool industry than in the port industry. We would thus say that England has a *comparative advantage* in the wool industry (though an *absolute advantage* in both industries).

If England has a comparative advantage in the wool industry, it must mean that it has a *comparative disadvantage* in port. This means that England's absolute advantage in wool is proportionately greater than its absolute advantage in port.

England's comparative advantage in wool means Portugal has a comparative disadvantage in wool. But England's comparative disadvantage in port corresponds to Portugal's comparative advantage in port. Portugal is less productive than England in both industries, but it is at less of a disadvantage in port production; this is where its comparative advantage lies. Looked at this way, the least skilled and least productive nation must have a comparative advantage in something, because there will be some industry in which it is least disadvantaged. But, if England is better at producing port than Portugal, why doesn't England produce its own wine rather than importing it? The reason is because England finds it cheaper to concentrate on producing what it's really good at — wool — and trading this wool for port.

This principle of comparative advantage is really a simple one but one which people sometimes don't grasp. Consider yourself as an example. Suppose when you graduate from college you are the world's best tennis player and also the world's best wheat farmer. Should you grow your own wheat *and* play your own tennis? Of course not. The time spent growing wheat would be time away from tennis. Assuming you could earn more playing tennis than growing wheat, you would play tennis and buy wheat from some wheat farmer who isn't as good a wheat farmer as you, but who isn't as good a tennis player either. This farmer would then have a comparative advantage in growing wheat.

Prices and the Gains from Trade

The price of goods in the two countries will determine if trade takes place. Let's assume that wool and wine are produced in competitive markets in both countries and that, as a result, prices reflect the opportunity costs of production as stated in Table 16-2. We can thus see what prices are necessary for trade to be beneficial. Examine Table 16-3, which is derived from Table 16-2. The table shows what the world price of wool and port has to be in order for England and Portugal to engage in trade. Let us begin by assuming that 1 bale of wool sells for .8 of a cask of port. The price of a cask of port is thus 1.25 bales of wool. A quick check of Table 16-3 shows that the price of wool and port falls in the range that makes trade mutually beneficial to both countries.

TABLE 16-3   **Prices at Which Trade Takes Place**

England

    If 1 bale of wool sells for more than ½ cask of port,
       England gains by selling wool.

    If 1 cask of port sells for less than 2 bales of wool,
       England gains by buying port.

Portugal

    If 1 bale of wool sells for less than 1 cask of port,
       Portugal gains by buying wool.

    If 1 cask of port sells for more than 1 bale of wool,
       Portugal gains by selling port.

Therefore:

    If the world price of port is between 1 bale of wool
       and 2 bales of wool, and if the world price of
       wool is between ½ cask of port and 1 cask of
       port, trade will be mutually beneficial.

Table 16-4 shows how the total output of wool and port will increase if firms in each country reallocate laborers to the product in which the country has a comparative advantage. The English wool industry hires a laborer away from the port industry, and the Portuguese port industry hires four workers away from the wool industry. The world output of port

TABLE 16-4   Gains from the Transfer of One Worker in England and Four Workers in Portgugal

	One English Worker	Four Portuguese Workers	Total Output
Wool	+6	−4	+2
Port	−3	+4	+1

has increased by 1 cask, and the world output of wool has increased by 2 bales.

Now assume that the English firm exports 3 bales of wool to Portugal. Since the price of a bale of wool is .8 casks of port, the trade yields England 2.4 casks of port. Both countries have gained from the exchange, and world output is greater than it was before specialization and exchange. To return to an earlier point, however, this example says nothing about how the gains from exchange are distributed between the two countries. A different set of prices, say 1 bale of wool equal to .7 casks of port, would have been more beneficial to Portugal, while a price of 1 bale of wool equal to .9 casks of port would have been more beneficial to England. But the important point is that as long as the world price falls in the range established in Table 16-3, both countries gain from specialization and exchange.

If constant costs prevailed in the production of port and wool, eventually all the wool would be produced in England, and all the port would be produced in Portugal. However, since increasing costs will likely occur at some point, the cost of producing port in Portugal and wool in England will rise, and trade will thus eventually be curtailed. This happens automatically, and, as a result, it is seldom the case that one country produces all of one commodity.

PROTECTIONISM

When England starts trading with Portugal and exports wool to import port, it cuts back on producing port and expands its wool industry. Given a price of port of somewhat less than 2 bales per cask, England as a nation is better off from the trade. However, some people in the English port industry are hurt by trade with Portugal. At the very least, some workers will be forced to leave the port industry to find new jobs in the wool industry. In realistic terms, this may involve moving hundreds or even thousands of miles and being unemployed for a certain period. Older workers may find it difficult to get new jobs. People specialized in the industries that are hurt may find their skills are worthless elsewhere, or valued less than before. Similarly, plants and equipment may be highly specialized. A small, one-industry town can be devasted when subjected to import competition. How would you like to be a grocer in such a town when half the work force is thrown out of work?

On the other hand, consumers benefit from lower import prices. People in the United States buy Datsuns, Toyotas, and Volkswagens because they think they are getting a better deal. Further, the factors in the export industry also benefit because of expanded employment and lower prices for imported raw materials and semifinished goods. In fact, as pointed out above, those who benefit from trade could compensate the losers and still be better off. But usually such compensation does not take place, and, as a result, those who are hurt may be successful in using the political process to protect their economic self-interest. To do this, they must prohibit the trade from taking place.

Firms can seek two different types of *protection*. One way is to attempt to get the government to establish a *quota*. Quotas are physical limits on the number of units of an item that can be imported. For example, the government might say that 1,000 casks of port can be imported from Portugal, and that is the limit. This type of protection shields the domestic industry from the foreign competition. Its economic impact is that it reduces the gains from specialization. Alternatively, the firm could attempt to have a *tariff* placed on the importation of the foreign good. You can easily see how a tariff can stop the flow of trade. In our earlier example we had a world price of 1 cask of port equal to 1.25 bales of wool. If the port-producing firm in England could get the government to enact a tariff of .76 bales of wool for each cask of port imported, it would transform the price of a cask of port to 2.01 bales of wool. Return to Table 16-3. At a price of 2.01 bales of wool, port will no longer be imported into England. The tariff is therefore prohibiting the flow of trade.

Economists as a group strongly favor free trade and oppose the use of tariffs and quotas that interfere with the free exchange of goods and services. Nevertheless, powerful political forces exist that favor increasing protection of U.S. industry. Because of these political pressures, it is worthwhile to examine some of the arguments for protection through either tariffs or quotas.

The Effects of Tariffs and Quotas

We can see the effects of tariffs and quotas by examining Figures 16-1 and 16-2. In Figure 16-1, D_F represents the home country's demand for a foreign-produced good, and S_F represents its supply. An equilibrium price of OP_1 and quantity of OQ_1 obtain. Now assume the government imposes a quota of OQ_2 per time period. The quota causes the supply curve to become perfectly inelastic at point A. The new price at import level OQ_2 is OP_2.

An interesting question once the quota is enacted is who benefits and who loses from the quota. Clearly consumers of this good lose. Its price

FIGURE 16-1   **The Effects of a Quota**

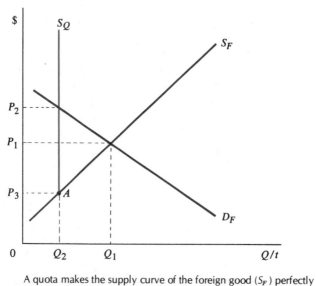

A quota makes the supply curve of the foreign good (S_F) perfectly
inelastic at the quota amount (point A). As a result, consumers pay a
higher price for the good.

has risen, and less of the good is available for consumption. Who gains?
Remember the discussion in Chapter 9 about the need to prohibit entry
into monopolized markets? This is one way to prohibit entry. A monopolist who can persuade the government to keep foreign competition out
has a very effective artificial barrier to entry. Additionally, those im-
porters who have the good fortune (or have made the payoffs) to be the
ones importing OQ_2 can make a huge profit. Foreign suppliers will supply OQ_2 at a price of OP_3, but domestic consumers will pay OP_2. The
difference is a profit to the importer who has the right to import OQ_2.
You can see how import licenses can be very valuable when quotas are
being used. Of course, if the government auctioned off permits to import
the good, this profit would be captured as revenue for the federal Treasury rather than as a gain for a fortunate importer. Of course, it's not
done this way.

Figure 16-2 shows the effect of a tariff. The demand for the foreign
good is D_F and the supply of the foreign good is S_F. In the absence of any
government interference, OQ_1 of the good would be imported at price
OP_1. Now assume the government imposes a tariff of t per unit of the
good imported. This shifts back the supply curve, exactly as a tax did in
Chapter 4. The price rises to OP_2 and imports fall to OQ_2. There are two
effects. First, there is a *revenue effect* of the tariff. This is the amount of
revenue generated for the government. The revenue is the amount of the

FIGURE 16-2   The Effects of a Tariff

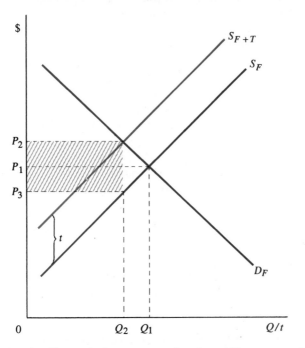

A tariff per unit of output causes the price paid by consumers to rise and the price received by suppliers to fall. This decreases the amount of the good that is imported.

tariff times the amount imported. In Figure 16-2 the revenue effect is $(OP_2 - OP_3)OQ_2$, which is the shaded area in the diagram. Second, there is a **protective effect** of the tariff. This is similar to a quota in that it keeps foreign competition out of domestic markets. Domestic firms are now able to sell at a higher price because some output, in this case $OQ_1 - OQ_2$, has been kept out of the market. In colonial American history, and even today in some less developed countries, the revenue generated by tariffs was and is an important source of government revenue. Since income taxation and other forms of taxation may prove to be difficult to collect because of inadequate record-keeping, tariffs can play a large role. At the present time, however, tariffs generate an insignificant portion of federal revenue in the United States.

Arguments for Protection

There are several arguments for the use of tariffs and quotas. Some of them are nonsensical from an economic viewpoint, but they often are used as reasons to decrease trade and should be seen for what they are.

Keep the Money at Home. It is reported that Abraham Lincoln once remarked: "I do not know much about the tariff, but I know this much, when we buy manufactured goods abroad we get the goods and the foreigner gets the money. When we buy the manufactured goods at home we get both the goods and the money."[1] Many economists have pointed out that the only thing correct in the statement is the first eight words. The problem is that many people would accept this argument. Do you? An economist wouldn't. Foreign countries and their citizens export goods because they want to buy goods of other countries. They don't want money. Think how great it would be if all they wanted was our currency. We could print money, send it to foreigners, and get cars, television sets, and caviar in return. But, of course, foreigners want to spend that money on our goods or on the goods of other countries, who in turn spend it on our goods. The argument confuses money as a *measure* of wealth with money as wealth. Money is only wealth because it represents the ability to buy goods and services.

The Cheap Foreign Labor Argument. It is obvious to anyone who has traveled outside the United States that wages vary significantly between countries. (They even vary considerably within countries.) Some industries and labor unions use this differential in wages to argue that a tariff is needed to protect American workers from cheap foreign labor.

This is clearly a fallacious argument. First, as we saw in earlier chapters, labor is only one of the factors of production. As a result, commodities embodying a lot of labor can be produced cheaply where labor is cheap, just as some countries will be able to cheaply produce commodities embodying a lot of capital if capital is cheap, or land, if land is cheap. Second, low wages imply low productivity. The reason wage rates are low in some places is because the labor is relatively unproductive compared to labor in high-wage places. Third, and perhaps most important, this argument ignores the concept of comparative advantage. In our earlier example, where labor was the only factor of production and one country was absolutely more efficient at producing both goods, there still were gains from trade. And, notice that there was no need to mention nominal (or money) wages for the argument. They are simply not relevant.

Employment Protection. This is similar to the cheap foreign labor argument. Foreign goods compete with domestic goods, and, since labor demand is derived from the demand for domestically produced products, imports will decrease the demand for domestic labor.

This argument ignores the two-way nature of trade. We export goods because foreigners demand our goods. This creates a derived demand for labor that is used to produce these exported goods. These goods wouldn't

---

[1]Cited in Asher Isaacs, *International Trade* (Homewood, Ill.: Richard D. Irwin, Inc., 1948), p. 229.

be demanded if we didn't import goods from the countries we now export to.

The Infant Industry Argument. This may be one of the oldest protectionist arguments and was a favorite of Alexander Hamilton, the first Secretary of the U.S. Treasury. The argument is that, in a country where industry is just beginning to develop, production costs may be high, and protection is therefore necessary for it to survive. On a more sophisticated level, the argument is that there are potential economies of scale in an industry that can't be realized because the industry is being undersold by a mature foreign industry that has already reached these economies of scale. It is thus argued that the industry should be protected until it "grows up" and can compete with the foreign industry.

The difficulty with this argument is that there is some economic sense to it. The problem is that it is impossible to determine *a priori* which industries will be able to compete when they mature and which ones won't be able to compete. There is no magic theory or formula to determine when an industry is no longer in need of protection, and it has been observed time and time again that tariffs, once enacted, are hard to get rid of.

Further, and this is an important point regarding all tariffs and quotas, the tariff is the same thing as a subsidy to the infant industry. In other words, consumers of the good are subsidizing domestic producers of that good by not being allowed to purchase the good at a lower price. So, if an argument can be made that an industry should be helped to reach maturity because it is in the interest of the country to have such an industry, it is much more equitable that such a subsidy should be paid out of general tax revenues. This would insure that all citizens pay the subsidy, not just the consumers of a particular product.

National Defense. "No price is too high to pay for the defense of our country." How can anyone disagree with such a statement? So imagine yourself as a monopolist seeking to keep foreign competition out of your industry. Think of the impact of going to Congress and arguing that if foreign competition destroys your industry, the country could be cut off from its source of supply in a time of national crisis. This is a politically powerful argument and the refuge of almost every industry pleading its case before Congress.

The argument, while politically sound, has several problems. First, how is one to decide what is essential for national defense? Prior to World War II we thought a cut-off of natural rubber would be a disaster. However, if we had had a domestic natural rubber industry, we may not have had the rapid development of synthetic rubber. The second problem is similar to one we discussed above. The national defense argument is an argument for a subsidy. If an argument can be made that it is essential to protect an industry for defense reasons, it should be done through a very visible subsidy rather than a hidden subsidy paid via a tariff or

Bruce Wolfe/UNIPHOTO

The Department of the Treasury

The Department of the Treasury

The Department of the Treasury was created by Congress in 1789. Alexander Hamilton was its first Secretary, and a statue to his memory stands outside the present Treasury building. The original role of the Treasury was to collect and disperse the public revenue. Hamilton, who was a federalist (meaning he wanted the federal government to be strong and active), made the Treasury a source of funds for promoting economic development.

The basic role of the Treasury is to develop and recommend tax and fiscal policy, to manufacture and coin currency, to serve as a financial agent for the United States, and to enforce certain laws, including those that relate to international trade and commerce.

The modern-day Treasury and the Secretary of the Treasury are active participants in developing economic policy. The Secretary often becomes the economics spokesperson for the president. In this role, the Secretary represents the United States in financial matters and in dealing with foreign governments and international agencies, such as the International Monetary Fund.

There is often much competition in government over who has the most influence on the president concerning economic matters. The Secretary of the Treasury is usually in the center of this competition, along with the chairperson of the Council of Economic Advisers and the chairperson of the Federal Reserve System. For these reasons, it is important that the Secretary be an experienced and politically astute bureaucrat as well as an experienced economist.

The individual chosen as Secretary of the Treasury has often come from the financial and banking community. Two recent Secretaries have had extensive training in economics: W. Michael Blumenthal, President Carter's first Secretary of the Treasury, and George Schultz in the Nixon administration. Schultz has written a book, *Economic Policy Beyond the Headlines* (1978), that presents his view of economic policymaking while he was Secretary of the Treasury. Blumenthal has a Ph.D. in economics from Princeton and had extensive experience in business before he went to Washington. As a result, he was able to move back into the business world with relative ease.

quota. For many years it was argued that we should have a tariff on imported oil for national defense reasons. The argument was that if we didn't protect the domestic industry we could be caught in time of war without a domestic oil industry. The result of the tariff was that we used our own oil instead of cheap foreign oil. The program might well have been labeled "Drain American First." The net result is that we have larger national defense problems now than we would have had if we had heeded some sage economic advice: "Buy where the goods are cheapest."

Tariffs and Quotas: The Bottom Line

Although there is considerable confusion and heated rhetoric concerning the use of tariffs and quotas, the basic economics is quite simple. A tariff or quota causes the price of goods to be higher than they would be in the absence of the tariff or quota. This produces a subsidy for the protected industry. So, every argument for a tariff or quota is basically an argument of a special interest for a subsidy.

The Rise of Protectionism

Almost all economists, unless they are working for a special interest group, are advocates of free trade and proponents of the ideas expressed in this chapter. Why, then, is there a rising trend of protectionism in the world? The answer is to be found in the political process.

The group that benefits from free trade is large. It is comprised of consumers of imported goods and exporters and producers of our exported goods. They gain by being able to consume goods at the lowest possible price. Many of this group's members may not even be aware that they are beneficiaries of free trade. The groups that can be hurt by free trade are composed of inefficient firms that would be forced out of business by freer international trade, of firms that are at a comparative disadvantage, or of firms that are monopolists and would have some of their monopoly profits destroyed by foreign competition. Laborers in each of these industries could be hurt because they would have to move to other industries. These groups are smaller than the group that gains, so you would think that free trade would be politically popular. The problem comes from the fact that those who are hurt know they are hurt by trade, and they are hurt a great deal. As a result, it makes good economic sense for those hurt to organize a special-interest lobby. Those that gain only gain a little, and even if they know they gain, it is much more difficult to organize a large group. Thus, politicians tend to be overcome by special-interest groups, and the result is an increase in protectionism.

DETERMINATION OF THE EXCHANGE RATE

So far, we have not discussed the *exchange rate*, or the rate at which two currencies trade for each other. In examining the law of comparative advantage and the basis for mutually beneficial trade, we didn't need to

consider exchange rates and money to see the main points concerning
the benefits of trade. However, the exchange rate plays a major role in
international trade and must be considered because disequilibrium exchange rates can impede trade flows.

Let's look at demand and supply in an exchange market where U.S.
dollars are exchanged for British pounds. For example, if you spend the
summer traveling in Great Britain, you will have to make your transactions there in pounds, so you want to buy pounds at the bank (either here
or in Great Britain) with your dollars. Figure 16-3 shows that the greater
the number of dollars required to buy one pound, the smaller the quantity of pounds people want to buy; the demand curve has a negative slope.
This makes sense. If it becomes more expensive to buy pounds, you'll
cut short your stay, buy fewer gifts for the folks back home, or just not go
at all. We also see that the supply curve has a positive slope. The equilibrium exchange rate is OE_1, where the demand and supply curves intersect and the quantity demanded equals the quantity supplied, OQ_1.

FIGURE 16-3   **Demand and Supply in the Foreign Exchange Market for U.S.
Dollars and British Pounds**

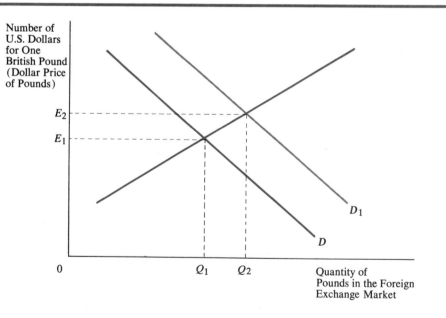

A floating exchange rate is determined by the underlying conditions of
supply and demand for the currency. An equilibrium price emerges as
the exchange rate. If the demand for the currency increases, as from D to
D_1, the exchange rate will rise.

Governments naturally are very interested in the exchange rate of their currency versus some (or many, or all) foreign currencies. At one extreme, they may adopt a hands-off attitude and allow the rate to be determined by the forces of demand and supply, as in Figure 16-3. When governments allow demand and supply to determine the exchange rate, it is said to be a *floating exchange rate* or *flexible exchange rate*. At the other extreme, they may attempt to keep the exchange rate in a tight zone or band.

If the exchange rate is flexible or floating, the basic forces of supply and demand will determine the exchange rate, which is simply the price of one currency in terms of another. Suppose, for example, that travel to Great Britain becomes the popular thing to do. This means that tastes change in favor of vacations to Great Britain and against vacations in the United States and other countries. This, in turn, means that U.S. citizens will demand more pounds. In terms of Figure 16-3, the demand for pounds shifts from D to D_1. If rates are floating, the dollar price of pounds rises from OE_1 to OE_2. It now takes more dollars to buy a pound. Another way of saying the same thing is to say that the dollar has *depreciated* relative to the pound or that the pound has *appreciated* relative to the dollar.

Figure 16-4 shows a case of a *pegged exchange rate* or *fixed exchange rate* in the band of $2.02 to $1.98 for each British pound. That is, one or both of the governments want to keep the price of a pound between $2.02 and $1.98. With demand and supply of D_1 and S_1, the equilibrium rate is in this band, and there is no problem meeting the exchange rate target. Suppose, however, that there is an increase in the demand for pounds in the foreign exchange market to D_2. This would lead to an equilibrium exchange rate above $2.02 per pound. To prevent this, either the United States or the British government (or both) can *intervene* in the foreign exchange market to keep the rate at $2.02. To do this, they must sell the additional pounds (AB) that people want to buy at $2.02 per pound. In this way, they can prevent the exchange rate from rising above $2.02 per pound. Or, if demand fell to D_3, people would want to supply more pounds than others demanded at $1.98, and the governments could intervene by buying these pounds (CE) and preventing the exchange rate from falling below $1.98 per pound. Notice that governments can set the limits to the exchange rate, but this pegging means they have to buy or sell as many dollars or pounds as the market wants based on demand and supply. In effect, the governments are setting both a price ceiling and a price floor (see Chapter 4 for a review) and are actively intervening to make the ceiling or floor effective.

From the point of view of governments, both freely floating exchange rates as well as pegged or fixed exchange rates can cause problems. For example, suppose the exchange rate is floating and there is an increase in demand, as when demand shifted from D_1 to D_2 in Figure 16-4. This will cause the dollar price of a pound to rise. Since pounds are now more

FIGURE 16-4   Exchange Market Intervention to Peg the Exchange Rate

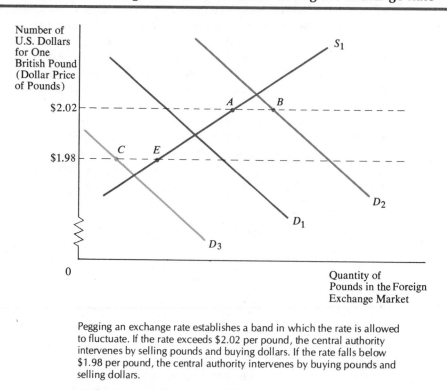

Pegging an exchange rate establishes a band in which the rate is allowed to fluctuate. If the rate exceeds $2.02 per pound, the central authority intervenes by selling pounds and buying dollars. If the rate falls below $1.98 per pound, the central authority intervenes by buying pounds and selling dollars.

expensive, Americans will tend to cut back on their trips to Great Britain, on their purchases of British Fords and Rolls Royces, on their purchases of Scotch, and of other goods. This is damaging to British exporters and will tend to reduce Great Britain's national income. Naturally, then, the British government wants to pay attention to the exchange rate and may be tempted to intervene in the exchange market to keep the rate from going up.

However, intervention to peg or control the exchange rate has its own problems. Assume the British government wants to peg the dollar price of the pound between $2.02 and $1.98, as in Figure 16-4. First, suppose that demand is D_3, so that with a floating exchange rate the dollar price will fall below $1.98 per pound. Britain can prevent this by buying up the extra pounds (distance *CE* in Figure 16-4) that represent the difference between the number of pounds people are willing to demand and supply at $1.98. To buy these pounds, Great Britain uses its *international reserves*, which are its stocks of assets that are liquid and readily acceptable internationally. For example, its international reserves include its holdings of gold, dollar deposits, and its deposits and credit lines with the International Monetary Fund (IMF) in Washington, D.C., as well as other assets. Further, it may be able to mobilize extra reserves quickly by, for example, borrowing from foreign central banks. If Great Britain must keep buying up pounds with its international reserves day after day and month after month, it will sooner or later run out of reserves. As reserves fall, Great Britain eventually has to give up and *devalue* the pound (let it *depreciate*), resulting in a new, lower dollar price of the pound. Thus, while the intervention may be able to work for a time, often the country has to give up in the end. In the meantime, the government wastes the reserves it uses up. Further, if you are engaged in trade, you have a good deal of uncertainty about when or if devaluation will occur. Of course, with a freely floating exchange rate, you don't know from one day to the next what the rate will be, so perhaps the two forms of uncertainty are equally unpleasant.

Suppose that demand is D_2 in Figure 16-4. To keep the dollar price of a pound at \$2.02, the British government would have to supply the extra pounds (distance AB in Figure 16-4) beyond what the market will supply. One way for the government to supply these pounds is simply to print them. Thus, intervention to keep the dollar price of the pound from rising would expand the British money supply. Monetarists and many Keynesians would argue that this would eventually lead to higher inflation for Great Britain. Thus, intervention to keep the price of currency from rising can lead to loss of control of the money supply, excessive monetary expansion, and inflation.[2]

Note that while Great Britain is selling AB pounds in the previous example, it is using them to buy dollars, and this increases British international reserves. If the exchange market sometimes has demand of D_3 and at other times D_2, the reserves lost in one period can be rebuilt in the next, and government intervention would keep the rate in the target band. However, if demand permanently rises to D_2, the country can be dragged into inflation; or if demand permanently falls to D_3, it can engage in a futile and costly struggle to stop devaluation. The problem is, how do governments know which are permanent changes and which are only temporary?

FROM FIXED TO FLOATING RATES

After World War II, a system of *fixed but adjustable exchange rates* was adopted. The idea was to peg rates, but if demand and supply became permanently unbalanced at the target rate (say D_2 or D_3 in Figure 16-4), the exchange rate would be adjusted. The system seemed to work satisfactorily up through the mid- and late 1960s, but in many ways those were stable years economically. The 1970s were much more turbulent. The pegged but adjustable rate system was abandoned during the early

---

[2]To see how this would happen, you should review Chapters 7 and 11 in the companion volume to this book.

1970s. Thus, large, sharp movements in exchange rates occurred, and massive shifts of funds became commonplace. Most economists agree that the pegged rate system could not have been maintained in these turbulent times, and there was no alternative but to go to floating rates. However, many countries continued to peg their rates. A great many less developed countries pegged their rates to the dollar, while some European countries floated against the dollar but pegged against each other (for example, Germany and the Netherlands). In addition, even countries that didn't peg all the time would often intervene on occasion, sometimes to a large extent. Because of the extent of pegging and intervention, the float (or the floating exchange rate) was referred to as *dirty floating*, with *clean floating* meaning no intervention in the exchange market.

Economists have mixed views on the success of the dirty float. Most argue that pegged rates couldn't have been maintained. However, some argue that floating has not worked well, with exchange rate movements resulting that are too large, erratic, and unrelated to underlying economic fundamentals. They urge greater fixity of rates and an attempt to move toward a system with more pegging. Other economists argue that the float worked about as well as could be expected. The large and frequent changes in exchange rates were often justified, in their view, and they doubt the wisdom of government intervention in financial markets to bring about better performance. These economists often view financial markets — stock and bond markets, as well as exchange markets — as working well, while those on the other side of the debate tend to have doubts about how well financial markets work. Notice that this is very similar to the philosophical split we saw in Chapters 4 and 15. Those who think markets work pretty well would like the governments to stay out of them, while others think that government actions can improve market performances.

Summary

This chapter has extended our discussion of the market mechanism to include trade across national borders. We saw that the motivations for such trade and the benefits of such trade are no different than those for trade between two individuals who are residents of a single country.

The principle of comparative advantage shows that the gains from trade depend on different relative costs in each country. Absolute advantage in all goods does not mean there are no gains from trade. Countries with an absolute disadvantage should produce and trade the goods they are least inefficient in producing; those countries with an absolute advantage in all goods should produce and sell those goods that they are most efficient in producing.

Not all parties gain from trade. Some firms and the labor within these firms will be hurt. This is no different than inefficient domestic firms being hurt by domestic trade. However, when foreign nations are involved, the damaged parties often call on the government to keep the foreign competition out by the use of tariffs and quotas.

There are many arguments for protection through tariffs and/or quotas. A few have a solid basis, but even these must be recognized as arguments for a subsidy to a particular industry. If they are recognized as a subsidy, the argument for a tariff or quota rather than a governmental transfer loses much of its force.

Exchange rates, or the price of one currency in terms of another, are determined by the forces of supply and demand just as prices of other commodities are determined. If the government stays out of these markets and allows them to reach market clearing prices, we say we have a flexible exchange rate or a floating exchange rate system. If the government intervenes by establishing price floors and ceilings, we have a pegged exchange rate or a fixed exchange rate system. Sometimes the government intervenes from time to time in a floating rate system, and as a result we refer to this as a dirty float.

New Terms

expected gains
gains from trade
absolute advantage
comparative advantage
protectionism
quota
tariff
revenue effect
protective effect
exchange rate
floating exchange rate

flexible exchange rate
depreciated
appreciate
pegged exchange rate
fixed exchange rate
exchange market intervention
international reserves
devalue
fixed but adjustable exchange rates
dirty float
clean float

Questions for Discussion

1 Diagram the effect of each of the following events on the pound-dollar exchange rate and on the dollar-pound exchange rate. (Hint: Use two markets, the market for pounds and the market for dollars.)
   (a) Bourbon becomes more popular in the United States and Great Britain than Scotch.
   (b) Because of the increased cost of gasoline, Americans begin buying motorcycles produced in great Britain.
   (c) You marry a British citizen and send a

$500 Christmas present to your new in-laws.

2 "If we trade with the Japanese we will lose our jobs to the Japanese because they don't allow American goods into their country." Do you agree with this statement? Analyze it.

3 Why might a U.S. monopoly seek a tariff on the good it produces? Might organized labor support this plea? Who gains and who loses?

Suggestions for Further Reading

Amacher, Ryan C., Gottfried Haberler, and Thomas D. Willett (eds.). *Challenges to Liberal International Order*. Washington: American Enterprises Institute, 1979.

Institute for Contemporary Studies. *Tariffs, Quotas, and Trade: The Politics of Protectionism*. San Francisco: Institute for Contemporary Studies, 1979.

Kindleberger, Charles P., and Peter H. Lindert. *International Economics*, 6th ed. Homewood, Ill.: Richard D. Irwin, Inc., 1978.

Root, Franklin R. *International Trade and Investment*, 4th ed. Cincinnati: South-Western Publishing Co., 1978.

CHAPTER 17

THE ECONOMICS OF ALTERNATIVE SYSTEMS

LEARNING OBJECTIVES

After studying the materials found in this chapter, you should be able to do the following:

1 Define
   (a) capitalism,
   (b) socialism,
   (c) communism,
   (d) fascism.

2 Outline the details of Karl Marx's interpretation of capitalism, including
   (a) the labor theory of value,
   (b) surplus value,
   (c) exploitation,
   (d) the reserve army of the unemployed.

3 Describe the major features of the types

of and differences in the economic systems found in
   (a) Russia,
   (b) China,
   (c) Cuba,
   (d) Yugoslavia.

4 Calculate input coefficients given physical data in an input-output table.

5 Define
   (a) shadow prices,
   (b) the socialist controversy,
   (c) the competitive solution.

We often talk about and refer to other economic systems without really knowing how to define such terms as *capitalism, socialism,* and *communism*. What are the key differences between these systems and to what degree do these differences affect economic outcomes? In Chapter 1 we began our study by saying that all economic systems are mixed systems and that the economics we would cover in the intervening chapters would serve to allow us to analyze any economic system. We stand by that statement 17 chapters later. So you might well ask, If the economics we have already learned is good for all systems, why include a chapter on alternative systems? The answer is that politics and ideology mix with economics to create widely differing economic-political systems. It is, therefore, enlightening to examine the political, economic, and historical settings of the various institutions that comprise the different economies we may wish to analyze.

In order to introduce you to the subject of comparative economics, we will begin with an attempt to define ideological systems. We will then examine some of the dominant, but different, forms of communism. We will next switch gears to present a decision-making approach to the analysis of differing systems, and then conclude with a treatment of the advantages and disadvantages of economic planning.

IDEOLOGIES

In Chapter 1 we divided economic systems into three major groups, which we labeled *traditional, planned,* and *market*. The field of comparative economic systems breaks this categorization into smaller parts so classification of economies can be made more easily. A very common approach, and perhaps the oldest, is to classify systems according to the underlying political philosophy *and* the basis of ownership of the factors of production. This might be called the *isms* approach because it concentrates on four major *isms*: capitalism, socialism, communism, and fascism.

This approach makes it difficult to be specific when we talk about alternative economic systems because we are used to thinking in terms of communism, socialism, and capitalism as if these three systems were the only three alternatives of economic organization. There are, however, a myriad of economic systems in the world. The term capitalism is often applied to the economic systems found in Western democracies, but the differences between economic institutions in the United States, Great Britain, France, and Sweden are significant. Likewise, we may be used to referring to the economic organization in Eastern Europe and the USSR as communism, but there are significant differences between the institutions in the USSR, Yugoslavia, and Romania. In this complexity lies the difficulty of separating the critical elements of difference between and among various economic systems. We must determine the differences in institutions and then determine if these differences (or similarities) cause economic behavior to be different between the systems. In doing so, the *isms* approach focuses primarily on the ownership of the factors of production.

Capitalism

Capitalism is a system based on the idea of private ownership by individuals (or groups of individuals) of the factors of production. These individuals must then be free to use the property as they see fit. Any limitations on the use of the property diminishes its value. These private-property holders are the center of the decision-making process in capitalism.

The system that evolves is usually thought of as individuals maximizing their own well-being, whether that be phrased in terms of profit or utility. This categorization can be and is viewed very broadly to allow for a great deal of government intervention. It thus is possible for systems as divergent as the U.S. economy and the British economy to be labeled by some observers as capitalism.

Socialism

Under a system of *socialism*, the nonhuman means of production are owned by society, or the state. Socialism is seen by its advocates as a way of shifting the decision-making structure, or the authority, from individual entrepreneurial agents to a central authority. This central authority then makes the major economic decisions. Socialism is advocated as a way of promoting equality and/or economic development. The key to understanding socialism is the central-authority concept. Utopian socialists see this central authority as promoting the "common good," however that is defined. Writers critical of socialism point out that this authority may be perverted into a centralist, personal dictatorship, as in the case of Stalin, and perhaps best exemplified in present-day Eastern Europe by Romania's President Nicolae Ceausescu.

As in capitalism, there are many types of socialism. There is utopian socialism and its variants, including some, such as the Fourier movement, that were actually practiced in the United States. Some variations, particularly those espoused by the Social Democrats, have become forceful political movements in Western Europe. In short, today it is almost meaningless to label someone a socialist or a set of institutions as being socialistic.

Communism

To Karl Marx, *communism* was the final stage of the progression from capitalism, with socialism representing the middle stage of the transition. Under communism, Marx saw the end of scarcity, the end of conflict among the classes, and the creation of a new social order. A member of this new order might be viewed as the antithesis of the economic human we discussed in Chapter 1. In the final stage, each individual would receive goods and services according to his or her needs and the state would wither away to a point where all it did was administer the economy. The organizational structure which Marx foresaw under communism is not at all clear. One must presume that everyone would contribute his or her labor in exchange for all the goods and services needed. A major problem would be the definition and determination of needs. The motivation driving the system and creating incentives would have to lie in the development of this new noneconomic order.

Fascism

In the countries in which it has been practiced, which include Spain, Portugal, and pre-World War II Germany and Italy, *fascism* combines monopoly capitalism, private property, and a strong authoritarian central government personified by a dictator. Fascism is in essence an authoritarian state imposed upon a capitalistic system. As a result, it is a strange permutation that promotes monopoly and then imposes "national interests" on that monopoly structure. This destroys the large degree of personal freedom that is a characteristic of free-enterprise capitalism. There are very few real-world examples of fascism.

Weakness of Isms Approach

The problem of the *isms* approach to systems analysis is that it is often too simplistic and does not include many of the keys to determining control over resources. The *isms* approach equates ownership with control and control with decision-making power over the factors of production. This distinction is becoming less clear over time. Consider just a few examples. In the Soviet Union, the leaders of the government do not own much of anything, yet they unmistakably control the system. In the United States, many people "own" oil reserves, but they do not have control over them because of the regulations of a controlling federal government. So, all in all, the *isms* approach, while often used in political-economic classification schemes (and political rhetoric), is not very useful. In fact, to apply this classification scheme across countries would likely produce just two sets of systems, capitalism and socialism. Yet no serious analyst would consider the United States, France, and Great Britain in one classification that revealed anything significant. Likewise, the Soviet Union, Yugoslavia, and China are too diverse to be labeled socialist and still have the term contain any meaning.

MARX, MARXISTS, AND MARXISM

Perhaps no other economist has had more effect on the political shaping of the world than Karl Marx, who with Friedrich Engels published the

Communist Manifesto in 1848. This book, along with Marx's magnum opus, *Das Kapital*, published in three volumes in 1867, 1885, and 1894, form the philosophical basis for a widely divergent group of socialistic-communistic, economic-political systems. Since such a diverse group of communists lay claim to being the true Marxists, it is necessary to distinguish between Marx and Marxism (or Marxists).

Marx's Writings

Although Engels was a collaborator on the *Communist Manifesto* and finished the final two volumes of *Das Kapital* from Marx's notes after his death, history has given the predominant position to Marx. Marx's economics was a product of the English Classical School. His labor theory of value was derived from the work of David Ricardo, a famous Classicial English economist (see biography on page 355), and his historical determinism was derived from the German Historical School, in particular the writings of the German philosopher Georg Wilhelm Friedrich Hegel (1770–1831). Of the writings of Marx, the *Communist Manifesto* is the most rhetorically revolutionary and *Das Kapital* is the most scholarly. In the *Communist Manifesto*, Marx calls, in the final paragraph, for revolution:

> Let the ruling class tremble at a Communist revolution. The proletarians have nothing to lose but their chains. They have the world to win. Workers of the world, unite![1]

In *Das Kapital* we get a better idea of Marx's view of how communism would evolve. Marx saw all societies passing through the historical stages of: (1) primitive society (tribal communism), (2) slavery, (3) feudalism, (4) capitalism, (5) socialism, and finally (6) communism. This final stage was the stage at which Marx argued that scarcity would disappear and workers would produce without material incentives. To Marx, the important stage was the decay of capitalism and the transition to socialism. Marx felt that the transition would come about because of fundamental weaknesses inherent in capitalism. These major weaknesses came from Marx's **labor theory of value** and the class struggle between the proletariat and the capitalists that would emerge. To Marx, all value in produced goods was derived from labor. The machines that were used in the production process were simply embodied or congealed labor from earlier production. All commodities were to be reduced to a common denominator of the labor time embodied in the product. The relative prices of goods would thus be determined by the labor time it took to produce them. If a wagon took five times longer to produce than a harness, it would sell for five times the price of the harness.

---

[1]It should be obvious why this rhetoric frightened many U.S. citizens and turned them against the early labor unions, as we saw in Chapter 14.

This labor theory of value produced a struggle based on Marx's observation that capitalists only pay workers the minimum amount necessary to survive. He argued that wages always tend toward subsistence because capitalists, seeking profits, only pay the lowest amount necessary. This amount, Marx said, was the amount necessary to keep workers alive. The difference between the labor value of the good produced and the subsistence wage the workers received was called *surplus value* by Marx. This surplus value represented capitalistic exploitation of workers.

Given this theory, Marx foresaw the eventual decline of profits as capitalists accumulated more and more capital. The private economy would become very monopolized, and business cycles would increase in severity. As a result of all these forces, a large group of unemployed laborers would result, called *the reserve army of the unemployed*. These unemployed workers would unite, and socialism would ultimately develop.

Marx's Writings Appraised

Marx does not win high grades as an economist. His economic reasoning was primitive even in his own day. His labor theory of value is not a particularly good theory. As we saw earlier in this book, price is determined by the interaction of supply *and* demand. It is true that labor costs play a large role in determining supply, but other costs of production also play a role. Marx's subsistence theory of wages also does poorly when compared to the marginal productivity theory of wages we developed in Chapter 13.

His prognosis for the future did not fare much better than his economics. It is true that industrialization spread through much of the world after the Industrial Revolution in Western nations, but the Industrial Revolution did not result in just a few industrialists acquiring all the wealth at the expense of the working masses. In fact, the material well-being of workers increased rapidly with spreading industrialization.

What, then, is the significance of Marx's writings? It is curious that in the countries where communism has spread, the level of industrialization has been very low, the exact opposite of what Marx predicted. The significance is not in Marx himself, nor, for that matter, in his writings, but rather in the rhetorical, philosophical movement his work has spawned. A widely divergent group of communist parties consider themselves Marxists and appeal to the writings of Marx to justify their views on various issues. In some respects they have similar roots. They all condemn the exploitation of workers by monopoly capitalism and eschew the use of the term profit. They all claim to have "full employment" economies and claim to have overcome the problem of the capitalistic army of unemployed workers. But after these simplistic notions are out of the way, wide differences come into focus. Countries as diverse as China, Yugoslavia, the Soviet Union, Albania, Romania, and Cuba all claim to be the true Marxists. Herein lies the significance of Marx — as the father of a political, rather than an economic, movement.

LEADER-ISMS

Socialism was Marx's intermediate stage between capitalism and communism. We saw earlier that under a system of socialism the decision-making authority is shifted from individual entrepreneurs to a central authority. These central authorities have historically almost always been personified by strong, dominant individuals. It is thus possible to view many of the offshoots of Marxism as the products of these strong-willed leaders.

Leninism

Vladimir Lenin (1870–1924) was active in developing the Communist Party of Russia and led the successful Bolshevik revolution in Russia. He claimed to be a follower of Marx but developed new directions for the achievement of communism. Lenin refused to wait for the maturation of capitalism and instead developed a formula for revolution based on four essential ingredients: (1) a small, revolutionary elite; (2) economic underdevelopment (the opposite of Marx's industrialization); (3) an estranged peasantry; and (4) war against an outside force. Lenin's formula worked in Russia and has worked in Yugoslavia, China, Vietnam, and Cuba. In fact, Lenin's formula is the way communism has almost always taken root. The exceptions are those countries of Eastern Europe where communism was imposed by the Soviet Union following World War II.

Lenin engineered and led the Bolshevik revolution and became the first communist to be faced with the task of setting up an economic system after the political system was secure. The first system that was implanted in Russia by Lenin is often referred to as *War Communism* because the Communist Party was engaged in civil war with the non-Communist White Russians throughout the period. This system substituted rigid administrative control of the economy for the previous market economy in an attempt to marshal the requisite resources to engage in war. Widespread nationalization took place throughout this period, and all private trading was outlawed. All labor movements were rigidly controlled, and money as an exchange mechanism virtually disappeared. This period is difficult to evaluate, and some economic historians claim that Lenin instituted War Communism only because of the pragmatic concern of carrying out a war.[2] In any event, in 1921 Lenin aban-

---

[2]Others claim Lenin instituted War Communism out of a desire to see such a system evolve as the economic application of communism. For this view, see Paul Craig Roberts, *Alienation and the Soviet Economy* (Albuquerque: University of New Mexico Press, 1971).

doned War Communism and instituted a program referred to as the *New Economic Policy (NEP)*, which was an attempt at *market* socialism with rigid plans for only the key industries in the economy. The remainder of the economy was to be organized under basic market principles. There was very rapid economic growth during this period, and the Soviet economy quickly recovered from the protracted civil war. Lenin died in 1924, and in 1926 the New Economic Policy came to an end for a variety of reasons. A major cause was that the re-marketization of the economy during NEP greatly reduced the power of the Communist Party to channel and direct the course of economic development.

Stalinism

From 1924 to 1928, open debate took place in the Soviet Communist Party. It is referred to as *the Great Industrialization Debate*.[3] The debate consisted of differing views on how the Soviet economy should develop. The left wing, led by economist E. A. Preobrazhensky, argued that the country should make a "big push" and pursue rapid industrialization of key sectors of the economy. This would be carried out by the central allocation of investment expenditures. N. I. Bukharin, who was the spokesperson for the right wing, disagreed with this position and stressed balanced growth of the economy. Bukharin argued that all sectors of the economy must grow together because they all support and feed one another.

Joseph Stalin (1879–1953) was both an observer and a participant in the debate. Stalin played one side against the other while consolidating his own power base. At the time of Lenin's death, Stalin allied himself with the right wing of the Party in order to counteract the power of Leon Trotsky and the left wing of the Party. This allowed him to discredit and weaken the left wing, and he accomplished this by 1927. He then turned on the right wing, and by 1928, had the leaders of the right wing denounced by the Party. Stalin was then in complete control, since he purged any dissidents.[4] The planning system that Stalin adopted was centrally directed and was set up in five-year increments. The five-year time increment was chosen since most investment projects can be completed in such a period. Stalin's first five-year plan was an extreme version of the left-wing superindustrialization plan. Its achievement required very centralized planning, investment in heavy industry, and extreme measures in the agricultural sector, which was expected to supply food and raw materials. The costs of this policy were great in human terms. Millions of people were purged or starved to death. Industrialization was very rapid, however. By the 1960s the Soviet Union had become

---

[3]See Alexander Erlich, *Soviet Industrialization Debate, 1924–1928* (Cambridge: Harvard University Press, 1960).

[4]For an excellent economic history of the Soviet Union, including this period, see Alec Nove, *An Economic History of the U.S.S.R.* (London: Penguin, 1975).

the second most powerful country in the world, second only to the United States.

The Soviet Union and its rigid central planning is the legacy of Stalin. Today Stalinism signifies a ruthless dictatorship as well as an extreme, severe, and highly centralized planning structure. However, Stalinism is not openly practiced in any communist country today. Romania perhaps comes the closest by combining the rigid, very centralized planning of Stalinism with a strong leader in the person of its president, Nicolae Ceausescu. Ceausescu has not, however, demonstrated the bloody ruthlessness that characterized Stalinism.

Titoism

Marshall Tito broke with Stalin in 1948 over Soviet interference in Yugoslavia's internal affairs. Tito was not a puppet of Stalin, since he had carried out his own revolution in Yugoslavia rather than having been installed by the Soviets, as had happened in the other Eastern European communist countries in the post-World War II period. Tito formulated his own "road to socialism," which began as a Stalinist-prototype centrally planned economy, but has become a market-planned economy with less central control than some Western market economies (France, for example). A key element, and one that is unique in the world, is the Yugoslav concept of *workers' self-management*. The concept is that all the workers, including what we would call blue-collar and white-collar workers, help direct the firm for which they work and have a financial stake in its outcome. Such a system could only have economic meaning if the firm were autonomous, and, as a result, a great deal of central authority has withered away in Yugoslavia. Tito and Yugoslav communists claim that such self-management by the workers is the true Marxist ideal because it removes the alienation of the worker.

Titoism, or the Yugoslav brand of communism, is unique in the world. It too, however, draws heavily on and owes much to the strength and personality of one man, Tito. What will follow after his death is impossible to forecast.

Castroism

Fidel Castro learned the lesson of Lenin's formula for revolution very well. He had a small group of committed revolutionaries, a large, estranged peasant class, an undeveloped economy, and the United States as an outside enemy. In many ways the Cuban system is most like Chinese communism in that Castro has placed heavy emphasis on the creation of a "new man."[5] The goal is to remove all social inequities and

---

[5]For a good view of Castro's Cuba, see Carmelo Mesa-Lago (ed.). *Revolutionary Change in Cuba* (Pittsburgh: University of Pittsburgh Press, 1971).

motivate workers by moral incentives rather than material incentives. This is very close to the Marxist view of the final stage of communism. In Cuba, this policy was in large part the work of Che Guevara and was received skeptically by the Soviets, who were financially underwriting the Cuban economy and, therefore, had a large economic interest in Cuba.

The Cuban experience also relied heavily on agriculture. Rather than attempting to rapidly industrialize the Cuban economy, Castro instead concentrated on agriculture and sought to exploit the export potential of the sugarcane industry. This required the transfer of labor from cities to rural areas, the exact opposite of the experience of all the European communist regimes. The planning in Cuba is carried out in a system referred to as the System of Budgetary Finance. This is an extreme central-planning system that views the economy as a single firm, to be rigidly controlled by the central authority.

As in many of the other communist countries, Cuban communism is uniquely the product of one man, Castro. Like Stalin in the Soviet Union, Tito in Yugoslavia, and Mao in China, Castro is such a strong leader that we may not see the true face of communism in Cuba during his lifetime. That is why it is perhaps most correct to refer to communism in Cuba as Castroism, at least for the present.

Maoism

In China, the Communist Party came to full power in October, 1949, after decades of struggle. Mao Tse-tung was the revolutionary leader who had taken command, much as Lenin's formula for communist revolutionaries had dictated. In the early years of Chinese communism, the goal was industrialization, much as it had been in the Soviet Union, but this policy was formulated without the help of Moscow. The Chinese Communist Party, from the very beginning, was fiercely independent of the Soviet Union.

In 1958, the *Great Leap Forward* took place. The Great Leap Forward was an impossibly overambitious plan to increase per capita income in China by 25 percent in five years. Many of the programs were foolishly conceived, including such programs as the production of steel on a small scale in backyard furnaces. The result was a worthless product. The regime then took a strange twist in the *Cultural Revolution* that took place in 1966 through 1969. This period represents the high point in the adulation of Mao. We see in this time span the essence of Maoism. The Cultural Revolution embraced the primacy of revolutionary values. Mao saw a completely classless society, organized as a collective operation rather than as a state enterprise as in the Soviet Union. The motivation for the society was to be completely altruistic. Here we have the concept of the "new man" who responds to social rather than material incentives. The system used moral and honorific rewards to motivate the labor force.

To some degree, this technique has had some influence, but it is not clear to what degree this new man has in actuality been motivated by indoctrination and coercive administrative controls.

The Chinese economy has changed often and in radically different directions. There is at present not enough information to get any real feel for the success of Maoism relative to economic development. Several economists have traveled to China, and one receives strikingly different reports from them. For example, Professor John Gurley of Stanford argues that China has made great strides and has eradicated poverty, while Professor James Tobin of Yale University argues that there was not much economic progress under Mao.[6]

Interesting developments in China are occurring at the present time. Despite the incredible power of Mao and the development of Maoism, since Mao's death in 1976 the new leaders have pursued a very pragmatic development stategy that often seems openly hostile to Mao. The new leaders, led by Premier Hua, have openly attacked the so-called "Gang of Four," consisting of Mao's widow and three other radicals. In attacking the Gang of Four, the leaders have attacked the ideas of the Cultural Revolution and, in fact, Mao himself, although they have been very careful not to attack Mao by name. *Newsweek* reports that Chinese officials argue that "Chairman Mao was deceived by the Gang of Four."[7]

It will be interesting to observe the new course of Chinese communism over the next few years. Yugoslav-style workers' self-management is being considered. As we saw earlier, this requires decentralization or it doesn't work. The leadership is moving quickly to open trade with the West, which is a significant break with Mao's policy of self-reliance and self-development. This Westernization will bring with it the influence and ideas of Western capitalism, as has already happened in the communist countries of Eastern Europe. Premier Hua is already using Western terminology when he speaks of plans to modernize China. He insists "the law of value" must be applied with a strict system of "economic accounting" to all projects with the aim of "increasing profits."[8] Teng Hsiao-ping's visit to the United States in early 1979 was yet another manifestation of China's new orientation. The main thrust of Teng's visit was to lay preliminary groundwork for what China wants most — modern technology for agriculture and industry.

While in the United States, Teng talked of new programs aimed at the *four modernizations*. The four modernizations are the plans to modernize farming, industry, science, and technology in three phases. In the short term, Teng hopes to mechanize agriculture. The next phase calls

---

[6]John Gurley, "Maoist Economic Development," and James Tobin, "The Economy of China: A Tourist's View," in Edwin Mansfield, *Economics: Readings, Issues, and Cases* (New York: W. W. Norton & Co., Inc., 1977).

[7]*Newsweek* (October 30, 1978), p. 50.

[8]Vermont Royster, "Chinese Communism's Many Faces," *The Wall Street Journal,* October 25, 1978.

for the modernization of industry, and the final phase calls for a further increase in industrial production, including consumer goods and high-technology electronic goods. In all, the plans call for China to catch up with the industrialized world by the year 2000.

ORGANIZATION AND DECISION-MAKING APPROACH TO THE STUDY OF SYSTEMS

Up to this point, we have been looking at alternative economic systems largely in terms of ideology and the effects this ideology has on the organization of the system. In many cases this resulted in the study of how a dominant personality shaped an entire system. Some of you may have found this an exciting and useful way to categorize the world. Others of you may have found this frustrating, requiring a study of each individual system or country, and thus a technique that worked against the development of any general principles of how differing systems are organized and how they affect behavior. This approach has been the dominant way economists have historically examined alternative systems. In recent years, however, a new approach has been developed. This newer approach, instead of looking at individual countries, attempts to formulate organizational principles based in part on the economic theory we developed in previous chapters to develop a coherent analytical framework in which to view alternative economic systems.[9]

The System

To understand the system, it is necessary to examine the organizational setting for the production of goods and services *and* the institutional setting for the distribution of those goods and services. The important questions concern the structure of decision-making in production and distribution. Perhaps the most important question concerns which individuals at which levels make the important decisions concerning production and distribution. In the United States, production decisions would be made at the entrepreneurial level; in the Soviet Union, these same decisions would be made at the planning level. At this stage of analysis we would inquire as to which level in the planning hierarchy the decisions are made.

Once the level of decision-making is determined, it is necessary to examine the motivational structure at this level of decision-making. How do the decision-makers bear the costs of wrong decisions or reap the rewards of correct decisions? Additionally, it is necessary to determine

---

[9]For a comprehensive development of this path-breaking approach, see Egon Neuberger and William J. Duffy, *Comparative Economic Systems: A Decision Making Approach* (Boston: Allyn and Bacon, Inc., 1976).

how one person influences another. This is different than individual rewards and punishments to the extent that it is possible to change another individual's internal values. In other words, do institutions affect individuals' value systems?

Once these two aspects of the decision-making structure are determined, we can turn to the informational structure in the system. This concerns the way in which individuals learn about their options so they can act on these options. In the U.S. economy, prices are an important source of information; but in the Soviet economy, the plan plays this role. As the decision-making becomes centralized, more and better information is critical because the costs of wrong decisions are so much larger.

The Environment

After examining the system, we turn to a country's environment; that is, its social structure, physical conditions, and international situation. Some of the more critical aspects of the environment in terms of possible impact on the system are: the level of economic development, the size of the country in area and population, the availability of natural resources from within and from safe allies, the values of the people (religious, cultural, and so on), the political system, the size of the country relative to its near neighbors, the level of development relative to the rest of the world and relative to near neighbors, and the sphere of influence the country is in (United States, Soviet, or Chinese, for example). These are only a few of the environmental considerations that can influence a system, but they are representative of the concept of environmental infuence.

Performance

The way in which an economy performs can have a powerful effect on the environment and the system. Economists usually focus on the performance of gross national product and examine per capita growth in production, stability of production (cycles can be socially destabilizing), and equity in the distribution of this production.

Policy

Policy changes can be made within a system without changing the underlying fabric of the system. Policy, in effect, thus refers to marginal changes in the system and its environment in order to affect performance. Policy changes can influence the system in a positive or negative way. A "good" system might develop "bad" policies that produce "bad" performance and in turn result in a negative change in the "good" system.

Interactions of Systems, Environment, Performance, and Policy

Of course, all these organizational elements interact in a simultaneous fashion. But using this terminology can help in understanding the slippery concept of why economic systems differ and why they are similar. For example, consider a small country having the USSR or the United States as a close neighbor. How would this affect the development of the system? It has had a profound effect on the communist countries of Eastern Europe. Likewise, being close to the United States has had effects on Canada, Mexico, and Cuba. What environmental factors caused the Industrial Revolution to spread from England to the United States, but not to Russia? How might "performance" influence an economic system? It's part of Lenin's formula: If things get bad enough, there might be a revolution. On the other hand, if they start to get good enough in communist countries, there might be a move toward capitalism or market socialism. Of course, we can't begin to answer all these complex questions. This approach may, however, give you a start in finding the answers.

PLANNING

Throughout this chapter, whether we were using the *isms* approach to systems or a more structured organizational approach, we continually flirted with the question of planning. Such questions as who directs production, who makes decisions, and who bears the costs for wrong decisions or receives the rewards for correct decisions kept coming to the forefront. This is the essence of the problem of understanding systems. The question is not whether planning should take place, but rather who should do the planning. General Motors plans, home-builders plan, wheat farmers plan — and so do you. The question is the degree of centralization of planning and control. At extremes, the market position would be that individual consumers and entrepreneurs should plan, and at the command end of the spectrum, the position would be that the central authority should plan.

The Socialist Controversy[10]

Marx had little to say about the actual workings of the economic system under socialism. Instead, Marx criticized capitalism and left the development of the economics of socialism to his followers. In 1922 a professor at the University of Vienna, Ludwig von Mises, wrote a famous

---

[10]For a thorough discussion of the socialist controversy, see Paul R. Gregory and Robert C. Stuart, *Soviet Economic Structure and Performance* (New York: Harper and Row Pubs., Inc., 1974).

article, "Economic Calculations in the Socialist Commonwealth."[11] This article purported to show that national economic calculations were impossible under socialism. Von Mises based his argument on a number of factors, but the essence of the argument was quite simple. If the state owned the factors of production (other than labor), it would have to allocate them between competing uses. Without a market to determine prices, this would be an impossible task. A simulated market (*shadow prices*, in the jargon of planners) could not supply correct prices because of the absence of the profit motive. In fact, von Mises argued that "the most serious menace to socialist economic organization" was the lack of reward for correct managerial decisions and penalty for incorrect managerial decisions. This article kicked off a debate known as the *socialist controversy*.

Professor Oskar Lange, a famous Polish economist who at the time was on the faculty at the University of Chicago, responded to von Mises by developing a model sometimes referred to as the *competitive solution*. In the model, Lange tried to prove that a socialist economy with central *and* local decision-making can arrive at the same efficiency standards as the model of pure competition we developed in Chapter 8. Prices are arbitrarily set by the central authority. Local managers are told to maximize profits, although they cannot keep these profits. They are solely accounting profits. If shortages or surpluses develop, the price is changed, and in this way an equilibrium price is finally reached. One of the most telling criticisms of Lange's solution is that if equilibrium prices are sought, why not use a market in the first place?[12]

The debate has never been resolved as to the technical feasibility of centralized planning. Is it possible for a central authority to make the necessary calculations to produce efficiently? In an article that might be considered a continuation of this debate, F. A. Hayek, Nobel prizewinning economist, says no.[13] Hayek argues that information is the friction in the system that causes economic models to diverge from the textbook ideal of either von Mises or Lange. We must, therefore, examine which type of system needs less information because economizing on costly information is necessary for efficient production. Hayek goes on to argue that market systems need less information than do command systems. Consider once again a simple example that we discussed earlier in the text. An earthquake destroys a copper mine in the United States and a copper mine in the USSR. In both countries, copper is now more scarce and needs to be used more sparingly. What happens in each economy? In

[11]Ludwig von Mises, "Economic Calculations in the Socialist Commonwealth," in F. A. Hayek (ed.), *Collectivist Economic Planning* (Clifton, N.J.: Augustus M. Kelley Publishers, 1967), p. 103.

[12]Paul Craig Roberts, "Oskar Lange's Theory of Socialist Planning," *Journal of Political Economy* (May–June, 1971).

[13]F. A. Hayek, "The Use of Knowledge in Society," *American Economic Review* (September, 1945).

Oskar Lange and F. A. Hayek

Oskar Lange (1904–1965)

F. A. Hayek (1899–   )

Oskar Lange and *F. A. Hayek* represent polar extremes in debates on the efficacy of economic planning. As we saw in this chapter, Professor Lange was instrumental in beginning the debate that compared the efficiency characteristics of socialism and capitalism. The debate was joined by the Austrian economist Ludwig von Mises and later expanded on by Professor Hayek.

Lange was born in Poland but educated in the United States at the University of California and at Stanford. He returned to Poland in 1947 and was active in the postwar communist government. In the early years of the communist government he served as Polish ambassador to the United States (1945–1946) and Polish delegate to the U.N. Security Council (1946–1947). He eventually became chairperson of the Polish Economic Council (1957–1962). He was also associated with the University of Warsaw. As expounded upon in his famous "On the Economic Theory of Socialism," published in the *Review of Economic Studies* in 1937, Lange believed it was possible that, through trial and error, prices would adjust to equilibrium levels in a socialist economy. He theorized that the same efficiency that characterizes the model of pure competition would eventually evolve in a planned system.

Nobel prizewinning economist F. A. Hayek vigorously disagrees with this theoretical solution. Hayek argues that the information needed to organize production efficiently is very costly. He points out that a market system economizes on the information that is needed while a planned system demands huge quantities of information. This fact, Hayek argues, insures that planning cannot approach the efficiency of laissez-faire capitalism. Many of Hayek's ideas can be found in his book, *The Road to Serfdom* (1944).

the United States, the price of copper will rise, reflecting its increased scarcity (decrease in supply). Profit-minded entrepreneurs will substitute cheaper metals in order to minimize costs. The entrepreneur does not need any information other than the fact that the price of copper has risen. In the Soviet Union, the planner must first be informed of the disaster. The planner must then make some estimate of the severity of the scarcity. Each user of copper must be informed that in the future less copper will be supplied and that other metals should be substituted. Producers of other metals will also need to be contacted and told to ship to the enterprises which had been using copper. Additionally, the planner will have to set priorities as to how the available copper is to be utilized. In the market system this priority-setting was done by the increase in price. So Hayek's position is quite simple — central planning can never be as efficient as a market system because it requires too much information in order to work. The market system, on the other hand, economizes on the amount of information needed.

How to Plan

Whether we view central planning as efficient or inefficient does not change the fact that it is done. The truth is that most socialist countries rely heavily on central planning in order to achieve the desired performance of the economy. We should, therefore, examine in a simplified version how planning is done in the Soviet Union, the command economy with the most experience in planning.

First, priorities must be established; the decision has to be made as to what to produce. In the early years of Soviet planning, this was only done at the most aggregate level. The first plan was, in fact, called the State Plan for the Electrification of Russia. Today this planning is done in the State Planning Commission, commonly called the *Gosplan*. At the most aggregate level, the decision can be made on whether to produce consumer or investment goods. This was one of the early uses of planning in the Soviet Union. The goal of the leaders was rapid economic growth. They therefore made the decision to produce investment goods at the expense of consumer goods. As a result, consumers didn't have very much to consume and were forced to save. This led to heavy investment and very rapid rates of economic growth. Yet there were, and still are, significant shortages of consumer goods in the Soviet Union. Tourists traveling in the Soviet Union are well aware of these shortages and familiar with Soviet citizens' attempts to buy items from them.

Once the decision of what to produce is made, the planners must turn their attention to how much to produce. This is a difficult planning problem because the amount depends on the productive capacity of the existing industry and on the resources that will be available during the period. Production uses up resources; therefore, the planners must plan for the production of the resources that will be used for the final output.

At this stage of planning, the various industries are brought into the picture, and the *ministries*, one for each major industry, make their plans based on the overall plan. Once these plans are finalized, they must be communicated to all the productive enterprises so they can take the necessary action to put the plan into operation. This is an ongoing process, and even though the planning period is usually expressed in five-year increments, it is a continuous exercise in revision and implementation.

This process in itself uses up a great deal of productive capacity. The individuals engaged in this planning are highly trained engineers and economists, people who are taken out of their productive capacities in order to plan. It is not, therefore, difficult to understand the burden that planning places on the economy. Many of the poorest countries, where most communist revolutions have taken place, are the very ones that can least afford to plan in an opportunity-cost sense of the personnel used in the planning process.

Input-Output Analysis

The complexity of planning can easily be seen by examining an input-output table for a small, fictitious economy in which there are only a few industries to control. *Input-output analysis* was developed by Nobel prizewinning economist Wassily Leontief and shows that everything depends on everything else. These interrelationships are what make planning so difficult, because specific plans must be made as to how much of each good is to be produced, by whom, and for whom.

To begin, we look at an aggregate economy in Table 17-1 that has only three industries — electricity, trucks, and steel. In addition, these individual industries supply inputs to the other industries. We also show a labor sector and a corresponding category of consumption. The input to labor is consumption. Reading across the rows of Table 17-1 gives us the output of each industry and the labor sector, as well as showing how that output is distributed. One of the reasons that input-output tables are especially useful in the communist economies is that the units are expressed in physical units, and prices of these outputs and inputs are not needed for the analysis.

To interpret our input-output table, read across the row. For example, the steel industry had an output of 20,000 tons, which was sold or allocated by the central authority to the following sectors: 5,000 tons to the electricity industry, 3,000 tons to the truck industry, 8,500 tons to the steel industry, and 3,500 tons were consumed by the labor sector. Reading down a column tells us the inputs that were needed to produce the output. Take steel as an example again. In order to produce the 20,000 tons of steel, the steel industry used inputs. These inputs were: 6,000 kilowatts of electricity; 2,000 trucks; 8,500 tons of steel; and 3,500 person-days of labor. Once we understand the simple arithmetic of input-output, we can use it to plan future output.

Wassily Leontief

Wassily Leontief (1906–   )

Wassily Leontief was born in Russia and received an M.A. degree at the University of Leningrad in 1925. In 1928 he received a Ph.D. from the Free University of Berlin. Later he emigrated to the United States and taught at Harvard University. At Harvard he established the Harvard Economic Research Project on the structure of the American economy. He was director of the project for more than 20 years until 1975 when, citing his unhappiness with the Harvard economics department, he accepted an appointment at New York University.

While at Harvard, Leontief completed his earlier work on input-output analysis. His ideas were first published in his book *The Structure of the American Economy, 1919–1929* (1941). In 1973 Professor Leontief was awarded the Nobel Prize in Economics for his work on input-output analysis.

As we have seen in this chapter, the essence of input-output analysis is the recognition of the many interdependencies throughout the economy. This concept, however, was certainly not new with Leontief. As early as 1758 in his *Tableau économique*, François Quesnay (1694–1774), personal physician to Louis XV, drew upon his understanding of the interrelated flows in the body to hypothesize interrelated flows in the economy. Quesnay's work was extended by many other economists, but Leontief was the first to develop a system that could quantify these interrelationships and simulate the economy based on extensive data sets.

Input-output analysis is an extremely important tool of planners, whether these be central government planners in the Soviet Union or economists in the planning department of a capitalist corporation. The technique is so necessary in socialist economies that the Soviets are fond of noting that the technique was developed by a Russian, without noting that he is now a U.S. citizen.

TABLE 17-1   **Input-Output Table for a Simple Three-Industry Economy**

Input↓ Output→	Electricity	Trucks	Steel	Consumption	Total Output
Electricity (Kilowatts)	1,000	500	6,000	1,500	9,000 Kilowatts
Trucks (Number of Trucks)	1,000	1,000	2,000	1,000	5,000 Trucks
Steel (Tons)	5,000	3,000	8,500	3,500	20,000 Tons
Labor (Person-Days)	2,000	500	3,500	0	6,000 Person-Days

The key assumption used in input-output analysis is that production takes place in all industries at *constant* costs. There are no economies or diseconomies of scale. This means that if we want to double the production of the steel industry, all we need to do is double the inputs. Regardless of the level of output planned, the amount of inputs required per unit of output remains the same. However, for large increases in output this is a very unrealistic assumption, as we saw in Chapter 7.

We can use Table 17-1 to calculate the input needed to produce additional units of output. The numbers we calculate are referred to as *input coefficients* in the jargon of input-output analysis. An input coefficient signifies the ratio of a particular input to the total outputs in that industry. Each input coefficient in Table 17-1 can be calculated by dividing each cell in a column by the total output of that industry. For example, the input coefficient of electricity in the truck industry is .10 kilowatts/trucks (= 500/5,000). Table 17-2 reproduces a part of Table 17-1 with input coefficients instead of physical units. Each input coefficient represents the amount of input needed per unit of output.

We can then use the input coefficients to plan increases in output. Reading Table 17-2 gives us a clue to the use of the input-output technique. Examine the column for trucks. The input-coefficient tells us what increase we need from each supply industry to get an increase in output in the truck industry.

We can use our input-output system in Tables 17-1 and 17-2 to plan our economy. Suppose we want to expand the output of the electricity industry by 2,000 kilowatts. A 2,000-kilowatt expansion in output would require 220 kilowatts of electricity, 220 trucks, 1,120 tons of steel, and 440 person-days of labor. These needed inputs are found by multiplying the input coefficient by the desired increase in output. We would, therefore, know how to direct these industries to deliver the required inputs to

TABLE 17-2   **Input Coefficients**

Input↓	Output→ Electricity	Trucks	Steel
Electricity	.11	.10	.30
Trucks	.11	.20	.10
Steel	.56	.60	.425
Labor	.22	.10	.175

produce the planned output. You should note that there are feedback effects in this simultaneous system. In order to produce more electricity, more electricity must be consumed in the production of the additional output. This happens throughout this interdependent system. The example assumes that there are no bottlenecks in the capacity of any sector of the economy. In fact, however, this may not be the case. In order to produce more electricity, it may be necessary to build new power generators. This may require time and, as a result, may disrupt the plan.

The problems encountered in actually using input-output analysis for planning stem from the fact that the coefficients are constant and are calculated on the basis of the historical record. In other words, the required inputs are calculated on the assumption that the input mix is constant and the same as that used when the data for the table were compiled.

Problems of Central Planning

We can see that the technique of planning is relatively simple. The physical calculations for a realistic economy can soon become overwhelming, however. Consider an input-output table for an economy with 100 industries, 1,000 industries, or maybe 5,000 industries. The interdependencies between the industries become mind-boggling, not to mention computer-boggling.

Perhaps more significantly, the problems of planning really begin after the plan has been created. These are the problems of implementing the plan, as well as the problems of creating and maintaining incentives that get workers and managers behind the plan. It is not surprising that plans are often announced with a great deal of publicity and fanfare, while the results are often played down.

The more an economy grows, the more sophisticated it becomes and the more difficult it is to control the complexity of the interrelationships between the sectors. This increased complexity explains, in part, the move in several of the communist countries to introduce market forces to replace some aspects of the plans.

Summary

The study of comparative systems allows the economist to analyze different institutions and how they can affect economic outcomes. The most common approach to the study of systems is to classify the systems according to the dominant ideology. This approach is not too useful because almost all systems must be labeled as capitalism or socialism. Since systems can differ considerably within these general labels, the approach is limited.

Marx's writings form the basic political framework on which all the communist countries are based. The economic systems of these countries are, however, widely divergent. The development of these varying systems has been, in many cases, the result of very significant and dominant political leaders. As a result, it is possible to distinguish between Leninism, Stalinism, Titoism, Castroism, and Maoism as separate variants of communism.

A separate and distinct approach to the analysis of different systems examines the organizational and decision-making differences in alternative systems. This approach looks at the levels at which decisions are made and the informational requirements and motivation of the decision-making units. This approach examines the interactions of systems, environment, performance, and policy to determine how each affects the other.

Planning is carried out in all economies, and the key difference between systems is the level at which the planning is carried out. The higher the level of planning, the greater the informational requirements of the system. For this reason, Professor F. A. Hayek has argued that central planning can never be more efficient than entrepreneurial planning through the market system.

Central planning requires the determination of what to produce. In the Soviet Union such planning resulted in rapid growth, because the central authority decided not to produce many consumer goods. This forced the population to save and generated high rates of investment.

The planning technique is exemplified in input-output analysis. Input-output analysis presents the historical experience of the inputs necessary to produce a given output. This experience can then be used to determine what inputs are necessary to produce a desired output. Input-output analysis assumes that this historical production record will hold in the next period.

After all the technical problems of planning are worked out, it is necessary to put the plan into operation. This requires the transmitting of the plan to the production units and the creation of the proper incentives to bring about the desired production.

New Terms

capitalism	surplus value
socialism	the reserve army of the unemployed
communism	War Communism
fascism	New Economic Policy (NEP)
labor theory of value	the Great Industrialization Debate

workers' self-management
Great Leap Forward
Cultural Revolution
four modernizations
shadow prices
socialist controversy

competitive solution
Gosplan
ministries
input-output analysis
input coefficients

Questions for Discussion

1 Does the *isms* approach to systems cloud the real economic issues in systems analysis?
2 How did Lenin change the theories of Marx? Which of the two appears more important as the inspiration of communist revolutions?
3 Is planning an important function in all economies? Is it more important in market or in command economies?

4 How would allowing the input coefficient to vary complicate input-out analysis? Is the assumption of fixed coefficients a damaging one?
5 Try to list as many problems of maintaining proper incentives under a central planning system as you can. Do these problems only exist in centrally planned economies?

Suggestions for Further Reading

Gregory, Paul, and Robert C. Stuart. *Soviet Economic Structure and Performance*. New York: Harper and Row Pubs., Inc., 1974.
Grossman, Gregory. *Economic Systems*, 2d ed. Englewood Cliffs, N.J.: Prentice-Hall, Inc., 1974.
Laidler, Harry W. *History of Socialism*. New York: Thomas Y. Crowell Co., 1968.
Neuberger, Egon, and William J. Duffy. *Comparative Economic Systems: A Decision-Making Approach*. Boston: Allyn and Bacon, Inc., 1976.
Schnitzer, Martin C., and James W. Nordyke. *Comparative Economic Systems*, 2d ed. Cincinnati: South-Western Publishing Co., 1977.

CHAPTER 18

THE ECONOMICS OF BEING AN ECONOMIST

Now that you have completed your first course in microeconomics, it is appropriate to reflect on what you have learned, to consider the possibility of other economics courses, and perhaps even to consider economics as a major field of study. In this chapter we will discuss a potpourri of material related to majoring in economics, career opportunities for economists, and graduate study in economics. We will also present a guide to material that can help you stay current in economics.

WHY MAJOR IN ECONOMICS?[1]

The great English economist Alfred Marshall (see page 26 for a biographical sketch) wrote that, "Economics is a study of mankind in the ordinary business of life."[2] You will find that an economics major prepares you for almost any professional career, because economics offers a way of thinking that is clear, concise, and rigorous. As a result, job recruiters and graduate school admissions' counselors alike are attracted to economics majors.

In choosing a major in college, it is helpful to consider a number of

---

[1]This entire chapter draws very heavily from a handbook prepared by Dr. Laurence E. Leamer and the Center for Economic Education and Public Policy of the State University of New York at Binghamton. Dr. Leamer graciously permitted us to use his ideas, his format, and in many cases his exact words.

[2]Alfred Marshall, *Principles of Economics* (8th ed.; Don Mills, Ontario: The Macmillan Co. of Canada, Ltd., 1920), p. 332.

important and related questions. First and foremost, what profession(s) do you have in mind? Second, does the major offer flexibility in the sense that if your originally chosen profession suddenly becomes unattractive, you will still have sufficient opportunities within the field without having to switch majors? Third, if you have selected a profession that can be approached through a number of different avenues, are there distinct advantages in choosing one major over another? Lastly, will the major be useful in everyday life as well as providing the necessary training for your life's work? With these questions in mind, why choose economics?

The most basic and enduring strength of economics is that it provides a logical, ordered way of looking at various problems and issues. It draws upon history, philosophy, and mathematics to confront topics ranging from how an individual household or business can make sound decisions, to societal issues such as how to fight unemployment, inflation, and environmental decay. As a result, economics is widely recognized as a solid background for many jobs and professions.

An undergraduate major in economics can be ideal preparation for work on a Master of Business Administration (M.B.A.) degree at a graduate business school. In many organizations, an M.B.A. is an important credential for getting a desirable job. Most business graduate schools (but not all) prefer their students to have a broad, liberal-arts background, which an economics major provides. Most business graduate schools don't require an undergraduate economics major, but they encourage students to take at least some economics courses, and they certainly don't have a prejudice against admitting students with economics majors.

If you can get into an M.B.A. program without a major in economics, why bother with economics? One reason is that a fair portion of the content of an M.B.A. program is based on economics. In the competition to see who does well in the program, you are at an advantage if you have already seen and worked with the central ideas in economics. Further, one of the things an M.B.A. program does is to expose you to different ways of looking at business and policy problems, and one way that is stressed is economic reasoning. It is certainly no disadvantage to have experienced this sort of thinking as an undergraduate.

If your goal is to become a lawyer, economics offers an excellent preparation. Many law schools now believe that economics represents one of the best backgrounds for success because of its logical, ordered approach to problems. Specific courses recommended for the prelaw student include the major economics requirements, industrial organization, and antitrust economics. Public administration, such as jobs with the government and other nonprofit organizations, provides many job openings to those with economics degrees. Specific economics courses recommended for this area include public finance, economics of human resources, economics of state and local government, and urban economics. Private business also employs many economists. Business firms (banks and other financial institutions included) employ economists to undertake specialized economic analysis in evaluating their market positions and profit possibilities, the federal government's domestic economic policies that have important implications for their businesses, and international economic events that affect the operations of their firms. Business firms also employ economics graduates to do nonspecialized work in sales and management because business officials believe economic training to be very desirable for these positions. For these positions, the economics major is well trained to compete with majors in the other business or liberal-arts fields. Many economists are employed in colleges and universities, both as professors and administrators. In general, graduate degrees are required for such positions. Economists are involved in community, state, and regional planning. Also, a large number of economists are employed in planning positions in foreign countries by the Agency for International Development, the United Nations, and U.S. State Department. Finally, economists engage in private research and act as consultants to both large corporations and government agencies.

As this listing demonstrates, economics majors have a wide range of choices and a great deal of flexibility when deciding on an interesting and challenging profession. To repeat a point made earlier, the reason for this flexibility is that the logical and encompassing approach of economics enables an individual to analyze many diverse topics, both in a professional capacity and in private, day-to-day living. Indeed, the career opportunities for economists are so diverse that we will return to describe them in more detail after we examine economics as a major field of study in greater detail.

WHY STUDENTS CHOOSE ECONOMICS — WHY STUDENTS AVOID ECONOMICS

So you are about to choose a major (or perhaps you are already an economics major and wonder why). This is one of your most important academic decisions.

The choice of a major is a choice of one of several desirable alternative future courses for your life. An economics major is at the "cost" of one in humanities, in a science, in another social science, or in a professional area such as business, and thus probably strongly influences the type of person you might become.

You have learned in economics that intelligent choices require a knowledge of one's alternatives. The purpose of this section is to make you more knowledgeable of some of the benefits and costs of majoring in economics. We hope you can then compare an economics major with other majors and apply the economic principles of choice to your own decision.

Benefits of an Economics Major: Reasons for Studying Economics

You are already aware, from your study of introductory economics, of reasons why many students find economics a challenging area for undergraduate study, while others choose to avoid it. Here are some reasons for studying economics.

Economics Deals with Really Vital Current Problems. Inflation, unemployment, monopoly, economic growth, pollution, free enterprise versus planning, poverty, income distribution, and so forth, are all covered in the study of economics. Economics is a problem-based social science, and the problems with which it is especially concerned are among the most disturbing of our age. They fill our newspapers and pervade our politics. Not only is economics relevant to the big problems of society, but it also relates to personal problems, such as one's job, wages, unemployment, the cost of living, taxes, voting, and so on.

Probably more than any other reason, its relevance attracts students to economics. We like to be knowledgeable of a subject that so many feel is important. Even a person with only a little knowledge of economics too rapidly becomes an "authority" because so many others feel economic events are important but baffling.

Economics Is a Successful and Prestigious Social Science. The actual accomplishments of economics have established it as perhaps the most successful social science. For example, you are the first generation in decades never to have experienced a major depression, thanks in part to economists. No other social science has had equivalent success in applying reason and science to the shaping of our social destiny. Our nation has a Council of Economic Advisers; no such permanent agency exists for any other social, biological, or natural science. Indeed, few scientists of any kind have as wide a following as such economists as Galbraith, Samuelson, or Friedman.

Economics has had many notable successes. Of course, past successes do not assure great future developments; but since science is cumulative, it is probable that in your lifetime past successes of economics will be dramatically overshadowed by future breakthroughs. Students may therefore choose to major in economics due to their desire to be intellectually in on where the action probably will be.

Economics Is Attractive Because of Its Theoretical Structure, Its Models, and Its Use of the Scientific Method. Students sometimes become impatient with the seemingly endless world of fact and conjecture which characterizes much of the social sciences. Economics is often their refuge, because it is a social science which has developed models, or simplifying constructs, for organizing facts and for thinking about policy alternatives. Economics has a highly theoretical content. Development of theory is a measure of any science. Because economics

Charles L. Schultze

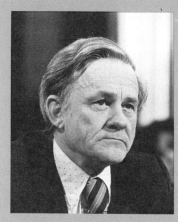

**Charles L. Schultze
(1924–   )**

Charles L. Schultze is, at this writing, chairperson of the Council of Economic Advisers (CEA). Membership on the CEA is one of the most prestigious governmental posts for a professional economist. The CEA consists of 3 members and a small staff of about 20 professional economists. The role of the CEA changes with each president, but the group functions largely as the economic consultant to the president.

The CEA was created in 1946. Since then, there have been eleven CEA chairpersons. Perhaps the two most influential were Walter Heller, who was chairperson during the Kennedy administration, and Alan Greenspan, who was chairperson during the Ford administration. The successes of Heller and Greenspan grew out of the personal relationships they developed with the presidents they worked for. Heller sold Kennedy on a tax cut to spur economic growth. The CEA under Heller was a politically powerful part of government. Greenspan convinced Ford to propose the tax rebate in 1975 that helped the economy recover from recession.

Schultze has competed against other economists in and out of government for the president's ear on economic matters. Such is the plight of the governmental economist. It is not enough to be capable of sound economic analysis; it is also necessary to gain access to policymakers. This requires political skills as well as intelligent handling of difficult policy problems.

Schultze is no stranger to the Washington political stream. After receiving an A.B. (1948) and M.A. (1950) from Georgetown University in Washington, Schultze earned a Ph.D. from the University of Maryland (1960). He has taught economics at Maryland but has been more active in governmental roles than in academic ones. Schultze was an adviser to President Kennedy and served as director of the Bureau of the Budget in the Johnson administration. When the Republicans won the White House in 1968, Schultze moved to the Brookings Institution as a senior fellow. (The Brookings Institution often serves as a refuge for advisers to Democratic administrations when the Republicans hold the White House.) Schultze was one of the first economists President Carter turned to when he began to put his administration together after the 1976 election.

deals to such a large extent with prices and numbers, because so many of its magnitudes are measurable, economic theory is more fully developed than most social theory. Many students find this attractive.

Economics Gives Students Who Are Proficient in Mathematics an Opportunity to Put Their Math to Real Use. Sometimes students view math as a fascinating game or language but are impatient at not being able to use it for really important human problems. While mathematics is increasingly used by all the social sciences, economics has long been in the forefront in its usage. A student with a background in algebra, geometry, calculus, and statistics finds a place to use these skills in economics.

An Economics Major Opens up a Great Variety of Future Options. Some majors are dead-ends, one-ended, or lead to relatively few alternative futures. An economics major, like other majors, may lead to graduate study and therefore possibly to the development of a professional scholar or teacher of the subject. For the nation as a whole, approximately 10 out of every 100 economics majors complete an M.A. in the subject, and 1 of these 10 continues to complete a Ph.D. Most graduates use their economics as a stepping stone to other occupations.

Alternatives for economics students are unusually varied. These include business, law, journalism, teaching, educational administration, politics, finance and banking, government service, public and private overseas service, labor leadership, or graduate study in a second discipline or another professional area. But there are other employment advantages of an economics major. Employers looking for liberal-arts graduates, due to their broad backgrounds, often favor economics majors because the students have already shown an interest related to the employment being sought. This is particularly true of business employers. In addition, one great advantage of an economics major is that, in the eyes of many employers, an economics graduate is a preferred employment risk. The demands of the economics major itself tend to drive those looking for an easy major away; the less ambitious in college avoid economics, and many better minds are attracted to it. Thus, to be a graduate in economics may itself be a valuable credential. A good grade point average in economics speaks for itself.

As a result, the salaries of economists, both academic and nonacademic, tend to be higher than those of other social scientists. This has been fostered by the accelerated growth in the use of economists in an increasing variety of roles. Indeed, economists often tend to rise to pivotal positions; for example, David Rockefeller and Arthur Burns in finance; Michael Blumenthal, Juanita Kreps, and James Schlesinger in government; Clark Kerr in education; Gabriel Hauge of Manufacturers Hanover Trust, Jane Pfeiffer Cahill of IBM, and Carl Madden of the Chamber of Commerce in business; Leonard Silk of the *New York Times* in journalism.

U.S. Department of Commerce

Juanita Kreps (1921–   )

Juanita Kreps

Juanita Kreps is, at this writing, Secretary of Commerce. This position makes her the highest ranking female economist in this presidential (or any other)administration. She is without question the most visible woman economist involved in economic policy. Her credentials and experience suited her for the task.

Secretary Kreps received an A.B. degree from Berea College and an M.A. and Ph.D. (1948) from Duke University. She has been on the economics faculty at Denison, Hofstra, Queens College, and Duke University. Before President Carter selected her to be Secretary of Commerce, Kreps was James B. Duke Professor of Economics and vice-president of Duke University.

Kreps's area of expertise is labor economics. She has an impressive publication list that includes numerous articles and books. Her views can be found in her text, *Contemporary Labor Economics* (1974), and *Sex in the Marketplace: American Women at Work* (1971). Kreps feels that top management must have goals of employing larger numbers of women and promoting women to high executive positions, and she also feels that women must work with each individual company to insure that this comes about.

Since becoming Secretary of Commerce, Kreps has worked to increase U.S. exports. She has argued that the Japanese market must become more open to U.S. exporters. Secretary Kreps has also drawn attention to the cost of regulations in industry. She has proposed a regulatory budget that would show how much each set of regulations costs. This would allow a determination as to whether the benefits from regulation are worth the costs. In 1979 Secretary Kreps took an active role in promoting U.S.-Chinese trade. Her trip to China broke an impasse over the payment of former claims held by the U.S. against China and will likely result in an increase in the volume of U.S. trade with China.

Citing personal reasons, Secretary Kreps resigned her Commerce position in October of 1979 and returned to Duke University.

An Economics Major Prepares Students Who Aspire to a Vocation or Avocation in Which a Knowledge of Economics Is Vital. Some disciplines are more easily learned on the job or in one's spare time than others. But if you are ever to develop a basic background in economics, it will probably be in college, not later. A knowledge of economics and an understanding of current economic institutions and problems is essential in certain occupations or for advancement in these occupations. For example, business leaders are usually expected by the general public, and often by colleagues, to be knowledgeable of economic phenomena.

Or, economics and economic issues may be your avocation. As a person knowledgeable of the subject, you may well play a leading role in a local or national political party, on a civic club committee concerned with the local economy, as a bargaining agent for a union or teacher's association, or as an informed commentator on current issues at your club or at home. With the media so full of economic matters, few disciplines are equal to economics for preparing one to be an interested, interesting, and understanding observer and interpreter of passing events.

Costs of an Economics Major: Reasons for Avoiding Economics

There are many reasons why students may want to avoid economics or to choose another major. In part, another discipline may simply be more attractive; something else may "turn you on." But also, students may be disenchanted by the nature of economics itself. Here are some reasons for avoiding economics.

You May Prefer to Avoid a Quantitative Social Science Which Employs Algebra, Geometry, and Calculus. Perhaps mathematical thinking is difficult for you, or you have an aversion to it, or you simply lack a mathematical background or interest. Possibly you should look for a major elsewhere. While it is true that much of economics (probably most of undergraduate economics) is presented in narrative-descriptive form, mathematics is still frequently employed as a second way to understand economic phenomena because of its greater precision and clarity. Yet it is indeed possible for a student who does not plan to go on to graduate study of economics, but who is really interested in the subject, to major successfully in economics with only a limited basic knowledge of algebra, geometry, and calculus.

You May Dislike Abstract Thinking and Theory. Some students have an aversion to theoretical thinking. They may defend their aversion by closing their minds to theory as "impractical" or "useless." Their minds thrive on the concrete, the real, but are closed to the theoretical. If that is you, you'd better look elsewhere for a major.

Still, you do have a point. The teachers of a science that has developed an impressive theoretical system, like economics, sometimes make their theory the prime goal of their teaching, rather than a tool for understanding real problems. Thus, students may legitimately complain that while economics is potentially the most relevant of social sciences, it is sometimes taught as if it is hardly related to the real world. You can overcome this problem by mixing theory courses and policy courses to obtain the desired blend.

You May Have an Aversion to Scientific Methods. Science, even social science, is a bore to some students and a threat to others. They come to the study of economics with preconceived ideas and with closed minds. Their aim is not to learn or to scrutinize ideas, but to convert others and to argue. They are sure the teachings of economics are wrong, and they are therefore unwilling to study the subject to see what economists think they know and why. They are unwilling to employ a method which begins with careful observation, proceeds to hypotheses, then to testing and possible verification, and finally to a tentative conclusion. If you are unwilling to try the methods of science, you had better look elsewhere.

Perhaps You Really Want to Avoid the Difficult; You Want a Snap Course of Study. Frankly, economics has a long tradition of being a difficult subject. Reasons for its difficulty are suggested by the three points above. To study the economic world in terms of the infinite trade-offs and complexities we find in this field is much more complex than a simple world of cause and effect. To study the economic world, in which there is often no cause or effect, but rather more intricate functional patterns of mutual or reciprocal causation, is challenging but difficult. Simple answers are lacking. To understand takes real effort. And then, what one eventually learns is not a final truth but only an approximation in the making. If you thrive best in a simpler world that is largely descriptive, and in an environment of students you can easily surpass, avoid economics.

You May Prefer a Broadly Focused Discipline for Study Rather Than a Relatively Narrowly Focused One. Other social sciences often study society or societies as a whole, including their economic aspect (for example, anthropology or sociology). History employs such an approach but adds an explicit time perspective. These subjects and most of the other social sciences usually concern themselves with the economic aspects of their subject. But economics, as it is typically taught and studied, tends to exclude many very important subjects. It usually takes as given (and thus for study by those other than economists) the wants, the politics, and the goals of society. It is thus usually regarded as a science of means toward these given or accepted ends.

If it is the social sciences or social philosophy that you really want to study, then you should consider another major. Or, if the economic side of life really fascinates you, and you want the fullest understanding of economics courses, use your electives outside of economics to broaden this sometimes narrowly focused discipline.

You May Find Economic Reasoning Stifling. Economics has been called the "dismal science," and perhaps not without reason. It is always counting costs; that is, it is always reminding us that choices are usually at the cost of other things of value. Thus, it is a conservative science; it may make one afraid of the possible costs of change. The economic way of thinking may make one obsessed with efficiency, with improving the organizations of society for attaining whatever society values. In their defense, economists such as Alfred Marshall have responded that economics is a science concerned with the "material means to a refined and noble life." Before we can be creative, we must learn to be productive.

You might try to design a major to combine both the economic and the creative worlds. As a result, you might become an intellectual leader of the effort to define a new, more appropriate scope for economics, or develop new applications of old methods and/or new methods for old or new purposes. Remember, economics continues to be an evolving social science.

CAREER OPPORTUNITIES FOR ECONOMISTS

One of the greatest economics educators and the teacher of many great American economists, Jacob Viner, was reported to have remarked that, "Economics is what economists do." The truth in this statement is demonstrated by the wide range of job opportunities open to economists.

But what is an economist? An obvious answer would, of course, be someone who has a college or university degree in economics. According to the National Science Foundation, an economist is someone who has had professional training in economics at the graduate level and is identifiable as a member of a professional group, such as the American Economic Association or the National Association of Business Economists. According to this definition, there were 15,000 economists in this country in 1970, about 7,000 of whom were employed by academic institutions, about 3,000 by various levels of government, and about 5,000 by business firms. This is a small number when you compare it to the more than 200,000 physicians and almost 500,000 lawyers in the same year. Perhaps this helps to explain the great demand for economists at all levels of government and business. But this number from the National Science Foundation is most certainly too low. For example, the U.S. Civil Service Commission states that more than 36,000 persons worked as economists in 1972. The difference lies in classification, and as we saw in earlier chapters of this book, any classification scheme has its problems. So let's not worry too much about classifying people as economists. Rather, let's examine some of the opportunities for economists.

Most jobs for undergraduate economics majors are not classified as jobs for economists. Instead, they are jobs that make use of training in economics as a background for positions in personnel, management, marketing, education, or some other field. This is not surprising, since very few undergraduate degrees lead to jobs where the job classification is the same as the student's major. Accounting and engineering would perhaps be two exceptions to this principle. In other words, if you want to be an *economist*, you will need graduate training in economics in most cases. But before we discuss graduate studies, let's examine the three major career paths of economists.

The Academic Economist

Almost one half of all professional economists are engaged in college teaching. This will likely change in the future as college enrollments decline, and the graduates of graduate programs shift to government and business employment. In order to teach at the college level, it is virtually essential now to have a Ph.D. Junior college instructors usually have an M.A. in economics, but even here a Ph.D. or work toward a Ph.D. may be required.

A new Ph.D. generally begins an academic career at the assistant professor level. Starting salaries in 1980 ranged from about $18,000 to $21,000 for nine months. The salary, of course, depends on the type of school and the area of the country in which it is located. Responsibilities include teaching from 2 to 4 courses, which constitutes a 6 to 12 credit hour load on a semester basis. Promotion to associate professor usually occurs from 5 to 7 years after the original appointment. As the job market tightens, schools are increasingly becoming "publish or perish" institutions, meaning the faculty member must publish books and articles in journals in order to be promoted. Promotion to the (full) professor rank usually occurs from 5 to 15 years after the promotion to associate professor. The elapsed time depends in large part on the research record, publications, and teaching ability of the faculty member. Mobility in large part depends on publications, and mobility speeds up promotion by giving the faculty member more options.

Academic economists supplement their incomes by writing textbooks and other educational materials, and by consulting. Consulting opportunities for the academic economist are numerous, the most common being economic analysis for government, business, and the legal profession. Almost anywhere economists are employed on a full or part-time basis provides consulting opportunities for the academic economist. In many cases, academic economists are sought out by government and the legal profession because of their objectiveness and impartiality.

The Business Economist

Undergraduate economics majors are recruited by business firms in all size ranges, from small, local companies to the very largest multinational corporations. In this regard an economics degree prepares students to compete with students from marketing, management, and finance, as well as students from liberal-arts majors such as history and political science. These jobs are general-purpose jobs for which employers are interested in bright, highly motivated students who can learn a specific business through on-the-job training.

The Growth of Economics as a Business Tool. The profession of business economist requires graduate training in economics. This is a rapidly growing professional field and reflects the rising prominence of economics as a business tool. It is a fairly recent phenomenon, because for many years the business community disdained academic training and expressed a preference for "practical experience." In fact, the prestigious Wharton School of Business and the Harvard Graduate School of Business did not open their doors until 1884 and 1908, respectively. So business education is literally less than 100 years old.[3] Additionally, business schools have, until only very recently, looked upon economics as too theoretical. The image of the economist in business was that of the ivory-tower dreamer. The famous industrialist, Bernard Baruch, was reported to have defined an economist as a man with a Phi Beta Kappa key on his watch, without the watch! This attitude toward economics is in large part explained by the role that these early business schools played. The business schools were largely a training ground for middle managers and were founded to teach accounting and management skills. Any contact that these early business students had with economics was accidental and usually unsatisfactory.

This has all changed in the complex modern environment in which business finds itself today. This is reflected in the training of general business majors and the emphasis placed on economics. More importantly, however, it is reflected in the ever-increasing role that graduate-trained economists play in the business community and on the faculty of business schools. In the 1950s economists were only to be found in the research departments of large banks and manufacturing firms, but the economists of the 1970s are found throughout the business community from top management positions down through the company hierarchy. This rapid growth of the role of the economist has come from the awareness and the experience that economic reasoning can help solve business problems, as well as help formulate business policy in a complex and changing environment.

Jobs for the Business Economist. It is impossible to list all the individual jobs that are performed by the business economist, but it is most likely that an economist would begin a career with business in the firm's "think-tank" or economics department. These organizational divisions

---

[3]See Robert A. Gordon and James E. Howell, *Higher Education for Business* (New York: Columbia University Press, 1959).

undertake a variety of tasks, including forecasting the general business environment and how it might affect the particular firm in question, interpreting the effects of governmental policy, and gathering and processing economic data and intelligence. From this beginning, the doors to upward mobility are open. The economist may remain in the role of the economist, or may move into the management side of the business organization. In this role the economist is following the earlier lead of the professional engineer, accountant, and lawyer in moving into the top management positions in both large and small business firms.

Business economists receive excellent salaries. This results from the simple fact that the demand for professional economists is great. The largest employers of economists, according to the National Association of Business Economists (NABE), are firms engaged in manufacturing, banking, business services, and securities and investments. In 1976, NABE conducted a survey of business economists' salaries. This survey showed that the median salary nationwide was $33,000, and in the New York area it was $37,500. These salaries have kept pace with inflation in recent years, making the incomes of business economists very attractive.

The future market for economists in business will likely expand. More and more business firms are coming to appreciate the skills and abilities of professional economists. Economists are being asked to join lawyers, accountants, engineers, and other business professionals in solving business problems. In addition, the business economist is increasingly being drawn into top management positions. All these demands for intelligent economic thinking make the profession of a business economist a career with great potential.

The Government Economist

Since the New Deal era of Franklin Roosevelt, economists have moved into the forefront of governmental policy analysis. In recent years economists have begun to displace political scientists and lawyers in the top administrative posts in government. Recent presidential cabinets have had more economists than any other identifiable profession.[4]

Economists in the Federal Government. This area of employment for economists is growing because economists have displayed the tools necessary for analysis of public issues. In the federal government there are positions for economists in every governmental agency. A few positions are available at junior grades for undergraduate economists, but most governmental positions in which one works as an economist require a Master's or a Ph.D. degree in economics. A wide spectrum of

---

[4]For an interesting view of the economist as a policy adviser from a professional economist with extensive high-level governmental experience, see George P. Shultz and Kenneth W. Dam, *Economic Policy Beyond the Headlines* (New York: W. W. Norton and Co., Inc., 1978).

jobs is open, many of which follow the traditional field areas of economics. In other words, there are jobs for labor economists, international economists, development economists, and population economists, as well as macro- and microeconomists. The duties of a governmental economist are very diverse and in large part depend on the particular governmental agency. For example, an economist for the State Department (or the CIA) might become an expert on the economy of a particular country, while an economist at OMB (Office of Management and Budget) may be an expert in cost-benefit analysis.

The governmental economist sometimes takes on the role of being an advocate for a particular agency. This is a change for the economist, *qua* scientist, who has been trained to use positive, scientific analysis. Governmental economists often take on duties that turn the role of the economic analyst into that of an administrator. In this sense, as in opportunities in business and academics, economics can lead to high level administrative jobs in government. However, it was the authors' experience in government that economists don't have to take positions or defend positions they don't believe in. This is not to say you might not have to avoid public disagreement with your boss.

Employment on Capital Hill (working for Congress) is a relatively new area of opportunity for economists. Until very recently, except for the Joint Economic Committee, very few congressional committees or individual congressional staffs hired economists. This is changing rapidly. Legislation and the issues facing Congress are becoming increasingly complex and economic in nature. As a result, Congress is turning to economists to give them expert advice on these issues.

Above all, the economist in Washington, whether a permanent career economist or a business or academic economist on temporary duty in Washington, must operate in a political environment. This is one of the problems for the many academic economists who move into short-term Washington jobs. The professional bureaucrat looks with derision on the analyst who cannot operate in the political environment. In Washington the term "academic economist" is not used as a complimentary term. "Good economists" and "academic economists" are not necessarily synonymous in Washington. This does not mean that academics cannot be viewed as "good economists," but this is a label that has to be earned in the bureaucratic environment.

The economist in government is well paid. In 1978 an individual with a B.A. or B.S. degree and at least 21 semester hours in economics could get a beginning job as a GS5 or GS7 which paid an annual salary of $10,507 and $13,014, respectively. An M.A. degree in economics qualified one to start work as a GS9 at $15,920 per year, and a Ph.D. qualified an individual to start work as a GS13 at $23,087 per year.

Economists in State and Local Government. Perhaps the fastest growing area of employment for economists is in state and local government. This, of course, follows the very rapid growth of state and local governments in the last decade. State economists play a wide variety of roles, just as they do in the federal government, but there are a few differences. State economists are more likely to be involved with microeconomic problems and issues because states do not carry out independent monetary and fiscal policy. At the state and local level of analysis, the primary areas of research by economists are labor market analysis, school finance issues, state and local taxation and tax reform, environmental issues, and budgetary expenditure analysis. Of course, as in all the other areas we discussed, economists can and are moving into important administrative responsibilities in state and local government.

GRADUATE SCHOOL IN ECONOMICS

All of the career positions that we have discussed place important emphasis on graduate training. It is never too early to plan your career education goals, so we will now turn to a discussion of graduate education in economics.

Graduate schools in economics currently award about 800 Ph.D. degrees and about 2,000 Master's degrees annually. Many of the jobs we discussed in the previous sections require a Ph.D. or a Master's degree. In fact, holding a job with the designation of "economist" usually requires graduate work. This section will introduce you to some of the items you should consider in preparing yourself for graduate study in economics.

There are over 100 graduate schools in the United States offering Ph.D.'s in economics (plus a number of others offering a Master's only). Which ones would you like to attend? To which ones should you apply? What should you do as an undergraduate to prepare for graduate school and to increase the likelihood of being admitted to the schools of your choice?

Your Undergraduate Preparation

First let us assume you are an undergraduate, still to complete your course of study. If you aspire to graduate study in economics (or if you are unsure but want to keep that possibility open), there are certain guidelines you might well keep in mind.

Mathematics. Most graduate departments require a background in mathematics. You should as a minimum take calculus. Some schools offer a course called *Mathematical Analysis for Economists*. Some graduate departments allow you to make up deficiencies in mathematics after entrance, but this is a less than satisfactory compromise; you should begin graduate study with your "tools" ready for use.

Theory. Macro and micro theory are the foundations on which most graduate study is based. You have been introduced to these in this book and its companion volume. Your first graduate courses will probably be in micro and macro theory again, but in greater depth and with the assumption that you already have a firm foundation in basic theory. Economics is a science based on theory; there is no more important part of your undergraduate economics study than your theory courses for preparing you for graduate study.

Grades. If you are to go on to graduate school, your undergraduate grades really matter. A *C* or even a *C*+ average, especially in economics courses, usually means that you will not be admitted. For consideration for admission to the most prestigious schools, an *A* average or close to it is indispensible. An upward-moving grade average may indicate blooming promise; a falling grade average may spell disaster for graduate school admission.

Product Differentiation. Graduate study of economics is usually very specialized. You have little time for broadening your education. Thus, whether or not you become any more than a narrowly trained technical economist is probably determined by what you have done with your undergraduate electives.

For example, your knowledge of foreign languages may be a major determinant of how you later use your economics. An economist with a working knowledge of Chinese, Russian, or Arabic may have an indispensible product differentiation in the future (for research, for government service, for a multinational corporation, or for other international agencies). Likewise, an economist with a strong foundation in accounting, in law, in politics, and so on, may well have a combination of talents of unusual value. An economist who is skilled in communication — in listening and understanding, in writing and speaking — has one of the scarcest talents in the profession. With the expansion of knowledge and with economics alienating itself from the average citizen by its use of a specialized vocabulary and language, it is probable that the synthesizer or communicator of knowledge will become indispensible.

The foundations of all these skills (language skills, knowledge of related disciplines, communication skills) must be laid in undergraduate school. Indeed, your undergraduate education is likely more important than your graduate training for determining whether you become any more than a technically competent economist. Give some thought to your personal product differentiation.

Determining Your Goals

By the time you are a senior, your past is an unchangeable prologue to graduate study. Before trying to select a school, review and possibly revise your goals, for they may influence the school you should select. The following tabulation is meant to remind you of possible goals. Which do you now value? You might check your choices (or determine tentative priorities).

Professional Goals (that is, toward what professional roles do you aspire?).

		In a —
		Prestigious University
		Graduate School
		Prestigious College
ACADEMIC	Teaching	State College
	Research and Writing	Small Private College
	Administration	Junior College
		Secondary School

RESEARCH: { In a Private Economic Research Organization
{ In a Public Economic Research Organization

BUSINESS: { Economic Adviser to a Business Firm
{ Finance and Banking
{ Economic Consulting Agency
{ International Business

SPECIAL INTEREST
GROUPS (e.g., business,
labor, agriculture):   Economic Adviser, Interpreter, Defender

GOVERNMENT: International, Federal, State, Local, Political Parties

COMMUNICATIONS: Economic Journalism, TV, Freelance Writer

Personal Intellectual Goals.

AREA OF KNOWLEDGE — Is there some aspect of economics, some area of knowledge, which you would like to develop as a specialty (something about which you would seek to know as much as any other economist)?

AREAS OF SKILL — Are there particular personal skills which you hope to develop to a very high level of proficiency? For example:
Application of mathematical methods in economics.
Teaching of economics.
Clear writing, oral explanation, or argument.
Interpreting economic ideas, synthesizing and clarifying professional and/or political issues.

Personal Status Goals (that is, from whom do you seek deference and recognition for your professional accomplishments?).

FROM PROFESSIONAL ECONOMISTS GENERALLY — You should apply to as prestigious an institution as will admit you.

FROM GOVERNMENT, BUSINESS, AND OTHER NON-ECONOMIST LEADERS — Similar to the above, but since there is prestige in being an economist, you may be judged by your proficiency in serving leaders' objectives. Thus, less prestigious schools may serve as well or better.

FROM THE PUBLIC — Here your status may depend on your ability to relate to the public and to articulate their unformulated desires. The status of your school will count for little.

FROM YOURSELF — This is for you to answer. What kind of school is necessary to give you a sense of self-confidence and personal pride?

Enough, then, on goals. There are no doubt others we have overlooked. These are for you to formulate and relate to criteria for the choice of a graduate school.

Constraints on Your Choice

One more preliminary before looking at graduate schools: What constraints are likely to limit or influence your choice? Here are several that may apply. You should determine whether they are relevant to you.

Money. Do you have the financial resources to attend any school (up to $5,000–$10,000 a year for a minimum of three years)? If not, are you able and willing to work? Do you have any salable talent? What about fellowships, assistantships, borrowing, and so forth?

Your Academic Qualifications.

GRADES

STATUS OF YOUR COLLEGE — Being a college graduate is a good credential, but you will be in competition with good graduates of other, perhaps even more prestigious, private liberal-arts colleges and state universities.

ACADEMIC PREREQUISITES — Do you have the math and the economic theory to qualify you for serious consideration?

Geographic Location.

LOCATION OF STUDY — Are there constraints on you personally, or personal preferences, to study in one part of the country or another?

LOCATION OF FUTURE EMPLOYMENT — Where would you like to be employed upon graduation? Some graduate schools have a national reputation and placement market. Others are regional, and if you are interested in a particular geographic area, you may be better off going to school in that area, particularly if you are interested in business or state government.

Schools Offering Ph.D.'s in Economics

With your goals and constraints in mind, you are ready to survey your options for graduate study. Table 18-1 presents a list of all universities offering Ph.D.'s in economics, with the top ten ranked in order of the rated quality of their faculty.

This listing order is based upon a 1969 survey by the American Council on Education as to the quality of each school's graduate faculty as judged by representative economists from institutions awarding two percent or more of all Ph.D.'s in economics. This procedure tends to favor the larger departments (which as a result are more likely to have graduates in positions to be known or to vote). For similar reasons, it favors long-established departments and departments with faculty that are highly visible due to their publications (prestigious departments tend to dominate the prestigious journals). Indeed, the ratings may be largely self-fulfilling (the lesser centers tend to seek faculty from the prestigious departments and thus, in effect, rate their own judgments high). In this sense they suffer from many of the same problems as college football polls. Consequently, this rating tends to overlook the new programs, those with few graduates, those serving primarily a regional area (this was a national poll), and those whose primary aim has been something other than educating economic scholars (for example, teachers, public servants, business). Also, none of the departments offering only an M.A. degree have been listed.

How, then, may this table be used to identify departments for further study? Following is a list of criteria which you may want to employ in evaluating departments. Note that individual criteria are not listed in order of their importance, but in order of the introduction of relevant information. You determine what is important.

Professional Status of the Department (that is, how each department is viewed in the eyes of the profession nationally). Would you prefer to attend one of the more prestigious departments (and do you have the qualifications)? If yes, then Table 18-1 is your guide.

Keep in mind that in the past, economics, especially academic, has been a very stratified community. To be a graduate of one of the more prestigious centers may be an important credential for your future employment. Your academic-social mobility may be horizontal or downward, but is usually not upward. Thus, a graduate of a prestigious department may be employed by another prestigious one and may avidly be sought by lower rated ones, while a graduate of a little-known department is likely to move to another little-known one, or possibly into government or business, or into some employment in which one is judged more by what one can do than by what school one graduated from. Of course, with the recent increase of new Ph.D.'s, it is possible that this academic stratification will decrease in the future.

TABLE 18-1   Economics Departments Offering Ph.D.'s
(Listed by Rated Quality of Graduate Faculty)

Top 10 by Rank

1–2	Harvard M.I.T.
3	Chicago
4	Yale
5	University of California (Berkeley)
6	Princeton
7–10	Michigan Minnesota Pennsylvania Stanford

Other Schools Offering Ph.D.'s

(by region)

Northeast	North Central	South	West
Brown	Case	Alabama	Arizona
*Bryn Mawr	Catholic	*Arkansas	*Arizona State
Carnegie-Mellon	Cincinnati	Duke	Claremont
Columbia	Illinois	Florida	Colorado
Connecticut	Indiana	*Florida State	*Colorado State
Cornell	Iowa	Georgia State	Davis (U. of CA)
Johns Hopkins	Iowa State	Houston	Los Angeles (U. of CA)
Massachusetts	Kansas	Kentucky	*New Mexico
New York University	Kansas State	L.S.U.	Oregon
Penn State	Michigan State	Maryland	Riverside (U. of CA)
Pittsburgh	Missouri	Miami	*San Diego (U. of CA)
Rochester	Nebraska	*Mississippi	Santa Barbara (U. of CA)
*R.P.I.	*Northern Illinois	*Mississippi State	Southern California
*SUNY-Albany	Northwestern	North Carolina	Utah
*SUNY-Binghamton	Notre Dame	North Carolina State	*Utah State
SUNY-Buffalo	*Ohio	Oklahoma	Washington (Seattle)
SUNY-Forestry	Ohio State	Oklahoma State	Washington State
Syracuse	Purdue	Rice	*Wyoming
	*St. Louis	*South Carolina	
	Southern Illinois	Southern Methodist	
	Washington (St. Louis)	Tennessee	
	*Wayne State	Texas	
	Wisconsin	Texas A & M	
	*Wisconsin (Milwaukee)	Tulane	
		Vanderbilt	
		Virginia	
		Virginia Polytechnic	
		*West Virginia	

Continued on page 416

TABLE 18-1   (continued)

| | Metropolitan Areas | | |
New York	Washington	Boston	Other
*Fordham	American	Boston College	Hawaii
*Hunter	Catholic	Clark	*Temple
New School	Georgetown	Tufts	
Rutgers	George Washington		
*SUNY-Stony Brook			

*New Degree Programs Since 1965

Location of the Department. If you have a preference as to the part of the country in which you want to study, the listings in Table 18-1 should assist you in identifying schools in your preferred region. Also, as mentioned earlier, the location of schools, particularly of the less prestigious, may determine the part of the country in which you are most likely to find employment.

Recency of Development of the Doctoral Program. You may prefer one of the older and thus more mature departments or one of the newer programs. Trying to prove themselves rapidly, the newer departments may try harder. Being smaller, and knowing that the reputation which they have yet to build will be through their products, they may invest much more time in the development of individual students. Or, being insecure, they may be more conservative and more traditional; they may seek to copy the prestigious centers rather than to strike out innovatively on their own. The asterisks in Table 18-1 enable you to identify the newer programs; that is, those Ph.D. programs which did not exist in 1965 when an earlier study was made by the American Economic Association. Recently established graduate programs in economics may have much to offer; study them to be sure they have what you want.

Effectiveness of Doctoral Programs. In 1969, the economists whose views are summarized in Table 18-1 were also asked to rate the effectiveness of doctoral programs. The resulting ratings were approximately the same as the ratings of faculty. Therefore, they are not repeated. You might, however, like to inspect them. See Roose and Anderson, *A Rating of Graduate Programs*, American Council on Education, 1970. When the same economists rate a department's program significantly different from the quality of its faculty, it may be important. In any case, remember the limitations mentioned above of this manner of securing ratings.

Survey of Departmental Flyers

The list of all economics departments should enable you to select some to investigate more thoroughly. Take a look at the advertising flyers that are likely posted in your department; others are included in the latest Peterson's *Annual Guides to Graduate Study — Economics*, or the American Economic Association's *Graduate Study in Economics, 1977*. These have varied summaries (usually one page or less) of each department and its program. While you should perhaps focus on your selected schools, browsing is really in order, for you may discover possibilities you have not previously considered. What are some more of the criteria to watch?

Curriculum Design. Largely prescribed or elective? Narrow in focus or broad? Confined to economics courses or permitting others? Prerequisites? Math requirements? Traditional in design, innovative, or experimental? Adequate course alternatives? Adequate areas of specialization? (For example, can you study labor economics there, if you wish?)

Departmental Product Differentiations. Is there any evidence that the department is trying to make anything special of itself? Beware of the aim of general or all-round excellence; this may merely be a cover for trying nothing or for deluding oneself by words. Are the specialties of the department of real interest to you? Are they marketable?

The Department's Real Values. Watch for clues as to what the department really values. What is stressed about its faculty members or its graduates — their scholarship, their teaching, their status, their number of publications? What is stressed about its view of economics — its rigor, its relevance, the place of applied or institutional economics? In the description of the goals of the department's Ph.D., what seems of primary or of secondary importance? How does the department seem to value teaching, research, and public service?

Department Size (number of graduate students). A class of around 50 graduate students has been suggested as a minimum size for efficient and effective operation, which should be large enough to permit a reasonable variety of courses and to foster an effective intellectual community of students. In very large departments, one's choices and contacts may be increased, but possibly at the expense of impersonalization. The reverse may occur in very small departments.

Costs, Assistantships, Student Aid, and the Cost of Living. If these are important to you, get information from the aforementioned flyers and department guides.

Student Body. Full-time, part-time? Foreign, and from where? Percent supported by assistantships?

Study of Graduate Catalogs and Materials

From your survey of departmental flyers and national guides to economics graduate departments, you have narrowed and focused your choice to several which meet your goals and fit your constraints. You are ready to write to the departments for information and application blanks. (Or you may inspect catalogs found in the library.) In addition to the above criteria, here are others to which the catalog may relate.

Departmental Efficiency, Courtesy, and Imaginativeness. A department may reveal itself to you by the way it responds to your interest. Promptness? Has it been imaginative and really helpful in designing materials to aid your choice? On the other hand, beware of "all sales but no substance."

Teaching. How seriously does the department take its teaching? For example, are new graduate students just out of undergraduate school immediately assigned to teaching? (This may be a clue to a department which really does not take teaching seriously and exploits cheap student labor to free faculty time for research.) Is there a teaching seminar for graduate students who are being trained to teach? Is there a carefully planned teaching apprenticeship as part of the Ph.D. program? Or does the department let these things take care of themselves?

Quality of Faculty. By inspecting the list of faculty, or perhaps brief biographies the department may provide, you can see where faculty members have been granted their degrees, what their scholarly interests are, and where and how recently they have been published. How many faculty members really seem to have a currently vital professional specialty?

Employment Market. Where are its graduates placed? Does it have contacts with markets for the kind of employment you want?

Special Facilities and Programs. Library, computers, data banks, lecture programs, outside guests, visiting professors, outside funding and grants?

Finally. As you study catalogs and flyers, watch for the unusual. Also watch for what is *not* said. Remember, sometimes a catalog bears little relation to what you will find; it may give an idealized picture. Be alert.

Calendar for Graduate School Applicants

SOPHOMORE AND JUNIOR YEARS — Prepare (see above for suggestions).

EARLY SENIOR YEAR — Review your goals and constraints.

FALL SEMESTER, SENIOR YEAR — Survey flyers, write for information, register for Graduate Record Exam (GRE) and take it. The GRE is like the College Boards, only harder. Many schools require it for you to be considered.

JANUARY, FEBRUARY — Apply to several schools (including a sure one).

MARCH, APRIL — Await the results.

ECONOMICS AS AN AVOCATION

After all our discussion of economics careers and graduate schools, the truth of the matter is that most of you finishing this course will not major in economics. And even those majoring in economics will not be employed as economists. So for the majority of you, economics will be at most an avocation. The avocation of economics is a very important one. It will make you a more informed citizen. Some of the economics you have learned in this course will be superseded by new theories, new institutions, and even new problems. Ten years ago no economic textbooks devoted space to the energy problems that now face all of us. You have, however, learned principles that will allow you to sort through new problems if you continue to inform yourself. Your avocation should be one of continuing interest in economics and thus of continuing examination of the issues. The course you have just finished and this book will have been successful if they opened your eyes to the economy and activated your continuing interest in it. To aid you in your continued study of economics, we offer the following guide to economics as an avocation.

Calendar of Recurring Economic Events

"Economy watching" as a hobby is facilitated by the fact that many economic events and the reporting of them occur at regular times. They usually set off reactions in the form of interpretive news articles, editorials, comment by columnists, and TV reporting and commentary. The following calendar should alert you to the monthly cycle and yearly patterns of recurring economic events.

MONTHLY

First Week — Unemployment for prior month, both actual rate and seasonally corrected rate.

Second Week — Producer Prices (wholesale price index) for prior month, both actual and seasonally corrected index.

Third Week — Consumer price index for prior month, both actual and seasonally corrected index.

— Industrial production index for prior month.

— Personal income for prior month. This is the only monthly national income figure and thus a monthly measure of aggregate output.

Fourth Week — Balance of payments for prior month.

        — Index of leading indicators for prior month. This is an index of variables that tend to "lead" real output; that is, tend to indicate when booms or recessions are likely to be coming.

ANNUALLY

January

Early in month — Annual economic review of the prior year and forecasts for current year abound in newspapers and periodicals; for example, the *New York Times*.

After mid-month — Gross national product for the October–December quarter. Revised figures are often issued one month later.

Last week — President's annual economic message and annual *Economic Report of the President*.

February

Hearings by the Joint Committee on the Economic Report. Prominent economists usually appear. Their views are reported in the press.

March

Final report of the Joint Committee on the Economic Report.

Around the 20th — Balance of payments for the prior year.

April

Fourth week — Balance of payments for the first quarter.

After mid-month — First quarter gross national product.

May

June

Late in month — Mid-year report of Council of Economic Advisers.

July

After mid-month — Second quarter gross national product.

August

September

Third week — Second quarter balance of payments.

October

After mid-month — Third quarter gross national product.

November

December

Last week — American Economic Association annual meeting.

Annotated Bibliography of Sources of Economics Information to Follow Current Economic Events

NEWSPAPERS

New York Times — The general daily and Sunday publication offers the fullest coverage of economic events, frequent editorials on economic issues, and ably written interpretive features by Leonard Silk, Edwin Dale, Selma Golden, Eileen Shanahan, and others.

The Wall Street Journal — Excellent economics coverage and numerous well-written interpretive features. Especially valuable for those interested in business and financial matters. Usually briefer than the *Times* and more focused on economic events. Excellent summary column on first page. *The Wall Street Journal* is available at a very low subscription price for students.

Christian Science Monitor — Its interpretive news articles and features are especially valuable. They deal ably with many important topics of lasting importance that are sometimes overlooked by other newspapers in their focus on daily events.

The Economist (London) — To see ourselves and our economy from the perspective of an outsider is often useful. Here is a well-known, quality publication to serve that purpose.

WEEKLY NEWSMAGAZINES

Newsweek — Economic news is usually found in the "Business and Finance" section. The weekly columns by Milton Friedman or Paul Samuelson make this a particularly valuable magazine to see how economists with very different economic philosophies view events and policy.

Time — The most widely read weekly newsmagazine. Watch its "Economy and Business" section for economic news. A board of economists frequently contributes a variety of views.

Business Week — Usually provides the most complete weekly coverage of economic events. Frequent excellent interpretive features.

U.S. News and World Report — Full reporting of economic news, usually including well-drawn charts.

TELEVISION

CBS, NBC, ABC "Evening News" — Coverage of economic news, usually by a TV journalist specializing in the subject.

NBC's "Today," CBS's "Morning News," ABC's "Good Morning America."

AN ECONOMICS MAGAZINE
FOR THE GENERAL READER

Challenge — The Magazine of Economic Affairs. International Arts & Sciences Press, Inc., 901 N. Broadway, White Plains, New York 10603. $9.00 a year (six issues). A bimonthly magazine featuring articles of current and lasting significance, usually written by leading economists especially for the general reader. An economics magazine in a class by itself.

JOURNALS OF OPINION

Conservative — *National Review*

Liberal — *New Republic, Nation, New York Review of Books* (a recent survey revealed that this is the periodical read by more intellectual opinion leaders than any other).

MAGAZINES WHICH INCLUDE
ESSAYS ON CURRENT ISSUES

General — *Atlantic Monthly, Harper's Magazine, Commentary, The New York Times Sunday Magazine, The Public Interest.*

Magazines in which each issue is built around a single theme — *The Annals, Daedalus.*

Business oriented — *Fortune.* Excellent, well-illustrated articles. Its "Business Roundup" is a good way to follow the economy.

Digests — *Current* (ably edited cuts from many current magazines on current issues).

TV INTERPRETIVE AND OPINION PROGRAMS

NBC's "Today" and CBS's "Morning News" — Both include excellent interpretive interviews on current economic issues. In addition, ABC, NBC, and CBS occasionally feature documentaries or other special programs on economic issues during evening hours (for example, on the oil shortage).

PBS "Washington Week in Review" (Friday evenings) — A show in a class by itself. Often an economic journalist is included in the panel of five. "Wall Street Week," which follows it, relates economic events to the behavior of the stock market.

To Locate Economics Information

ECONOMIC STATISTICS

World Almanac, Information Please Almanac, New York Times Almanac, Readers' Digest Almanac — Each of these has a section of economic statistics in which you are likely to find whatever information you seek (but not accurate figures for the current or last year). If available in your library, the latest annual *Economic Report of the President* has the most useful statistical appendix for data for the past years back to 1929, including last year. Or, for greater detail, see the U.S. Commerce Department's biennial *Economic Statistics* or the annual *Statistical Abstract*. Latest monthly data is found in daily newspapers or weekly newsmagazines at the time indicated on the "Calendar of Recurring Economic Events."

ECONOMIC DICTIONARY OR ENCYCLOPEDIA

The McGraw-Hill Dictionary of Modern Economics: A Handbook of Terms and Organizations. Second edition, 1973. The most complete dictionary.

GUIDES TO ARTICLES ON ECONOMIC SUBJECTS

Readers' Guide to Periodical Literature — You will probably find listed by subject most of the materials you want. But if you want to look further for articles in other, less widely read periodicals, see *Social Science and Humanities Index*.

To Locate and Choose Books on Economics to Read

BOOK REVIEWS

New York Times Book Review — Watch for new books reviewed. The lists of best sellers, both hardcover and paperbacks, and of newer recommended books, may give you ideas.

New York Review of Books — Provocative reviews, usually by well-known writers.

Economics Books for Leisure Reading

ECONOMIST WRITERS AND
BOOKS YOU SHOULD KNOW

Heilbroner, Robert L. *The Worldly Philosophers: Lives, Times, and Ideas of Great Economic Thinkers*. The author is probably the most widely read and one of the most successful of all modern popularizers of economics. This book has sparked an interest in economics in many beginners. You'll enjoy it and will benefit by its placing of economics in the context of the history of thought. You may also enjoy other books by the same author.

Galbraith, John K. *Economics and the Public Purpose.* Galbraith, with his facile pen and his iconoclasm, is the modern economist with whom almost everyone must be acquainted. If you have never read a "Galbraith," this, one of his latest books, is a place to start. He is so much a part of our modern culture that you're expected to be knowledgeable of him.

Friedman, Milton. *Capitalism and Freedom.* An ably presented conservative view of the economy and how it could solve our major socioeconomic problems. Every economics student should be acquainted with Friedman as the most widely read conservative economist, just as Galbraith and Heilbroner are noted for a liberal economic philosophy.

BIOGRAPHY

Douglas, Paul H. *In the Fullness of Time: The Memoirs of Paul H. Douglas.* A delightful autobiography of an economist who entered politics after a distinguished career as an academic economist. You who are interested in political economy will enjoy the experience of Senator Douglas.

Harrod, Roy F. *The Life of John Maynard Keynes.* A near-classic biography of this greatest of modern economists. It reveals the breadth of his education, the variety of his interests, and his many areas of public service. He was no narrow specialist, in scholarship or in service. You may prefer a shorter and very readable biography, Robert Lekachman's *The Age of Keynes.*

Nearing, Scott. *The Making of a Radical: A Political Autobiography.* An autobiography of an economist who was dismissed from his academic appointment because of his political beliefs and who then devoted his remaining life to writing and action in support of the radical causes he favored.

Summary

This chapter was intended as a potpourri of information for those interested in economics as a career-oriented major or as an avocation. The essential point to keep in mind is that economics as an undergraduate major can open the door to a wide range of professional careers. The job classification of *economist*, however, requires graduate training in economics. Perhaps the best advice of all is to select some senior economics majors and ask them how they view the experience they have completed. Most schools have economics clubs that can facilitate such a dialogue.

Suggestions for Further Reading

Cartter, Allan. *An Assessment of Quality in Graduate Education*. Washington: American Council on Education, 1966.

National Association of Business Economists. *Business Economics Careers*. Washington: September, 1974.

Norton, Hugh S. *The World of the Economist*. Columbia: University of South Carolina Press, 1973.

GLOSSARY

absolute advantage The absolute difference in productivity between countries.

acreage allotment A farm program that sets a limit on the total number of acres that can be placed in production.

adjustable exchange rates Exchange rates that are changed from time to time but are for the most part fixed by intervention.

administered prices A term coined by Gardiner Means to describe price inflexibility in concentrated industries. Means labeled prices that were relatively rigid or changed only infrequently as administered prices.

AFL-CIO The merged Federation of Labor and Congress of Industrial Organizations. The merger took place in 1955 and gave labor a more unified political stance.

agricultural support program The political response to the pressure to increase farm incomes. Most programs in agricultural support are aimed at decreasing supply or increasing demand for raw agricultural production.

allocative efficiency The efficient level of production from the consumers' point of view has been reached when price is equal to marginal cost. Firms are expanding production exactly to the level consumers desire, as measured by the market price.

American Federation of Labor (AFL) Founded by Samuel Gompers in 1886, the AFL was the first business union. The AFL was an exclusive union organized for skilled workers.

American Federation of State, County, and Municipal Employees (AFSCME) One of the few growing unions, AFSCME is a union of public employees. Jerry Wurf is the president of AFSCME.

appreciated In exchange rate terminology, a currency that has appreciated has become more valuable in terms of other currencies. The other-currency price of this particular currency has risen.

arbitration A third party hears the arguments of both sides in a labor dispute and renders a decision. In binding arbitration, the sides must abide by the decision.

assumptions Suppositions about the state of the world on which a theory can be based.

average fixed cost Total fixed costs of production divided by output. Average fixed costs decline as production is increased.

average physical product The total physical product (output) divided by the number of units of the factor.

average revenue Total revenue divided by the quantity sold. A demand curve is an average revenue curve.

average total cost Total costs of production divided by the number of units of output.

average variable cost Total variable costs divided by the number of units of output.

barriers to entry Natural or artificial obstacles that keep new firms from entering an industry.

bilateral monopoly Monopolies dealing with each other as buyers and sellers, such as when a monopoly labor union sells labor to a monopsonistic firm.

black markets Market processes in which people buy and sell goods or services at prices above imposed price ceilings.

board of directors The individuals elected by the stockholders of a corporation to select the managers and oversee the management of the affairs of the corporation.

bonds Interest-earning certificates issued by governments or corporations as a way of borrowing money.

budget constraint A given level of income that limits the amount of goods that may be purchased by an individual.

budget line The graphing of the budget constraint, indicating achievable levels of consumption given the prices of goods and the consumer's income.

business firm An organization formed by an entrepreneur to transform inputs into marketable outputs.

business union Samuel Gompers' description of a union that worked for economic goals without wanting to change or destroy the business organization in which it worked.

capital The durable or long-lived, but depreciable, input in the production process. Machines, tools, and buildings are capital. The return to capital is interest.

capitalism An economic system based on the idea of private ownership of the means of production.

cartel A group of independent firms which agree not to compete. Perfect cartels behave as monopolies.

Celler-Kefauver Antimerger Act Passed in 1950, this act made it illegal in certain circumstances for a firm to merge with another by purchasing its assets. This strengthened the Clayton Act.

ceteris paribus A Latin term that means "holding everything else constant."

chiseling Cheating on a cartel arrangement by lowering prices in an attempt to capture more of the market.

Class I oligopolies Firms in oligopoly that are unorganized and uncollusive. Their behavior is characterized by independent action.

Class II oligopolies Firms in oligopoly that are organized and collusive. Their behavior can be characterized by perfect joint action.

Class III oligopolies Firms in oligopoly that are unorganized, but still collusive. Their behavior is characterized by imperfect joint action.

Clayton Act Passed in 1914, the Clayton Act prohibited the acquisition of the stock of a competing company if such an acquisition would "substantially lessen competition."

clean float A floating exchange rate system in which there is absolutely no intervention by governments.

closed shops Firms where workers are forced to become union members before employment.

Coase theorem A solution to externality problems which shows that in the case of small numbers of affected parties, a property right assignment is sufficient to internalize any externality that is present.

coefficient of price elasticity of demand The numerical measure of price elasticity of demand. The percentage change in quantity demanded divided by the percentage change in price.

coefficient of price elasticity of supply The numerical measure of price elasticity of supply. The percentage change in quantity supplied divided by the percentage change in price.

collusion Agreements between firms in an industry to set certain prices or to share markets in certain ways.

communication Firms' ability to signal their intentions to each other. This is important in oligopoly where there are few firms.

communism The final stage in the theory of Karl Marx. Marx saw under communism the end of scarcity, the end of conflict among the classes, and the creation of a new social order.

comparative advantage The relative difference in productivity between countries which allows countries to trade regardless of absolute levels of efficiency.

competitive fringe In markets with one, large, dominant firm, there is sometimes a substantial number of small competitors, which would be referred to as the competitive fringe.

competitive solution The name given to the

model developed by Oskar Lange to show that a planned economy could, theoretically, reach the same efficiency solutions as a market economy.

complements Those goods that are jointly consumed. The consumption of one good enhances the consumption of the other good. Complements have a negative cross elasticity of demand.

concentration ratio An index of the relative degree of concentration in an industry. The one most commonly used is the percentage of sales of an industry accounted for by the four largest firms in that industry.

Congress of Industrial Organizations (CIO) An affiliation of industrial unions that was organized when the AFL decided not to promote unions in the mass production industries. John L. Lewis was the CIO's first president.

constant cost industry An industry in which an industry-wide expansion does not cause average costs to rise. The long-run supply curve is perfectly elastic.

constrained sales maximization Occurs when a manager's primary goal is to increase the sales of the firm because managers are rewarded by stockholders for increasing the firm's relative share of the market.

consumer surplus The extra utility gained from the fact that some consumers pay less for an item than they would be willing to pay. The total value of the utility of an item is often worth more to consumers than the total amount that is paid for the item.

coordination Firms' ability to relate their production decisions to the other firms in an industry. This is important in oligopoly where there are few firms.

corporation The form of business enterprise where stockholders are the legal owners of the firm. Their legal liability is limited.

cost Cost and price are separate concepts. The cost of a factor of production includes both price and productivity. The cost of a factor of production could rise even if its price remained constant (if productivity fell).

cost-plus pricing The practice in price regulation of allowing firms a markup on average costs of production. This is the most common form of price regulation.

craft unions Unions composed of skilled workers, such as plumbers and carpenters.

cross elasticity of demand A measure of the responsiveness of changes in the quantity consumed of one product to changes in the price of another product.

crowding out The increased demand for loanable funds by government causes the interest rate to rise; this attracts funds away from business investment, thus crowding out business investment.

Cultural Revolution The revolutionary reevaluation of the Chinese economy that took place from 1966 through 1969. This period represents the high point in the adulation of Mao.

decrease in demand A shift in the demand curve indicating that at every price consumers demand a smaller quantity than before.

decrease in supply A shift in the supply curve indicating that at every price suppliers will supply a smaller quantity than before.

decreasing cost industry An industry in which an industry-wide expansion causes average costs to fall in the long run. The long-run supply curve has a negative slope.

demand The desire and ability to consume certain quantities at certain prices.

demand curve A graphical representation of a demand schedule, or a graphical representation of the quantity demanded at various prices.

demand-determined price If supply is perfectly inelastic, the price is determined by changes in demand only.

demand schedule A tabular listing which shows the quantity demanded at various prices.

dependent variable The variable that changes in response to the independent variables in an equation.

depreciate A reduction in the value or usefulness of fixed assets through wear.

depreciated In exchange rate terminology, a currency that has depreciated has become worth less in terms of other currencies. The other-currency price of this particular currency has fallen.

derived demand A demand that results from the demand for another product. The demand for labor is derived from the demand for the good the labor is used to produce.

devalue In exchange rate terminology, a devaluation occurs when a country allows a fixed or pegged exchange rate to depreciate closer to its equilibrium level.

diamond-water paradox The problem classical economists faced when they argued that value in use could not determine price (demand) because diamonds, while less useful than water, were more expensive than water.

differentiated oligopoly An oligopoly market structure that produces a heterogeneous or differentiated product.

differentiated product A good that has real or imagined identifiable characteristics that are different from other goods.

diminishing marginal utility The fact that marginal utility declines as consumption increases. Less satisfaction is obtained per unit as more units are consumed.

dirty float A floating exchange rate system in which there is some intervention to move the rate adjustment in a certain direction or at a certain speed that is different from the market rate.

discounting The term given to the technique of calculating present values.

diseconomies of scale Increases in average cost that are due to increased plant size. Increasing long-run average costs.

distributive justice Arguments for a fair distribution of income. These are normative arguments for a particular distribution of income.

dominant firm The most influential firm in an industry, usually the price leader. The dominant firm is often the largest firm, but it can be the low-cost firm.

dumping The practice of selling in foreign markets at lower prices than in domestic markets. This is a form of price discrimination.

economic approach A way of thinking about and analyzing problems that relies heavily on the basic tools of economic theory.

economic efficiency The least-cost method of production.

economic profit Return to the firm in excess of the explicit and implicit costs of production.

economic rent A payment greater than the amount necessary to bring a factor into productive use.

economies of scale Declines in average cost that are due to increased plant size. Declining long-run average costs.

economize Since wants are insatiable and resources are scarce, individuals must make choices; they must economize.

egalitarian Programs and individuals that are concerned with promoting a more equal distribution of income.

elasticity A measure of the sensitivity or responsiveness of quantity demanded or quantity supplied to changes in price (and other factors).

encouragement phase The period (1930–1947) in which government support by legislation greatly increased the power of unions.

Energy Resources and Development Administration (ERDA) A federal agency created in 1974 to take over the energy research functions which were formerly the responsibility of the Atomic Energy Commission. The research is not limited to nuclear energy.

entrepreneurship The input that represents management, innovation, and risk-taking. The return to entrepreneurship is profit.

ex ante A Latin phrase meaning "before the event." The concept of utility is an *ex ante* concept. This means that consumption behavior based on utility is based on utility before buying or consuming a commodity. It is based on anticipated utility.

excess capacity Underutilization of existing plant size. In monopolistic competition, the firm produces less than the efficient capacity of the plant.

exchange market intervention The action taken by governments to establish an exchange rate other than a market-determined rate.

exchange rate The price at which one currency sells for another.

excise tax A tax that is placed on the sale of a particular item, such as liquor, cigarettes, or electricity. It is a narrow-based tax.

exclusive union A union that restricts supply and maintains a higher than competitive wage by excluding workers from the profession. Craft unions are exclusive unions.

expectations Individual forecasts for the state of the future.

expected gains The anticipated utility a consumer foresees when engaging in trade. Trade and consumption are based on expected rather than actual gains.

explicit cost Bookkeeping cost or money outlay.

externalities Costs or benefits that are imposed on economic units. These units bear the costs without any compensation or gain the benefits without paying for them.

factor markets Markets in which owners of factors of production are selling these factors' services to producers or consumers.

factors of production   The inputs that a firm uses to produce output. Land, labor, capital, and entrepreneurship constitute the factors of production.

fair rate of return   The idea that a regulated industry must earn a normal profit or it will go out of business.

fascism   An economic system that combines monopoly capitalism, private property, and a strong authoritarian central government. Fascism is in essence an authoritarian state imposed upon a capitalistic system.

featherbedding   The maintenance of jobs that management claims are unnecessary or redundant. Unions often insist on featherbedding in industries that are declining.

Federal Power Commission (FPC)   An independent agency that controls hydroelectric projects and regulates the interstate sale of electricity and natural gas.

Federal Trade Commission Act   This act established the Federal Trade Commission (FTC) to police "unfair" business practices.

fixed but adjustable exchange rates   The exchange rate system that existed from 1945 until the early 1970s. This system consisted of a pegged system that could be adjusted when demand and supply moved permanently out of balance.

fixed exchange rate   An exchange rate that is fixed at a predetermined rate by intervening governments; sometimes called a pegged exchange rate.

fixed factors   The factors of production that cannot be varied in the short run, such as the size of a plant.

flexible exchange rate   An exchange rate that is determined solely by the underlying forces of supply and demand; sometimes called a floating exchange rate.

floating exchange rate   An exchange rate that is determined solely by the underlying forces of supply and demand; sometimes called a flexible exchange rate.

four modernizations   The latest development project in China, which plans for modernization of farming, industry, science, and technology.

free-riding behavior   Free-riders mask their time demands and indicate they don't want a public good because they know once it is produced they can consume it without paying for it. As a result, less than the optimal amount will be produced.

fundamental questions   Questions which must be addressed by every society. What is to be produced? How much is to be produced? In what way, or how, are things to be produced? Who shall have the right to consume the goods and services produced, and how much will each person get?

gains from trade   The extra satisfaction an individual anticipates when voluntarily engaging in trade.

Gosplan   The State Planning Commission in the Soviet Union.

grain reserve program   A program that attempts to persuade farmers to store their own surplus grain. The government pays farmers the cost of storage.

Great Industrialization Debate   An open debate that took place in the Soviet Union from 1924 to 1928 concerning the correct way to industrialize the economy.

Great Leap Forward   Communist China's highly overambitious modernization plan that was launched in 1958.

holding companies   Single firms set up for the sole purpose of owning and controlling other firms.

Humphrey-Hawkins Full Employment Bill   A bill passed in 1978, after Senator Humphrey's death, that sets national goals to reduce unemployment from its current rate to 4 percent by 1983 and to reduce inflation to 3 percent by 1983 and to zero by 1988.

imperfect competition   The market structures of oligopoly and monopolistic competition.

implicit cost   The cost implied by the alternatives given up. The opportunity cost of production.

inclusive union   A union that attempts to organize all the workers in an industry and maintain a strong bargaining position vis á vis management.

income-consumption curve   A curve in indifference-curve analysis that shows how the consumption of two goods changes as income changes. It is found by connecting the tangencies of indifference curves and budget lines as the budget line is shifted, representing changes in income.

income effect   As the price of a good falls (rises), the consumer's real income rises (falls) and the consumer buys more of all normal goods.

income elasticity of demand   A measure of the way in which quantity consumed responds to changes in income.

increase in demand   A shift in the demand curve indicating that at every price consumers demand a larger quantity than before.

increase in supply   A shift in the supply curve indicating that at every price a larger quantity will be supplied than before.

increasing cost industry   An industry in which an industry-wide expansion causes average costs to rise in the long run. The long-run supply curve has a positive slope.

independent variable   The variable or variables in an equation which are determined outside the equation.

indifference curve   A graphing of an indifference set. An indifference curve shows all combinations of the two commodities among which the consumer is indifferent.

indifference curve analysis   A technique of analyzing consumer behavior that does not require the concept of measurable utility.

indifference map   A series of indifference curves representing higher levels of satisfaction for the consumer.

indifference set   A ranking of bundles of goods among which a consumer is indifferent. The bundles yield equal satisfaction.

industrial organization   A subfield of economics which examines industrial structure in theory and in practice.

Industrial Reorganization Act   A bill which has been under consideration in Congress which seeks to codify into law the Market Concentration Doctrine. The bill was advocated by the late Senator Philip Hart of Michigan.

industrial unions   Inclusive unions such as the Steelworkers, Autoworkers, and Teamsters that gain power by organizing all (or a large share) of the workers in an industry.

industry   A group of firms producing similar or related products.

industry studies   Investigations of particular industries to determine the degree of competitive behavior in the industry.

inferior good   A good for which demand decreases as income increases.

injunctions   Court orders that were used in the labor union-management disputes to order labor back to work. The Clayton Act (1914) limited the use of injunctions, but this section was later declared unconstitutional.

input coefficients   In input-output analysis, the ratio of a particular input to the total outputs in that industry.

input-output analysis   An attempt to quantify the flows between different sectors of the economy. Input-output analysis is useful in economic planning.

interest   The return to the factor of production, capital.

internalize   The idea that the cost of an externality that is borne by society should be taken into account in the production process.

international reserves   Stocks of assets that are liquid and readily accepted as international payment.

International Workers of the World (IWW)   An international union that organized American steelworkers after World War I. The IWW was viewed as socialistic in the United States, and this contributed to its demise.

interpersonal utility comparisons   Attempts to compare levels or amounts of utility between consumers. This is impossible because utility is subjectively determined.

intervention stage   The period since the Taft-Hartley Act (1947) in which the government has intervened in labor disputes and taken away some of labor's earlier gains.

jointly interdependent demand   The demand for a factor of production depends on the amount of other factors the firm plans to use. The demand for a factor is thus interdependent on the demand for other factors of production.

kinked demand curve   A model of pricing in oligopoly used to explain price rigidity. The kink comes from the pricing behavior. If firms cut prices, other firms follow suit and there is very little increase in the price-cutters' market share. A price increase, however, is not matched and the price rise will result in a loss of a market share.

Knights of Labor   Organized by Uriah Stevens in 1869, the Knights of Labor was a secret organization. It won the first major strike in the United States against the railroad industry. The Knights had political reformist goals, which led to its demise.

labor   The factor of production that represents

the human element in the production process. The return to labor is wages.

labor theory of value   A central theme in the writings of Karl Marx. All commodities were reduced to a common denominator of the labor time embodied in the product.

land   The factor of production that represents resources that are fixed or nonrenewable. The return to land is rent.

Landrum-Griffin Act   Passed in 1959 and aimed at further curbing union power. The act made unions more democratic and restricted Communist party members and convicted felons from union leadership. It made picketing under certain circumstances illegal.

law of demand   The quantity demanded of a good or service is an inverse function of its price, *ceteris paribus*.

law of supply (not quite)   The quantity supplied of a good or service is usually a positive function of price, *ceteris paribus*.

least-cost combination   The lowest attainable per unit cost for a given sized plant. The minimum point on the short-run average cost curve.

limited liability   The fact that the stockholders of a corporation cannot be sued for failure of the corporation to pay its debts; only the corporation itself can be sued.

local monopoly   A firm which has monopoly power in a geographic region. Even though close substitutes exist, the distance between sources of supply creates monopolies.

logically indeterminate   The theoretical model will not give a precise answer. Instead, a range of answers will be obtained from the model.

logrolling   Vote trading in a legislative process. Legislators vote for a colleague's program in return for a vote on their program.

long run   A period of time long enough that all inputs, including plant and equipment, can be varied.

long-run average cost curve   The lowest attainable average cost of producing any given output. A curve tangent to all the possible short-run cost curves.

long-run profit maximization   The argument that even if managers follow satisficing behavior or constrained sales maximization, they do this only because this leads to higher profits in the long run.

Lorenz curve   A geometric construction which traces the cumulative percentage of income households receive, ranked from the lowest to the highest.

lumpy   Indivisibilities in consumption. Consumption of houses is lumpy, for example, because 10 percent of a house cannot be easily purchased and consumed.

macroeconomics   The study of the economy as a whole. Macroeconomics is concerned with policy issues such as the level of employment and the overall price level.

marginal analysis   A technique used to analyze problems in which the results of small changes in quantities are examined.

marginal cost   The change in total cost of producing one more (or one less) unit of output.

marginal cost pricing   A theoretical technique for forcing a monopoly to behave exactly as a competitive firm by regulating the monopoly price so that it is equal to marginal cost and average revenue.

marginal physical product   The change in physical output that is produced by a unit change in a factor of production.

marginal productivity theory   A theory originally exposited by John Bates Clark which explains how the distribution of income comes about. Each factor is paid according to its contribution, or its marginal productivity.

marginal rate of substitution   The consumer's trade-off between two goods represented on an indifference curve. The slope of the indifference curve represents this trade-off.

marginal resource cost   The cost of each additional unit of a productive resource.

marginal revenue   The change in total revenue from selling one more (or one less) unit.

marginal revenue product   The amount that an additional unit of the variable factor of production adds to a firm's total revenue.

marginal utility   The amount of utility that an additional unit of consumption adds to total utility.

market clearing price   The equilibrium price. It is market clearing because there are no frustrated purchasers or suppliers.

Market Concentration Doctrine   A hypothesis that holds that the degree of concentration in an industry is a reliable index of the degree of monopoly power in that industry.

market demand   The summation of all the individual consumer demand curves. A market demand curve shows what quantity will be demanded by all consumers at various prices.

market economy   A market economy answers the fundamental questions through the forces of supply and demand. There are elements of market forces in all economies.

market equilibrium   The price and quantity that will exist in the market if no impediments are placed on the free working of the market.

marketing quota system   A farm program which specifies how much output a farmer can bring to market.

market power   The ability of firms or buyers to affect price. Large numbers of buyers and sellers insure that no one buyer or seller affects price.

market structures   The models of pure competition, monopolistic competition, oligopoly, and monopoly, which describe ways in which firms in an industry interact and react to changes in demand and/or costs of the factors of production.

market supply   The summation of all the individual firm supply curves. A market supply curve shows what quantity will be supplied by all firms at various prices.

mediation   Third party intervention in a strike. The mediator attempts to keep the parties together and talking by offering suggestions and clarifying issues.

microeconomics   The study of individual market interactions. Microeconomics concentrates on the individual unit, the consumer, the firm, and the industry.

minimum wage   A price floor imposed by a governmental unit in labor markets.

ministries   State agencies in the Soviet Union that make plans for and coordinate an industry. There is a ministry for each industry.

mixed economy   An economy that contains elements of tradition, planning, and the market. All economies are mixed.

monopolistic competition   The market structure in which a large number of firms produce a differentiated product. Entry into the industry is relatively easy.

monopoly   The market structure in which there is a single seller of a product that has no close substitutes.

monopoly power   The ability to exercise some of the economic effects as predicted in the model of pure monopoly.

monopsonistic competition   The market structure in which a large number of firms produce a differentiated product. Entry into the industry is relatively easy.

monopsonistic exploitation   The underpayment of wages due to monopsony power. Labor receives less than it would receive in competitive markets.

monopsony   The case of a single purchaser of a factor of production.

National Labor Relations Board (NLRB)   Established by the Wagner Act (1935), the NLRB was empowered to investigate unfair business practices and to determine legitimate bargaining agents for labor when there were competing unions.

National Labor Union   The first successful union in the United States that had a national scope. Founded in 1867 by William Sylvis, the union quickly grew to 600,000 members but fell apart rapidly after Sylvis' death in 1869.

National Recovery Administration (NRA)   The NRA was a major New Deal program aimed at business recovery. The NRA was anticompetitive, since it allowed and encouraged agreements between firms. It was eventually declared unconstitutional.

natural monopoly   A monopoly that emerges because of economies of scale. The size of the market is such that there is room for only one optimally sized firm.

negative income tax   A transfer from the government to the poor based on a formula, similar to the present income tax system. A negative income tax has two components: an income guarantee and a negative tax rate.

New Economic Policy (NEP)   An attempt at market socialism from 1921 to 1926 in the Soviet Union.

non-price competition   Competing with rivals through advertising, style changes, color changes, and other techniques other than lowering price.

normal good   A good for which demand increases as income is increased.

normal profit   The opportunity cost of capital and entrepreneurship. This is the level of profit that is necessary for a firm to remain in a competitive industry.

normative economics   A set of propositions about what ought to be. Value judgments about the world.

Norris-La Guardia Act   A law passed in 1932 that (along with the Wagner Act of 1935) vastly strengthened the power of labor unions and set the stage for their rapid development.

oligopoly The market structure in which there are few firms. The fewness of the firms causes them to recognize the mutual interdependence among them.

oligopsony The market situation in which there are few buyers of a factor of production.

opportunity cost Because of scarcity, every decision to consume or produce means that we forego consuming and producing something else.

optimal-size plant The short-run average cost curve with the lowest possible attainable per-unit costs. The minimum point on the long-run average cost curve.

parity Parity prices are an attempt to define fair prices. Fair prices are defined as those prices which establish agricultural purchasing power at some past level. 1910–1914 is usually viewed as the golden age of agriculture and parity is often linked to this period.

partnership The form of business enterprise where there is more than one owner, and these owners and the firm have no legal distinction.

pegged exchange rate An exchange rate that is fixed at a predetermined rate by intervening governments; sometimes called a fixed exchange rate.

perfectly elastic A price elasticity of demand coefficient of infinity. The quantity demanded responds in an infinite way to a change in price. The demand curve is a horizontal line.

perfectly inelastic A price elasticity of demand coefficient of zero. There is no response in quantity demanded to changes in price. The demand curve is vertical.

planned economy A planned economy answers the fundamental economic questions through central command and control. There are elements of planning in all economies.

planning curve The long-run average cost curve. In the planning stage, a short-run curve on the long-run curve can be selected.

positive economics A set of propositions about what is rather than what ought to be.

positive theory A theory that leads to implica-tions and a hypothesis about the consequences of certain actions. A positive theory makes no judgments about the moral correctness of these implications.

present value The capitalized value of an item to be paid for or sold in the future. A future value discounted to the present.

price The value, usually in money terms, for which goods and services exchange.

price ceilings Prices imposed by a governmental unit that are set as a limit. The ceiling is a price that cannot be exceeded.

price clusters Groupings of prices for similar, but not homogeneous, products.

price-consumption curve A curve in indifference curve analysis that shows how the consumption of two goods changes as the price of one of the goods changes. It is found by connecting the tangencies of indifference curves and the budget line as the budget line is shifted, representing a change in price of one of the goods.

price discrimination The practice of charging different consumers different prices or a particular consumer different prices for different quantities purchased.

price elasticity of demand A measure of the responsiveness of the quantity demanded to changes in price.

price elasticity of supply A measure of the responsiveness of the quantity supplied to changes in price.

price floors Prices established as minimum prices. A governmental unit sets a price which cannot be undercut.

price leadership The practice of industry pricing in which other firms follow the pricing initiatives of a particular firm, the price leader.

price searcher A firm that sets price in order to maximize profits. A price-searching firm has monopoly power.

price taker A firm in pure competition is a price taker because the firm views itself as having no influence on price. It can sell any amount at the market clearing price.

principle of diminishing marginal rates of substitution As a consumer receives more and more of a particular good, its value in terms of other goods declines. This is represented by the changing slope of the indifference curve.

principle of diminishing returns An increase in variable inputs given a set of fixed factors will eventually produce an increment in output that is smaller than the increment in input.

principle of increasing costs   As more of a particular good is desired, the opportunity cost will increase. This is because resources that are less well suited to producing the good will have to be drawn into production.

principle of increasing returns   An increase in variable inputs given a set of fixed factors may produce an increment in output larger than the increment in input.

product differentiation   The technique of making a product different from other products through design, color, styling, quality, or advertising.

production   The transformation of inputs into marketable outputs.

production function   A description of the technical relationships that transform inputs into outputs. Production functions can generally be described by mathematical relationships.

production possibilities curve   A graph which depicts the concept of opportunity cost by showing production trade-offs between two goods in a hypothetical economy. It depicts the fact that more of one good can be produced only by giving up some of the other good.

product group   A market for a good that is differentiated but has a large number of close substitutes.

product markets   Markets for the goods and services produced by firms or individuals.

profit   The return to the factor of production, entrepreneurship. Profit is a residual and the signal that drives the market mechanism.

progressive income tax   An income tax which applies a higher tax rate to taxpayers with higher levels of income. The tax rate and income level are positively correlated.

property rights   The basic institution of a market economy. Markets and exchanges can only occur if individuals have property rights to goods, services, and labor.

proportional income tax   An income tax which applies the same tax rate to all taxpayers regardless of their level of income.

protectionism   The desire to limit imports into a country in order to protect national firms from foreign competition.

protective effect   The protective effect of a tariff is the degree to which it limits imports, thus protecting national industry from foreign competition.

public goods   Those goods that generate external benefits that are jointly consumed. It is difficult (impossible) to exclude people from consuming a public good.

pure competition   The market structure in which there are many sellers and buyers. The firms produce a homogeneous product and there is free entry and exit of these firms to and from the industry.

pure oligopoly   An oligopoly market structure that produces a homogeneous product.

quantity demanded   A change in the amount of a good or service that is being purchased as price changes. Quantity demanded responds to a price change. It is a movement along the demand curve.

quantity supplied   A change in the amount of a good or service that is being supplied as price changes. Quantity supplied responds to a price change. It is a movement along the supply curve.

quota   Physical limits on the amount of a commodity that may be imported.

rent   The return to the factor of production, land.

rent control   Price ceilings that are imposed by governmental units on apartment rentals.

representative firm   A firm used to represent the firms of an industry; an average firm.

repression phase   The early years of the labor movement in which government and the courts were hostile to union activity.

reserve army of the unemployed   The large group of unemployed laborers that Marx predicted would unite, ultimately developing socialism.

resources   The inputs that can be used to produce goods and services. All resources are relatively scarce.

revenue effect   The revenue effect of a tariff is the amount of tax revenue it raises for the government.

revolutionary unions   Those unions that sought changes in the social order.

right-to-work laws   State laws that allow people to hold jobs without belonging to unions. Federal law leaves up to the states the choice between right-to-work laws and union shops.

risk aversion   Most individuals will, *ceteris paribus*, avoid risk unless they are compensated for assuming risk. This negative utility from risk is a general phenomenon, and economists refer to it as risk aversion. Some individuals may not conform to this and may display a taste for risk. We generally view these individuals as unstable. This does not mean that stable individuals will not do risky things. It means, instead, that they will only bear risk if adequately compensated.

robber barons   The very successful turn-of-the-century entrepreneurs who amassed fortunes by setting up trusts and holding companies.

rule of reason   Indicated that monopolies that behaved well did not violate the Sherman Act. The court held that the existence of competitors was sufficient to demonstrate "reasonable behavior."

satisficing   Management does not seek to maximize profits, but rather seeks target levels of output and profits that are satisfactory to the interests of ownership.

scarcity   The fact that there are not sufficient resources to produce everything that individuals want.

secondary boycotts   Union actions to stop one employer from doing business with another employer. This involves action to create pressures on third parties.

self-interest   A basic assumption of economic theory that individual decision-makers behave in a selfish manner; they do what is best for themselves.

separation of ownership and control   Corporations are run by hired managers, not owners. These managers might operate by some principle other than profit maximization. This behavior would result if managers have goals different than the owners' and if the owners cannot control the managers.

shadow prices   Simulated market prices. Shadow prices are used by economic planners.

shared monopoly   A recent term used to describe a highly concentrated industry in which a few firms control the industry. The term is often used by lawyers rather than economists.

Sherman Antitrust Act   Passed in 1890, the Sherman Antitrust Act was the first antitrust law. Section 1 of the act declared every contract, combination, or conspiracy in restraint of trade to be illegal. Section 2 made it illegal to monopolize or attempt to monopolize.

shortage   The amount that consumers wish to purchase at some price exceeds the amount suppliers wish to supply. A shortage can only occur on a lasting basis when a price ceiling is in effect.

short run   The period of time too short to vary all the factors of production. This period of time varies from industry to industry. Short-run decisions are those concerned with using the existing plant more or less intensively.

short-run supply curve   The supply curve in the short run, the period in which the size of the plant cannot be varied. In price competition, the short-run marginal cost curve is the short-run supply curve.

shutdown point   The price and output at which the firm loses less if it ceases operation. The minimum point on the average variable cost curve.

single tax   A tax on land proposed by Henry George to tax away the economic rent on land. His proposal developed a political movement.

socialist controversy   A debate started by Ludwig von Mises and Oskar Lange concerning the feasibility of planning without markets.

social costs   Costs that are borne by society or some group without compensation. Externalities impose damages, or social costs, on groups in the population.

Social Darwinism   Charles Darwin's theory of evolution of the species applied to business enterprise. Under that view, stronger firms were justified in getting bigger by swallowing up the smaller ones.

socialism   An economic system in which the nonhuman means of production are owned by society, or the state.

soil bank program   A program which attempts to raise farm income by paying farmers who allow their land to lay idle.

sole proprietorship   The form of business enterprise where no legal distinction is made between the owner and the firm.

Standard Industrial Classification (SIC) system   A classification system devised by the U.S. Census Bureau for classifying industries. The SIC system divides the economy into about 400 four-digit industries. The four-digit industries are then aggregated and disaggregated.

stocks Certificates of ownership in a corporation.

stockholders The owners of a corporation.

substitutes Goods that replace the consumption of other goods. Substitutes have a positive cross elasticity of demand.

substitution effect When the price of a good falls (rises), it becomes less (more) expensive relative to all other goods and more (less) of it is consumed, substituting for other goods.

supply The quantity of goods offered for sale at a particular time or a particular place.

supply and demand The organizing principles in a market economy. These forces also operate in planned and traditional economies.

supply curve A graphical representation of a supply schedule. A graphical representation of the quantity supplied at various prices.

supply schedule A tabular listing which shows quantity supplied at various prices.

support prices Price floors in agriculture that were used before 1973.

surplus The amount that suppliers wish to supply at some price exceeds the amount that consumers wish to purchase. A surplus can only occur on a lasting basis when a price floor is in effect.

surplus value In the writings of Karl Marx, the difference between the labor value of goods produced and the subsistence wages received by workers.

tacit collusion Unorganized and unstated attempts to practice joint action. Gentlemen's agreements and price leadership are two forms of tacit collusion.

Taft-Hartley Act Passed in 1947, the act was designed to reverse some of the labor excesses created by the Wagner Act. President Truman vetoed the act but Congress overrode the veto. The Taft-Hartley Act shifted some rights back to employers.

tangency solution In indifference curve analysis, a consumer is maximizing satisfaction where an indifference curve is tangent to a budget line. This represents the highest attainable indifference curve.

target prices Prices that the government determines are fair to farmers. After the market clearing price is determined, the government pays each farmer the difference between the target price and the market price.

tariffs Taxes that are placed on the importation of goods into a country. A tariff can be a fixed amount per item or it can be a percentage of the value of the item.

tax incidence The place where the burden of any tax actually rests; those who pay the tax after all shifting has occurred.

technical efficiency A method of choosing a production technique that minimizes inputs according to some physical rule.

technologically determined demand The demand for a factor of production is determined by the techniques of production and the level of technology used. The demand for a factor is thus technologically determined.

testable hypothesis An inference from economic theory that can be subjected to empirical testing.

theory The development of a set of principles that can be used to make inferences about the world.

total cost The summation of all the costs of production.

total fixed cost The cost of the fixed factors of production. Total fixed cost does not vary in the short run.

total physical product The amount that a firm produces in physical units.

total revenue The quantity of a good or service that a firm sells times the price of the good or service.

total variable cost Costs that vary directly with output, increasing as more output is produced.

traditional economy Sometimes called a subsistence economy, the traditional economy answers the fundamental questions by appeals to tradition. There are elements of tradition in all economies.

treble damages A provision under the Sherman Act that victims of monopoly can recover three times the damages they have sustained.

trusts Legal organizations set up to control the stock of other companies through boards of trustees.

tying contracts Agreements between producers and retailers whereby a retailer must agree to handle certain items as a prerequisite to handling other items.

union shops Union membership is necessary for a worker to remain employed. Federal law leaves up to the states the choice between right-to-work laws and union shops.

United Mine Workers   The industrial union for mine workers. John L. Lewis was the most colorful and powerful leader of the UMW.

unit elastic   A price elasticity of demand coefficient of one. The change in quantity demanded responds at the same rate as any change in price. The demand curve is a rectangular hyperbola.

util   An arbitrary unit used to measure utility.

utility   The satisfaction that an individual receives from consuming a good or service.

utility function   A preference function ordering a consumer's desires to consume differing amounts of goods. These functions consist of assigned numbers.

utility interdependence   The fact that some individuals gain satisfaction from the consumption of others. Utility is gained from increases in the utility of others.

utility maximization   The way a consumer adjusts consumption, given a budget constraint and a set of prices, in order to maximize the total amount of satisfaction.

value in exchange   Price, or value in exchange, is determined by marginal utility. Scarcity is related to value through utility.

value in use   Usefulness, or value in use, is often thought of as the total utility an item supplies. Water is thus very valuable in use, but not very valuable in exchange (price) because it has a low marginal utility.

value of the marginal physical product   The value of the marginal physical product is found by multiplying the marginal physical product by the price the firm can sell the product for.

variable factors   The factors of production that can be varied in the short run.

wages   The return to the factor of production, labor.

Wagner Act   A law passed in 1935 that (along with the Norris-La Guardia Act of 1932) vastly strengthened the power of labor unions and set the stage for their rapid development.

wants   Individuals' desires for various goods and services. Wants are insatiable.

War Communism   The economic system that was imposed by Lenin in Russia immediately after the Bolshevik revolution. It is called War Communism because there was continuing civil war.

welfare economics   A branch of economics which evaluates the economic order from an ethical perspective.

welfare unions   Those unions that had lofty ideals of social welfare and sought to establish worker cooperatives.

wildcat strikes   Local strikes that are unauthorized by the national union.

workers' self-management   The system in Yugoslavia in which workers direct and have a financial stake in the firm in which they work.

yellow-dog contracts   Contracts in which an employee must agree to refrain from union activity as a precondition for employment.

INDEX

N

O